10 TESTS FOR ENGLAND

Scorebook and Journal
for 1988

BILL FRINDALL

COLUMBUS BOOKS
LONDON

First published in Great Britain in 1989 by
Columbus Books Limited
19-23 Ludgate Hill, London EC4M 7PD

Designed by Martin Bronkhorst

British Library Cataloguing in Publication Data

Frindall, Bill
Ten Tests for England: scorebook and journal for 1988
1. Cricket. English teams. Test matches.
I. Title
796.35′865

ISBN 0 86287 874 8

Phototypeset by Falcon Graphic Art Ltd
Wallington, Surrey
Printed and bound by
Butler and Tanner Ltd
Frome, Somerset

CONTENTS

PREFACE

Between 29 January and 30 August 1988 England played ten Test matches against Australia, New Zealand, West Indies and Sri Lanka. In that little span of just over seven months Peter May's selection committee called upon four different captains and employed the extraordinary total of 32 players. The grand product of their efforts was a result line reading: four defeats, five draws and a solitary victory against Sri Lanka.

This highly eventful period began just five weeks after the calamitous mission in Pakistan and with several careers very much in the balance, not least that of the normally cheery captain, Mike Gatting. An early diversion to join in Australia's birthday romp added further colour. Then there was Richard Hadlee's imminent Test bowling world record; who would be the unlucky English batsman forever remembered as wicket number 374?

England's tourists had a meagre two-week respite between returning home and reporting to their counties in preparation for the longest professional cricket season ever devised. No other generation of cricketers had been called upon to cope with such an excess; not in the entire history of first-class cricket which began in earnest in 1864 when 'overhand bowling' was legalized and *Wisden* was first published. Could we find players with the stamina to meet such a demanding schedule and prevent West Indies from achieving a third consecutive 5-nil blackwash?

Ten Tests for England chronicles these matches, reproducing the special scoresheets which I originally designed to assist the BBC's radio commentators. From these records it is possible to reconstruct each match ball-by-ball and in great detail. To put some flesh on the bones I have added a journal compiled from my criticisms, observations and reports for *The Mail on Sunday* and *Cricket World*. These tawdry efforts are really just an excuse to publish a selection of evocative photographs by Graham Morris.

The first cricket book I bought for myself was Alex Bannister's *Cricket Cauldron*, an account of MCC's 1953-54 tour of the Caribbean under Len Hutton's captaincy. It inspired my ambition to accompany an England team on an overseas tour as a cricket correspondent. To be paid to spend a large chunk of Britain's nastier winter months in comfort and sunshine *and* to watch cricket had to be a dream beyond dreams.

Although I had been on several England tours this was the first on which I had travelled at the expense of someone else; once I stopped feeling guilty, it became highly enjoyable. I am immensely grateful to *The Mail on Sunday* for entrusting me with such an assignment, particularly to Ken Haskell, Roger Kelly and Trevor Bond for their encouragement, good humour and for inspiring confidence.

My previous visits to Australia and New Zealand had given much pleasure and enabled me to meet many famous past and present cricketers who had featured heavily in my reading, none more so than Sir Donald Bradman and Harold Larwood. It was a great privilege to visit them both again and I am very grateful to them for finding time to see me.

Test match schedules in England are always hectic affairs and I am indebted to everyone who assisted me throughout the summer, not least Debbie Brown and Alison Mitchell.

Finally, much gratitude is due to Medwyn Hughes and Gill Rowley of Columbus Books for their indulgence and many kindnesses.

BILL FRINDALL
Hereford, October 1988

AHSAN ABOUT IN PAKISTAN

England's winter schedule and three touring teams · The Reliance World Cup · England's subsequent tour of Pakistan · Haseeb Ahsan and the background to the Shakoor Rana/Gatting confrontation · TCCB intervention · Aftermath

When England's itinerary for the winter of 1987-88 was first scheduled it involved just a normal tour of Pakistan and New Zealand, merely a repeat of the successful format of similar tours in 1977-78 and 1983-84. At that stage it was assumed that the 1987 World Cup would be staged in England like its three predecessors. When India and Pakistan were granted the franchise for that tournament it had to be added to England's list of winter chores. Then came a commemorative Test and one-day international to help Australia celebrate its bicentenary of white settlement. The grand result was a ridiculous programme that allowed England's key cricketers barely a fortnight's break at the end of an exhausting home season, a three-week hiatus at Christmas, and only another fortnight before reporting back for pre-season training with their counties. Talk about overkill!

Not surprisingly David Gower decided this was a good winter to take a sabbatical, Ian Botham signed a three-year contract with Queensland, Graham Gooch opted for half-measures only and Vic Marks preferred to become a father. Phil Edmonds, a stateless entrepreneur having had his relations with Middlesex severed, made himself available for the Pakistan sector only, an offer which the selectors found they could refuse.

Faced with such a schedule the tour selectors chose separate combinations for the winter's three distinct phases: the Reliance World Cup in Pakistan and India, the tour of Pakistan, and the post-Christmas tour of New Zealand and Australia.

Graham Dilley was selected for the World Cup but did not recover from injury in time. Paul Jarvis took his place and ironically, because of various maladies, was one of only two players among the eight fourteen-man squads who did not play in a single match. The other was Tony Gray, who fractured an arm; unusually for a West Indies fast bowler, it was one of his own.

WORLD CUP	PAKISTAN	AUSTRALASIA
M. W. Gatting (Captain)	M. W. Gatting (Captain)	M. W. Gatting (Captain)
J. E. Emburey (Vice-captain)	J. E. Emburey (Vice-captain)	J. E. Emburey (Vice-captain)
C. W. J. Athey	C. W. J. Athey	C. W. J. Athey
B. C. Broad	B. C. Broad	B. C. Broad
P. A. J. DeFreitas	D. J. Capel	D. J. Capel
P. R. Downton	N. G. B. Cook	P. A. J. DeFreitas
N. A. Foster	P. A. J. DeFreitas	G. R. Dilley
G. A. Gooch	G. R. Dilley	N. H. Fairbrother
E. E. Hemmings	N. H. Fairbrother	N. A. Foster
P. W. Jarvis	N. A. Foster	B. N. French
A. J. Lamb	B. N. French	E. E. Hemmings
D. R. Pringle	G. A. Gooch	P. W. Jarvis
R. T. Robinson	E. E. Hemmings	M. D. Moxon
G. C. Small	P. W. Jarvis	N. V. Radford
	R. T. Robinson	C. J. Richards
	R. C. Russell	R. T. Robinson

There were no surprise inclusions among England's World Cup list. The accent was very much on experience, to such an extent that their average age had exceeded 30 by the time they began the tournament by defeating the West Indies on 9 October.

Only six of the side that drew the fifth Test against Pakistan had survived; David Gower, Ian Botham and Phil Edmonds opted out, while Martyn Moxon and Bruce French have seldom excelled at the one-day game. There were recalls for Graham Gooch (at long last), Paul Downton, Allan Lamb, Derek Pringle and Eddie Hemmings. The other nine (plus Lamb) had helped to win two one-day trophies in Australia the previous winter.

Gooch could hardly have been omitted after proving the complete restoration of his confidence and technique at the Lord's Bicentenary. Nothing will convince me that he would not have achieved it a lot sooner had he been brought back for the last two Tests against Pakistan.

Downton deserved his return. No one works harder at his game and, with 1,052 runs and 61 dismissals, he had enjoyed a fine season with Middlesex under Gatting's selectorial eye. Importantly, he had done well – and stayed fit – on two previous tours of the subcontinent.

Lamb is such an outstanding limited-overs cricketer that his must have been one of the first names on the final list. With Gower and Botham gone, his experience should have made him an automatic choice for the winter's other tours as well.

The unenviable task of taking on Botham's mantle fell on Pringle, just as it did in 1986 during the living legend's suspension for unacceptable hobbies. The Essex all-rounder has become a tougher competitor than in his premature days at Test level but is still rather injury-prone. His bowling earned him the nod over David Capel.

I was delighted that Hemmings was chosen. He is a supreme competitor and an aggressive, attacking bowler. Now that Edmonds has gone he could well be the best slow bowling partner for John Emburey.

A stupendous sigh of relief was heard all over Hyderabad in Sind on 8 October when cricket's first World Cup to be staged simultaneously in two countries began with a little subcontinental derby between Pakistan and Sri Lanka. Such was the confusion both potential and imagined concerning the schedule that it is necessary to qualify Hyderabad. Its Indian version in Deccan staged a match two days later.

The three previous World Cups in England had been a doddle to organize with 60-overs matches culminating in finals at Lord's and with 'The Pru' as their sponsors. This extravaganza involved 50-overs games spread throughout India and Pakistan, two countries only recently at war. The final was expected to be between those two host nations, a match at which a volatile crowd of over 90,000 would test the organizers and police at Calcutta's renovated Eden Gardens stadium.

Apart from incredibly complex problems involving the transport and accommodation of eight teams with their officials and attendant press, media communications, crowd control and the ever-present political threat towards players with South African connections, the organizers had to invent a competition in which matches could be finished within seven hours of actual play. This meant reducing the games to 50-overs, starting play at 9 a.m. and levying severe fines on teams who failed to bowl their overs within 3½ hours.

Clive Lloyd, who captained West Indies to victory in the first two world cups, was a harsh critic of the playing conditions: 'It will just be a lottery with pitches varying appreciably between the two countries. The very early start will compel the side winning the toss to bat first because the overnight dew will keep the ball wet and the hot morning sun will prevent it swinging.'

The former Pakistan captain Mushtaq Mohammad agreed, adding: 'It's the worst time to play cricket in Pakistan – very hot and humid. February and March would have been much better.'

In the event neither the early start nor the weather proved a problem and the whole competition went off almost without a hitch. The organization, particularly in Pakistan, where President Zia took a personal interest and the army was called upon to improve amenities at some grounds, was exemplary. No side was fined for slow over-rates.

Before the England party left from Heathrow Airport on 28 September I wrote in *The Mail on Sunday*, referring to the comments of Lloyd and Mushtaq:

> These are all factors that could help England win their first world cup after being losing finalists once and losing semi-finalists twice. They are in the stronger group and must compete with favourites Pakistan, West Indies and Sri Lanka. They will be helped by having to field only 50 overs in that heat and must have a tremendous chance of winning their fourth one-day trophy of the year if Mike Gatting has reasonable luck with the toss.

To do so they must beat the West Indies, who will be hampered by the absence of Malcolm Marshall, Joel Garner, Gordon Greenidge and Michael Holding and frustrated by the 'no bouncers' rule. No one knows what a summer in Rishton has done for Viv Richards. But, as Imran Khan is quick to point out: 'West Indies will only win a 50-overs match if Viv comes in at three.'

Their rival semi-finalists are likely to be India and Australia, unless New Zealand's Martin Crowe can score enough runs to compensate for the absence of Richard Hadlee.

Injury, exhaustion or medical hazards real and imagined have robbed the tournament of too many star names for the organizers' comfort. Any world jamboree lacking Hadlee, David Gower, Ian Botham and four key West Indians must be heavily devalued in terms of standard and entertainment.

Perhaps it was. But it was great fun and appeared from a distance to be a fine advertisement for international cricket and goodwill. Analysed purely in cricket terms the competition did not prove very much. The winners could not claim to be world champions: only a tournament of five-day Test matches could decide that title. What it did do was to prove to the rest of the cricketing world that two of its poorer relations could stage a world event even more complex and splendiferous than the three held in Britain. It also revealed which side was best at playing 50-overs cricket in India and Pakistan in October.

Regrettably I have to write 'appeared from a distance', because while this tournament and England's subsequent adventures in Pakistan were taking place I was having my hands rearranged. This was not because I had decided to change from inswing to outswing or make a late conversion to bowling leg-breaks and googlies. For some reason yet to be fathomed by medical science I have for the past 25 years suffered from a condition known as Dupuytren's contractures. They first appeared in the arch of my left foot, and waited an entire decade before attacking its partner. Eight years ago they developed in the palm of my left hand and more recently they have afflicted the right.

Dupuytrens are benign fibrous growths that entwine themselves around nerves and ligaments cramping the fingers in towards the palm. They rarely affect the feet. In most cases they involve only the little fingers and, once removed by surgery, rarely recur. They are named after a Frenchman who studied them at length without ever discovering their cause. Normally they are hereditary.

Mine are not hereditary, nor do they respond to surgery. My feet have been surgically attacked three times and my hands a combined total of five. By the middle of the 1987 season both hands were again badly affected and John Strachan, a highly experienced Harley Street specialist, wanted me to have further surgery and radiotherapy in mid-season. As a freelance with a number of contracts to honour it was impossible for me to be out of action before the end of September. And so I underwent surgery on my right hand on 1 October and the left on 12 November. After each operation lasting 90 minutes and involving over 20 stitches I had a course of six sessions of radiotherapy to attempt to discourage the little blighters from returning.

And so my goal was to get both hands healed and in working order before leaving for Adelaide on 17 January. If some of my colleagues thought I was swinging the lead, I can assure them that I would sooner have endured the heat and unpleasant moments in Pakistan rather than the discomfort and frustration of my handicapped autumn in London.

The group matches went very much according to prediction, with India and Australia qualifying for the semi-finals from the weaker Group A and Pakistan and England heading Group B. Of those four, England had the poorest record having lost two games while the others were beaten only once. Gatting's side twice defeated a disappointing West Indies team and were themselves twice beaten by Pakistan. New Zealand's only successes were against Zimbabwe, who, like Sri Lanka, failed to win a match.

With the two host countries gaining home ties for the semi-final, all seemed set for them both to contest the final, just as the organizers had planned. But those semi-finals were to provide the most devastating blows ever inflicted upon cricket on the subcontinent. First, Australia beat Pakistan by 18 runs at Lahore, Craig McDermott taking 5 wickets, and then, the following day, England overwhelmed the holders by 35 runs at Bombay after Graham Gooch had literally swept his way to a very remarkable hundred.

Kapil Dev was swiftly separated from the

Indian captaincy. Leaders who lose the World Cup must expect the knife and Kapil would not have been surprised by the news that he had been succeeded by Dilip Vengsarkar. Ironically India would probably have won the trophy had Vengsarkar not been stricken by food poisoning shortly before the semi-final.

With an immaculate sense of timing Imran Khan had already announced his first retirement, although subsequently he allowed the President to persuade him to lead Pakistan on their tour of the Caribbean.

The semi-final shocks had horrific effects in both host countries. A Lahore student suffered a fatal heart attack soon after Pakistan's defeat, whilst, in Bombay, three rioters were shot dead by police when Hindus and Moslems fought pitched battles after England's victory. More than 20 people were injured in disturbances that involved stabbings and the throwing of bricks and acid bombs. Similar fights broke out in Baroda and Ahmedabad.

The Final itself was a triumph for the organizers and for Allan Border's young Australian team. Given a flying start by David Boon and Geoff Marsh, they managed to thwart England by just 7 runs in a most exciting contest. Few would have predicted their success, even fewer the identity of the two finalists.

Gooch, Lamb and Gatting had been England's outstanding batsmen. DeFreitas and Emburey were the most economical bowlers. Downton, Pringle, Lamb and Small had completed their winter's touring antics, the first two with such scant success that they probably thought they had played their last international cricket.

Poor Pringle conceded 83 runs off his 10 overs against the West Indies in England's opening match and failed with the bat. Next morning at breakfast, TV commentator Ray Illingworth was heard saying: 'I can't understand it. Keith Fletcher assured me that Pringle would be a banker both as a batsman and as a bowler.' 'Are you sure he said banker?' queried a colleague.

Allan Lamb's departure was greatly lamented. He had played a major part in winning two matches and averaged 59.80 in the tournament. With Gooch unavailable for the antipodean tour, England would be desperately short of experienced batting. Lamb returned home, signed a contract to play for Orange Free State in the Currie Cup, and promptly hit a career-best 294 against a strong Eastern Province side. His 394-minute marathon gained Lamb 50,000 rand for making the highest score in the history of the competition, another 50,000 rand for sharing a record South African 5th-wicket partnership of 355, and a further 15,000 rand for scoring 150 off fewer than 300 balls and 200 in under 400 balls. It was a strong message to Chairman May.

(Opposite) Watched by Kiran More, Graham Gooch (115) sweeps England to victory in the Reliance World Cup semi-final against India at Bombay.

(Above) Mike Gatting communes quietly with his Maker after joining Abdul Qadir's lengthy list of dubious lbw victims at Lahore.

England hardly had time to draw breath before their frenetic winter schedule entered its second stage with the rare treat of a three-day match. That game, against the President's XI at Rawalpindi, heralded the start of their sixth major tour of Pakistan, a 37-day affair which included 8 days of travel and 24 days of cricket: three Tests, three one-day internationals and two three-day games. England's 15 previous Test matches in Pakistan had resulted in 13 draws and one solitary victory – 26 years previously in their very first Test in Pakistan when Ted Dexter's side won by 5 wickets.

England's six new members arrived from England looking pale and interesting. David Capel, Nick Cook, Graham Dilley, Neil Fairbrother, Bruce French and 'Jack' Russell acclimatized quickly but not before French had added to an ever-growing list of bizarre injuries. These include being bitten by a dog on a training run (Heaven knows what would have happened if the dog had been running seriously). This time he was hit on the head by a ball during practice; it was thrown by a spectator. Walking across hospital grounds to have four stitches inserted in his gashed left eyebrow, he was knocked down but not damaged by an erratically driven car. He then completed an unlikely but notable hat-trick by smashing his head on an overhead light as he arose from the stitching operation.

Gladstone Small was retained as temporary cover for the ailing Paul Jarvis until the Yorkshireman managed his first match bowl of the tour at Rawalpindi: 17-2-51-1. Small returned home and so, soon afterwards, did Jarvis. Suffering from circulation problems in his bowling hand, he was to spend several days in hospital before regaining fitness just in time to join the flight to New Zealand.

After drawing a soporific encounter with the President's Men, England had to play three more one-day internationals, bringing their total for 1987 to 31. John Emburey had played in them all. Having already spent five weeks doing what Wilfred Rhodes once pithily described as 'swiping about' contesting a limited-overs tournament, it was astonishing that the respective cricket boards of Pakistan and England had agreed to include three more of the wretched matches before the Test series. This really was cricket prostitution. The three games, all won by England with increasing margins of comfort, were watched by a grand total of 20,000 spectators. It was a clear message from the public that enough is enough. Certainly the players did not want them. Javed Miandad had the sense to go missing for a week.

At last, on 25 November, two months after leaving London, England began a Test match. Within an hour they realized it was a mistake. Played on a pitch that proffered an extravagant degree of turn from the first hour, it was one of the most unsavoury games of cricket ever played, soured by some appalling umpiring by Shakil Khan standing in his third Test.

Tragically, the bitter controversy caused by Shakil's decisions completely overshadowed an historic display of leg-break and googly bowling by Abdul Qadir. He completely dominated the match from the moment he came on to bowl the 11th over after 45 minutes. In a spell of 37 overs broken only by scheduled intervals he returned figures of 9 for 56, the best analysis ever returned against England in 639 Tests since 1877. Only four superior analyses have been achieved in Test cricket – by Jim Laker (twice) in 1956, by George Lohmann in 1895-96 and by Richard Hadlee in 1985-86.

Bamboozling umpire and batsmen with a heady mix of leg-breaks, top-spinners, googlies and flippers, Qadir added four more wickets in the second innings as England mustered only a paltry 130, equalling their lowest total against Pakistan set at The Oval in 1954. With the dazzling figures of 13 for 95 from 73 overs, Qadir returned Pakistan's best match analysis against England, and took ten or more wickets in a Test for the fourth time in 49 appearances, and for the second match in succession (following his 10 for 211 at The Oval the previous August).

Thus, shortly after lunch on the fourth day, Pakistan completed their massacre. The final margin of an innings and 87 runs was the largest of their five victories in 45 Tests against England.

It is necessary to put on record the other side of the coin.

The tourists claimed that five of Qadir's lbw victims were not out. To those must be added Capel's second innings dismissal, given out caught at second slip off his arm.

Nor were England's batsmen alone in their suffering. Qadir himself was given out stumped when French had clearly bungled his first attempt and the batsman had recovered his ground before the second one. England surrendered much moral ground by not recalling him. Qadir, on the other hand, gave one of the worst (or possibly the best) displays of dissent when he angrily remonstrated with everyone in earshot.

But even this virtuoso performance dimmed in comparison with that of Chris Broad a little later. Given out caught at the wicket off a ball he missed by several inches, he simply refused to leave his crease until nanny Gooch came and led him gently away. That evening the tour manager, Peter Lush, called one of his more dramatic press conferences. He announced that Broad had been reprimanded but not fined, and then delivered a none-too-subtle broadside at the umpiring.

Broad should most certainly have been fined, if not suspended, and the right time and place for complaining about the umpires was certainly not a mid-match press conference.

I wish I could have seen this Test, not least because I regret having missed the greatest current exponent of a dying art completely dominating a major match. For too long we have been confronted with Test cricket governed by guileless pace and monotonous seam bowling. Watching a fleet-footed batsman unravelling the mysteries of flight and disguised spin provides the caviar and champagne of cricket.

I should also like to have witnessed for myself the reportedly blatant cheating of fielders claiming non-catches and the apparent ineptitude of umpire Shakil Khan. Having been marooned in London during this series it is impossible to make any judgement except from televised excerpts and press reports.

The key to all the unpleasantness at Lahore lies in the appointment for this match of Shakil Khan by the Board of Control for Cricket in Pakistan (BCCP). Pakistan's youngest Test umpire, he had officiated in the first of the three one-day internationals which preceded the First Test and had given a number of questionable decisions, the most significant being a highly imaginative lbw against Gatting.

Pakistan have favoured the appointment of 'neutral' umpires for some time and employed two Indian Test umpires, V. K. Ramaswamy and

Referee Bill Athey moves to separate his captain from Shakoor Rana as the infamous confrontation erupts.

P. D. Reporter, to stand in the Lahore and Karachi Tests against the West Indies in November 1986. Apparently the BCCP was prepared to employ umpires from India, Australia, New Zealand or the West Indies for this series but all were required to officiate in their own countries.

But why did the Board appoint an umpire whose performances in previous internationals had attracted much criticism when they had, in Khizer Hayat and Mahboob Shah, two experienced Test officials who had been members of the international panel which had just officiated throughout the Reliance World Cup?

The answer to that question involves Haseeb Ahsan, Pakistan's Team Manager and Chairman of Selectors, and his influence over other members of the BCCP. Haseeb has a very large axe to grind when it comes to umpires. As the leading off-spin bowler on Pakistan's 1962 tour of England he had returned home prematurely after doubts were expressed about his action. As manager of the 1987 Pakistan team, he had twittered round the touring circuit, bemusing and bewildering, his role as a media shield for his captain, Imran Khan, grossly underestimated. The TCCB treated him unwisely, curtly dismissing his plea to have David Constant suspended from the panel of Test umpires.

From that moment he seems to have masterminded his revenge brilliantly, happily casting himself in the role of Wicked Uncle against Gatting's hapless Babes in the Wood. First he ignored Imran's recommendation to appoint Ramiz Raja as his successor because his dastardly plot demanded that the mischievous Javed Miandad be cast in the role of *agent provocateur*. Then he selected his most compliant puppet umpires to stage-manage the kidnap of the series. His final malevolent touch was to ensure that a timid groundsman queered the pitch.

England had a short respite before the Second Test at Faisalabad. It involved a drawn three-day match against the Punjab Chief Minister's XI at Sahiwal. There they were cosily accommodated within the Montgomery Biscuit Factory, Montgomery being the name of the venue when it was part of India under the British flag.

The Faisalabad Test proved even more sinister than its hot, dusty, disreputable predecessor. Naughty Uncle Haseeb had found a second dubious official in Shakoor Rana and another turf wizard to under-prepare the pitch. But this time the pitch-doctoring backfired and, a few minutes before stumps on the second day, Pakistan had drifted to 106 for 5, still 186 behind England's first innings total of 292.

At that stage Shakoor Rana, standing at square-leg, decided to invoke Law 42 (notes 3 and 6) on the grounds of unfair play by Gatting, who was fielding in front of him at backward short-leg. Eager to squeeze in one more over, Gatting, having advised the batsman, Salim Malik, of his intentions, had surreptitiously moved Capel in a few years from long-leg as Hemmings was starting his delivery approach.

That Law states:

Note 3. Intervention by the Umpire. The umpires shall intervene without appeal by calling and signalling 'dead ball' in the case of unfair play, but should not otherwise interfere with the progress of the game except as required to do so by the Laws.

Note 6. Incommoding the Striker. An umpire is justified in intervening under this Law and shall call and signal 'dead ball' if, in his opinion, any player of the fielding side incommodes the striker by any noise or action while he is receiving the ball.

Clearly Rana was exceeding his powers. Salim Malik subsequently confirmed that Gatting had warned him the fielder was being moved and that he was in no way being incommoded.

The result was a furious confrontation between Gatting and Rana. Players close to the scene were adamant that the first abusive language came from the umpire who addressed the England captain as a 'f---ing, cheating bastard'. The appellation 'sahib' seems to have been omitted. Gatting's uncontrolled response was equally colourful and the two had to be separated by Athey, who had himself been involved in a row with Rana only a short time before.

There followed an unprecedented hiatus lasting more than a day when Rana refused to officiate until he had received an unconditional apology from Gatting. This the England captain was happy to provide just as soon as Rana apologized for his accusation of cheating.

The morning after the incident the England team took the field at the appointed hour of ten o'clock, and waited with a few groundstaff and photographers until 10.27 for the absent umpires and Pakistan batsmen. In their continued non-appearance everyone then trooped back to the pavilion for the remainder of a wasted sunny day.

By noon, draft statements of apology had been prepared for the two protagonists. Gatting agreed to sign his but, just when Rana was on the point of submission, Javed Miandad disrupted the truce by persuading him that his honour and that of his country had been besmirched. Rana declined to apologize and the stalemate resumed.

The appointment of Javed Miandad, the street-fighter urchin, to succeed Imran Khan, the warrior lord, was again the work of Haseeb Ahsan. A veritable Scargill of Test cricketers, Miandad's last stint of captaincy ended when he found himself isolated by a mutiny which left him commanding a team of one. With Pakistan in trouble in the current match, he had every reason for delaying the resumption as long as possible to safeguard his lead in the series.

Lush telephoned Lord's, where a scheduled meeting of the TCCB happened to be discussing the situation, and then went to Lahore, some two-and-a-half hours' drive, hoping to meet the BCCP President, General Safdar Butt. The general was otherwise engaged and they eventually met the following morning, on the rest day of the Test. With Haseeb Ahsan also present it is not surprising that nothing was achieved.

On the fourth day of the match, the TCCB, following talks with the Foreign Office, ordered Lush 'to take whatever action was necessary' to restart the match. Lush responded by instructing Gatting 'in the wider interests of the game... to write an apology to Shakoor Rana'. Under protest Gatting submitted a note, written in block capitals on lined paper, which read:

> Dear Shakoor Rana,
>
> I apologize for the bad language used during the 2nd day of the Test match at Fisalabad [*sic*].
>
> [signed] Mike Gatting 11th Dec. 1987

One of the more extraordinary and reluctant international peace treaties, it did allow play to resume one day and 35 minutes late.

The matter was far from over. Understandably angered by Rana's refusal to apologize to their captain and by their management having the ground shot from under them by Lord's officialdom, the English team was on the verge of mutiny. The tourists decided to continue the match but issued a statement after that day's play. This deplored the fact that the governing bodies of both countries could not effect a compromise solution, and registered 'a unanimous protest' against the TCCB's action. The statement ended with the poignant sentence: 'The incident was sad for cricket but the solution forced upon us is even sadder.' Pakistan eventually escaped with a draw.

Gatting threatened to resign the captaincy but changed his mind after talks with the TCCB's chairman, Raman Subba Row, and their chief executive, Alan Smith. Former Test cricketers both, they had flown to Karachi for crisis talks soon after the Faisalabad match had ended. These discussions eased the tension between the Board and the team who had been supported by Lush and Stewart throughout.

Like the Good Little Fairy Birds in *Babes in the Wood*, the arrival of the English officials demanded that Uncle Haseeb provide a decent pitch and unbiased umpires for the Third and final Test at Karachi. Mahboob Shah and Khizer Hayat duly officiated as Pakistan gained the better of a draw to maintain their unbeaten record at the National Stadium, 26 Tests there having produced 11 victories and 15 draws.

As soon as the TCCB duo flew home to Lord's, the naughty uncle was up to his wicked tricks again. Mysterious tapes of the notorious double-act featuring Gatting and Rana suddenly fell into his hands. He set up an official enquiry into the incident, appointing Omar Kureishi and Yawar Saeed as his 'independent' panel. Omar, himself a former manager of Pakistan touring teams, had criticized England's recent behaviour most scathingly in his newspaper reports and while commentating on television. But, alas, the good fairies must have doctored the tapes. Shakoor the Terrible could not be vindicated. Ranagate was doomed. Never in the uproarious history of pantomime had there been a more blatant display of Ahsan about.

During this series I took up John Arlott's generous invitation to convalesce at The Vines. 'Come and stay with me, Frindalius, and I'll get you pissed twice a day,' he promised. As ever, the Sage of Alderney was as good as his word and the

The Longest Day: Neil Fairbrother, Graham Dilley and Chris Broad during Test cricket's hiatus at Faisalabad.

treatment certainly improved my pain threshold – I felt none.

Tucked away on his beloved Channel Island, he had kept an ear half-tuned to the radio commentaries from Pakistan and had been greatly saddened by those events. A sensitive and supremely compassionate man, he would not be drawn into any criticism of the England team's behaviour. John is eminently suited to the role of President of the Cricketers' Association, an office he regards as his greatest reward from the game he broadcast for 36 summers, 'because it came from the players':

I felt immense sympathy for the players, the players on *both* sides. I don't think that the tour, even coming after a Pakistan series in England and the World Cup, was ill-conceived but, once the trouble started, I couldn't see how it could have been avoided. Once the unpleasantness began, I had no interest in the tour. Now I just want to forget it.

That must be the saddest testimony of all about a tour that did untold damage to the game's reputation.

The England team and press had been counting the days until flight BA146 left Karachi for London on 22 December. During a Christmas break lasting just over three weeks the management and captain had to submit tour reports and meet TCCB officials at Lord's. The captain and his entire team were given a free pardon for any displays of dissent and awarded a special bonus of £1,000 in view of the exceptionally traumatic nature of the Pakistan mission. This windfall, subsequently the subject of some criticism by the TCCB executive, was the brainchild of Raman Subba Row.

The controversial bonus and the TCCB's reluctance to censure England's players were probably not wholly unconnected to the fact that the Board had chosen to ignore a report by the selectors which predicted major conflict and strife.

Following Pakistan's malevolent 1987 tour of Britain, the England selectors had compiled a confidential report which warned of further trouble between two sides who were doomed to play each other in six different competitions during 1987. Had the TCCB cancelled the tour, relations with Pakistan's authorities would certainly have deteriorated even further.

Cricket's future historians will inevitably label 1987 as the year of the great umpiring fracas in Pakistan. Sadly, the year's greatest moments will have to take second billing to the lamentable behaviour of players, umpires and administrators during that traumatic series.

Forget about Australia's epic tied Test at Madras, the Lord's Bicentenary, or the Reliance World Cup. Never mind Sunil Gavaskar's unique 10,000th Test run, or the magnificent bowling feats of Qadir and Hadlee. When 1987 is recalled, their memory will be over-shadowed by that hideous confrontation between a captain and an umpire at the game's highest level.

It was the year in which an entire day's Test cricket was lost for reasons wholly unconnected with the weather, the year in which a batsman actually refused to walk after being given out, and the year in which a team's persistent dissent was punished by a £1,000 bonus. It must also be remembered as the year in which a young club umpire in India died from head injuries received when he was attacked by a stump-wielding player during a minor match.

Perhaps cricket's current troubles date back to 1775. That was the year in which wickets, then just a foot high and only six inches wide, gained a third stump. Was it merely a coincidence that the very same year saw William Waterfall of Derby become the first man to be convicted of manslaughter on the field of play?

England's tour of New Zealand had hardly started before there were dramatic changes at the helm of Pakistan's cricket. Imran Khan, finally succumbing to the pressures of student hunger-strikes, fasting and an audience with President Zia ul-Haq, was persuaded out of retirement to captain his country on their Caribbean tour in March and April. One suspects that the subsequent resignations of the BCCP president and his three-man selection committee, including the notorious Haseeb Ahsan, were the result of a deal leading to Imran's return.

Dynamically led by Imran and astutely managed by the highly respected Intikhab Alam, Pakistan were to redeem the 1987-88 season with some outstanding cricket and, although held to a draw in a pulsating three-match series, did manage to inflict the first home defeat on the West Indies for ten years.

ENGLAND'S TASK IN THE ANTIPODES

Setting the scene for the New Zealand Tour and Sydney's Bicentenary Test · Gatting under pressure · The new recruits · Statistical profiles of the touring team · Assessment of the New Zealand side

Refreshed by his 22-day Christmas recess and determined to put all memories of Pakistan firmly behind him, Mike Gatting reported to Heathrow's Sheraton Skyline Hotel to lead a somewhat revamped touring team on the final lap of their convoluted winter.

His first task was to spearhead the launch of Kwik Cricket, a mini version of the game, simplified for boys and girls from tots to teenagers. After a dozen local schoolchildren had demonstrated the game at the hotel, Gatting was persuaded to have a bat. The England captain, with 3,691 runs from 61 Tests, faced the bowling of a robust 11-year-old. Over went the young lad's arm, the blue plastic ball pitched on a length and down went the blue plastic off stump. It seemed a bad omen, especially as the young demon bowler was named Dipak Patel. His older namesake, a Kenyan-born Worcestershire all-rounder, had recently established himself in New Zealand's team.

No England captain can have embarked on a tour of New Zealand under the mental pressures borne by Gatting. Even buoyed up by enormous public support, he must have realized that his little contretemps with Shakoor the Terrible would inevitably feature as one of the most shameful acts on any cricket field. Bearing in mind that Keith Fletcher reckoned that he had been replaced as captain merely for tapping a bail from his stumps during a Test in India, Gatting must have wondered if chairman of selectors Peter May was oiling the rack and thumb screws in readiness for his return in March. Meanwhile David Gower, refreshed after his winter's sabbatical and reappointed as Leicestershire's leader, was waiting eagerly in the wings.

Gatting's comments at a conference given shortly before the team's departure revealed that he regarded his tenure of the England captaincy as anything but secure. 'I will do the captaincy job as I see it but, if people are not happy with the way that I perform, then I will stand down,' he said. 'I will give 100 per cent as I always do but, if I cannot be captain, I would still love to continue playing for England.'

He is such a whole-hearted cricketer that one instinctively wished him well and hoped this tour would bring many happier moments for him. I have known him since he was a teenage club cricketer and have delighted in his success after his early setbacks at international level.

Tour manager Peter Lush was well aware of the pressures caused by the Pakistan tour. 'We must put Pakistan behind us and get on with it. We are aware of what is expected in behaviour on the field. We will take the rough with the smooth and will not query umpires' decisions or publicly discuss them,' he promised.

The 16 players and four officials who boarded British Airways flight BA11 included three changes from the party which had endured the pre-Christmas ordeal. Inevitably the ranks would be hugely depleted by the absence of Graham Gooch, who had completed his agreed stint of touring. Yorkshire's Martyn Moxon, his replacement, was an opener of sound technique who learned much from his turbulent years as Sir Geoffrey's understudy – not least the art of surviving dodgy calling. His international career had been tinged with catastrophe. Twice he had been compelled to interrupt earlier tours, once when his father was taken seriously ill, and later when he died. A week before this flight his father-in-law had passed away suddenly but his family had urged him not to withdraw from the tour. Competition for places in the current England team was fiercest among opening batsmen and Moxon realized that he was embarking on a tour that could make or break his international career.

Other newcomers to the ever-changing England party were Worcestershire's bustling seam bowler Neal Radford (for the left-arm spin of Nick Cook) and Surrey's wicket-keeper 'Jack' Richards (for 'Jack' Russell). Both selections were open to criticism.

If only two spinners were required surely Cook's left-arm leg-breaks would provide more variety in attack than two off-spinners. With a Test scheduled for the spinner's paradise of Sydney, this was likely to prove a mistake. The selectors argued that only one spinner would be employed in New Zealand and that Emburey and Hemmings were very dissimilar in style.

Radford arrived straight from Transvaal where he had been in cracking form. The leading wicket-taker in English first-class cricket last season with 109 wickets, he had just taken 23 Currie Cup wickets in only three matches on plumb former Test pitches at The Wanderers and Newlands. Even so, he knew that he must compete for one of three Test match places with Dilley, Foster, DeFreitas and Jarvis.

Richards was the fourth 'keeper to be involved in this winter's gadabout. He would have been a much sounder choice for the World Cup. Having chosen Russell for the Pakistan section it made little sense to jettison him now. By the end of the 1987 season most professional observers of county cricket, players and umpires included, rated him the best of a highly-talented crop of young 'keepers. It would surely have made more sense to have given him as much experience of international cricket as possible.

One omission put even those selectorial blunders in the shade. Bereft of the experience of Gooch, Gower and Botham, the batting desperately needed the class of Allan Lamb; his absence was extraordinary.

Apart from their captain, England's batting line-up looked terribly brittle. Their bowling had often been vulnerable and erratic in Pakistan; it tended to struggle to dismiss sides twice. Only a brave spirit would have backed this ensemble to add to the meagre tally of two Test victories so far gained under Gatting's eighteen-match reign.

THE TOURING PARTY

(Statistics updated to 13 January 1988; * denotes not out)

CAPTAIN

GATTING, Michael William. Born Kingsbury, Middlesex, 6 June 1957. 5 ft 10 in tall. Educated at John Kelly High School. Sturdily-built, pugnacious right-handed batsman who can bowl medium-paced seamers. Middlesex debut 1975; capped 1977; captain since 1983; benefit 1988. Cricket Writers' Club Young Cricketer of 1981. One of *Wisden*'s Five Cricketers of 1983. Created MBE in 1987. 61 Test appearances for England having made his debut against Pakistan at Karachi in January 1978, 18 as captain (won 2, lost 5, drew 11). Highest Test score 207 *v*. India (Madras) 1984-85; best bowling 1-14. 74 limited-overs internationals, 30 as captain (won 21, lost 9). Previous tours: Australia 1986-87 (captain); West Indies 1980-81 and 1985-86; New Zealand 1977-78 and 1983-84; India and Sri Lanka 1981-82 and 1984-85; Pakistan 1977-78, 1983-84 and 1987-88; Zimbabwe 1980-81 (for Middlesex). 1,000 runs in a season nine times in UK and once overseas; most – 2,257, in 1984. Highest first-class score 258 Middlesex *v*. Somerset (Bath) 1984; best bowling 5-34 Middlesex *v*. Glamorgan (Swansea) 1982.

VICE-CAPTAIN

EMBUREY, John Ernest. Born at Peckham, South London, 20 August 1952. 6 ft 2 in tall. Educated at Peckham Manor Secondary School. Off-spin bowler and increasingly prolific eccentric right-handed batsman. Middlesex debut 1973; capped 1977; benefit 1986. One of *Wisden*'s Five Cricketers of 1983. Played for Western Province 1982-83 and 1983-84. 49 Test appearances for England having made his debut against New Zealand at Lord's in August 1978. Highest Test score 75 *v*. New Zealand (Trent Bridge) 1986; best bowling 7-78 *v*. Australia (Sydney) 1986-87. 47 limited-overs internationals, 3 as captain (won 2, lost 1). Previous tours: Australia 1978-79, 1979-80 and 1986-87; South Africa 1981-82 (for

South African Breweries England XI); West Indies 1980-81 and 1985-86; India 1979-80 and 1981-82; Pakistan 1987-88; Sri Lanka 1977-78 (for D.H. Robins' XI) and 1981-82; Zimbabwe 1980-81 (for Middlesex). 100 wickets in a season once – 103 in 1983. Highest first-class score 133 Middlesex *v.* Essex (Chelmsford) 1983; best bowling 7-36 Middlesex *v.* Cambridge University (Fenner's) 1977.

ATHEY, Charles William Jeffrey. Born at Middlesbrough, Yorkshire, 27 September 1957. 5ft 9½in tall. Educated at Stainsby Secondary School and at Acklam Hall High School. Stylish right-handed batsman who can bowl medium-paced seamers. Played for Yorkshire 1976-83; capped 1980. Gloucestershire debut 1984; capped 1985. 20 Test appearances for England having made his debut against Australia at Lord's in August 1980. Highest Test score 123 *v.* Pakistan (Lord's) 1987. 29 limited-overs internationals. Previous tours: Australia 1986-87; West Indies 1980-81; New Zealand 1979-80 (for D.H. Robins' XI); Pakistan 1987-88; Sri Lanka 1985-86 (for England B). 1,000 runs in a season six times; most – 1,812, in 1984. Highest first-class score 184 England B *v.* Sri Lanka (Galle) 1985-86; best bowling 3-3 Gloucestershire *v.* Hampshire (Bristol) 1985.

BROAD, Brian Christopher. Born at Bristol, 29 September 1957. 6ft 4in tall. Educated at Colston's School (Bristol) and at St Paul's College (Cheltenham). Left-handed opening batsman who, very occasionally, is allowed to bowl right-handed at medium-pace. Played for Gloucestershire 1979-83; capped 1981. Nottinghamshire debut and cap 1984. Played for Orange Free State (captain) 1985-86. 17 Test appearances for England having made his debut against West Indies at Lord's in June 1984. Highest Test score 162 *v.* Australia (Perth) 1986-87. 26 limited-overs internationals. Previous tours: Australia 1986-87; Pakistan 1987-88; Zimbabwe 1984-85 (for English Counties XI). 1,000 runs in a season six times; most – 1,786, in 1985. Highest first-class score 171 Nottinghamshire *v.* Derbyshire (Derby) 1985; best bowling 2-14 Gloucestershire *v.* West Indians (Bristol) 1980.

CAPEL, David John. Born at Northampton, 6 February 1963. 5ft 11in tall. Educated at Roade Comprehensive School. Right-handed all-rounder who bowls medium-fast. Northamptonshire debut 1981; capped 1986. Played for Eastern Province 1985-86 and 1986-87. 4 Test appearances for England having made his debut against Pakistan at Headingley in July 1987. Highest Test score 98 *v.* Pakistan (Karachi) 1987-88; best bowling 1-8. 6 limited-overs internationals. Highest first-class score 134 Eastern Province *v.* Western Province (Port Elizabeth) 1986-87; best bowling 7-46 Northamptonshire *v.* Yorkshire (Northampton) 1987.

DEFREITAS, Phillip Anthony Jason. Born Scotts Head, Dominica, 18 February 1966. 6ft tall. Educated at Willesden High School, London. Right-handed fast-medium bowler and long-hitting lower order batsman. UK resident since 1976. Leicestershire debut 1985; capped 1986. 7 Test appearances for England having made his debut against Australia at Brisbane in November 1987. Highest Test score 40 *v.* Australia (Brisbane) on debut; best bowling 5-86 *v.* Pakistan (Karachi) 1987-88. 30 limited-overs internationals. Previous tours: Australia 1986-87; Pakistan 1987-88. Highest first-class score 106 Leicestershire *v.* Kent (Canterbury) 1986; best bowling 7-44 (13-86 match) Leicestershire *v.* Essex (Southend) 1986.

DILLEY, Graham Roy. Born Dartford, Kent, 18 May 1959. 6ft 3in tall. Educated at Dartford West Secondary School. Right-handed fast bowler and left-handed lower order batsman. Played for Kent 1977-86; capped 1980. Worcestershire debut and cap 1987. Cricket Writers' Club Young Cricketer of 1980. Played for Natal 1985-86. 31 Test appearances for England having made his debut against Australia at Perth in December 1979. Highest Test score 56 *v.* Australia (Headingley) 1981; best bowling 6-154 *v.* Pakistan (The Oval) 1987. 34 limited-overs internationals. Previous tours: Australia 1979-80 and 1986-87; West Indies 1980-81; New Zealand 1983-84; India 1979-80 and 1981-82; Pakistan 1983-84 and 1987-88; Sri Lanka 1981-82. Highest first-class score 81 Kent *v.* Northamptonshire (Northampton) 1979; best bowling 7-63 Natal *v.* Transvaal (Johannesburg) 1985-86.

FAIRBROTHER, Neil Harvey. Born Warrington, Lancashire, 9 September 1963. 5ft 8in tall. Educated at Lymm Grammar School. Left-handed batsman and outstanding fielder who can bowl left-arm medium-paced seamers. Lancashire debut 1982; capped 1985. 2 Test appearances for England having made his debut against Pakistan at Old Trafford in June 1987. Highest Test score 3. 6 limited-overs internationals. Previous tour: Pakistan 1987-88. 1,000 runs in a season four times; most – 1,395, in 1985. Highest first-class score 164* Lancashire *v.* Hampshire (Liverpool) 1985; best bowling 2-91 Lancashire *v.* Nottinghamshire (Old Trafford) 1987.

FOSTER, Neil Alan. Born Colchester, Essex, 6 May 1962. 6ft 3in tall. Educated at Philip Morant Comprehensive School. Right-handed fast-medium bowler and improving lower-order batsman. Essex debut 1980; capped 1983. Cricket Writers' Club Cricketer of 1983. One of *Wisden's* Five Cricketers of 1988. 21 Test appearances for England having made his debut against New Zealand at Lord's in August 1983. Highest Test score 39 *v.* Pakistan (Lahore) 1987-88; best bowling 8-107 *v.* Pakistan (Headingley) 1987. 44 limited-overs internationals. Previous tours: Australia 1986-87; West Indies 1985-86; New Zealand 1983-84; Pakistan 1983-84 and 1987-88; India and Sri Lanka 1984-85. 100 wickets in a season once: 105 in 1986. Highest first-class score 74* England XI *v.* Queensland (Brisbane) 1986-87; best bowling 8-107 England *v.* Pakistan (Headingley) 1987.

FRENCH, Bruce Nicholas. Born Warsop, Nottinghamshire, 13 August 1959. 5ft 6in tall. Educated at the Meden Comprehensive School. Specialist wicket-keeper who bats right-handed. Nottinghamshire debut 1976 when aged 16 years 287 days; capped 1980. 12 Test appearances for England having made his debut against India at Headingley in June 1986. Highest Test score 59 *v.* Pakistan (Old Trafford) 1987. 9 limited-overs internationals. Previous tours: Australia 1986-87; West Indies 1985-86; Pakistan 1987-88; India and Sri Lanka 1984-85. Highest first-class score 98 Nottinghamshire *v.* Lancashire (Trent Bridge) 1984.

HEMMINGS, Edward Ernest. Born Leamington Spa, Warwickshire, 20 February 1949. 5ft 10in tall. Educated at Campion School. Off-break bowler who bats right-handed. Played for Warwickshire 1966-1978; capped 1974. Nottinghamshire debut 1979; capped 1980; benefit 1987. 6 Test appearances for England having made his debut against Pakistan at Edgbaston in July 1982. Highest Test score 95 and best bowling 3-68 *v.* Australia (Sydney) 1982-83. 13 limited-overs internationals. Previous tours: Australia 1982-83; South Africa 1974-75 (for D.H. Robins' XI); West Indies 1982-83 (for International XI); Pakistan 1981-82 (for International XI) and 1987-88. Highest first-class score 127* Nottinghamshire *v.* Yorkshire (Worksop) 1982; best bowling 10-175 International XI *v.* West Indies XI (Kingston) 1982-83.

JARVIS, Paul William. Born Redcar, Yorkshire, 29 June 1965. 5ft 10in tall. Educated at Bydales Comprehensive School, Marske. Right-handed fast-medium bowler and stylish lower-order batsman. Yorkshire debut 1981 when aged 16 years 75 days – Yorkshire's youngest representative; capped 1986. Has yet to play Test cricket or appear in a limited-overs international. Previous tours: West Indies 1986-87 (for Yorkshire); Pakistan 1987-88. Highest first-class score 47 Yorkshire *v.* Essex (Chelmsford) 1986; best bowling 7-55 Yorkshire *v.* Surrey (Headingley) 1986.

MOXON, Martyn Douglas. Born Barnsley, Yorkshire, 4 May 1960. 6ft tall. Educated at Holgate Grammar School, Barnsley. Right-handed opening batsman who can bowl at medium pace. Yorkshire debut 1981, scoring 5 and 116 *v.* Essex (Headingley); capped 1984. Played for Griqualand West 1982-83 and 1983-84. 3 Test appearances for England having made his debut against New Zealand at Lord's in July 1986. Highest Test score 74 *v.* New Zealand (Lord's) on debut. 5 limited-overs internationals. Previous tours: West Indies 1986-87 (for Yorkshire); India 1984-85; Sri Lanka 1984-85 and 1985-86 (for England B). 1,000 runs in a season three times; most – 1,447, in 1985. Highest first-class score 168 Yorkshire *v.* Worcestershire (Worcester) 1985; best bowling 3–26 D. B. Close's XI *v.* Sri Lankans (Scarborough) 1984.

RADFORD, Neal Victor. Born Luanshya, Northern Rhodesia (now Zambia), 7 June 1957. 5ft 11in tall. Educated at Athlone Boys' High School, Johannesburg. Right-handed fast-medium bowler and lower-order batsman. Brother of W. R. Radford (Orange Free State). Has played for Transvaal since 1978-79. Played for Lancashire 1980-84. Worcestershire debut and cap 1985. One of *Wisden's* Five Cricketers of 1985. 2 Test appearances for England having made his debut against India at Edgbaston in June 1986. Highest Test score 12★ *v.* New Zealand (Lord's) 1986; best bowling 2–131 *v.* India (Edgbaston) on debut. No limited-overs internationals. 100 wickets in a season twice; most – 109, in 1987. Highest first-class score 76★ Lancashire *v.* Derbyshire (Blackpool) 1981; best bowling 9–70 Worcestershire *v.* Somerset (Worcester) 1986.

RICHARDS, Clifton James ('Jack'). Born Penzance, Cornwall, 10 August 1958. 5 ft 11 in tall. Educated at Humphrey Davy Grammar School, Penzance. Specialist wicket-keeper and enterprising right-handed middle-order batsman who can also bowl off-spin. Surrey debut 1976; capped 1978; benefit 1988. Played for Orange Free State 1983-84. 6 Test appearances for England having made his debut against Australia at Brisbane in November 1986. Highest Test score 133 *v.* Australia (Perth) 1986-87. 21 limited-overs internationals. Previous tours: Australia 1986-87; West Indies 1982-83 (for International XI); New Zealand 1979-80 (for D.H. Robins' XI); India and Sri Lanka 1981-82. 1,000 runs in a season once: 1,006 in 1986. Highest first-class score 172★ Surrey *v.* Kent (The Oval) 1987; best bowling 2–42 Surrey *v.* Somerset (The Oval) 1985.

ROBINSON, Robert Timothy. Born Sutton-in-Ashfield, Nottinghamshire, 21 November 1958. 6 ft tall. Educated at Dunstable Grammar School, High Pavement Sixth Form College and Sheffield University. Right-handed opening batsman whose medium-paced seam bowling is usually kept well concealed. Nottinghamshire debut 1978; capped 1983; appointed captain for 1988. One of *Wisden's* Five Cricketers of 1985. 23 Test appearances for England having made his debut against India at Bombay in November 1984. Highest Test score 175 *v.* Australia (Headingley) 1985. 20 limited-overs internationals. Previous tours: West Indies 1985-86; India and Sri Lanka 1984-85; Pakistan 1987-88. 1,000 runs in a season five times; most – 2,032, in 1984. Highest first-class score 207 Nottinghamshire *v.* Warwickshire (Trent Bridge) 1983; best bowling 1–22.

OFFICIALS – *Manager:* Peter M. Lush. *Team manager:* Michael J. Stewart. *Physiotherapist:* Laurie G. Brown. *Scorer:* S. Peter Austin.

The schedule for this tour had been complicated by Australia's Bicentennial celebrations. After two three-day warm-up matches in New Zealand they were required to nip across to Sydney for a one-off commemorative Test, followed by a one-day international in Melbourne. Returning to the Land of the Long White Cloud, they would have another three-day game before embarking on the nitty-gritty of the tour: three Test matches and four one-dayers. Within a month of their return home the longest English first-class season ever devised was scheduled to begin.

New Zealand could no longer be described as a cosy push-over tagged on to tours of Australia. After waiting a record 26 years and 45 matches for their first Test victory, they had notched up 17 wins in the last ten years. Their home record was even more impressive. Since going down to Pakistan in 1978-79 they had not lost a series in New Zealand. All six opponent countries had been defeated with two other series drawn. Contrast that magnificent achievement with England's dismal home record over the last four seasons: defeats at the hands of West Indies, India, New Zealand and Pakistan had been interspersed by a solitary success against probably the weakest Australian team ever to visit our shores.

Although several key players, including their admirable captain, Jeremy Coney, had retired since England's last visit in 1984, the Kiwis had in Martin Crowe and Richard Hadlee two outstanding and highly competitive potential match-winners. Crowe had enjoyed reasonable success in 1987, scoring 4,045 first-class runs average 79.31. The most recent of six previous instances of a batsman scoring 4,000 runs in a calendar year was achieved back in 1948 by Len Hutton. Hadlee remained a superbly fit and mean bowling machine, even at the advanced international fast bowling age of 36. Blessed with the analytical ability of his accountant father, Walter, and inevitably spurred on by his own Lancaster Park crowd, he would cause many a palpitation amongst England's early order batsmen as he strove for the dismissal that would gain him the outright mantle of Test cricket's leading wicket-taker.

My Scoring Method

'Fergie' · How the method was devised · The system revealed

Appropriately, the first of the ten Test matches involving England during 1988 took place in Sydney, for it was that city which produced the man who, in 1905, during the first of 41 international tours, devised a revolutionary scoring system which is the basis of the method I use.

W. H. Ferguson was a remarkable character who began his working life as a filing clerk for a Sydney directory. As a respite from the tedium of filing cards with names of householders and streets all day, he used to spend his lunch hour on the waterfront gazing longingly at ships bound for exotic destinations.

At the age of 24 'Fergie' determined to escape from the bondage of his filing chores by travelling abroad. He discovered that the Australian cricket team was about to sail for England and needed a baggage master and scorer. Fearing that a written application to the tour manager would be lost amongst a mountain of pre-tour correspondence and also realizing that he had no qualifications for the job, Fergie decided upon a more painful approach. Monty Noble, considered by many to have been Australia's greatest all-rounder, had a dental practice in Sydney. During several visits for gold fillings Bill Ferguson persuaded his dentist to recommend him for the tour. Noble did so but the team set sail for England via New Zealand and Canada without him.

Then, just as his hopes had vanished, a letter arrived from Frank Laver, the tour manager, from the SS *Manuka* 'at sea near Auckland'. Dated 3 February 1905 and carefully preserved until his death, it offered Fergie the position of scorer and baggage master at £2 a week plus train fares.

He made his scoring début at London's Crystal Palace. The opposition was a Gentlemen of England team led by W. G. Grace and including Pelham Warner, Charles Fry, Archie MacLaren and Gilbert Jessop. In near-freezing conditions he opened the brand-new tour scoring book for the first time. Astonishingly, he had managed to camouflage the fact that he had never scored a cricket match in his life. Using a pencil and cribbing from his English colleague he carefully recorded the first of 1,207 tour matches. Back in his hotel room each night he would ink in the details using one of his street directory mapping pens. It must have given him special pleasure to record Monty Noble's innings of 60 and 162 in that match.

Not many matches had passed when Fergie realized that the traditional method of scoring a cricket match was extremely cumbersome and actually recorded very few of the more intricate details of an innings. Using a school exercise book he evolved the bones of the system which I use today. That book, now preserved in the Sydney offices of the New South Wales Cricket Association close to where Bill Ferguson filed his directory cards, also contains his first radial scoring charts of individual innings showing the area of the field into which each scoring stroke was played. The original 1905 tour scorebook was bought from Victor Trumper's estate by a private collector and is now the property of 'Swan' Richards, managing director of Gray-Nicholls of Australia and organizer of the Melbourne-based Crusaders touring team. Like many others preserved in the MCC Library at Lord's and at Board offices around the world, it contains many of Fergie's sketches of pavilions and scenery surrounding each ground. These were carefully drawn in the margins surrounding the scoring section of the page and made his books unique.

By an odd coincidence I happen to have the

same initials as William Henry Ferguson. We met just once. Towards the end of their 1953 tour, the Australians played the Combined Services during the Kingston Festival at Hawkers Sports Ground and, during a tea interval, a certain truant schoolboy had the temerity to visit the scorers' box and ask to see Fergie's famous book. A small, frail old man wearing a brown trilby, he was very kind and patiently showed me the latest sample of his handiwork. His meticulous contributions to the directory had given him a perfect training for scoring and it was very evident that he took a great delight in his work.

After scoring 204 Tests out of the 299 played during his working span of 49 years, he died at Bath in 1957 at the age of 77. In the course of guiding cricketers' luggage on world tours totalling an estimated 614,000 miles, he never lost a bag. Robert Menzies paid him the ultimate tribute when he wrote in the foreword to Fergie's autobiography, *Mr Cricket* (Nicholas Kaye, 1957): 'There is no better-loved man in the entire cricket world.'

When continuous ball-by-ball radio commentaries were introduced, my BBC predecessors soon discovered that the orthodox system of scoring a cricket match did not provide sufficient information for the commentators. Additional sheets had to be kept to record the number of balls faced by each batsman and, short of using a different colour for each bowler, it was impossible to analyse an innings in any detail. Arthur Wrigley (1912-65) and Roy Webber (1914-62) were the pioneer scorers for radio and television respectively. Each adapted the Ferguson method in designing their own sheets.

After Wrigley's death I practised the method by scoring from the radio commentaries on England's 1965-66 Ashes series in Australia. By the last Test I had re-designed all three sheets and made various alterations to the system itself. Apart from adding columns to the bowling sheet to record boundaries conceded, I have not needed to change my original designs. These sheets are reproduced within the chapters on each of the four Test matches played on this tour and are used by all scorers at BBC radio and television commentaries.

The method follows the basic conventions of the standard system as described in *Cricket Umpiring and Scoring*, a textbook for umpires and scorers compiled by R. S. Rait Kerr, who was secretary of the MCC from 1936 until 1952.

During BBC commentaries my system involves the use of three types of scoresheet: a ball-by-ball record of play (*Sheet 1*); an innings scorecard (*Sheet 2*); and a cumulative record of bowling analyses and extras (*Sheet 3*). As *Sheet 3* is essentially a commentator's aid which extracts data already recorded on *Sheet 1*, it has not been included in the Test match chapters. A sample is reproduced on page 28 to show the complete range of my output as a commentary-box scribe.

From a brief study of the three sheets you will see that the method accommodates many more details of the play than the conventional system and yet is still simple to follow.

Sheet 1, the ball-by-ball record of play, forms the basis of the scoring method but, unlike the other two sheets, it is not used by the commentators. It contains three sections: one for the bowlers, one for the batsmen, and one for recording the totals at the end of each over, or at the fall of a wicket, interval or unscheduled stoppage of play. Each line across these columns records one over, the time when the bowler commences the over being entered in the first column.

The sample *Sheet 1* shows the start of the First Test between New Zealand and England at Christchurch. You will see that there are two bowling columns (one for each end of the ground), and two batting columns which list the batsmen in the positions (left or right) in which their scores are shown on the scoreboard. The elaborate scoreboards in New Zealand and Australia give the complete batting order of the innings in progress and list the two not-out batsmen by name. My sheets were designed for use in England where most boards identify the players only by their number on the scorecard. The left/right separation identifies the batsmen in the end-of-over totals.

My sheet shows that umpire Aldridge is standing at the City (press box/commentary box) End, whilst umpire Woodward is at the Southern End with his back to the Port or Cashmere Hills. England, having won the toss, elected to bat and the names of Broad and Moxon are entered in the batting columns, with 'LHB' noted alongside the

1st DAY	BOWLERS (BL ALDRIDGE) CITY END		(SJ WOODWARD) SOUTHERN END		BATSMEN SCOREBOARD LEFT			SCOREBOARD RIGHT			ENGLAND 1st INNINGS	END-OF-OVER TOTALS					
TIME	BOWLER	O.	BOWLER	O.	SCORING	BALLS	6s/4s	SCORING	BALLS	6s/4s	NOTES	O.	RUNS	W.	'L' BAT	'R' BAT	EXTRAS
					BROAD		LHB	MOXON									
11.00			HADLEE	1	x L x 7 7 · · · · 2 ·	6						1	2		2		
04	MORRISON	1			· ·	8		· · · 3 1	4			2	3			1	
08			"	2				6 6P Y. x x · · · · ⊙ · · ·	11		(NB) NB 1	3	4				1
13	"	2			· · 4 · · · 3 2	14						4	6		4		
17			"	3				P6/5 · · · · · ·	17		M1	5					
21	"	3			· · 5 9 · · · 1	18		L 7/8 · W	19	-		6	7	1	5	1	1
24								ROBINSON								0	
26			"	4	x 8/7 · · 3	21		· P 5(6) ⊙ · · 2	4		(NB) NB 2	7	13		8	2	2
31	"	4			↑ LB · · · ·	25		L · · ·	6		(LB) M2	8	14				3
36			"	5	8 · · 2 8 P 2 · · ② ⊙ · ·	33					(NB) NB4	9	19		12		4
40	"	5						2 4 ↑ 3 2 2 · · · 1	12			10	24			7	
44	(5-1-9-1)		"	6				· ↑ · 3 · · · · · · · ·	18		M3	11					
48	CHATFIELD	1			· x 1 · · · · 3 ·	38		9 1	19			12	28		15	8	
52			"	7	· LB · 7 · · · 1	42		9 L 1 LB	21		(LB)(LB)	13	32		16	9	6
56	"	2	(7-2-16-0)		x 3 2 · · · 1 · ·	47		8 1	22		1HR	14	34		17	10	
12.00 04	DRINKS		SNEDDEN	1				· EP8 · · · · · · 1	28			15	35			11	
08	"	3			·	48		· · · 9 · · · · 1	33			16	36			12	
10			"	2	· x 8 · · 2	51		· 8 8 · 2 1	36			17	41		19	15	
15	"	4						· · 5 9 2 · · · · 2 · ·	42			18	43			17	
19			"	3	· · LB L 3 · · · · ·	56		LB ·	43		M4 (LB)(LB)	19	45				8
22	"	5						· ↑ · · · · · · · · ·	49		† Hit on box (5 min. delay for repairs) M5	20					
30			"	4	T · E3 6 5/6 · · · · · 2	62						21	47		21		
34	"	6						4 5/4 · P E2 · 2 · · · ·	55			22	49			19	
37	(6-1-11-0)		"	5	3 1	63		6 · 2 5 · · · · · · ·	60			23	50		22		
41	HADLEE	8			P · 2/3 P · 7 · · 4 · · ·	69	1					24	54		26		
45			"	6	9 3S 2 1	71		· · LB · · · ·	64		(LB) 50 p'ship · 82'	25	58		29		9
49	"	9	(6-1-12-0)		· 2 P x 8/7 · · · · · ·	77					M6	26					
53			CHATFIELD	7				x E2 P · · G · · · · · ·	70		G - Hit on rt. glove. M7 2HR	27					
59	" (10-3-28-0)	10	(7-2-11-0)		E1 · 7 4 · ⊙ 1	81	2	5 5 · 2 ·	73	-	(NB) NB5	28	66	1	34	21	10
1.03	LUNCH										M7 NB5		L	U	N	CH	
1.40			CHATFIELD	8	· · · 7/8 · 7 · · · 2 · 2	87						29	70		38		
44	HADLEE	11						7 · · · · 3 · · · · · 4	79	1		30	74			25	
47			"	9	P 3S · 1	89		8 E1 · · 2 · ·	83			31	77		39	27	
51	"	12			P 3 6 8 · · 1 1	93		7 1 ·	85			32	80		41	28	
55			"	10	3 7 7 · · 1	96		· · 3 · · ·	88			33	81		42		
59	"	13			3 · P 7 4 · · ⊙ 1 ·	101		· 4 · 1	90		(NB) NB 6	34	84		43	29	11
2.03			"	11				4↑ · · · 2 · · · · ·	96		† Dropped WRIGHT - 1-handed mid-off.	35	86			31	
06	"	14			LB · 3 EP x · · · · ·	106		3 1	97		(LB)	36	88			32	12
2.10	(14-3-39-0)		" (12-2-25-0)	12		106	2	7/8 · · 4 4 · 4 · · · · ·	103	2	M7 NB 6	37	92	1	43	36	12

former to denote that he is a left-handed batsman.

Hadlee is about to bowl the first ball of the series from the far end and I enter his name on the next line of the 'Southern End' column. I put a '1' in the square alongside it to show that it is his first over. When Aldridge calls 'Play', I enter the time in the first column and start my three stop-watches; one for each batsman and one for the England innings as a whole.

I am now ready to record the first ball, which is faced by Broad and allowed through to the wicket-keeper. As no run has been scored this is entered as a dot just as in the standard system. Broad plays at the next ball and misses it, his error being recorded by putting an 'X' above the dot.

The third ball hits Broad's pad and Hadlee appeals unsuccessfully for lbw. This is shown by putting an 'L' above the dot. Had there been no appeal the fact that the ball had struck the batsman's pad would have been recorded with a 'P'.

Broad is beaten by the fourth ball (another dot surmounted by an 'X') before hitting the next towards the mid-wicket boundary and taking two runs. This is recorded by entering a '2' for the runs and adding a smaller '7' above it to show in which area of the field those runs were scored. This is a cryptic form of charting the scoring strokes of a batsman's innings and is based on the following key which, as in Broad's case, is reversed for left-handed batsmen:

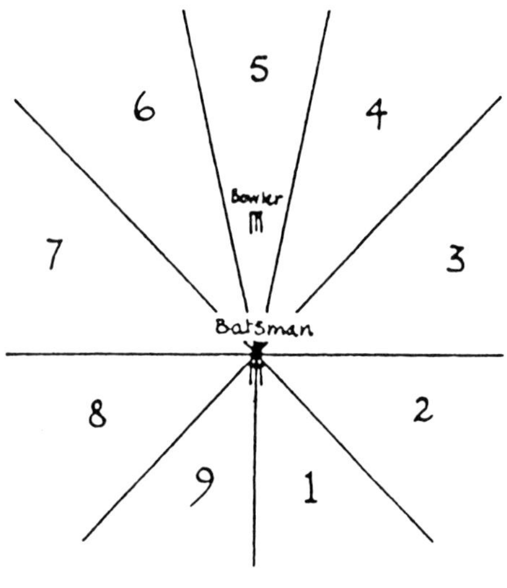

This method is only approximate but it does show if a batsman has a favourite scoring area. It also reveals if a bowler is prone to conceding runs to a particular stroke. My scoring charts are constructed from these little numerals.

After Viv Richards had scored 232 against England at Trent Bridge in 1976, the England captain, Tony Greig, asked me for a set of charts showing the batsman's scoring strokes against each of the six bowlers he faced. I was able to construct these from my sheets and I also separated the 313 balls received by Richards to show his scoring rate against each bowler. After Richards had amassed 291 in the final Test at The Oval, still the highest innings I have scored at any level of cricket, Greig publicly destroyed my charts!

The final delivery of Hadlee's opening over is a dot. The balls-received column is updated if that batsman has faced any of the over just bowled; in this instance a '6' is entered in Broad's section and Moxon's is left blank.

The end-of-over totals require entries only when they have changed during that particular over, so I enter '1' on the 'O' (Over) column, '2' in the Runs (England Total), and '2' in Broad's (L Bat) column.

Morrison is about to begin the second over of the match. I note the time and enter his name in the other bowling column. It is Moxon's turn to take strike; scoring is done in his column until he scores a single towards cover off the fourth ball and loses the bowling. At the end of this over any totals which have changed are updated, i.e. the Balls columns of both batsmen and the totals for Overs, Runs and Moxon (R Bat).

I then record the time at which Hadlee starts his second over; as he bowled the previous one from that end there is no need to write his name: ditto marks (") are sufficient. Moxon edges the second ball into his pad ('EP' above the dot). The next is a yorker ('Y').

Hadlee's fourth ball is called a 'no-ball' by umpire Woodward and is missed by Moxon. This is recorded as ⊙, just as in the traditional system of scoring. If the no-ball had been hit for four runs it would have been shown as ④ in the batsman's section – similarly with any other number of runs scored off a no-ball. A no-ball counts as a ball received because, unlike a wide which is not included, the batsman can score off it. As with wides, one run is added to the total runs conceded by that bowler for each no-ball that is not scored off.

Like other extras, no-balls are itemized in the Notes column (NB) and a tally is kept of them immediately alongside: 'NB 1' denotes the first no-ball call of the innings. This facilitates a check of the number of balls received by each batsman. I usually do this during drinks intervals, at the end of each session of play, or when I am bored. The total number of overs is multiplied by six and the number of no-balls is added to that total. This is then compared with the total number of balls received by the dismissed and not-out batsmen. When lunch is taken three minutes late because Hadlee's four-minute over started just one minute before the scheduled interval, 28 overs have been bowled, including 5 no-balls: 28 × 6 + 5 no-balls = 173. Broad (81) + Moxon (19) + Robinson (73) = 173.

Although no runs were scored off Hadlee's second over, because of the no-ball it is not a maiden. His next over is a maiden and the six dots are underlined and 'M 1' is marked in the Notes column to show that it is the first maiden of the innings and to facilitate a check with the bowling figures.

I use the Notes column to record the weather at the start of each day's play, the daily attendance figures, substitution of fielders (this became slightly congested during Pakistan's tour of England in 1987), dropped catches, unsuccessful appeals for anything except lbw, injuries, bowlers changing from over to round the wicket, any exceptional pieces of fielding and unusual incidents. Even the most obscure and apparently useless piece of data can prove invaluable.

The first ball of Hadlee's third over struck Moxon's pad but did not encourage an lbw appeal ('P'). The fifth ball was a bouncer ('↑'). Shooters are shown as arrows in the direction of down.

The last ball of Morrison's third over produces the first wicket, Moxon being caught by Andrew Jones fielding slightly forward of square-leg. The fall of a wicket produces a pressure point in any scoring system but practice soon helps to evolve the best sequence of action and there is normally a period of two minutes in which to complete it before the new batsman starts his innings.

First, I stop the watch recording Moxon's batting time. It shows 24 minutes and this is recorded on *Sheet 2*, together with the other essential details and statistics: 'ct Jones b Morrison 1', the fall of wicket '1-7', boundaries '-', balls received '19', and a note of how he was out. A red 'W' with '7/8' (to denote that the catch was taken on the line dividing areas 7 and 8 on my scoring chart), is entered in Moxon's batting column on *Sheet 1*.

All the totals are completed in the end-of-over totals section, Moxon's column in that section and his own batting column are ruled off in red, and his Balls Received and '6s/4s' columns are carried down. The time of Moxon's dismissal (11.24) is entered on both sheets.

The name of the new batsman (Robinson) is entered on the next line of the vacant batting column. Had the dismissal occurred from any of the first five balls of Morrison's over it would have been continued on the line below Robinson's name, together with the time it restarted. In this case the time of the start of Hadlee's fourth over is entered alongside Robinson's name on *Sheet 2*, and the stop-watch is set to zero and restarted.

The batsmen take a leg-bye from the fourth ball of Morrison's fourth over. This is shown as a dot (not counting against the bowler) with 'LB' above it. It is also shown in the Notes column and added to the extras column at the end of the over. Byes ('B') are treated similarly. If more than one run is taken they are shown as '2LB', '4B', etc.

When Chatfield replaces Morrison at the City End his name is entered in that bowling column and Morrison's figures (5-1-9-1, denoting 5 overs, 1 maiden, 9 runs and 1 wicket) are in that column on the line below the last over of his spell.

And so the process continues. It quickly becomes routine with a logical sequence of recording, adding and checking. Reduced to its bare essentials, the system requires only one digit to record each scoring stroke. Less recording is necessary while the over is in progress than with the traditional scoring method. Instead of marking each run in the batting, bowling and innings tally sections of the standard scorebook, my method requires just one entry. It is also immediately possible to tell exactly what has happened to each ball; who bowled it to whom, from which end, at what time, and how the batsman reacted. Unless a wicket falls, all the totalling is done at the end of the over while the fielders are changing positions and when there is no action to record.

The first ball of the final pre-lunch over is edged through the slips for four runs by Broad. I add a small 'E1' above the '4', 'E' signifying the edged stroke. For routine scoring such elaborate refinements are obviously superfluous, but for Test match broadcasts I need to record many minor details in order to answer the commentators' diverse questions. Brian Johnston and Trevor Bailey relish setting me such posers as: 'How many times did Moxon play and miss against Hadlee?', or 'How many of Broad's runs have come from edged strokes?'

At noon, after exactly an hour's play, a drinks interval was taken and noted. I always record the time of the start and finish of such intervals but, by tradition, this counts as playing time and cannot be deducted from the individual batting times. This came about because of the difficulty in noting such things in a normal scorebook. It has always seemed nonsensical and has convinced me that the only accurate and logical measurement of the duration of an innings is the number of balls received. This scoring system makes such a calculation extremely simple.

As the first hour of the innings has been completed I note '1 HR' in the Notes column and record 14 overs/34 runs in the appropriate section on *Sheet 2*.

At lunch, as at the end of any session or at a stoppage for rain or bad light, the three watches are stopped and all the totals on *Sheet 1* are carried down. The lunch score and not-out batsmen's details are entered in the largest box on *Sheet 2*.

Unfortunately there is no instance of a wide in this sample *Sheet 1*. Wides are recorded in the batsman's column as + just as in the standard system. Four wides would be shown ⁜. It does not count as a ball received because the batsman cannot score from it. The likelihood of a batsman being stumped off a wide the first ball he received and therefore not facing a ball is so remote that it can safely be ignored. Wides are marked as 'W' in the Notes column.

Before we leave *Sheet 1*, here is a list of the symbols which I use in the batting columns:

B	Bye
E	Edged stroke
EP	Edged ball into pads
F	Full toss
G	Hit on glove
L	Hit on pad – lbw appeal
LB	Leg-bye
P	Hit on pad – no appeal
S	Sprinted run
T	Hit on thigh pad
X	Played and missed
Y	Yorker
●	Blocked
↑	Bouncer
↓	Shooter
∩	Bowler used shortened run-up.

The last of those symbols was introduced in Australia in 1979-80 when Rodney Hogg, suffering from heat exhaustion, frequently bowled *à la* Keith Miller off only five or six paces. After straining his calf muscle during the last over before tea on the first day of the Christchurch Test, Hadlee delivered what were to be his last two balls of the series from a mini run.

Sheet 2, the Innings Scorecard, is the commentator's main source of reference. It records the start and finish times of each batsman's innings, its length in balls and minutes, his score and number of boundaries, the total at which his wicket fell and the manner of his dismissal.

The lower part of the sheets shows the final bowling analyses, the hourly run and over rates, the time taken for each 50 runs scored by the team, the full details of each wicket partnership, the total and individual scores at the end of each session of play, details of when a new ball was taken, and notes of any records set during the innings.

Coloured inks are used to highlight the more important entries and to make it easier for the commentator to select essential items from a sheet containing so much data. Names and run totals are shown in blue, as is the close of play or 'stumps' score. Red is used for hundred partnerships, lunch and team totals, and any other data of special interest.

Sheet 3, the Cumulative Record of Bowling Analyses and Extras, is essential only to radio and television commentators. It is illustrated here but has not been included in the scoresheets of the

ENGLAND 1ST INNINGS v NEW ZEALAND (FIRST TEST) at LANCASTER PARK, CHRISTCHURCH on 12, 13, 14, 16, 17 FEBRUARY, 1988.

IN	OUT	MINS	No.	BATSMAN	HOW OUT	BOWLER	RUNS	WKT	TOTAL	6s	4s	BALLS	NOTES ON DISMISSAL — TOSS: NEW ZEALAND
11.00	5.38	341	1	B.C. BROAD	ct SMITH	SNEDDEN	114	4	219	·	11	244	Edged low to 'keeper's left.
11.00	11.24	24	2	M.D. MOXON	ct JONES	MORRISON	1	1	7	·	-	19	Defensive push to short-leg.
11.26	4.06	223	3	R.T. ROBINSON	ct SMITH	MORRISON	70	2	175	·	7	181	Edged leg-side flick.
4.08	4.31	23	4	M.W. GATTING *	ct SUB (M.J. GREATBATCH)	MORRISON	8	3	187	·	1	19	Cut long-hop to cover.
4.33	12.00	114	5	C.W.J. ATHEY	ct SUB (M.J. GREATBATCH)	MORRISON	22	6	241	·	1	79	Drove half-volley low to cover.
5.40	11.44	31	6	D.J. CAPEL	ct BRACEWELL	CHATFIELD	11	5	237	·	1	25	Edged low to 2nd slip.
11.46	2.30	124	7	J.E. EMBUREY	ct JONES	MORRISON	42	10	319	·	5	93	Drove low to cover.
12.02	12.12	10	8	B.N. FRENCH †	ct SMITH	CHATFIELD	7	7	248	·	1	4	Edged leg-cutter to 'keeper.
12.13	12.23	10	9	P.A.J. DeFREITAS	ct MORRISON	CHATFIELD	4	8	260	·	-	14	Skied hit to wide mid-on.
12.25	1.54	49	10	P.W. JARVIS	ct SMITH	CHATFIELD	14	9	285	·	1	37	Edged lifting away-seamer.
1.56	(2.30)	34	11	G.R. DILLEY	NOT OUT		7			·	-	14	
				EXTRAS	b - lb 11 w 1 nb 7		19			-[6]	28[4]	729 balls (inc 8 no-balls)	

* CAPTAIN † WICKET-KEEPER

TOTAL (120.1 OVERS; 500 MINUTES) 319 ALL OUT at 2.30 pm on 2nd day.

14 OVERS 2 BALLS/HOUR
2.65 RUNS/OVER
43 RUNS/100 BALLS

UMPIRES: B.L. ALDRIDGE and S.J. WOODWARD.

BOWLER	O	M	R	W	W/NB
HADLEE	18	3	50	0	-/8
MORRISON	21.1	3	69	5	1/-
CHATFIELD	42	13	87	4	-
SNEDDEN	33	9	86	1	-
BRACEWELL	6	1	16	0	-
			11		
	120.1	29	319	10	

2ND NEW BALL taken after 35.1 overs at 5.50 pm 1st day - ENGLAND 223-4.

HRS	OVERS	RUNS
1	14	34
2	13	24
3	16	60
4	16	51
5	13	33
6	15	22
7	14	41
8	14	25

RUNS	MINS	OVERS	LAST 50 (in mins)
50	97	22.1	97
100	163	39.1	66
150	223	54.4	60
200	287	69.2	64
250	403	97.3	116
300	483	116.1	80

LUNCH: 66-1 [28 OVERS, 123 MIN] BROAD 34* (123'), ROBINSON 21* (97')

TEA: 171-1 [60 OVERS, 243 MIN] BROAD 88* (243'), ROBINSON 68* (217')

STUMPS (1ST DAY): 235-4 [90 OVERS, 370 MIN] ATHEY 18* (94'), CAPEL 10* (27')

2ND DAY - START DELAYED 40 MINUTES (RAIN)

LUNCH: 278-8 [108 OVERS, 450 MIN] EMBUREY 11* (74'), JARVIS 11* (35')

WKT	PARTNERSHIP		RUNS	MINS
1st	Broad	Moxon	7	24
2nd	Broad	Robinson	168	223
3rd	Broad	Gatting	12	23
4th	Broad	Athey	32	65
5th	Athey	Capel	18	31
6th	Athey	Emburey	4	14
7th	Emburey	French	7	10
8th	Emburey	DeFreitas	12	10
9th	Emburey	Jarvis	25	49
10th	Emburey	Dilley	34	34
			319	

Test matches which follow. For this book I have added the bowling figures to *Sheet 1* and they appear in their appropriate bowling column at the end of each spell and at the foot of each sheet.

Entries are made only at the end of each over or at the completion of a session of play. A red line is ruled under a bowler's figures when he is taken off. Intervals, close of play ('stumps') and interruptions for rain and bad light are also shown, thus enabling the commentator to calculate quickly the length of each individual bowling spell. The number of boundaries conceded by each bowler is shown cumulatively, the result of my pandering to a special plea from Brian Johnston.

Extras are recorded in separate columns on the right. No-balls and wides are also recorded against the name of each bowler.

This sheet facilitates a number of cross-checks. The total of the overs delivered by each bowler should equal the number bowled so far in the innings (10 + 5 + 7 + 6 = 28 at lunch). The total of maidens, runs conceded, wickets, no-balls and boundaries can be checked in the same way.

Over the years various publications have held competitions in which entrants were asked to score 50 consecutive overs of a current Test match using my scoring method. Usually their only guidance was an illustration of part of a Sheet 1 accompanied by a very brief explanation of the system. Most of the entries were of a very high standard and many came from the 12-to-16 age group. One even typed his entire 50-overs. It all goes to show that the method is very much simpler than it appears at first sight – otherwise I could not have coped with it.

In 1972 I designed a looseleaf scoring system based on this method, complete with rexine-covered board binders for clubs and individuals who simply enjoy scoring cricket matches for fun. The *Frindall Cricket Scoring Sheets* are now marketed exclusively by 3-D Cricket Ltd at The Runnings, Cheltenham GL51 3NJ.

NEW ZEALAND BOWLING — FIRST INNINGS

HADLEE — NB 𝍸 III — WIDES

O	M	R	W	4s
1	0	2	0	
2	0	3	0	
3	1	3	0	
4	1	9	0	
5	1	14	0	
6	2	14	0	
7	2	16	0	-
8	2	20	0	1
9	3	20	0	
10	3	28	0	2
LUNCH				
11	3	32	0	3
12	3	35	0	
13	3	38	0	
14	3	39	0	
15	3	40	0	3
16	3	44	0	4
17	3	48	0	
18	3	50	0	4
TEA				
STUMPS (1st DAY)				
LUNCH				

MORRISON — NB — WIDES I

O	M	R	W	4s
1	0	1	0	
2	0	3	0	
3	0	4	1	
4	1	4	1	
5	1	9	1	-
LUNCH				
6	1	18	1	2
7	1	23	1	3
8	1	27	1	4
TEA				
9	2	27	2	
10	2	29	2	
11	2	30	2	
12	2	32	3	
13	2	36	3	5
STUMPS (1st DAY)				
14	2	38	3	
15	3	38	3	
16	3	42	4	6
17	3	49	4	7
18	3	54	4	8
19	3	58	4	9
20	3	63	4	
21	3	69	4	10
LUNCH				
21.1	3	69	5	10

CHATFIELD — NB — WIDES

O	M	R	W	4s
1	0	4	0	
2	0	6	0	
3	0	7	0	
4	0	9	0	
5	1	9	0	
6	1	11	0	-
7	2	11	0	-
LUNCH				
8	2	15	0	
9	2	18	0	
10	2	19	0	
11	2	21	0	
12	2	25	0	1
13	2	27	0	
14	3	27	0	
15	3	35	0	2
16	4	35	0	
17	4	38	0	2
TEA				
18	5	38	0	
19	5	39	0	
20	6	39	0	
21	6	41	0	
22	6	44	0	
23	6	48	0	
24	7	48	0	
25	8	48	0	
26	8	52	0	
27	8	56	0	2
STUMPS (1st DAY)				
28	9	56	1	
29	10	56	1	
30	11	56	1	
31	11	59	2	
32	11	60	3	
33	11	61	3	
34	11	62	3	
35	12	62	3	
36	13	62	3	
LUNCH				
37	13	64	3	
38	13	67	4	2

SNEDDEN — NB — WIDES

O	M	R	W	4s
1	0	1	0	
2	0	6	0	
3	1	6	0	
4	1	8	0	
5	1	9	0	
6	1	12	0	-
LUNCH				
7	1	15	0	
8	1	17	0	
9	1	23	0	1
10	1	33	0	3
11	2	33	0	
TEA				
12	2	37	0	
13	2	42	0	4
14	2	46	0	
15	3	46	0	
16	3	55	0	5
17	4	55	0	
18	4	56	0	
19	5	56	0	
20	5	60	0	
21	5	62	0	
22	6	62	0	
23	7	62	1	
24	7	66	1	6
25	7	67	1	
26	7	70	1	6
STUMPS (1st DAY)				
27	8	70	1	
LUNCH				
28	9	70	1	
29	9	72	1	
30	9	73	1	
31	9	74	1	
32	9	80	1	7
33	9	86	1	7

BRACEWELL — NB — WIDES

O	M	R	W	4s
1	0	1	0	
2	0	6	0	1
3	1	6	0	
4	1	7	0	
5	1	12	0	2
6	1	16	0	3
TEA				
STUMPS (1st DAY)				
LUNCH				

CHATFIELD/2 — NB — WIDES

O	M	R	W	4s
39	13	70	4	2
40	13	77	4	3
41	13	84	4	4
42	13	87	4	4

EXTRAS

B	LB	W	NB	TOT
	1	1	1	
	2		2	
	3		3	
	4		4	
	5		5	
	6		6	
	7		7	
	11			

CRICKET SCORING SHEET No. 3

AUSTRALIA'S BICENTENARY TEST

Australia celebrates · Flotillas and fireworks · Match report · Bradman's lap of honour and Broad's disgrace · Bill O'Reilly retires · Boris completes a unique double

After warming up in New Zealand with two three-day matches in Wellington and Hamilton, the England team flew to Sydney to join Australia's biggest party in its brief history. The celebrations were for 200 years of white settlement, a nicety emphasized by a well-orchestrated but totally peaceful Aboriginal protest. The First Fleet with Governor Phillip and its enchained prospective residents had sailed into Botany Bay in January 1788. One banner pointed out that the first feet were Aboriginal.

To the visitor it was all great fun. After spending a week in Adelaide I flew into Sydney on Australia Day. Our landing approach passed over the harbour, giving us a magnificent view of the First Fleet re-enactment vessels surrounded by a 10,000-strong armada of small boats. It was a spectacular parade of sail festooned with flags, balloons and bunting. One cannot imagine a more magnificent sight than Sydney Harbour bathed in sunlight, but that night's firework display certainly rivalled it. Centred on the famous bridge, it lasted over an hour and could be seen for miles. Dining at the Rushcutters Bay Travelodge with my great-aunt, I was treated to a grandstand view of this Star Wars extravaganza. As the first rocket exploded into a thousand cascading glow-worms I tried unsuccessfully to convince Aunt Eadith I had arranged it all especially for her.

After that tremendous piece of theatre, the Bicentenary Test match was clearly going to have a lot to live up to. That it failed to produce a pulsating climax was no fault of the players.

Commemorative Tests are becoming as commonplace as commemorative stamp issues and this specimen never earned its first day cover. Although it certainly produced cricket worthy of Test status, it did not develop into a grandstand finish as the organizers had intended. No doubt they had hoped for a repeat of last year's tussle between the two countries on the same ground, which had resulted in Australia winning in the final over. You cannot label a match 'Australia *v.* England', give it Test status and expect it to be played as a celebration game with the festival atmosphere of the MCC Bicentenary match at Lord's in 1987. A contest between Australia and a Rest of the World XI would have been far more appropriate and entertaining.

The New South Wales Cricket Association spared no effort in their presentation of the match, providing abundant hospitality for the teams and a galaxy of specially invited former Ashes cricketers. For them it was a superb five-day beano and a constant battle against overwhelming alcoholic temptation.

The match was a great disappointment for the Australian cricketers. Fresh from their World Cup success, they had also narrowly won a three-Test rubber against New Zealand before gaining a comprehensive victory over their neighbours in the World Series Cup. With England jaded and disillusioned after their Pakistan experiences, Allan Border's men certainly fancied their chances of avenging their 1985 and 1986-87 defeats, even though the Ashes were not at stake.

Certainly Australia would have derived little satisfaction from the first two days. Their lapses in the field cost them dearly. Their outfielding was often sloppy and, when Bruce French led the tailend assault, the throwing and stopping became a shambles.

The difference in tactical approach between the short, stereotyped limited-overs game and five-day Test cricket is vast. Border struggled to make the conversion and was too inflexible in the handling of his attack. Even allowing for the fact that his options were severely reduced by Craig McDermott's knee injury, he seemed to rotate his bowlers according to a pre-match list and not in response to the dictates of the situation. It was astonishing that he did not employ spin at both ends until the 147th over. Neither of his spinners, the two Peters, Sleep and Taylor, found it easy to transform their bowling techniques from the dictates of limited-overs cricket. In trying to recapture the variations of flight that had been put into cold storage during the pyjama interlude, they frequently overpitched. In 140 previous Test matches I have never recorded as many full-tosses as the 17 presented to England's batsmen during 172.5 overs in this innings. They were all Bicentenary birthday presents gratefully received.

Although the pitch was still damp at the start, with patches of green and brown grass, Gatting made the correct decision in choosing to bat. It took spin slowly at first but, by the close of England's 676-minute innings, Peter Sleep's wrist spin was turning square. The pitch was also two-paced – Athey's dismissal was the result of a ball that 'stopped' – and its bounce became progressively more uneven, especially at the Randwick End. In short, it was a far from ideal surface for a Test match given as much hype as this one.

When Australia collapsed against some fine out-cricket and were compelled to follow-on 221 runs behind, England's third victory in 26 Tests since 1985 looked very much in prospect. That they were unable to complete the task by bowling out Australia a second time was largely the result of a combination of circumstances beyond their control. Their efforts in the second innings were thwarted mainly by a pitch that dried out into a featherbed. But the deciding factor was a masterly display from David Boon who, for more than four hours, was supported by the phlegmatic Geoff Marsh. Boon's squat, defiant figure and pouting moustache dominated the last five sessions of play. His was one of Test cricket's greatest match-saving knocks, and he was a most deserving winner of the match

David Boon's squat, defiant figure and pouting moustache during his epic match-saving Bicentenary Test innings.

award. I wonder how many times during his 491-minute vigil he cast his mind back twelve months to the moment he was discarded into the wilderness by his selectors.

Boon's heroic rearguard action was made slightly easier by the recurrence of Foster and Dilley's knee injuries; the former's proved so severe that he returned home for surgery and took no further part in the tour. Foster's departure was a grievous blow to England's fortunes. Their lack of recent success had arisen mainly from their inability to bowl sides out a second time. Foster was their main strike force. An engaging character with a fruity Colchester accent, he puts tremendous effort into his bowling, frequently psyching himself up to a warlike state that has earned him the title of 'Mr Angry'.

England were unlucky to be victims of a bizarre interpretation of the regulations governing light when, at 4.11 p.m. on the third afternoon, Australia were 164 for 7. Who knows what would have happened in the remaining 109 minutes? If Boon had been dismissed, the match would probably not have lasted beyond the fourth day.

Foster and Hemmings were the pick of England's attack in the first innings, although Capel revealed a golden arm and fine competitive temperament. One suspects that he has yet to convince his captain that he is a Test match bowler. Dilley recaptured glimpses of his form from his last Australian tour but Emburey, although the epitome of accuracy, managed only one dismissal in 68 overs. Since claiming 7 for 78 in the second innings of the Fifth Test at Sydney a year earlier, he had bowled 299 overs and taken only 8 wickets at 78.50 runs apiece. His striking rate of a wicket every 224 balls showed that his method had become too static, too predictable. His bowling lacked ingenuity and variety. Over after over he trundled away like a metronome, pitching middle and leg, and aiming for a bat/pad catch to short-leg. Emburey has had to endure a ridiculous amount of limited-overs cricket in the past twelve months, including 32 one-day internationals. The widely differing demands of the two games greatly affect slow bowlers.

By contrast, Hemmings the Whale in action was like a breath of fresh air. His variations in flight, pace and angle continuously probed the batsmen's concentration and technique.

For Saturday's crowd of 27,164, the high point of the entertainment probably occurred during the lunch interval when Sir Donald Bradman slowly lapped the SCG boundary in a vintage open-top Rolls-Royce at the head of a motorcade of veteran cars. The Don, in his 80th year, was at his most animated, waving vigorously to acknowledge a tumultuous reception on the ground where he had completed his 100th first-class century. But it was Geoffrey Boycott who unwittingly stole the show when his car spluttered to a halt after a few yards. He briefly helped to push it before sneaking a lift on the running board of Ray Lindwall's vehicle. I wonder if some victims of his eccentric calling would have spotted an allegory there.

An hour earlier the enthusiastic crowd had witnessed one of the most stupid acts ever perpetrated on that famous ground. Few cricketers can have emulated Chris Broad and changed from hero to villain in a few seconds. One moment he was playing a match-winning innings and frustrating Australia's bowlers to despair. The next saw him turn his back on a short ball from Steve Waugh. It swung into him late, caught his elbow and fell on to his wicket.

Broad simply could not believe that he had been the victim of such a bizarre dismissal. He had been determined to score a double century, and found his disappointment too much to bear. He swung his bat with a ferocity more savage than most of the blows which had brought him 13 boundaries in his epic 434-minute marathon in near sauna conditions. The leg stump flew from the ground as Broad began his long, lonely trudge back to the pavilion. I found it hard to believe what I had just witnessed as a crescendo of booing greeted the replay on the giant computerized scoreboard to prove that it had not been an illusion. It was an extremely sad and embarrassing finale to a major innings.

Instead of receiving congratulations for his historic hundred he was reprimanded and fined £500 by tour manager Peter Lush.

'He had no excuses. It was a stupid thing to do and he knew that he had done wrong,' said Lush barely half an hour after the incident. 'All the players were warned about their behaviour before this tour. He knows the form. It was a sad end to a great innings.'

Indeed it was and, having admired his supreme tenacity for more than seven hours on a difficult pitch, one could only feel desperately sorry for him. Tragically, that sour ending to his innings will be recounted long after his magnificent contribution to England's highest total at Sydney since 1965-66 is forgotten.

Broad is a dignified and charming man but his recent displays of outrageous petulance reveal a childish streak which he must control. Apart from his previous offences in Pakistan, he has gained a reputation on the county circuit as a player who never thinks he is out. Umpires from his school days in Bristol still have clear memories of similar tantrums. Heaven forbid that any of the millions watching his demolition act replayed on television will be prompted to repeat it in matches at any level. Sometimes it seems that professional sportsmen are totally oblivious to the example they set the young.

Christ Broad reacts to his bizarre Bicentenary dismissal with an expensive display of stump abuse.

The extent of Broad's contribution is shown by the scorecard. No other batsman reached 50, although, apart from Hemmings, they all made double figures. Had Hemmings acquired another two runs it would have been the first time since 1928-29, by coincidence also at Sydney, that every member of an England team had scored at least 10 runs in the same innings.

After England had forced the follow-on, Australia, thanks to Boon's gutsy display, saved the match with ease. They were helped by a pitch that dried out into a slow surface which gave the bowlers no assistance at all. From lunchtime on the fourth day a draw was inevitable and far more interest was evoked by a commemorative computer Test displayed, session by session during the various intervals, on the SCG's new computerized scoreboard. Programmed by a Sydney resident, it not surprisingly produced an Australian victory.

Star of the computerized Australian success was Bill O'Reilly, and it was appropriate that it should coincide with his being the central figure of a special press box ceremony on that final afternoon. Attended only by the writers and broadcasters covering the Bicentenary Test, it marked 'Tiger''s retirement from reporting Test cricket for the *Sydney Morning Herald* and consisted of a tea-time presentation of a copy of David Frith's magnum opus, *Pageant of Cricket*.

The Tiger is now 82, and his trenchant comments will be much missed by his vast readership. A humane and entertaining companion, he was always worth listening to. We first met in Adelaide in 1978, when our identical tour holdalls became mixed up at the airport. He found himself with my mobile library and scoring paraphernalia while I became the puzzled guardian of four pairs of large black shoes.

It was great fun to attend Australia's 200th birthday party, but the whole hype was put into perspective by Boris, a Russian taxi-driver. He revealed that celebrating Bicentenary Day among the hundreds of boats in Sydney Harbour had completed a notable double for him. At the age of eight he had been in Moscow when that city had celebrated its 800th anniversary.

1ST DAY	BOWLERS P.J. McCONNELL PADDINGTON END		AR CRAFTER RANDWICK END		BATSMEN SCOREBOARD LEFT			SCOREBOARD RIGHT			ENGLAND 1ST INNINGS NOTES	END-OF-OVER TOTALS					
TIME	BOWLER	O.	BOWLER	O.	SCORING	BALLS	6s/4s	SCORING	BALLS	6s/4s	NOTES	O.	RUNS	W.	'L' BAT	'R' BAT	EXTRAS
					BROAD		LHB	MOXON			No cloud. 27°c						
11.00	McDERMOTT	1			. 3/2 · 1	2		2 : . . :	4			1	1		1		
04			DODEMAIDE	1	8 x P 8 2 . . . 3	8						2	6		6		
08	"	2			7/8 9 2 . . 1	12		9 . 1	6			3	10		9	1	
12			"	2				x 7 : 2 P · 2 · 2 . .	12			4	14			5	
16	"	3			15 x : (·) : . . 8	19					(NB) NB 1	5	15				1
21			"	3	. x 5/4 · 4	23	1	• 6E · 1	14		• Dropped sh. sq leg (BOON)	6	20		13	6	
25	"	4						L ↑ : 7/6 2 . . . 2 .	20			7	22			8	
29			"	4	. . . 5(4) 2 : x	29						8	24		15		
33	"	5			4B ↑ . .	31		. Y . 9 : . 1	24		(4B)	9	29			9	5
37	(5-0-9-0)		"	5	P .	32		x ! ↑ 6 . . . 1	29			10	30			10	
41	TAYLOR	1			: : 7	35		. 3 7/2 : . 1	32			11	31			11	
45			"	6	7 LB . .	37		9 1 . . .	36		(LB)	12	33			12	6
49	"	2			: 6 . † . : P	43					M1 † Round wkt	13					
51			"	7	3 6 2 · 2	46		Y 7 . : 1	39			14	38		19	13	
55	"	3	(7-0-23-0)					4 5† : : : 2	45		† Good stop (bowler)	15	40			15	
58			WAUGH	1	: : : : 4/3 3	51		:	46		1 HR	16	43		22		
12.02 / 05	DRINKS "	4			6/7 4 : : : : P	57	2					17	47		26		
08			"	2				: • E1 9/1 2 . : :	52		• Dropped Border (1st slip)	18	49			17	
12	"	5			: 5 2LB F4	63					(2LB) 50 p'ship: 72 min M2	19	51				8
14			"	3	:	64		: : : : 5/6 1	57			20	52			18	
17	"	6						P 4 4 7 9 3	63			21	55			21	
21			"	4				: 6 x . P	69		M3	22					
23	"	7			: : : : 6/7 1	69		:	70			23	56		27		
26			"	5	8/7 · 8 3 L · 2	75						24	58		29		
30	"	8			: : : :	79		7 8 : 1	72			25	59			22	
33	(8-2-12-0)		"	6				: 4 : : 3 :	78		M4	26					
36	McDERMOTT	6			. : : ↑ 2 9 . . 1	85					2 Diving stop - gully (Marsh)	27	60		30		
41			"	7	E1 •4 . . : 7 1	90	3	P .	79		• Over slips	28	65		35		
43	"	7	(7-2-13-0)		: . . P 8 F5 . . .	96					M5	29					
48			SLEEP	1				7 4 x 4 . . . :	85	1		30	69			26	
50	"	8			↑ 7 3 : . . 1	100		: L .	87			31	70		36		
56			"	2	7 . . 3 x 4 . .	106					M6	32					
58	(9-1-12-0)	9	(2-1-4-0)		: •SF4L . .	110	3	6 9 · 1	89	1	• Dropped - head high (bowler)	33	71	0	36	27	8
1.02	LUNCH										M6 NB1 2 1 1 R			LUNCH			

1ST DAY	BOWLERS (McCONNELL) PADDINGTON END		(CRAFTER) RANDWICK END		BATSMEN SCOREBOARD LEFT			SCOREBOARD RIGHT			ENGLAND 1ST INNINGS	END-OF-OVER TOTALS					
TIME	BOWLER	O.	BOWLER	O.	SCORING	BALLS	6s/4s	SCORING	BALLS	6s/4s	NOTES	O.	RUNS	W.	'L' BAT	'R' BAT	EXTRAS
					BROAD	110	3	MOXON	89	1	M6 NB1 2HR	33	71	0	36	27	8
1.40			SLEEP	3	. . : P P	114		2LB . 1B 1	91		(2LB) • wide of slip	34	74			28	10
44	McDERMOTT	10						5 7 4 4 : :	97		M7	35					
48			"	4	P 2 P 2/3 : : : 1	118		5 8 : 1	99			36	76		37	29	
51	"	11			. : 3	120		: (·) · 2 (·) 3 4/5F	105		(NB)(NB) NB3	37	81			32	12
57			"	5				: . : . . 4 3/4	111	2		38	85			36	
2.00	"	12			. . 5 2/3 P .	126					M8	39					
04			"	6				: 6 x x : 4 6/5	117	3		40	89			40	
07	"	13			x . . : 4 . 4 3	132	4					41	93		41		
12	(13-3-21-0)		"	7	}			: W x	119	3		41[2]	93	1	41	40	12
12½					}			ROBINSON								0	
14			"	7	} 1E 1	133		: 5 LB	3		(LB)	42	95		42		13
17	DODEMAIDE	8			: . 1E : 4	139					Just short of 2nd slip M9	43					
21			"	8	: 7 :	142		3 4 7/8 1	6			44	96			1	
24	"	9						. . : : . 2 6	12			45	98			3	
28			"	9	. . 3 6 1	146		3 3	14			46	99		43		
31	"	10			7S 1	147		. : . : .	19			47	100		44		
35			"	10	. : x . 2 1 7	153					3HR	48	102		46		
38	"	11						6 . : 4 4 :	25		M10	49					
40 44	DRINKS		"	11	. 1 8/7	155		3 3 7 : : 2 .	29			50	105		47	5	
47	"	12			. : 3 4	158		6 . 4 2 : :	32		Broad's 50 · 190'	51	110		50	7	
51	(12-2-31-0)		"	12	P : P . 4 2 6/7 4	164	5					52	116		56		
54	WAUGH	8			7 7 2 1	166		4 4 3/2 . . . 3	36			53	122		59	10	
58			"	13	: PA 6 7 4 : . 3	171		:	37		A · short leg.	54	125		62		
3.01	"	9	(13-1-32-1)		: 4 1 . 6	175		: 6 3	39			55	129		63	13	
05			TAYLOR	9				3 : 2 3 4 : 4	45	1		56	133			17	
08	"	10			: : : 4 6 7	181					M11	57					
11			"	10				! : 3 7 : x	51		M12	58					
15	"	11			. : 8 1	184		. 4 6/5 4	54	2		59	138		64	21	
18	(11-3-28-0)		"	11	. F6 : 4 : 1E	190					M13	60					
21	McDERMOTT	14			x : 8 9w . . 4	194	6	. 4 1 8	56		(W) • Mr. w/k. 50 p'ship: 72'	61	144		68	22	14
26			"	12	:	195		: : 6 : 8 1	61			62	145			23	
29	"	15						. . : : . 3•	67		• Just short of cover M14	63					
34			"	13	7F 9/8 4 2 : : 4 F9/8	201	8					64	155		78		
37	(16-4-28-0)	16	(13-4-27-0)		:	202	8	: : 6 : 6 1	72	2	4HR	65	156	1	78	24	14
3.41	TEA										M14 NB3			T	E	A	

1ST DAY	BOWLERS (McCONNELL) PADDINGTON END		(CRAFTER) RANDWICK END		BATSMEN SCOREBOARD LEFT			SCOREBOARD RIGHT			ENGLAND 1ST INNINGS Attendance: 25462 NOTES	END-OF-OVER TOTALS					
TIME	BOWLER	O.	BOWLER	O.	SCORING	BALLS	6s/4s	SCORING	BALLS	6s/4s		O.	RUNS	W.	'L' BAT	'R' BAT	EXTRAS
TEA					BROAD	202	8	ROBINSON	72	2	M14 4HR NB 3	65	156	1	78	24	14
4.00			SLEEP	14				: : 2 : . :	78		M15	66					
03	McDERMOTT	17			: P LB ⊙ 4	207		7 9 2 1	80		(LB) (NB) NB 4	67	161			27	16
09			"	15				9 3 2 : . 1 2 : 2 2	86			68	167			33	
13	"	18			: : : x . :	213					M16	69					
17			"	16				. : : : : :	92		M17	70					
19	"	19			: : x 4 . x	219					M18	71					
24			"	17				. 6 4 4 6 x 4	98	3		72	171			37	
28	"	20			: : : 4 1 4 .	225	9					73	175		82		
33			"	18				. x : 4 . .	104		M19	74					
35	"	21			: 5 1 3	228		: 5 :	107			75	178		85		
41	(21-6-39-0)		"	19	: 8/7 1	230		: 1E 6 :	111		Round wkt	76	179		86		
45	DODEMAIDE	13			3 3	231		6 8 2 . 6 2/3 4	116	4		77	188		89	43	
49			"	20	F5 4 P : 6/7F 4 :	237	10					78	192		93		
52	"	14						: : . E1 W	120	4		78.4	192	2	93	43	16
54								GATTING								0	
56	"	14						: :	2		M 20 SHR	79					
58			"	21	P . : . . P LB	243					(LB) M21	80	193				17
5.01 04	"	15			: : 4 3S 1	247		: .	4			81	194		94		
08			"	22	: . P . 8/7 3 4 2	253	11				BROAD'S 100: 313' at 5.10pm	82	200		100		
11	"	16						L : : : : 2	10		M 22	83					
15	(16-4-41-1)		"	23	: : 3 5 P 4F 1	259						84	201		101		
17	McDERMOTT	22	(23-5-54-1)		1E : . 4 2 1E 3	265					E - short of 2nd slip • In air mid. cover	85	204		104		
22			DODEMAIDE	17	† 7 2 : 8 8 8 2 1 1	271					† NEW BALL	86	209		109		
27	"	23			. † : P 4 4 Y.	277					† Turned ankle on foothold M23	87					
31			"	18	: : 3	280		: : 7 1	13		GATTING 38' on 0	88	210			1	
36	"	24			7 1	281		. 8 1 . † :	18			89	212		110	2	
40			"	19	4 1E 4 ⊙ : : : 6 (1)	287	12	: :	20		† Round wkt NB 5 6 (NB)	90	218		115		18
46	"	25			† † : : 4 1	292		:	21			91	219		116		
50			"	20	: : : . ⊙ L	299					(NB) NB 7	92	220				19
54	"	26			: † x : :	303		: 8 1	23		† Round wkt	93	221			3	
59	(26-7-46-0)		(21-5-54-1)	21		303	12	: : : 7 :	29	-	M24 NB7 6HR	94	221	2	116	3	19
6.02	STUMPS		(1ST DAY)									STUMPS					

2ND DAY	BOWLERS (McCONNELL) PADDINGTON END		(CRAFTER) RANDWICK END		BATSMEN SCOREBOARD LEFT			SCOREBOARD RIGHT			ENGLAND 1ST INNINGS	END-OF-OVER TOTALS					
TIME	BOWLER	O.	BOWLER	O.	SCORING	BALLS	6s/4s	SCORING	BALLS	6s/4s	NOTES	O.	RUNS	W.	'L' BAT	'R' BAT	EXTRAS
					BROAD	303	12	GATTING	29	–	M24 NB7 6HR	94	221	2	116	3	19
11.00	McDERMOTT	27			P 7 : 4 7 . 1	309						95	222		117		
05			DODEMAIDE	22	. . x . : E1	315					M 25	96					
09	"	28			4 . . . 3	319		: 8/9 1	31			97	223			4	
13			"	23	5 EP2 . 7 3	323		: EP7 1	33			98	227		120	5	
17	"	29			. † . : . : †	329					† Round wkt M 26	99					
22			"	24	6 3 2E .	331		2 3 L . 8 1	37			100	234		123	9	
26	"	30	(24-6-65-1)					8 4 P F4 P : :	43	1	Gatting 92' for 1st 4	101	238			13	
31			WAUGH	12	7 1	332		: 4 : : :	48			102	239		124		
34	"	31			†† ⊙ : ⊙ 5(6) 3	337		: EP P	51		† Round wkt (NB) NB 8 9 (NB)	103	244		127		21
41			"	13	: 8 1	339		E1 . W	53	1	50 p'ship: 106'	103⁴	245	3	128	13	21
42								ATHEY								0	
44			"	13				: 6	2			104					
46	"	32			: 2 : . . 2 3	344		7 1	3		Round	105	249		131	1	
51	(32-8-61-0)		"	14	† † : E1 4 4	349	13	9 1	4		• over slips 7 HR	106	254		135	2	
54	DODEMAIDE	25			8 5 † . 2 2 2	354		5(4) 3	5			107	261		139	5	
59	(25-6-72-1)		"	15	7 6 : 6 :	359		7 1	6			108	262			6	
12 02 05	DRINKS SLEEP	24						3 P 4 : P 5	12		M 27	109					
08			"	16	4 X† : W	361	13				† Played on via elbow – no stroke.	109²	262	4	139	6	21
09					CAPEL										0		
11			"	16	: : : :	4					M 28	110					
14	"	25						: x P 8/7 4 : :	18	1		111	266			10	
17			"	17	: : x 4 4 : :	10	1					112	270		4		
20	"	26			x : : : : :	15		7 1	19			113	271			11	
24			"	18				: : 4 4 : : .	25	2		114	275			15	
27	"	27			9 : : : 2 4 :	21	2					115	279		8		
30			"	19				: † 9 4 † P : :	31	3		116	283			19	
33	"	28			3 3	22		: 8 : : 8 1	36			117	287		11	20	
36	(28-6-67-1)		"	20				: 3 2 . . : :	42			118	289			22	
40	McDERMOTT	33			: : . : : 6 2	28						119	291		13		
45	"		"	21	: : RO :	32		(6)5 : 1	44		• Waugh direct hit on stumps.	120	292			23	
49	"	34	(21-4-51-2)		6 : . .	34		: . : 9 1	48		8 HR	121	293			24	
54			SLEEP	29	: :	36		: : x 7 1	52			122	294			25	
56	(35-8-65-0)	35	(29-6-68-1)		† 2 : 3 . .	41	2	7 1	53	3		123	295	4	13	26	21
1.00	LUNCH										M28 NB 9		LUNCH				

2ND DAY	BOWLERS (McCONNELL) PADDINGTON END		(CRAFTER) RANDWICK END		BATSMEN SCOREBOARD LEFT			SCOREBOARD RIGHT			ENGLAND 1ST INNINGS	END-OF-OVER TOTALS					
TIME	BOWLER	O.	BOWLER	O.	SCORING	BALLS	6s/4s	SCORING	BALLS	6s/4s	NOTES Hughes sub (McDermott)	O.	RUNS	W.	'L' BAT	'R' BAT	EXTRAS
LUNCH					CAPEL	41	2	ATHEY	53	3	M28 NB9	123	295	4	13	26	21
1.40			SLEEP	30	x . . : :	45		: 8 1	55			124	296			27	
43	DODEMAIDE	26						7 3 : : : :	61		M29	125					
47			"	31	8/7 2 : : 2 4F 3	51						126	298		15		
51	"	27						: : 6 2 : 4 :	67			127	300			29	
55			"	32	3 8 . 1 :	54		: : 7 1	70			128	302		16	30	
58	"	28			: : . : 5 2	59		3/4 1	71			129	305		18	31	
2.02			"	33				: 4 : 5 4 4 7 1	77	4	over bowler's head	130	310			36	
05	"	29	(33-6-78-1)		: 4 : 9E 2	64		9/8 1	78		Partnership: 50 in 78 min.	131	313		20	37	
10			TAYLOR	14				: : 5 5 W	82	4		131 (4)	313	5	20	37	21
12								EMBUREY								0	
14			"	14				9 2 : :	2		M30	132					
15	"	30			: : . 6 : 7	70					M31	133					
19			"	15				: : : : : :	8		M32	134					
22	"	31			3 1	71		: : : 4 :	13			135	314		21		
26			"	16	2/3 : 7 4 4 4 W	77	2				M33	136	314	6	21	0	21
29					FRENCH										0		
31	"	32						: : : . . 3	19		M34 9HR	137					
34			"	17	3.P 4 4 6 :	6					M35	138					
37	"	33						: 1E 4 2 x : 1E 4 .	25	2	• (low chance to WK's right.	139	322			8	
41 DRINKS 45			"	18	: : : : : :	12					M36	140					
47	"	34						: : 7/8 4 : 4 :	31	3		141	326			12	
52			"	19	. 3 8 1	15		: 3 7 1	34			142	328		1	13	
55	"	35			: E1 : : :	20		LB	35		• low to 2nd slip (LB) M37 (wang)	143	329				22
59			"	20	7 :	22		4/5 2 . 8 1	39			144	332			16	
3.02	"	36			4 . 7 2 2 . . 2	26		8 1	41			145	337		5	17	
06	(36-10-98-1)		"	21				: : P : P	47		M38	146					
09	SLEEP	34			2 x 2/3 . 3 .	32					M39	147					
13			"	22				6/5 4 . 2 . P .	53	4		148	341			21	
16	"	35			4F : : : 8 1	38						149	342		6		
20			"	23	: 6 1	40		7F 2 : : 8	57			150	345		7	23	
22	"	36			3 7F 1	42		: x W	59	4		150 (4)	346	7	8	23	22
24								FOSTER								0	
26	"	36						x :	2			151					
28			"	24	: 3 : 8 4 3	47		P	3			152	349		11		
32	"	37			8 1 : : 8 1	51		: 7/8 1	5		10HR	153	352		13	1	
35			"	25	P 1E 4 : : x 5 3	57	1				• High c & b.	154	359		20		
38	(38-7-85-2)	38	(25-10-49-2)		6 . 9E 6 3 9 2	63	1		5	-	• Dropped Marsh backward point	155	361	7	22	1	22
3.41	TEA										M39 NB9			T	E	A	

2ND DAY	BOWLERS (McCONNELL) PADDINGTON END		(CRAFTER) RANDWICK END		BATSMEN SCOREBOARD LEFT			SCOREBOARD RIGHT			Att: 27,164 NOTES Hughes sub (McD)	ENGLAND 1ST INNINGS END-OF-OVER TOTALS					
TIME	BOWLER	O.	BOWLER	O.	SCORING	BALLS	6s/4s	SCORING	BALLS	6s/4s		O.	RUNS	W.	'L' BAT	'R' BAT	EXTRAS
TEA					FRENCH	63	1	FOSTER	5	-	M39 NB9	155	361	7	22	1	22
4.00			TAYLOR	26	3 : : :	66		: 8/7 2 4 1	8			156	364			4	
03	SLEEP	39						EP 6/7 · 4 x 1 : · 3/4 4 ·	14	2		157	372			12	
07			"	27	7/8 1 5† 4 4 1	69	2	1 6/5 2 1 :	17		† hit sightscreen 1st bounce	158	381		28	15	
11	"	40			: 2 1	71		: 3/4 4 3 1 : ·	21	3		159	386		29	19	
15			"	28	EP9 1	72		: : E! W	24	3		159^{4}	387	8	30	19	22
16								HEMMINGS								0	
18			"	28	:	73		9 1	1			160	388			1	
20	"	41			: 7† 1	75		8 1 x : :	5		† Air shot - just clear	161	390		31	2	
23			"	29	5 · 7 2 2/3 2 : · 7/6F 4	81	3					162	398		39		
26	"	42						x : : 3 9 : :	11		M40	163					
29			"	30	x 4F : 1	83		7 2 : : :	15			164	401		40	4	
33	"	43			3† · 1	85		x L · L : :	19		† Jones misfielded	165	402		41		
37			"	31	7 1	86		: : : : : :	24			166	403		42		
40	"	44			1 8/7 2 1 7 · 8 2 · ·	91		4 1	25			167	409		47	5	
43			"	32	6 3 x : · W	94	3	7 7 : 1	27			167^{5}	410	9	47	6	22
45					DILLEY		LHB								0		
47			"	32	7 4	1	1					168	414		4		
48	"	45			P 6†4 5(4) · 2 2 2	5		x 8 · 1	29		† Air shot - no field 11HR	169	421		10	7	
52	(45-8-114-2)		"	33	: x :	7		P · 4/3 : · 1	32		x Dyer hit on nose	169^{5}	422		10	8	
56	DRINKS										Valetta WK 13th man: ROSS TAYLOR (N. Distr) Sydney.						
5.00			"	33	:	8						170					
01	WAUGH	22						: : : : 7 :	38		M41	171					
05			"	34	: EP : 7 2 P6 · 1	14						172	425		13		
08	" (22.5-5-51-3)	23	(34-10-84-4)		4 · x : : x W	19	1		38	-		172^{5}	425	10	13	8	22
5.10	ALL OUT										M41 NB 9		ALL OUT				
											1046 balls						

2ND DAY	BOWLERS (McDONNELL) PADDINGTON END		(CRAFTER) RANDWICK END		BATSMEN SCOREBOARD LEFT			SCOREBOARD RIGHT			AUSTRALIA 1ST INNINGS	END-OF-OVER TOTALS					
TIME	BOWLER	O.	BOWLER	O.	SCORING	BALLS	6s/4s	SCORING	BALLS	6s/4s	NOTES	O.	RUNS	W.	'L' BAT	'R' BAT	EXTRAS
					BOON			MARSH									
5.22			DILLEY	1	4 · · 4 · 1	5	1	·	1		(W)	1	6		5		1
28	FOSTER	1			· · 2 · · ·	11						2	8		7		
32			"	2				· · · · · ·	7		M1	3					
36	"	2	(2-1-6-0)		· · · · · ·	17					M2	4					
40			EMBUREY	1				· 4 · · · ·	13		7 Robinson hit (leg) M3	5					
43	"	3			· · 1	20		· · ·	16			6	9		8		
47			"	2	· · · · · ·	26					M4	7					
50	"	4			· · ·	29		· · 1	19			8	10			1	
54			"	3				· · · · · ·	25		M5	9					
56	(5-1-8-0)	5	(3-3-0-0)		4 · · · · ·	35	2		25	–		10	14	0	12	1	1
6.00	STUMPS		(2ND DAY)								M5 NB –		STUMPS				

3RD DAY	BOWLERS (McDONNELL) PADDINGTON END		BOWLERS (CRAFTER) RANDWICK END		BATSMEN SCOREBOARD LEFT			BATSMEN SCOREBOARD RIGHT			AUSTRALIA 1ST INNINGS	END-OF-OVER TOTALS					
TIME	BOWLER	O.	BOWLER	O.	SCORING	BALLS	6s/4s	SCORING	BALLS	6s/4s	NOTES	O.	RUNS	W.	'L' BAT	'R' BAT	EXTRAS
					BOON	35	2	MARSH	25	-	M5 NB -	10	14	0	12	1	1
11.00			DILLEY	3	·· P	37		7 · E½ ···3	29			11	17			4	
05	FOSTER	6						·:···† x	35		† Bat/pad chance (ROBINSON) M6	12					
10			"	4	4F · P 4 ······	43					M7	13					
14	"	7			·6···G1 W	48	2	8 1	36			14	18	1	12	5	1
17					JONES										0		
19			"	5				·······	42		M8 1HR	15					
23	"	8			7 † 3† ··1	3		·:·	45		† 1000 RUNS in TESTS	16	19		1		
27			"	6	⊙ 6· 6(B) 6(F) ···2·3	10					(NB) NB1	17	25		6		2
33	"	9	(6-3-15-0)		········	16					M9	18					
37			CAPEL	1				·E9 ···W	49	-		18^4	25	2	6	5	2
40								BORDER		LHB						0	
42			"	1				T ··	2		M10	19					
44	"	10			·3 ···1	20		8 2·	4			20	28		7	2	
48			"	2	····2 4:	26	1					21	32		11		
52	"	11	(2-1-4-1)					········	10		M11	22					
57	(11-4-13-1)		EMBUREY	4	:9 2:··P	32						23	34		13		
12.00	CAPEL	3						· E9† 9† ···W	15	-	† Legside catch (WK)	23^5	34	3	13	2	2
03								VELETTA								0	
06	"	3						:	1		M12	24					
07			"	5	···6 1	36		··	3			25	35		14		
11	"	4			·· x 4/5 ··3	41		4/5 2	4			26	40		17	2	
16			"	6	·P·5LB ······	46		·	5		(LB) M13 2HR	27	41				3
19	"	5			4PP ·····	52					M14	28					
24			"	7	···8/9 1	56		7 1 :	7			29	43		18	3	
26	"	6			4··3 ···4··	62	2					30	47		22		
31	(6-3-13-2)		"	8	::·	65		4·7 4·1	10	1		31	52			8	
33	FOSTER	12	(8-4-10-0)		:7 1	67		4s† 1 †·T	14		† Ro attempt (FOSTER)	32	54		23	9	
39			HEMMINGS	1	7:7 ··1 :	71		3LB 2·	16		(LB)	33	58		24	11	4
42	"	13			3 1	72		8 1 ····	21			34	60		25	12	
46			"	2	9EP · 7 8/7 · •·22··	78					• Low chance to leg-slip's rt hand (EMBUREY)	35	64		29		
49	"	14						·† ½ 6 ··2···	27			36	66			14	
53	(14-4-19-1)		"	3	·8 ·1	80		·· ·5(4) ···1	31			37	68		30	15	
56	EMBUREY	9	(3-0-9-0)		2LB P ··	82	2	8·7 8 ··21	35	1	(2LB)	38	73	3	30	18	6
1.00	(9-4-13-0) LUNCH										M14 NB1		LUNCH				

3RD DAY	BOWLERS (McCONNELL) PADDINGTON END		(CRAFTER) RANDWICK END		BATSMEN SCOREBOARD LEFT			SCOREBOARD RIGHT			NOTES	AUSTRALIA 1ST INNINGS END-OF-OVER TOTALS					
TIME	BOWLER	O.	BOWLER	O.	SCORING	BALLS	6s/4s	SCORING	BALLS	6s/4s		O.	RUNS	W.	'L' BAT	'R' BAT	EXTRAS
LUNCH					JONES	82	2	VELETTA	35	1	M14 NB1	38	73	3	30	18	6
1.41			HEMMINGS	4	. . 3	85		. . 1	38		(NB) NB2	39	77		33	19	
45	DILLEY	7			: 1	87		. : 2 ⊙ 1	43		• Dropped Robinson diving mid-wicket	40	82		34	22	7
50			"	5				: . W	46	1	Cloud - welcome breeze	40³	82	4	34	22	7
51								WAUGH								0	
53			"	5				: : .	3		M 15	41					
55	"	8			: 2 ⊙ : ①	93		. 3	5		(NB) NB 3̶4	42	86		37		8
2.01			"	6	: 1	95		: . : 1	9		3HR	43	88		38	1	
04	"	9			3	96		: . 3 . .	14			44	94		41	4	
10	(9-3-30-0)		"	7	2 : 1	99		: : :	17			45	97		44		
13	EMBUREY	10			1	100		P : : : 1	22			46	99		45	5	
16			"	8	1	101		1 2 : . .	27			47	103		46	8	
20	"	11			P x• 6 . :	107					• st chance M16	48					
23			"	9				: : : :	33		M17	49					
25	"	12			: . 4 : P6	113	3				50: 147 min	50	107		50		
28			"	10	: : . 4	117	4	: 1	35			51	112		54	9	
32	"	13						: : : : :	41		• nr Amey on leg M18	52					
34			"	11	2 : : : :	123						53	114		56		
37	"	14						: : : : 2	47			54	116			11	
40			"	12	: W	125	4					54²	116	5	56	11	8
40	DRINKS				SLEEP										0		
44			"	12	4 : .	4	1					55	120		4		
46	"	15						: : : P : 1	53			56	121			12	
49			"	13				P : . : : :	59		M19	57					
52	"	16			P F : P . 2	10						58	123		6		
54			"	14	: 6 P	13		: : 1	62			59	124			13	
57	"	17						4 : : : 2 :	68	1		60	130			19	
59			"	15	: 1	15		: : : :	72		Mexican wave 4HR	61	131		7		
3.03	"	18			: P 6 P . EP	21					M20	62					
06			"	16	1	22		: : † . 1 4	77	2	† Round wkt (3.08) Paper on field (3.11)	63	137		8	24	
13	"	19			6 : . 1 2	27		1	78			64	141		11	25	
16			"	17				: 2LB 2 . : :	84		(2LB)	65	145			27	10
20	"	20	(17-3-43-2)		: : : : P 2	33					• Skier nr Hemmings (mid-wkt)	66	147		13		
24			DILLEY	10				W	85	2		66¹	147	6	13	27	10
25								DYER								0	
27			"	10	⊙ : 3	36		LB : .	3		(LB) (NB) NB5	67	152		16		12
32	"	21			. P : : P P	42					M21	68					
34	(21-8-36-0)		"	11				: ⊙ . W	7	-	(NB) NB6	68³	153	7	16	0	13
36								TAYLOR LHB									
38			(11-3-35-2)	11		42	1	: . .	3	-	• Hit on back of helmet	69	153	7	16	0	13
3.41	TEA										M21 NB6				T	E	A

3RD DAY	BOWLERS (McCONNELL) PADDINGTON END		(CRAFTER) RANDWICK END		BATSMEN SCOREBOARD LEFT			SCOREBOARD RIGHT			AUSTRALIA 1ST INNINGS Att: 29,511 NOTES	END-OF-OVER TOTALS					
TIME	BOWLER	O.	BOWLER	O.	SCORING	BALLS	6s/4s	SCORING	BALLS	6s/4s		O.	RUNS	W.	'L' BAT	'R' BAT	EXTRAS
TEA					SLEEP	42	1	TAYLOR	3	–	M 21 NB 6	69	153	7	16	0	13
4.00	EMBUREY	22			5/6F 3 P : :	45		P : 3 . . 1	6		overcast – breezy	70	157		19	1	
04			HEMMINGS	18	P .	46		P : P P 3/2 3	11			71	160			4	
07	(23-8-44-0)	23	(18-3-46-2)		8 1	47	1	P P : 1/2 3 P	16	–		72	164	7	20	7	13
4.11	BAD LIGHT										M21 NB 6			BL SP			
5.32	PLAY ABANDONED												STUMPS				
4TH DAY 11.00			DILLEY	12	LB .	48		↑x 1E 2 . . 4 2 .	21	1	(LB)	73	171			13	14
05	EMBUREY	24			: L . : : :	54					M 22	74					
08			"	13	5(6) 4 :	57		3 : : 2 1	24		5HR	75	172			14	
12	"	25						: 2 7 P P : 2 . .	30			76	174			16	
15			"	14	: ↑ 6/7 1	60		: . :	33			77	175		21		
19	"	26	(14-3-43-2)		. P P P : 8 1	66						78	176		22		
22			HEMMINGS	19	: 4 1	68		P x A 5	37		A – ct wk.	79	177		23		
26	"	27			Y L . 5 : :	74					M 23	80					
28			"	20				P : 6F : : 7 4	43	2		81	181			20	
31	"	28			6S 1	75		: P ! P :	48			82	182		24		
34			"	21	7 1	76		E1 W	49	2		82²	183	8	25	20	14
35								DODEMAIDE								0	
37			"	21				: : . :	4			83					
39	"	29			: . 2/3 2 P EP 4 . : :	82						84	185		27		
41			"	22	7 6 : 1	84		: 7 P LB . .	8		(LB)	85	187		28		15
44	"	30	(22-3-53-3)		3 6 7 3 6F : . 4 2 1	89	2	P :	9			86	194		35		
47	(30-10-57-0)		DILLEY	15	† . : . ↑ . 2	95					† NEW BALL M 24	87					
52	FOSTER	15						: : : . . 42	15		M 25	88					
57			"	16	. . Y. . 6 1	100		3/2 1	16			89	196		36	1	
12 01 05	DRINKS "	16			8/7 133 2 . . .	104		: 8 1	18		6 HR	90	199		38	2	
09			"	17	↑ 4 : 2 : :	108		6 LB . .	20		(LB)	91	202		40		16
14	"	17						9 P 3 : 4 x 4	26	1		92	206			6	
18			"	18	1/2 1	109		49 2 . X . 2	31			93	209		41	8	
23	"	18			: ↑ : . E1 W	114	2					93⁵	209	9	41	8	16
25					McDERMOTT										0		
27	"	18			↑	1					M26	94					
28			"	19				. 4 4 . 3 . 2 . 2 .	37			95	213			12	
33	"	19			9 1	2		. . X . 6 .	42			96	214		1		
38	(19-6-27-2)		(19.1-4-54-3)	20	6 W	3	–		42	1		96¹	214	10	1	12	16
12.38	ALL OUT										M 26 NB 6		ALL OUT				
											583 balls						

4TH DAY	BOWLERS (CRAFTER) PADDINGTON END		BOWLERS (McCONNELL) RANDWICK END		BATSMEN SCOREBOARD LEFT			BATSMEN SCOREBOARD RIGHT			NOTES	AUSTRALIA 2ND INNINGS END-OF-OVER TOTALS					
TIME	BOWLER	O.	BOWLER	O.	SCORING	BALLS	6s/4s	SCORING	BALLS	6s/4s		O.	RUNS	W.	'L' BAT	'R' BAT	EXTRAS
					MARSH			BOON									
12.50	FOSTER	1			. : . . . : 7 1	6						1	1		1		
54			CAPEL	1	4 4 . x : : : : :	12					M1	2					
58	" (2-1-1-0)	2	(1-1-0-0)			12	-	. 6 :	6	-	M2	3	1	0	1	0	-
1.01	LUNCH										Fairbrother sub for Emburey.		LUNCH				
1.40			DILLEY	1	. . : . x : 4 : :	18					M3	4					
45	FOSTER	3			LB .	19		: . 6S 1 ↑2 9 2 2	11		(LB)	5	7			5	1
49			"	2	2† 4 . : : 2 : 3 . 1	25	1				† over gully.	6	12		6		
53	"	4			4S 1	26		. . . : 7/8 7/8 1	16			7	14		7	6	
57			"	3	.	27		. 6 : . (NB)(NB) . 6 1	23		(NB)(NB) NB 2	8	17			7	3
2.03	"	5			:	28		P : P : 3 : 1	28			9	18			8	
08			"	4	2 : .	30		↑7 ↑ 4S . 4 . 1	32	1		10	23			13	
12	"	6						L : . . P : . : .	38		M4	11					
16			"	5	2 (4) 3 1 : : . . .	36	2	5/(6) 3	39		NB 3	12	31		12	16	
21	"	7	(5-1-21-0)		: . 1/2 4 .	40	3	L : 1 1	41		1 HR	13	36		16	17	
27	(7-2-14-0)		CAPEL	2				: 4 4 P : . : P :	47	2		14	40			21	
32	HEMMINGS	1			2B : . : 9 1	45		:	48		(2B)	15	43		17		5
37			"	3	. 2 : . 2/3 1	50		:	49			16	44		18		
40 DRINKS 43	"	2			: 9 1	52		P 4 : 6 : 4 : :	53	3	Round wkt	17	49		19	25	
47			"	4	LB .	53		. : 7 x 7 : 2	58		(LB) 50 p'ship; 78'	18	52			27	6
52	"	3			: P : P : :	59					M5	19					
55			"	5				. E1 : . . 8 4	64	4		20	56			31	
3.00	"	4			: 9/1 8 2 1	62		: : E3	67			21	59		22		
03	(4-1-9-0)		"	6	. 3 ↑ 2 ↑ 7 : : : :	68					M6	22					
08	EMBUREY	1	(6-2-11-0)		: : :	71		: 7 8 : 1	70			23	60			32	
11			HEMMINGS	5				P 4 P : : :	76		M7	24					
14	"	2			: P : P 9 P	77					M8	25					
16			"	6	4S 1 : 7	80		3/9 1 : 9 1	79			26	63		23	34	
19	"	3			: :	82		. 6P : 6 1	83			27	64			35	
21			"	7	: : . P	86		P 3 : 1	85			28	65			36	
24	"	4						P P : : : :	91		M9	29					
27			"	8	: 4 : 9 8 2 . :	92					2HR	30	67		25		
29	"	5			P 9 4 : 1 :	96		6 1 6 1	93			31	70		26	38	
32			"	9	8 1	97		6 : 7 8 2 : . 1 4	98	5		32	76		27	43	
35	"	6			: 4 2 : : P 4 3	103						33	81		32		
39	(6-2-10-0)		"	10	: : : 8 1	107	3	: :	100	5		34	82	0	33	43	6
3.40	TEA		(10-2-22-0)								M9 NB 3			T	E	A	

4TH DAY	BOWLERS (CRAPTER) PADDINGTON END		(McCONNELL) RANDWICK END		BATSMEN SCOREBOARD LEFT			SCOREBOARD RIGHT			Att: 13,049 NOTES	AUSTRALIA 2ND INNINGS END-OF-OVER TOTALS					
TIME	BOWLER	O.	BOWLER	O.	SCORING	BALLS	6s/4s	SCORING	BALLS	6s/4s		O.	RUNS	W.	'L' BAT	'R' BAT	EXTRAS
TEA					MARSH	107	3	BOON	100	5	M9 NB 3	34	82	0	33	43	6
4.01	EMBUREY	7			6 : : : : 2 2 : ·	113						35	84		35		
03			HEMMINGS	11	:	114		: : 4 : : 6 1	105			36	85			44	
06	"	8			: :	116		: : P 8 • · 1	109		• Running muddle	37	86			45	
09			"	12	7 :	117		4 : : 5 · P 8 · 1	114			38	87			46	
11	"	9						: 6 7 4 : : :	120	6	Boon's 50: 143'	39	91			50	
14			"	13	2 3 6 3†16 · · · ·	122		2/1 1	121		† Athey (s. pt) hit on shin.	40	95		38	51	
17	"	10			: : : :	126		: 8/7 1	123			41	96			52	
20			"	14	: · ·	129		: · 8 1	126		umpires conferred	42	97			53	
23	"	11	(14-2-29-0)		: 8 1	131		· † : 8 1 :	130		† Round	43	99		39	54	
26	(11-2-20-0)		DILLEY	6	2 : 8 2 ↑ ·	~~134~~	3		130	6	100: 159'	43.3	101	0	41	54	6
4.29	BAD LIGHT		(5.3-1-23-0)														
5.36	PLAY ABANDONED										M9 NB3		STUMPS				

AUSTRALIA 2ND INNINGS

5TH DAY TIME	BOWLERS (CRAFTER) PADDINGTON END BOWLER	O.	(McCONNELL) RANDWICK END BOWLER	O.	BATSMEN SCOREBOARD LEFT SCORING	BALLS	6s/4s	SCOREBOARD RIGHT SCORING	BALLS	6s/4s	NOTES	END-OF-OVER TOTALS O.	RUNS	W.	'L' BAT	'R' BAT	EXTRAS
					MARSH	134	3	BOON	130	6	M 9 NB 3	43³	101	0	41	54	6
11.00			DILLEY	6	: : .	137						44					
03	HEMMINGS	15						. : : : .	136		M 10	45					
06			"	7	+½ 1	138		: : ⊙⊙ : : : P	143		+ Round (NB) (NB) NB 5	46	104		42		8
11	"	16			P : : P : L	144					M 11	47					
14			"	8	: : .	147		: : ⊙ . ③ ¾	148		(NB) NB 7	48	108			57	9
19	"	17	(8-1-30-0)		8 3 : : : :	151		: 9 3	150		3 HR	49	111			60	
23			EMBUREY	12				: : : 9 : 8 1	156			50	112			61	
25	"	18			: 8 .	153		1E 2 : 7 6S 1	160		Best opening p'ship by M + B v Eng (p 113)	51	115			64	
28			"	13				: : 8 : : 4	166		M 12	52					
30	"	19			: : : : 3 2 :	159						53	117		44		
33			"	14	: 9 1	161		: : : 3 1	170			54	119		45	65	
36	"	20			P : 8 P P 9/4 1	167						55	120		46		
39			"	15	P 4 1 : : :	172		½ 3	171			56	124		47	68	
42	"	21						: : 7 2 7 . . 7 1	177		Record A v I (1st) at Sydney (p 126 = 1946-47) Barnes + Morris	57	127			71	
44			"	16	: : :	175		: 8 9 3	180			58	130			74	
47	"	22						: : 6 : : 4	186		M 13	59					
49			"	17	P 4 3 4 : : : .	181	4				MARSH'S 50: 209'	60	134		51		
53	"	23	(17-3-34-0)					: 4 : 2 2 : :	192			61	136			76	
56			FOSTER	8	7 1	182		: : : 7 2 ‡ :	197		x Missed hook - hit on ribs.	62	139		52	78	
12.00	"	24			6 4 7 : P :	188					M 14	63					
02 05	DRINKS		"	9				. : : P : :	203		M 15	64					
09	"	25			9 1	189		: 3 4 : : 8	208	7		65	144		53	82	
13			"	10	. 3 : : 1E :	195					M 16	66					
16	"	26			: :	197		: 7 : 5(6) : : 3	212		4 HR	67	147			85	
19	(26-6-51-0)			" 11	: : : :	201		7 LB	214		(LB) M 17	68	148				10
22	EMBUREY	18						6 4 : : P :	220	8	150 p'ship: 243'	69	152			89	
26			"	12	7S 1 : 2 1	204		4 2 . 1 †	223			70	155		55	90	
29	"	19			: 2 4 : 1	207		: : :	226			71	156		56		
32			"	13	2 : 4 : : 7	213					M 18	72					
35	"	20	(13-6-20-0)		. CP7 W	215	4	P 6 3/2 7 4 ⊙ 1	230	9	(NB) NB 8	72⁵	162	1	56	95	11
38					JONES										0		
40	"	20			P	1						73					
41			HEMMINGS	27	P : L P	5		? 8 1	232			74	163			96	
45	"	21			: 8 4 : :	9	1	: 1†	234		+ Gd running stop + return (Hemmings)	75	168		4	97	
48			"	28				: : : : . P	240		M 19	76					
51	"	22			. B :	11		P : : 4	244		(B) M 20	77	169				12
53			"	29	P : P : : .	17					M 21	78					
56	"	23						: 7 2 P : : 6 1	250		BOON'S 100: 278' at 12.58 pm	79	172			100	
59	(23-4-53-1)		"	30		17	1	: : : : .	256	9	M 22 NB 8	80	172	1	4	100	12
1.01	LUNCH		(30-9-52-0)									LUNCH					

5TH DAY	BOWLERS (CRAFTER) PADDINGTON END		(McCONNELL) RANDWICK END		BATSMEN SCOREBOARD LEFT			SCOREBOARD RIGHT			AUSTRALIA 2ND INNINGS Breeze 23°C	END-OF-OVER TOTALS					
TIME	BOWLER	O.	BOWLER	O.	SCORING	BALLS	6s/4s	SCORING	BALLS	6s/4s	NOTES Fairbrother sub	O.	RUNS	W.	'L' BAT	'R' BAT	EXTRAS
LUNCH					JONES	17	1	BOON	256	9	(Gatting - flu) M22 Emburey capt NB 8	80	172	1	4	100	12
1.40	EMBUREY	24			: : : P . 9 2	23						81	174		6		
43			HEMMINGS	31				: 7 7 : 7F 4	262	10		82	178			104	
46	•	25			: : : : : :	29					M23	83					
49			"	32				: : : : : :	268		M24	84					
51	•	26	(32-10-56-0)		8 1	30		: 3/2 : 8 . 1	273			85	180		7	105	
54	(26-5-57-1)		DILLEY	9	2/3 : . .	33		4 †3/2 8/7 : 4 1	276	11	† NEW BALL at 1.55 5HR	86	185			110	
59	FOSTER	14			. . 7 1 :	37		7 1 3 1	278			87	188		8	112	
2.03			•	10	•E1 . . 2 . .	42		↑7/8 3	279		• Dropped 2nd slip (Athey)	88	191			115	
08	"	15						6 3 6 . 4 2 . 2 . . :	285			89	195			119	
12	(15-6-27-0)		•	11	E1 5 L 5 4† 4 1	48	2				† Dwind stop (sub) DeFreitas sub (Foster) knee	90	200		13		
16	CAPEL	7			8 1 5(4) 4 4 :	51	3	x : LB	288		(LB)	91	206		18		13
23			"	12	↑ : :	54		: P 1/2 3	291		Boon replaced bat handle rubber.	92	209			122	
28	"	8						4 . . : : 7 2 2	297		2.31 Aus in lead	93	211			124	
33			"	13	: : . 4 : 8 2	60					Jarvis, sub (Moxon) 50 p'ship: 78'	94	213		20		
37	•	9	(13-1-48-0)		T 2 : :	62		2/3 4 7 2/1 . . . 1	301			95	214			125	
41 45	DRINKS		HEMMINGS	33				: : 5 L P . .	307		Moxon back M 25	96					
49	"	10	}		8 4 . . : 2 W	67	4					96⁵	218	2	24	125	13
51					BORDER		LHB								0		
53	•	10	}		3 :	1						97					
54			•	34				: : : : 1 2 :	313		6HR	98	220			127	
58	"	11			: 5(4) 3	3		: 6P8/7 . . 2 .	317			99	225		3	129	
3.03			"	35	† : : X L Ø 3 . . .	9					† Round wkt M26	100					
06	"	12			† : ↑ :	12		5(4) 7 . 4 1	320	12	† Round wkt	101	230			134	
11	(12-2-33-1)		•	36				4 : : : . E1 2	326			102	232			136	
15	EMBUREY	27			: 3 2 : : 3 2 .	18					Jarvis sub (Moxon)	103	236		7		
18			•	37	† : : : P . .	23		8 1	327		† Round wkt	104	237			137	
21	"	28			: 2 :	25		5 x 7 8 . . . 1	331			105	238			138	
24			"	38	:	26		8 7• : 8 . . . 1	336		• Nr sh. sq. leg (Robi'n)	106	239			139	
27	"	29			: 8 1	28		4 L 7 5(4) . . 1 3	340			107	244		8	143	
30			"	39	3 2 . 3 2 :	32		: 1 3	342		Boon's HS in Tests (prev 143 - NZ)	108	251		12	146	
33	"	30						: : : . . 7 1	348			109	252			147	
36			"	40	. 2 :	34		: : : 6 1	352			110	253			148	
39	" (31-5-71-1)	31	(40-12-70-0)		: : 9/8 1 :	38	-	4 1 8 1	354	12	Boon's 150: 400'	111	256	2	13	150	13
3.41	TEA										M26 NB 8			T	E	A	

5TH DAY	BOWLERS (CRAFTER) PADDINGTON END		(McCONNELL) RANDWICK END		BATSMEN SCOREBOARD LEFT			SCOREBOARD RIGHT			AUSTRALIA 2ND INNINGS Att 8,645 NOTES 3 subs as before Tea	END-OF-OVER TOTALS					
TIME	BOWLER	O.	BOWLER	O.	SCORING	BALLS	6s/4s	SCORING	BALLS	6s/4s		O.	RUNS	W.	'L' BAT	'R' BAT	EXTRAS
TEA					BORDER	38	-	BOON	354	12	M26 NB 8	111	256	2	13	150	13
4.00			HEMMINGS	41				. : ⑫3 5 : :	360		M27	112					
03	EMBUREY	32			7 3 † . 5(6) : 3	41		4 1 8 5 . 1	363		† Round wkt	113	264		19	152	
07			"	42	1 1	42		: 7 4 6 1 : :	368	13		114	270		20	157	
10	"	33			8 1	43		: 6/5 2 . : 6 .	373			115	273		21	159	
13			"	43	: : : : P :	49					M28	116					
15	"	34			: :	51		: P : 4 1	377		7HR	117	274			160	
17			"	44	† : : 2/1 3	54		7/4 2 8 1 7 .	380		† 1 overthrow (ricochet) † Round wkt	118	280		24	163	
21	"	35	(44-14-82-0)		3 3 2 1	56		: 6 1 . :	384			119	285		28	164	
25	(35-5-88-1)		CAPEL	13	: . : : . 3	62					M29	120					
30	HEMMINGS	45			† 3 : 2/3 1	64		7 7 : 8 1	388		† Round wkt to LHB	121	287		29	165	
33			"	14	. LB .	66		7 2 : :	392		(LB) M 30	122	288				14
38	"	46			5 : . 3/4 3	69		6 6 . 4 3	395	14		123	298		32	172	
42			"	15	5(4) 1	70		4 . LB . : X P	400		(LB)	124	300		33		15
47	"	47			: : : : 3 3 1	75		4 .	401			125	301		34		
50			"	16	. L . 3 5 1	78		: 4 † :	404		† Round wkt	126	302		35		
55	"	48			1 1 E1 .	80		: : P 8 1	408			127	304		36	173	
58			"	17	7 2 P .	82		: 5 : 2 1	412			128	307		38	174	
5 03 07	DRINKS "	49	(17-4-38-1)		3 4 : :	85	1	7 4 : 7 1	415		118' for 1st four (Border)	129	312		42	175	
11			EMBUREY	36	† : 8 1	87		: LB . : 9 2	419		(LB) Round to LHB	130	316		43	177	16
14	"	50			: 2 P . 1 2 . 5(6) 2	93					Radford sub (DEF) 8HR	131	320		47		
17			"	37	:	94		1 2 : 4 . 1 3	424			132	325			182	
21	"	51			: : : :	98		: 8 1	426			133	326			183	
24			"	38	8 1	99		: : : 3 1 7 .	431			134	328		48	184	
27	" (52-15-107-0)	52	(38-5-98-1)		: : : : : :	105	1		431	14	M31	135	328	2	48	184	16
5.30	STUMPS										M31 NB 8	MATCH DRAWN					
											818 balls						
											TOTAL ATTENDANCE :-						
											103,831						

ENGLAND 1ST INNINGS v AUSTRALIA at SYDNEY CRICKET GROUND ON 29, 30, 31 JANUARY, 1, 2 FEBRUARY 1988

IN	OUT	MINS	No.	BATSMAN	HOW OUT	BOWLER	RUNS	WKT	TOTAL	6s	4s	BALLS	NOTES ON DISMISSAL — TOSS: ENGLAND
11.00	12.09	434	1	B.C. BROAD	BOWLED	WAUGH	139	4	262	·	13	361	Turned back on lifting inswinger - played on via elbow.
11.00	2.12	154	2	M.D. MOXON	BOWLED	SLEEP	40	1	93	·	3	119	Off stump - down wicket - missed on-drive at leg-break
2.14	4.54	141	3	R.T. ROBINSON	CT VELETTA	DODEMAIDE	43	2	192	·	4	120	Fended sharply lifting ball to 2nd slip.
4.56	11.42	108	4	M.W. GATTING*	CT DYER	WAUGH	13	3	245	·	1	53	Edged outswinger - quicker ball.
11.44	2.12	108	5	C.W.J. ATHEY	CT AND BOWLED	TAYLOR	37	5	313	·	4	82	Drove waist-high direct to bowler.
12.11	2.29	98	6	D.J. CAPEL	CT SLEEP	TAYLOR	21	6	314	·	2	77	Miscued lofted straight drive to wide mid-off.
2.14	3.24	71	7	J.E. EMBUREY	ST DYER	SLEEP	23	7	346	·	4	59	Beaten by sharply-turning leg-break.
2.31	4.45	115	8	B.N. FRENCH†	ST DYER	TAYLOR	47	9	410	·	3	94	Missed pull at arm-ball.
3.26	4.16	31	9	N.A. FOSTER	CT BORDER	TAYLOR	19	8	387	·	3	24	Edged square-drive to slip.
4.18	(5.10)	52	10	E.E. HEMMINGS	NOT OUT		8			·	·	38	-
4.47	5.10	23	11	G.R. DILLEY	BOWLED	WAUGH	13	10	425	·	1	19	Missed lofted off-drive.
				EXTRAS	b 4 lb 9	w 1 nb 8	22			-6	38 4	1046	

*CAPTAIN †WICKET-KEEPER

TOTAL (172.5 OVERS; 676 MINUTES) 425 ALL OUT at 5.10pm 2ND DAY

15 OVERS 2 BALLS/HOUR
2.45 RUNS/OVER
40 RUNS/100 BALLS

UMPIRES: A.R. CRAFTER and P.J. McCONNELL

BOWLER	O	M	R	W	nb/w
McDERMOTT	35	8	65	0	6/1
DODEMAIDE	36	10	98	1	3/-
TAYLOR	34	10	84	4	-
WAUGH	22⁵	5	51	3	-
SLEEP	45	8	114	2	-
			13		
	172.5	41	425	10	

2ND NEW BALL taken at 5.22 pm 1st day
- ENGLAND 204-2 after 85 overs

HRS	OVERS	RUNS
1	16	43
2	17	28
3	15	31
4	17	54
5	14	36
6	15	29
7	12	33
8	15	39
9	16	21
10	16	38
11	16	69

RUNS	MINS	OVERS	LAST 50 (in mins)
50	72	18.3	72
100	173	46.1	101
150	235	63.2	62
200	313	82.0	78
250	416	105.1	103
300	497	126.3	81
350	597	152.1	100
400	637	163.3	40

LUNCH:	71-0	(33 OVERS 122 MIN)	BROAD 36* MOXON 27*
TEA:	156-1	(65 OVERS 243 MIN)	BROAD 78* (243') ROBINSON 24* (87')
STUMPS (1ST DAY):	221-2	(94 OVERS 365 MIN)	BROAD 116* (365') GATTING 3* (66')
LUNCH:	295-4	(123 OVERS 485 MIN)	ATHEY 26* (76') CAPEL 13* (49')
TEA:	361-7	(155 OVERS 606 MIN)	FRENCH 22* (70') FOSTER 1* (15')

WKT	PARTNERSHIP		RUNS	MINS
1st	Broad	Moxon	93	154
2nd	Broad	Robinson	99	141
3rd	Broad	Gatting	53	108
4th	Broad	Athey	17	25
5th	Athey	Capel	51	82
6th	Capel	Emburey	1	15
7th	Emburey	French	32	53
8th	French	Foster	41	31
9th	French	Hemmings	23	27
10th	Hemmings	Dilley	15	23
			425	

AUSTRALIA 1ST INNINGS [IN REPLY TO ENGLAND'S 425 ALL OUT]

IN	OUT	MINS	No.	BATSMAN	HOW OUT	BOWLER	RUNS	WKT	TOTAL	6s	4s	BALLS	NOTES ON DISMISSAL
5.22	11.17	55	1	D.C. BOON	CT FRENCH	FOSTER	12	1	18	.	2	48	Fast lifting ball flicked glove.
5.22	11.40	78	2	G.R. MARSH	CT FRENCH	CAPEL	5	2	25	.	.	49	Edged leg-glance.
11.19	2.40	160	3	D.M. JONES	CT EMBUREY	HEMMINGS	56	5	116	.	4	125	Edged off-break via pad to leg-slip.
11.42	12.03	21	4	A.R. BORDER *	CT BROAD	CAPEL	2	3	34	.	.	15	Hooked bouncer to long-leg.
12.06	1.51	64	5	M.R.J. VELETTA	CT EMBUREY	HEMMINGS	22	4	82	.	1	46	Edged off-break to leg-slip.
1.53	3.25	92	6	S.R. WAUGH	CT FRENCH	DILLEY	27	6	147	.	2	85	Edged push - low catch diving to right.
2.44	12.25	153	7	P.R. SLEEP	CT ATHEY	FOSTER	41	9	209	.	2	114	Edged off-glide low to 2nd slip's left - 2-handed diving catch.
3.27	3.36	9	8	G.C. DYER †	LBW	DILLEY	0	7	153	.	.	7	'Plumb'.
3.38	11.35	49	9	P.J. TAYLOR	CT FRENCH	HEMMINGS	20	8	183	.	2	49	Bottom-edged cut at shortish leg-break (to LHB).
11.37	(12.38)	61	10	A.I.C. DODEMAIDE	NOT OUT		12	.	.	.	1	42	
12.27	12.38	11	11	C.J. McDERMOTT	CT FOSTER	DILLEY	1	10	214	.	.	3	Spectacular diving catch running back at mid-on.
				EXTRAS	b - lb 10	w 1 nb 5	16			-	14	583 balls (inc 6 nb)	

* CAPTAIN † WICKET-KEEPER

TOTAL (96.1 OVERS; 387 MINUTES) 214 ALL OUT at 12.38 pm on 4th day.

14 OVERS 5 BALLS/HOUR
2.22 RUNS/OVER
36 RUNS/100 BALLS

BOWLER	O	M	R	W	nb/w
DILLEY	19.1	4	54	3	6/1
FOSTER	19	6	27	2	-
EMBUREY	30	10	57	0	-
CAPEL	6	3	13	2	-
HEMMINGS	22	3	53	3	-
			10		
	96.1	26	214	10	

2ND NEW BALL taken at 11.47 on 4th day - AUSTRALIA 194-8 after 86 overs.

HRS	OVERS	RUNS
1	15	18
2	12	23
3	16	47
4	18	43
5	14	41
6	15	27

RUNS	MINS	OVERS	LAST 50 (in mins)
50	129	30.1	129
100	194	46.1	65
150	267	66.4	73
200	359	90.2	92

STUMPS (2ND DAY): 14-0 (10 OVERS, 38 MIN) BOON 12*, MARSH 1*

LUNCH 73-3 (38 OVERS, 158 MIN) JONES 30* (101'), VELETTA 18* (54')

TEA: 153-7 (69 OVERS, 278 MIN) SLEEP 16* (57'), TAYLOR 0* (3')

STUMPS (3RD DAY): 164-7 (72 OVERS, 289 MIN) SLEEP 20* (68'), TAYLOR 7* (14')

211 BEHIND ON FIRST INNINGS

- INVITED TO FOLLOW-ON

WKT	PARTNERSHIP		RUNS	MINS
1st	Boon	Marsh	18	55
2nd	Marsh	Jones	7	21
3rd	Jones	Border	9	21
4th	Jones	Veletta	48	64
5th	Jones	Waugh	34	47
6th	Waugh	Sleep	31	41
7th	Sleep	Dyer	6	9
8th	Sleep	Taylor	30	49
9th	Sleep	Dodemaide	26	48
10th	Dodemaide	McDermott	5	11
			214	

AUSTRALIA 2ND INNINGS FOLLOWING ON 211 RUNS BEHIND

IN	OUT	MINS	No.	BATSMAN	HOW OUT	BOWLER	RUNS	WKT	TOTAL	6s	4s	BALLS	NOTES ON DISMISSAL
12.50	12.38	257	1	G.R. MARSH	Ct ATHEY	EMBUREY	56	1	162	·	4	215	Edged off-break to short square-leg via pad.
12.50	(5.30)	491	2	D.C. BOON	NOT OUT		184			·	14	431	(6th in TESTS; (2nd v ENGLAND. HS in TESTS.
12.40	2.51	92	3	D.M. JONES	Ct MOXON	CAPEL	24	2	218	·	4	67	Cut long-hop very hard above gully's head - Juggled catch
2.53	(5.30)	138	4	A.R. BORDER*	NOT OUT		48			·	1	105	
			5										
			6										
			7										
			8										
			9										
			10										
			11										
				EXTRAS	b 3 lb 7	w - nb 6	16			-6	23 4	818 balls (inc 8 no-balls)	

* CAPTAIN † WICKET-KEEPER

TOTAL (135 OVERS; 491 MINUTES) 328-2

16 OVERS 3 BALLS/HOUR
2.42 RUNS/OVER
40 RUNS/100 BALLS

BOWLER	O	M	R	W	nb
FOSTER	15	6	27	0	-
CAPEL	17	4	38	1	-
DILLEY	13	1	48	0	7
HEMMINGS	52	15	107	0	-
EMBUREY	38	5	98	1	1
			10		
	135	31	328	2	

2ND NEW BALL taken at 1.55 pm on 5th day - AUSTRALIA 180-1 after 85.1 overs

HRS	OVERS	RUNS
1	13	36
2	17	31
3	19	44
4	18	36
5	19	38
6	12	35
7	19	54
8	14	46

RUNS	MINS	OVERS	LAST 50 (in mins)
50	78	17.1	78
100	159	43.2	81
150	243	68.2	84
200	316	90	73
250	392	107.5	76
300	444	123.3	52

LUNCH: 1-0 (3 OVERS, 11 MIN) MARSH 1*, BOON 0*

TEA: 82-0 (34 OVERS, 131 MIN) MARSH 33*, BOON 43*

STUMPS (4TH DAY): 101-0 (43.3 OVERS, 159 MIN) MARSH 41*, BOON 54*

LUNCH: 172-1 (80 OVERS, 280 MIN) BOON 100* (280'), JONES 4* (21')

TEA: 256-2 (111 OVERS, 401 MIN) BOON 150* (401'), BORDER 13* (48')

MATCH DRAWN

MATCH AWARD: D.C. BOON

WKT	PARTNERSHIP		RUNS	MINS
1st	Marsh	Boon	162	258
2nd	Boon	Jones	56	92
3rd	Boon	Border	110*	138
			328	

BRADMAN AND LARWOOD

Visits to the homes of the two key protagonists of the most tumultuous Test series played during Australia's first 200 years of European settlement · Records and highlights of the extraordinary career of the world's master batsman together with some of his more topical opinions · Life and times of the world's most feared fast bowler

As a statistician I must have written or typed the name of Sir Donald Bradman more often than that of any other cricketer. During a career involving only 52 matches spanning twenty years, eight of which were lost to war, injury and illness, he almost totally rewrote the records of Test cricket. Such was his stature and influence on world cricket that, under Douglas Jardine's captaincy in 1932-33, England felt compelled to resort to the infamous leg-theory 'bodyline' attack to curb his exceptional talents.

No other batsman approaches his Test career average of 99.94 (had he scored 4 and not 0 in his final innings at The Oval in 1948 he would have averaged 100), nor his frequency of contributing a century every 2.75 innings. At the height of his career, newspaper vendors' posters frequently proclaimed 'HE'S OUT!', or 'BRADMAN *versus* ENGLAND', or 'BRADMAN BATS AND BATS AND BATS'.

Although many of Bradman's records have been surpassed, several of those he set on his first tour of England in 1930 have proved unassailable. His aggregate for that five-match rubber was a mammoth 974, average 139.14, from just seven innings including a record three double centuries: 8, 131, 254, 1, 334, 14 and 232. His 334, the first triple century in Test cricket and still the record score for Australia, included a record 309 runs on the first day; 105 were gathered before lunch, 115 in the afternoon session and another 89 after tea. No other batsman has scored 300 runs in a single day of Test cricket. His time of 214 minutes remains the fastest for achieving a Test match double century.

The Don is also alone in holding the record scores for two batting positions in Test cricket with 304 at number 5 (*v.* England at Leeds in 1934) and 270 at number 7 (*v.* England at Melbourne in 1936-37).

He is also the only batsman to score hundreds in six successive Test matches. His partnership of 451 with Bill Ponsford at The Oval in 1934 remains the highest, although equalled, at Test level. Although all his Test appearances were confined to Australia and England, no one has improved upon his record scores on four major grounds: Adelaide Oval (299 not out), Brisbane's 'Gabba' (226), Lord's (254) and Headingley (334). His 299 remains a unique score in all first-class cricket; compiled against South Africa in 1932, his innings ended when he ran out the last of his partners while attempting a vital single off the final ball of an over.

He was captain when the Australians at Southend in 1948 amassed the most runs in any day of first-class cricket (721 in 5 hours 48 minutes), contributing 187 in 125 minutes himself.

The first batsman to average over 100 runs during an English season (115.66 in 1938), he remains the only one to have done so twice. On each of his four tours of England he exceeded 2,000 runs and averaged over 80, surpassing the average of the leading home batsman of that year. In 1930 and 1938 he completed his 1,000th first-class run before June. The only batsman to have achieved this feat twice, he also holds the record for the earliest 1,000 runs in a season: 27 May (1938).

His 452 not out for New South Wales against Queensland at Sydney in January 1930 remained the world's highest first-class innings until Hanif Mohammad overtook it in Pakistan 29 years later. Bradman's 415-minute knock included 49 fours and, astonishingly, was scored in the second innings of the match. He was then only 21. Having scored 205 not out on the Saturday, he resumed on the Monday, adding 90 before lunch and a further 137 by tea when Alan Kippax closed the innings. Had he been allowed to bat through the final session he might well have extended the record beyond the 600-mark.

Playing for Bill Woodfull's XI against Jack Ryder's XI in the same season he completed a first innings century (54 to 124) before scoring a second innings double century the same day.

Bradman exceeded 1,000 runs in an Australian first-class season on 12 occasions, twice as many as any other batsman, and is alone in scoring 1,500 more than twice. His aggregate of 1,690 achieved in 1928-29, his first full season and the one in which he began his Test career, remains the Australian record. In 1931-32 he scored 1,190 runs against the touring South Africans, the record by one batsman against any visiting team. In 1947-48 his twelve first-class innings included a record eight centuries.

Born in the New South Wales township of Cootamundra, Bradman lived his early life in Bowral and unwittingly taught himself the basis of batting by throwing a golf ball against a large brick water tank and hitting the rebound two-handed with a small stump. His magnificent outfielding owed much to a similar exercise, which involved throwing a ball against the upper rail of an open fence and catching the rebounds.

His early cricket was played on concrete wickets with a matting cover. On those steeply-bouncing surfaces he evolved a technique which enabled him to keep the ball down and which stood him in good stead when he began playing grade cricket in Sydney on turf pitches.

Such was his mastery of the artificial surfaces that he once added 100 runs off 22 balls in three eight-ball overs. This incredible display occurred in November 1931 at Blackheath, a Blue Mountains town some 60 miles west of Sydney. Playing for Blackheath against Lithgow in a match celebrating the opening of an experimental malthoid pitch, Bradman, having scored 38 off the first over he received, later produced the following sequence: 66424461/64466464/ ★661★446. The asterisks denote singles scored by his partner, Wendell Bill.

He saw only two days of first-class cricket – during the Fifth Test at Sydney in 1921 – before embarking on his own first-class career. Bradman was completely self-taught as far as technique was concerned, and claims never to have deliberately copied any other player's method. He had an unusual stance with the bat between his feet rather than behind his back foot. His pick-up was not text book vertical but was angled towards the slips. Sometimes when he completed a pull shot he would finish up with one foot behind the stumps in the bowling crease.

Sir Neville Cardus wrote of him in 1930 during that first tour of England:

> Bradman is not a romantic ever. He is perpetually a realist with the oldest head a boy cricketer has carried on his shoulders since W. G. Grace.

Being a realist and an arch competitor would have counted for nothing if Bradman had not been blessed with exceptional co-ordination and superb judgement of a ball's potential length and direction from the moment it left the bowler's hand. Contrary to popular opinion, he did not possess above-average eyesight. He often moved into a preliminary position fractionally before the ball was released; forward against a slow bowler or back and across when facing the quicker stuff. Most vital to his method was his footwork. He had little feet and moved lightly and very, very quickly into the correct position.

I first met The Don in 1976, when Richie Benaud introduced us at Yalumba winery on the rest day of an Adelaide Test. It was like meeting royalty, appropriately enough I suppose, as he was undoubtedly a prince of cricket. His influence on the game had been immense, particularly in Australia and especially in Adelaide, his adopted home since 1934.

On first seeing him one is surprised by his lack of height and immediately struck by his alert eyes and incisive mind. He has a ready and sharp wit and easy sense of humour. He is justly proud of his achievements and has dedicated his later life to his family, his business interests and golf. In recent years he has given up all his ties with the administration of cricket, office by office, both nationally and in his state.

I was highly honoured when he accepted

Sir Donald Bradman with the author at Yalumba. ***(Adrian Murrell/All Sport)***

my invitation to write a foreword to the 1984 edition of the *Daily Telegraph Cricket Year Book*, and even more delighted when he agreed similarly to endorse the second edition of my *Wisden Book of Test Cricket*.

The Don is very much back in the news in Australia. After shunning the media for many years he has emerged in print and on radio to the vast delight of his many fans. First came two sumptuous volumes of *The Bradman Albums*, a condensed edition of 52 leather-bound volumes of the Don's career prepared by the State Library of South Australia from the original scrap-books kept by his mother, wife, relatives, friends and admirers. Then came the publication of the Bradman Tapes, *The Don Declares*, an ABC Radio biography composed of eight hour-long interviews in which he straightens the record on many aspects of his brilliant but often controversial career.

In his 80th summer, the first man to be knighted for his services to cricket still looks as spry and fit as in his heyday 50 years ago.

'I play golf every Saturday – A-grade – and can still get round in fewer strokes than my years,' he revealed, eyes sparkling with pride.

To visit his elegant two-storey house in Kensington, a leafy suburb of Adelaide, is to enter hallowed ground. The sitting room with its piano – he once recorded some pieces for the BBC – is a treasure house of cricketana. His portrait surmounts the fireplace. Watched by Lady Jessie, his serene and devoted wife for 55 years, he gave wise counsel on a variety of topics. Our discussion soon involved Mike Gatting's on-field row with umpire Shakoor Rana.

'An umpire's decision must be accepted, however incompetent he might be. If you don't accept his authority you have anarchy. The time to complain is off the field afterwards.

'I don't agree with the idea of selecting umpires for Test matches from a panel of the best officials, regardless of nationality. That would inevitably restrict the field to English and perhaps some Australian umpires because they are the most experienced. How would umpires from other countries ever gain the experience necessary to reach that level? I think that the home country's best umpires should officiate throughout each series.'

If that had happened in Pakistan, England would have had no cause for complaint.

Computerized scoreboards dominate the Test arenas at Sydney and Melbourne. Apart from the match details, the giant screens present the crowd with slow-motion replays of run outs and stumpings. Bradman is convinced that the umpires should be able to examine these replays before making their decision.

'It is ridiculous that millions of viewers should

have the benefit of this aid when umpires do not. But I would not support its use for lbw's. There the umpire's unique positioning to exercise judgement should remain dominant.'

Many retired players of Bradman's era hold scathing views on the use of helmets. The Don does not share them.

'If someone had produced a batting helmet during the 1932-33 (Bodyline) series I would certainly have worn it.'

As a statistician, I have long considered that maiden overs should be removed from bowling analyses and records. During the last hundred years the over has varied between 4, 5, 6 and 8 balls; to add such entities together is a mathematical absurdity. Maidens have no significance as far as the result of a match is concerned, nor do they affect personal averages. Since no-balls and wides became universally debited to bowling analyses in 1984-85, any over containing one of these penalties cannot be a maiden even if it includes no runs from the bat. Sir Donald shares my view: 'Any reference to maiden overs has long since become anachronistic and serves no useful purpose.'

John Inverarity, former captain of both Western and South Australia, lives two doors away from Bradman. How close was 'Invers' to becoming captain of Australia instead of Graham Yallop in 1978-79 when England won 5-1?

'I don't know. I wasn't a selector then. but he wasn't a good enough player to get in as a batsman and that prevented him from being captain. By the same token, Mike Brearley would never have skippered Australia.'

Bradman played his 52 Tests over a period of twenty years. Sunil Gavaskar amassed his world record aggregates of 10,122 runs and 34 hundreds during 125 Tests in just sixteen years. I asked The Don if he realized that, had he maintained his Test average of 99.94, with a century every 2.75 innings, and enjoyed the same number of completed innings as Gavaskar (198), he would have finished with the useful tallies of 19,788 runs and 77 centuries.

'What makes you think I would only have maintained my average?' he asked. 'If I had had the opportunity of playing in India, Pakistan and Sri Lanka I think I might have increased it!'

When I suggested that the local umpires might have made sure that he did not hang around too long, he retorted: 'They can't give you out if you hit it for four!'

He obviously has not been there!

Soon after my visit, the Bradmans flew to Sydney to attend the Bicentenary celebrations, including the commemorative Test against England when the Don led his motorcade on a lap of honour around the historic SCG turf. It was fitting that Australia's oldest surviving captain should ride in a vintage Rolls-Royce. His record as a leader is also a tribute to one of the greatest cricketers of all time: 24 Tests, 15 wins, 3 defeats and 6 draws.

Having enjoyed the privilege of visiting Sir Donald Bradman in Adelaide, my first mission on arriving in Sydney on the eve of the Bicentennial Test was to telephone his old adversary, Harold Larwood, a resident there since 1950, in the hope that I could present the other side of the coin. His eyes may have failed him, but 'Lol' 's voice, with its unblemished Nottinghamshire accent, was as strong and cheery as ever and I was soon off in a taxi to see him.

We had first met in 1977 when Nottinghamshire had flown him home to share their celebrations of the Royal Jubilee. He had sat next to me in the *Test Match Special* commentary box chatting about his career to Brian Johnston. It was during an interval of the Centenary Test in Melbourne a few months earlier that I had first set eyes on him. On that occasion he had taken a mid-pitch bow with his old bowling partner, Bill Voce, and received a tumultuous welcome from the vast crowd.

'Bit different from the last time we were here, Bill!' remarked Harold, referring to the 1932-33 tour. Voce's reply was to hand Larwood his coat and pace out his run at the end from which fellow left-armer John Lever had been bowling. It was a tribute to Bill Voce's strength that his run was barely half Lever's and his contemporaries insist he was a yard or two faster.

When a storm felled the famous Trent Bridge elm known as 'George Parr's Tree' in January 1976, former Nottinghamshire captain and England opening batsman Reg Simpson had arranged for his company, Gunn and Moore, to make a limited edition of miniature bats from

Harold Larwood, the most feared fast bowler of all time. ***(Author's collection)***

the timber. One of these tiny but noticeably heavy bats, bearing the signatures of Larwood and Voce, is a treasured possession.

Almost 55 years have passed since Harold Larwood ended his controversial Test career at the Sydney Cricket Ground. It was a notable finale which completed England's decisive 4-1 victory in the infamous 'Bodyline' rubber.

Larwood's five wickets in that match brought his tally for the series to 33 at a cost of 19.51 runs apiece. Furious at being sent to bat at number four as 'nightwatchman' after bowling 32.2 overs with a splintered bone in the ball of his left foot, he tried to run himself out before the close. He hit the ball to cover-point and called Hammond for an impossible run. Bradman collected the ball as they crossed mid-pitch, hurled it at the bowler's end stumps and missed. Larwood thus opened his account with a five.

Next morning the mob on the Hill exhorted the Australian bowlers to 'knock the bastard's bloody head off '. In 140 minutes he rattled up 98, hooking and square-cutting nine fours and straight driving a six. Going for his century in the grand manner, he miscued an on-drive and skied the ball to Bert 'Dainty' Ironmonger at mid-on. 'Dainty was a hopeless fielder,' grinned Larwood. 'Couldn't stop a tram. But the beggar clung on to that one.'

The crowd that had vilified him for bowling bodyline treated him to a rapturous reception as he returned to the pavilion. 'They gave me a standing ovation. They were cheering and jumping up in the air. They like a fighter in Australia.'

Since 1950 he has lived just three miles from that famous ground in a cosy house at Kingsford. If the wind is right he can hear the Hillites in full cry when a major match is in progress. Now 83 and blind, his handshake revealed the immense strength that had made this little ex-miner from Nuncargate the most feared fast bowler of all time. I was welcomed into his home, kept spick and span by Lois, his wife for more than 60 years, and remained enthralled for two hours as he recalled that turbulent series.

So turbulent was it that an exchange of cables between the Australian Board and MCC, then the governing body of English cricket, threatened to end the tour and sever relations between the two bodies.

Fast leg-theory involved short-pitched bowling aimed at the batsman's torso and head with a menacing ring of close legside catchers to take the ball as it was fended away. It was employed with the solitary objective of curbing Bradman's exceptional appetite for large scores. The Don's genius had created an imbalance between bat and ball which needed to be rectified if England were to regain the Ashes.

According to Larwood, during his innings of 232 in the Fifth Test at The Oval in 1930, Bradman had been uncomfortable when facing short-pitched bowling on his leg stump. The Don strenuously denies this and claims it was merely an excuse to justify the leg-theory plan with its packed onside field. Devised by England's captain, Douglas Jardine, around the accuracy and speed of Larwood and his left-handed Nottinghamshire partner Bill Voce, it proved outstandingly successful. Bradman – career Test average 99.94 – was confined to 396 runs at 56.67, four times falling victim to Larwood.

The actual term 'bodyline' was originated virtually by accident on the opening day of the series by Hugh Buggy of the *Melbourne Herald*. Soon after MCC's match against an Australian XI in Melbourne, Buggy had read an article by Jack Worrall. The former Victoria and Australia batsman had used the phrase 'half-pitched slingers on the body line'. Buggy had to send his match reports by telegraph and, needing a concise phrase to catch the lunch-time edition, sent: 'Voce was hit for six, again bodyline bowling.' It was only his shorthand telegraphed form of 'bowling on the line of the body'.

Back in the sports office of the *Melbourne Herald*, sub-editor Ray Robinson latched upon the word 'bodyline' and decided to use it as a headline. His editor, Syd Deamer, forbade it but allowed the word to remain within Buggy's report. And so, by an extraordinary sequence of events, the most contentious term in cricket's long history was originated.

Ray Robinson became one of Australia's greatest cricket writers. He overcame some massive heart surgery and partial blindness to report cricket until shortly before his death in 1982 at the age of 73. I had the pleasure of staying in his lofty house at Northbridge during my first three visits to Australia. A frail, kindly man of great humour and humility, he played down his own role in seizing upon Buggy's phrase. Robinson was a most concise writer, and compressed more facts and figures into a page of copy than any writer before or since. He admitted that as soon as he saw the word 'bodyline' he knew he had found the ideal term for a type of bowling that writers were struggling to describe using a single word.

Back in England after the tour, Larwood was told to apologize to the MCC for his bowling. As he had only been obeying Jardine's instructions, he not surprisingly refused. From that moment he was ignored by England's selectors and, disillusioned, he soon retired from first-class cricket. In 1950 he sold his confectionery shop in Blackpool and, accompanied by his wife and five daughters, sailed for Australia on the *Orontes*, the very ship that had carried the MCC team there in 1932.

He has found much happiness in Australia, and those five daughters have given him thirteen grandchildren and four great-grandchildren. Despite his disability he can easily find his way around the house he moved into soon after his arrival. As we looked at his team photographs, his memory of the whereabouts of each player was so uncanny that his blindness was soon forgotten. His impressions of his playing career are so vivid that it is hard to accept that he was describing events that occurred more than 50 years ago.

Sadly, the honours lists have continued to pass him by, and his lifestyle is in stark contrast to that of the Don in his affluent Adelaide suburb. Larwood's proudest possession is a silver ashtray presented by Jardine. It is inscribed: 'To Harold for the Ashes. 1932-33. From a grateful skipper.'

We had a beer together and he presented me with a revised edition of his book, *The Larwood Story*, sightlessly signing it for me with the aid of his wife. As I waited for my taxi I photographed them both in front of their house, two delightful people who still cared deeply about each other. Their diamond wedding anniversary (September 1987) was commemorated by greetings cables from the Queen and the Nottinghamshire County Cricket Club. They had also received one from H. S. T. L. 'Stork' Henry, the Australian Test all-rounder who, at the age of 92, was then enjoying his 62nd year of marriage.

As I once again felt myself on the receiving end of Larwood's powerful handshake, it was easy to reconcile the personality of this gentle old man with that of cricket's most devastating fast bowler.

CHRISTCHURCH
THE FIRST TEST

New Zealand's impressive recent home record · Pukekura Park · Lancaster Park · Richard Hadlee, the Mean Machine · Match report · The Dilley incident · Chatfield's Scrooge Award · Champagne for Jarvis

England's commendable showing at Sydney did much to restore their spirit and confidence which had been so sadly damaged in Pakistan. To compel a cock-a-hoop Australian side to follow-on was a magnificent achievement which augured well for their three-match series against New Zealand. Not that the tour management underrated the strength of the opposition, particularly on their home paddocks. They were only too well aware that New Zealand had not lost a home series since Pakistan beat them 1-0 in 1978-79, since when they had defeated all six opponent countries and lost only two of their 23 home Tests.

After losing a one-day international in Melbourne, Gatting's troops recrossed the Tasman to concentrate on the final leg of their winter jetabout. Their only respite before undertaking the pressures of another Test series took the form of a three-day match against a Shell XI in New Plymouth. Shell sponsor New Zealand's two major domestic competitions, the Shell Trophy being the national first-class championship and the Shell Cup being the limited-overs tournament. The scratch side contained a number of promising players on the fringe of Test selection and batted well to snatch a thrilling victory on the final evening.

More memorable even than that unexpected success was an introduction to Pukekura Park, which ranks extremely high on my list of the world's most delightful cricket grounds. A smallish playing area is surrounded on three sides by steeply-banked grass terracing surmounted by a framework of exotic trees. Perched precariously atop the middle summit, the press tent provided a perfect view down the pitch, over a colourful medley of roofs towards the shimmering Tasman. Around this terraced amphitheatre a thousand sparsely-clad spectators sat on slatted benches, their sun brollies adding more colour to a kaleidoscope of green.

The cricket ground is just a small part of a beautiful park with a huge variety of native trees, king ferns and rhododendrons. In the middle is a long, thin lake, its middle parted by the Poet's Bridge, named after the horse whose winnings paid for its construction.

Lancaster Park is anything but pretty. In fact I would relegate it well down the list of my favourite Test grounds. In fairness it is, like Carisbrook in Dunedin and Eden Park in Auckland, primarily a rugby arena with cricket a poor tenant. Its spectator amenities are virtually non-existent; unless you happen to be a committee member or invited to one of a handful of hospitality boxes, there is no watering hole from which you can watch the cricket. Nevertheless, the ground has been the venue for many historic cricket matches and the scene of five of New Zealand's 26 victories in 186 Tests, including a most notable one against England.

Gatting, the sole survivor from the 1984 debacle, would not wish to recall that last England visit to Lancaster Park when the Kiwis had won by an innings and 132 runs, their record margin of victory in this series, after only eleven hours and 41 minutes of actual play. For the first time since 1894-95, England had suffered the ignominy of being dismissed for under 100 in both innings. There were also spicy accounts of the England dressing-room door being lined with wet towels to confine the aroma of some interesting substances being smoked within.

The normal drama attending the opening

The delightful Pukekura Park at New Plymouth. ***(Author)***

morning of any Test series was spiced by the imminence of a world record being broken. Richard Hadlee needed to take just one wicket to overhaul Ian Botham's record Test match tally of 373. Six weeks earlier I had selfishly thanked the fates which had decreed that he should not gain that decisive wicket during a nerve-jangling final afternoon at Melbourne when Australia held out by their finger-nails to draw the match and win the series. Aware of England's itinerary with its opening Test in Christchurch, I could already see the headline to my piece: 'HADLEE BREAKS RECORD ON HIS HOME GROUND.' It would be the bowling equivalent of Boycott scoring his 100th first-class century in the 1977 Test against Australia at his native Headingley.

That drama was increased when Jeff Crowe won the toss and put England in. There had been much banter amongst the England party as to which unfortunate was going to have to bear the cross of being remembered as Hadlee's record-breaking victim. As Broad and Robinson had experienced considerable practice against him in the Trent Bridge nets, poor Martyn Moxon had become a clear favourite as the most likely fall guy, particularly as he had been his victim in each of his four innings during the 1986 series.

Not even his eventual record-breaking victim could deny that Richard Hadlee richly deserved that particular mantle. He equalled Botham's record aggregate of 373 wickets in 21 fewer matches and with 1,774 fewer balls. He also has the superior strike-rate of 51.0 balls per wicket compared with Botham's 55.7, and a lower average of runs per wicket: 22.32 compared with 27.86. Since economizing on his run he has become a master bowler, but it was surprising to discover that he has taken 196 wickets in 37 Tests overseas compared with 177 in 36 matches in New Zealand. His 32 instances of 5 or more wickets in an innings and 8 of 10 or more in a match are both Test records.

Richard Hadlee is a highly professional cricketer, almost as obsessive about his fitness and pre-match preparation as Geoffrey Boycott. He has a rigid training discipline and plans his playing schedule meticulously. His 1984 'double' for Nottinghamshire was the product of detailed target-setting. According to one former colleague, he used to fill one of his twin garages with an exhibition of Hadlee-ana, all personally autographed and surrounded by a purple rope, but that may be just another splendid example of the whimsical fantasy for which this player was noted.

There is nothing whimsical about Hadlee's bowling action. Magical perhaps. It is as rhythmic and as smoothly honed as any in the history of the game. Designed to produce maximum effect from a minimum of effort, it is a perfect sideways-on example from which his varied hand-actions and subtle changes of pace can propel a bewildering catalogue of deliveries. Richard Hadlee is the Mean Machine of Bowlers and is by far the most dangerous New Zealand have produced.

I am sure that the thought of Hadlee failing to capture a single wicket in this three-match series never entered anyone's mind. When the press box ran a sweep on the number of balls Hadlee would bowl before putting everyone out of their misery, the highest was 67 by Peter Roebuck (*Sunday Times* and captain of Somerset). John Thicknesse, a master bookie thinly disguised as cricket correspondent of the *London Evening Standard*, speculated upon the identity of victim No. 374. Predictably, Moxon was easily the favourite.

And just in case all that activity was insufficient to tempt fate, I had been rash enough to set as a question in a quiz in the *Playfair Cricket Annual*: 'Whom did Richard Hadlee dismiss to become the leading wicket-taker in Test cricket?'

Walter Hadlee, captain of the 1949 New Zealanders and Richard's father, sowed the first seeds of doubt when I asked him if the champagne was on ice.

'Remember Leeds in 1983, our first win in England? Richard bowled 47 overs in that match and didn't take a wicket,' Wally reminded me a trifle severely.

Conditions were perfect for swing bowling when Richard Hadlee took the new ball, a 'Kookaburra', at 11 a.m. on a battleship-grey morning. It was humid and the heavy cloud obliterating most of the Cashmere Hills would have done Old Trafford proud. His first ball, from the Southern End to the left-handed Chris Broad, was allowed through to wicket-keeper Ian Smith. His second pitched on off stump before snaking past the bat's groping edge. The third swung in late to strike the pad. Hadlee leapt in the air, forefingers aloft as he roared his appeal, and landed astride the pitch. 'Not out,' was Steve Woodward's verdict. Another play and miss from Broad before Hadlee's Nottinghamshire colleague safely middled the last two balls.

Those with numbers 7 to 12 in the sweep grinned knowingly as Hadlee began his second dramatic over, to Martyn Moxon. The first ball was pushed nervously to mid-on, the second edged into the pad, and the next, a swinging yorker, stabbed out at the last second. Hadlee polished the ball harder and, straining for extra pace and bounce on the slow surface, committed the rare mistake of over-stepping. Two deliveries later he beat the Yorkshire right-hander all ends up, shaving bat and off stump by the narrowest of margins.

And so the saga dragged on. Soon Hadlee looked under more pressure than the batsmen. The crowd, much smaller than anticipated, tried to boost his efforts with chants of 'Had-lee! Had-lee!' as he ran in with his distinctive arm action, arms parallel to thighs like a sprinter. It was all to no avail and he reluctantly ended his first spell after 56 minutes: 7-2-16-0.

The cricket press are accorded little sanctuary on any of New Zealand's grounds. Of the five grounds used to stage international matches during this tour, only Wellington's Basin Reserve did not owe its main allegiance to rugby football. At Lancaster Park the press area is immediately in front of the radio and television commentary boxes, and looks straight down the wicket at the City End. It is simply a dozen rows of terracing with desks and chairs. Alongside is a small area roped off as a VIP enclosure.

Wally Hadlee sat on the end of one of those rows, chatting animatedly with two other former Test players, Jack Kerr and Sir Jack Newman. Throughout those seven overs his every reaction to his son's frustrations was recorded by a TV camera crew standing on the stairway separating our territories. He handled it with great aplomb.

Richard Hadlee's balletic failure to intercept a straight-drive from Tim Robinson at Lancaster Park. Next ball he sprained his calf muscle.

England had reached 50 for 1 when Hadlee returned for the last three pre-lunch overs from our end. Broad was in touch by then and steered two offside boundaries. Five more overs after lunch were equally unsuccessful and Wally Hadlee's grim reminder about Leeds in 1983 began to bear more significance.

At 3.21 'Paddles' came back for the last three overs before tea from our City End. Robinson safely blocked a yorker and off-drove the second ball for four. A thundering straight-drive was brilliantly fielded by Hadlee, diving forward. Soon after, with two balls remaining before the interval, the bowler gingerly felt the back of his lower leg and completed his over off a four-pace mini-run. He had bowled 18 overs and been no-balled eight times, probably more than in an entire season of first-class cricket in England.

The camera crew left Walter Hadlee to have his tea. If his son did manage to snare his elusive wicket, Peter Roebuck would carry off the sweep, his 67 balls being the outsider in a closely packed field.

But Richard Hadlee did not return. He enhanced the irony of his injury when he said, 'I had never broken down in a Test before or left the field for more than fifteen minutes.'

The damage was diagnosed as a sprained calf muscle and it was packed in ice – probably that which had been ordered for the champagne. His father's wry look from across the gangway mimed, 'I told you so.'

The rest of the match was something of an anti-climax. It followed a similar pattern to the Sydney Bicentennial, with Broad scoring a century and England bowling well in the first innings before the opposition found refuge in plumb batting conditions to save the match.

Thanks to Broad and Robinson's second-wicket partnership of 168 England enjoyed a superb opening day to the series. When the second day began 40 minutes late because of light rain and poor light, Ewen Chatfield, wicketless after 27 of the unluckiest overs of his career, gained immediate revenge by dismissing David Capel with his first delivery. The pitch had quickened and a heavy cloud cover encouraged movement in the air and off the seam all day. Chatfield found a patch around off stump and hit it persistently. In just 52 balls England lost 4 wickets for 23 runs to plunge to 260 for 8, a sorry effort after being 175 for 1.

John Emburey would provide the perfect opening chapter for any book on bizarre batsmanship, but he was one of England's leading run-makers in 1987. He is to batting what Gerard Hoffnung was to chamber music. One could easily imagine him hitting the ball just as effectively with a carpet sweeper. Now he eschewed footwork and backlift to nudge, scoop, shovel and smear England past the vital psychological barrier of 300. He was capably supported by Paul Jarvis, who paraded a series of handsome cover drives, and by Dilley as 59 priceless runs were gathered for the last 2 wickets. Chatfield fully deserved to add 4 for 31 in 15 overs to his overnight 0 for 56, but Danny Morrison was greatly flattered by his first-ever 5-wicket haul in Test cricket.

Jarvis is already a confident and mature cricketer, a bustling third seamer who can bat a bit. His is a rags-to-riches story that will encourage any young cricketer beset by injury. After missing the entire World Cup programme and returning prematurely to England with an output of just 17 overs on the Pakistan tour, he endured ten days around Christmas immobilized on a drip feed to overcome circulation problems in his bowling hand. He then fought hard to regain fitness in time for the deadline set for this antipodean tour. When his confident appeal for lbw against Jeff Crowe was refused, he was within a whisker of becoming the first Englishman since Dick Howorth in 1947 to take a wicket with his very first ball in Test cricket.

An inspired spell of sustained accuracy and aggression by Graham Dilley gave England high hopes of enforcing the follow-on for the second Test in succession. At 83 for 4, with the out-of-form Jeff Crowe their only surviving batsman, New Zealand still required 37 runs to avoid that indignity. Borne by an Antarctic wind from the Cashmere Hills End, Dilley recaptured much of his old fire to dismiss the first four batsmen in a Test innings for the first time.

Jeremy Coney, Crowe's immediate predecessor as captain, was not in the least surprised by Dilley's performance: 'I always thought he had the capacity to bowl good sides out.'

Micky Stewart was fulsome in his praise. 'He has been rewarded for some very hard work on his bowling and his fitness. Only two bowlers in the world today have the ability to exploit this type of pitch: Hadlee and Dilley.'

Someone should have reminded him of Malcolm Marshall.

Dilley's 12-over spell, evenly divided by the tea interval, amounted to exactly a tenth of his entire output for Worcestershire in last season's Britannic Assurance County Championship. In the space of 29 balls he skimmed off the cream of New Zealand's batting at a cost of two singles and a no-ball. John Wright and Martin Crowe fell to sharp catches at short square-leg, while Trevor Franklin and Andrew Jones edged balls that lifted steeply and left them.

Dilley finished with the remarkable figures of 12-5-13-4 but admitted that he didn't feel as good as he did while taking 16 wickets in the series against Australia last winter. 'Then I ran up and knew exactly where the ball was going to go. I'm still slipping the odd one down the legside,' he admitted.

New Zealand's batsmen would have loved him to have strayed more often. Wright was never happy and Franklin looked far removed from the player who has notched up four Shell Trophy hundreds this season. At least he had the satisfaction of more than doubling a career aggregate of 9 runs from three innings before being savaged by a Gatwick Airport forklift truck eighteen months ago. He deserved a brief respite when Bruce French feigned an attempt at a catch heading for his captain at first slip.

Jones was the victim of a brutal ball that climbed from the middle and off to touch his gloves as it left him, French holding the catch above his head. Crowe exhibited little of the assurance of a player who scored 4,045 first-class runs during 1987. His demise was the tamest of all – a clumsily fended catch to short-leg.

It was tragic that yet another on-field incident involving an England player should have dominated the final day of an absorbing match which had provided some memorable cricket played in good humour. Dilley's lamentable outburst tarnished the game's image, detracted from his own magnificent effort with the ball, and brought renewed pressure on the management. Even his best analysis in Tests could not outweigh the slur he cast on his own reputation and that of the game. One way and another, cricket has taken a hammering this winter.

I found it impossible to excuse his vociferous swearing and sweater-dropping on the ground of frustration. It was the behaviour of a spoilt child, at least equal in 'criminal' magnitude to Broad's stump-chopping act at Sydney. In escaping with half of the fine meted out to Broad, Dilley received lenient treatment indeed.

Nor was Dilley the only one to express his feelings during three incidents, all of which contained sufficient doubt to justify umpire Brian Aldridge's decisions. After Martin Crowe's 'catch' to DeFreitas had been refused, the entire England team remained frozen like a Madame Tussaud's tableau. It was sad to see Gatting joining in instead of exerting his authority and ordering them back on duty immediately.

No wonder Peter Lush was tense and irritable at that evening's press conference. More than 20 writers, most with imminent deadlines, had been kept waiting half an hour before Lush and Stewart made their appearance in the players' dining room. Lush refused to make any announcement until the captain arrived, and

Chris Broad (114) drives Danny Morrison (5 for 69) at Christchurch.

Graham Dilley has his say at Christchurch. Athey, Gatting and Emburey seem to have heard it all before.

snarled abruptly at a journalist who attempted a question. Gatting arrived a full ten minutes later after Stewart had gone down to the dressing room to see what was going on.

The spectre of Pakistan continued to loom over Lush who, in spite of a three-year contract, perhaps regarded his own position as somewhat insecure as a result of the winter's events. His outburst about pitch microphones was so ill-timed as to appear an absolute red herring. The appliances, inserted in a tunnel within the base of the two outside stumps at each end, were switched off before Dilley's bellow, which was fully audible in the stands and hospitality boxes and probably startled the Wizard in the city square. For a manager to be under such pressure in New Zealand, the most hospitable of all host countries, was astonishing.

Chatfield bowled superbly, recording the enviable match analysis of 72-26-123-8 to win the match award. Some observers, one Geoffrey Boycott amongst us, thought that Broad's century, an outstanding achievement on such a sporting wicket, would have been a more just selection. Certainly Chatfield deserved a special Scrooge Award for economy.

Apart from the batting of Broad and Robinson, and the bowling of Dilley, England's greatest gain from Christchurch was the confident arrival on the Test scene of Paul Jarvis. His timing of the announcement of his engagement to Wendy Tester from Hastings on the final morning of this match proved most appropriate. It provided an excuse for a champagne celebration which did much to restore morale after the varied frustrations of a black final afternoon.

1ST DAY	BOWLERS (BL ALDRIDGE) CITY END		(SJ WOODWARD) SOUTHERN END		BATSMEN SCOREBOARD LEFT			SCOREBOARD RIGHT			NOTES	ENGLAND 1ST INNINGS END-OF-OVER TOTALS					
TIME	BOWLER	O.	BOWLER	O.	SCORING	BALLS	6s/4s	SCORING	BALLS	6s/4s		O.	RUNS	W.	'L' BAT	'R' BAT	EXTRAS
					BROAD		LHB	MOXON									
11.00			HADLEE	1	x L x 7 7 / · · · · 2 ·	6						1	2		2		
04	MORRISON	1			· ·	8		3 / · · · 1	4			2	3			1	
08			"	2				6 EP Y. x x · / · · · ⊙ · · ·	11		(NB) NB 1	3	4				1
13	"	2			4 3 / · · · · · 2	14						4	6		4		
17			"	3				P 6/5 / · · · · · ·	17		M1	5					
21	"	3			· 5 9 / · · · 1	18		L 7/8 / · W	19	-		6	7	1	5	1	1
24								ROBINSON								0	
26			"	4	x 8/7 / · · 3	21		· P 5(6) / ⊙ · · 2	4		(NB) NB 2	7	13		8	2	2
31	"	4			4 LB / · · · ·	25		L · / · ·	6		(LB) M2	8	14				3
36			"	5	8 · 2 8 P / 2 · · · ②⊙ · ·	33					(NB) NB4	9	19		12		4
40	"	5						2 4 4 3 / 2 2 · · · 1	12			10	24			7	
44	(5-1-9-1)		"	6				· 4 · 3 · · / · · · · · ·	18		M3	11					
48	CHATFIELD	1			· x 1 · / · · · 3 ·	38		9 / 1	19			12	28		15	8	
52			"	7	· LB · 7 / · · · 1	42		9 L / 1 LB	21		(LB)(LB)	13	32		16	9	6
56	"	2	(7-2-16-0)		x 3 2 · / · · 1 · ·	47		8 / 1	22		1HR	14	34		17	10	
12.00 / 04	DRINKS		SNEDDEN	1				· EP8 / · · · · · · 1	28			15	35			11	
08	"	3			·	48		· · 9 / · · · · 1	33			16	36			12	
10			"	2	· x 8 / · · 2	51		· 8 8 / · 2 1	36			17	41		19	15	
15	"	4						· · 5 9 2 · / · · · 2 · ·	42			18	43			17	
19			"	3	· · LB L 3 / · · · · ·	56		LB / ·	43		M4 (LB)(LB)	19	45				8
22	"	5						· † · · · / · · · · · ·	49		† Hit on box (5 min. delay for repairs) M5	20					
30			"	4	T · E3 6 5/6 / · · · · · 2	62						21	47		21		
34	"	6						4 5/4 · P E2 / · 2 · · · ·	55			22	49			19	
37	(6-1-11-0)		"	5	3 / 1	63		6 · 2 5 · / · · · · · ·	60			23	50		22		
41	HADLEE	8			P · 2/3 P · 7 / · · 4 · · ·	69	1					24	54		26		
45			"	6	9 3S / 2 1	71		· · LB / · · · ·	64		(LB) 50 p'ship · 82'	25	58		29		9
49	"	9	(6-1-12-0)		· 2 P x 8/7 / · · · · · ·	77					M6	26					
53			CHATFIELD	7				x E2 P · · G / · · · · · ·	70		G - Hit on rt. glove. M7 2HR	27					
59	(10-3-28-0)	10	(7-2-11-0)		E1 · 7 / 4 · ⊙ 1	81	2	5 5 / · 2 ·	73	-	(NB) NB5	28	66	1	34	21	10
1.03	LUNCH										M7 NB5		L	U	N	CH	
1.40			CHATFIELD	8	· · · 7/8 · 7 / · · · 2 · 2	87						29	70		38		
44	HADLEE	11						7 · · · · 3 / · · · · · 4	79	1		30	74			25	
47			"	9	P 3S / · 1	89		8 E1 · / · 2 · ·	83			31	77		39	27	
51	"	12			P 3 6 8 / · · 1 1	93		7 / 1 ·	85			32	80		41	28	
55			"	10	3 7 7 / · · 1	96		· · 3 / · · ·	88			33	81		42		
59	"	13			3 · P 7 4 / · · ⊙ 1 ·	101		· 4 / · 1	90		(NB) NB 6	34	84		43	29	11
2.03			"	11				4† · · · / 2 · · · · ·	96		† Dropped WRIGHT · 1-handed mid-off.	35	86			31	
06	"	14			LB · 3 EP x / · · · · ·	106		3 / 1	97		(LB)	36	88			32	12
2.10	(14-3-39-0)		" (12-2-25-0)	12		106	2	7/8 · · 4 4 · / 4 · · · · ·	103	2	M7 NB 6	37	92	1	43	36	12

1ST DAY	BOWLERS (ALDRIDGE) CITY END		(WOODWARD) SOUTHERN END		BATSMEN SCOREBOARD LEFT			SCOREBOARD RIGHT			ENGLAND 1ST INNINGS	END-OF-OVER TOTALS					
TIME	BOWLER	O.	BOWLER	O.	SCORING	BALLS	6s/4s	SCORING	BALLS	6s/4s	NOTES	O.	RUNS	W.	'L' BAT	'R' BAT	EXTRAS
					BROAD	106	2	ROBINSON	103	2	M7 NB6	37	92	1	43	36	12
2.13	HADLEE	15			8 · · · · 4S / · · · · · 1	112						38	93		44		
17	(15-3-40-0)		SNEDDEN	7	3 7 / 1 1	114		L · 7 · / · · 1 ·	107			39	96		46	37	
20	MORRISON	6			2 · · Y. 8 / 4 · · · 1	119	3	2 / 4	108	3	BROAD'S 50: 163'	40	105		51	41	
26			"	8	7 · x · · / 2 · · · · ·	125					100 p'ship: 143'	41	107		53		
30	"	7			4 / ·	126		4 4 ↑ 3 8 / · 4 · · 1	113	4		42	112			46	
34			"	9				7 4 · 6 6 / 2 · · 4 · ·	119	5	ROBINSON'S 50: 154' 3HR	43	118			52	
38	"	8	(9-1-23-0)		· · 47 · · / · · 4 · · ·	132	4					44	122		57		
42 45	DRINKS (8-1-27-1)		BRACEWELL	1	† P / ·	133		· · 5 6 8 / · · · · 1	124		† RO appeal (CROWE MD)	45	123			53	
49	CHATFIELD	13						· 4 · · · · / · 2 · · · ·	130			46	125			55	
53			"	2	3 · · P 8 / 4 · · · · 1	139	5					47	130		62		
55	"	14			P · 4 · 5/4 · / · · · · · ·	145					M8	48					
59			"	3				2 5 P 4 4 · / · · · · · ·	136		M9	49					
3.02	"	15			7 5/6 / 1 2	147		6 P x 7 / 4 · · 1	140	6		50	138		65	60	
05			"	4	2 / ·	148		· · P 6 3 / · · · · 1	145			51	139			61	
09	"	16						7 · · E4↑ · 3 / · · · · · ·	151		† Front edge over s. mid-off · M10	52					
12			"	5	· 3 · 4 8/7 / · 4 · · 1	153	6	· / ·	152			53	144		70		
15	"	17			x 5 8 / · · 1	156		6 9 · / · 2 ·	155			54	147		71	63	
18	(17-4-38-0)		"	6	3 · 2 / · · · 4 · ·	162	7					55	151		75		
21	HADLEE	16	(6-1-16-0)					Y. 4 · 6 · / · 4 · · · ·	161	7		56	155			67	
25			SNEDDEN	10	7/6 · 3 L 4 1E / 2 · · · 4 4	168	9				150 p'ship: 228'	57	165		85		
29	"	17			· 4 2 · 4 / · ⊙ · · 2	173		5 3 / · 1	163		(NB) NB7	58	169		87	68	13
33			"	11				· 7 4 6 7 3 / · · · · · ·	169		M11 4HR	59					
37	(18-3-50-0)	18	(11-2-33-0)		9 / 1	174	9	↑ 7 · / · · ⊙ · · nn	175	7	(NB) NB8	60	171	1	88	68	14
3.40	TEA										M11 NB8			T	E	A	
4.00			SNEDDEN	12	9 7 / 1 1	176		P · 6 6 / · · 1 1	179		GREATBATCH sub for HADLEE (calf).	61	175		90	70	
05	MORRISON	9						· 9 / · W	181	7		61 [2]	175	2	90	70	14
06								GATTING								0	
08	"	9						3 · · · / · · · ·	4		M12	62					
10			"	13	· 9 / · 1	178		5 3 2 6 / · · 4 ·	8	1		63	180		91	4	
14	"	10			· · P 8 / · · · 1	182		· 5 / · 1	10			64	182		92	5	
18			"	14	8 / 1	183		· 7 · / · · 3 · ·	15			65	186		93	8	
22	"	11			· 9 / · · 1	186		· / · · ·	18			66	187		94		
27			"	15	2 4 · · 7 / · · · · · ·	192					M13	67					
30	"	12						3 / W	19	1		67 [1]	187	3	94	8	14
31								ATHEY								0	
33	"	12			5/4 ↑ 8 / · · 1	195		8 / 1 ·	2		WARNING - Pitch damage (Morrison)	68	189		95	1	
37			"	16	5/4 P E1 P 9 / 3 · 4 · 1	200	10	3 3 / 1	3		BROAD'S 100: 282'	69	198		103	2	
43	"	13			7 7 7 7 / · 4 · · · ·	206	11					70	202		107		
4.47	(13-2-36-3)		(17-4-55-0)	17		206	11	6 · · · x · / · · · · · ·	9	-	M14 NB8	71	202	3	107	[illegible]	14

1ST DAY	BOWLERS (ALDRIDGE) CITY END		(WOODWARD) SOUTHERN END		BATSMEN SCOREBOARD LEFT			SCOREBOARD RIGHT			NOTES	ENGLAND 1ST INNINGS END-OF-OVER TOTALS					
TIME	BOWLER	O.	BOWLER	O.	SCORING	BALLS	6s/4s	SCORING	BALLS	6s/4s		O.	RUNS	W.	'L' BAT	'R' BAT	EXTRAS
					BROAD	206	11	ATHEY	9	-	M 14 NB 8	71	202	3	107	2	14
4.51	CHATFIELD	18			⁚ ⁚ ⁚ · ⁚ ⁚	212					M 15 5HR	72					
55			SNEDDEN	18	· ⁚	214		⁚ ⁚ · 1 (4)	13			73	203			3	
59	"	19			⁚ ⁚ · ·	218		⁚ 1 (3)	15			74	204			4	
5.03			"	19				· ⁚ ⁚ ⁚ · ⁚	21		M 16	75					
07	"	20			⁚ ⁚ · ⁚ ⁚ ⁚	224					M 17	76					
11			"	20	⁚ · 1 (3)	227		3 (4) ⁚ ⁚	24			77	208		108	7	
15	"	21			⁚ 1 (4)	229		⁚ ⁚ · 1 (5)	28			78	210		109	8	
19			"	21	1 (8)	230		· 1 (6) ⁚ ⁚ ⁚	33			79	212		110	9	
23	"	22			· 2 1 (7 7/8)	233		⁚ · ⁚	36			80	215		113		
27			"	22	⁚ P ⁚ ⁚ ⁚ ⁚	239					M 18	81					
32	"	23			1 (2)	240		· · 3 (7) · ⁚	41			82	219		114	12	
36			"	23	⁚ ⁚ · · W (E1)	244	11					82⁴	219	4	114	12	14
38					CAPEL										0		
40			"	23	⁚	2					M 19	83					
42	"	24						⁚ · ⁚ · ⁚ ⁚	47		M 20	84					
45			"	24	⁚ · 4 (3) ⁚ ·	8	1					85	223		4		
49	"	25						Pt. ⁚ · ⁚ ⁚	53		† NEW BALL M 21	86					
52			"	25	⁚ ⁚ · · 1 (8)	13		⁚	54		6HR	87	224		5		
56	"	26			⁚ 2 (6) · · 2 (2) ⁚	19						88	228		9		
6.00			"	26	⁚ · ⁚	22		⁚ · 3 (2)	57			89	231			15	
03	(27-8-56-0)	27	(26-7-70-1)		1 (7)	23	1	2 (4) ⁚ · 1 · ⁚	62	-		90	235	4	10	18	14
6.07	STUMPS										M 21 NB 8		S	T	UM	P	S
2ND DAY 11.00	RAIN										START DELAYED 40'						
11.40			MORRISON	14	1 (8)	24		· · · + · ·	67		(W)	91	237		11		15
44	CHATFIELD	28			W (E1)	25	1					91¹	237	5	11	18	15
					EMBUREY										0		
46	"	28			· · · · · ·	5					M 22	92					
49			"	15				⁚ ⁚ ⁚ · ⁚ †	73		M 23	93					
53	"	29			⁚ · ⁚ ⁚ · ⁚ ×	11					M 24	94					
57			"	16				⁚ ⁚ · 4 (†8) · W (3)	79	1		95	241	6	0	22	15
12.00								FRENCH								0	
02	"	30			⁚ × ⁚ · ⁚ ⁚	17					M 25	96					
06			"	17	† · · · × ·	21		4 (2) 3 (1)	2	1		97	248			7	
11	"	31						· W (P E1)	4	1		97²	248	7	0	7	15
12								DEFREITAS								0	
13	"	31						(4LB) · · 2 1 (7 8)	4		(4LB)	98	255			3	19
17			"	18	4 (1)	22	1	× × 4 4 · 1 (3)	9			99	260		4	4	
21	"	32	(18-3-54-4)			22	1	· - · (3) · W (6)	14	-		99⁵	260	8	4	4	19
12.23	(31⁵-11-59-3)										M 25 NB 8						

2ND DAY	BOWLERS (ALDRIDGE) CITY END		BOWLERS (WOODWARD) SOUTHERN END		BATSMEN SCOREBOARD LEFT			BATSMEN SCOREBOARD RIGHT			ENGLAND 1ST INNINGS	END-OF-OVER TOTALS					
TIME	BOWLER	O.	BOWLER	O.	SCORING	BALLS	6s/4s	SCORING	BALLS	6s/4s	NOTES	O.	RUNS	W.	'L' BAT	'R' BAT	EXTRAS
					EMBUREY	22	1	JARVIS	·	·	M25 NB8	99⁵	260	8	4	0	19
12·25	CHATFIELD	32			7/8 1	23						100	261		5		
26			MORRISON	19	x · 2 1 · x · · · 4 · ·	29	2				7HR	101	265		9		
31	"	33			· · L · · · ·	34		E1 1	1			102	266			1	
34			"	20	· 8 · 2	36		3 5 3 8 · · 2 1	5			103	271		11	4	
38	"	34			· · · · · ·	39		E2 E1† · · 1	8		† Dropped 2nd slip (BRACEWELL)	104	272			5	
42			"	21				3 †2/3 4 3 · 2 · 4 · ·	14	1	† 3 + 1 overthrow	105	278			11	
47	"	35	(21-3-69-4)		· · · · P · ·	45					M26	106					
51			SNEDDEN	27				· · 7 · 3P · ·	20		M27	107					
55	" (36-13-62-3)	36	(27-8-70-1)		x · 2 · · · · · ·	51	2		20	1	M28	108	278	8	11	11	19
1·00	LUNCH										M28 NB8		LUNCH				
1·40			SNEDDEN	28				· · · · · ·	26		M29	109					
45	CHATFIELD	37			P 8 · 1	53		· P 3 · · · 1	30			110	280		12	12	
48			"	29				P P · 3 · 1 · · · · · 2	36			111	282			14	
52	"	38			2 · x 7 2 · · 1	57		E1 W	37	1		111⁵	285	9	15	14	19
54								DILLEY		LHB						0	
56	"	38						P ·	1			112					
57			"	30	· · 7 · · 1	60		· · · · · ·	4			113	286		16		
2·01	"	39			7 · · 8 2 · · · · 1	66						114	289		19		
05			"	31	x 2 · 2 · · · · · 1	72					8HR	115	290		20		
08	"	40			· 7 · 5/4 7 · 2 · 4 1	77	3	·	5			116	297		27		
13			"	32	E1 L7 4 · 1	80	4	· · 9 · · 1	8			117	303		32	1	
17	"	41			F7/8 · E1 · · 2 · 4 · ·	85	5	8 1	9			118	310		38	2	
22			"	33	8 1	86		5/4 5 · 4 · 3 · · 2	14			119	316		39	7	
25	"	42	(33-9-86-1)		9/5 1E 2/3 7 · · · · 2 1	92						120	319		42		
29	(42-13-87-4)		MORRISON	22	3 W	93	5		14	-		120¹	319	10	42	7	19
2·30	ALL OUT		(21·1-3-69-5)								M29 NB8 729 balls		ALL OUT				

2ND DAY	BOWLERS (ALDRIDGE) CITY END		(WOODWARD) SOUTHERN END		BATSMEN SCOREBOARD LEFT			SCOREBOARD RIGHT			NEW ZEALAND 1ST INNINGS NOTES	END-OF-OVER TOTALS					
TIME	BOWLER	O.	BOWLER	O.	SCORING	BALLS	6s/4s	SCORING	BALLS	6s/4s		O.	RUNS	W.	'L' BAT	'R' BAT	EXTRAS
					WRIGHT		LHB	FRANKLIN									
2.41	DEFREITAS	1			. . 1	3		. . .	3			1	1		1		
48			DILLEY	1	. 1	5		. . . .	7			2	2		2		
54	″	2			. . 2 . . 2	11					† Nr. Emburey (slip)	3	6		6		
57			″	2				2	13			4	8			2	
3.01	″	3			. . . . . .	17					M1	5					
05			″	3				. . ⊙ 4 . . .	20	1	† Dropped GATTING (NB) NB1	6	13			6	1
10	″	4			2 . 1	20		. . .	23			7	16		9		
14			″	4	. . . . . .	26					M2	8					
18	″	5			⊙ ⊙ . . . 1	32		. 1	25		(NB) (NB) NB3	9	20		10	7	3
23			″	5	. . . . W	37	-					9[5]	20	1	10	7	3
26					JONES										0		
28			″	5	.	1					M3	10					
29	″	6						. . . . . .	31		M4	11					
33			″	6	. 1	3		. . . .	35			12	21		1		
37	″ (7-2-16-0)	7	(6-2-9-1)		. . 1	6	-	. . 3	38	1	1HR	13	25	1	2	10	3
3.41	TEA										M4 NB3			T	E	A	
4.00			DILLEY	7				. . . . 2 W	44	1	M5	14	25	2	2	10	3
04								MD CROWE								0	
06	CAPEL	1			. . . . 2 4	12	1					15	31		8		
10			″	8	. W	14	1	. . 1	3			15[5]	32	3	8	1	3
13					JJ CROWE										0		
14			″	8	.	1						16					
15	″	2			. . .	4		3 . .	6		(LB)	17	36			4	4
20			″	9	. . . . . .	10					M6	18					
24	″	3			2 . .	13		. . 1	9			19	39		2	5	
27			″	10				. . ⊙ W	13	-	(NB) NB4	19[3]	40	4	2	5	5
30								BRACEWELL								0	
32			″	10	.	14		① . .	3		(LB) † Ro chance (Rob'son) NB 5	20	42			1	6
35	″	4			1	15		. . 4 . .	8	1		21	47		3	5	
39			″	11	1	16		. . . . . .	13			22	48		4		
43	″	5			. 3	18		. . . .	17			23	51		7		
47			″	12	. . . . . .	24					M7	24					
52	″	6	(12-5-13-4)		1	25		. . 4 . 1	22	2		25	57		8	10	
55	(6-0-26-0)		JARVIS	1	. 1 4 . .	30	1	1	23		JARVIS close to wkt with first ball in Tests	26	63		13	11	
5.00	DEFREITAS	8						 2	29		2HR	27	65			13	
04 06	DRINKS		″	2	. . . . . .	36					M8	28					
09	″	9						 1	35			29	66			14	
14	(9-2-19-0)		″	3		36	1	. . 4 .	39	3		29[4]	70	4	13	18	6
5.16	BLSP		(2.4-1-10-0)								M8 NB5		BAD		LIGHT		

2ND DAY	BOWLERS (ALDRIDGE) CITY END		(WOODWARD) SOUTHERN END		BATSMEN SCOREBOARD LEFT			SCOREBOARD RIGHT			NEW ZEALAND 1ST INNINGS NOTES	END-OF-OVER TOTALS					
TIME	BOWLER	O.	BOWLER	O.	SCORING	BALLS	6s/4s	SCORING	BALLS	6s/4s	NOTES	O.	RUNS	W.	'L' BAT	'R' BAT	EXTRAS
					JJ CROWE	36	1	BRACEWELL	39	3	M8 NB5 (23 min lost)	29 (4)	70	4	13	18	6
5.39			JARVIS	3	. B	37		1 (8)	40		(B)	30	72			19	7
41	EMBUREY	1	(3-1-11-0)		. . : . B	42		.	41		(B) M9	31	73				8
44			DEFREITAS	10	. 2LB ⊙ . : . 4	49					(2LB) (NB) NB6	32	76				11
49	"	2			. 1 (2)	51		. 1 (8) . .	45			33	78		14	20	
51			"	11	. ⊙ : . . . L	58					(NB) NB7	34	79				12
55	"	3						. : . . : 7	51		M10	35					
59			"	12	1	59		2 (7) . 4 . ⊙ x	57		(NB) NB8	36	83		15	22	13
6.03	"	4			. : : . . .	65					M11	37					
05	(4-3-2-0)		"	13		65	1	. (7)	58	3		37 (1)	83	4	15	22	13
6.06	BLSP		(12-1-2-25-0)								M11 NB8		STUMPS				
3RD DAY 11.05			DEFREITAS	13				. . . 2 4 (4/8)	63	4	MIST delayed start	38	89			28	
09	JARVIS	4	(13-2-31-0)		: . . 3	69		. .	65		50 p'ship: 78'	39	92		18		
14			DILLEY	13	. . : . ⊙ . P	76					(NB) NB9	40	93				14
19	"	5			. : . . .	81		3	66		3HR	41	96			31	
22			"	14				W (E1)	67	4		41 (1)	96	5	18	31	14
23								HADLEE		LHB	(MD CROWE as RUNNER)					0	
25			"	14				. E1 x . 4	5		M12	42					
29	"	6			. . . : E1 . .	87					M13	43					
34			"	15				. . 2 (3) : 4 .	11	1		44	102			6	
37	"	7			. . . : . . .	93					M14	45					
41			"	16				: : . . . :	17		M15	46					
44	"	8			: P 6 . : :	99					M16	47					
49			"	17				P : ⊙ . . LB	24		(NB) (LB) NB10	48	104				16
54	"	9						. : 2 (9) . . :	30			49	106			8	
57			"	18	: . . . . :	105					M17	50					
12 02 06	DRINKS "	10						. : 4 . :	36		M18	51					
10			"	19	. . . 1 (9)	109		. . E1	38		JJ CROWE 60' on '0'. 11.12 to 12.12	52	107		19		
14	"	11			. x . : L 2 (8)	115						53	109		21		
19			"	20	. LB	116		4 (3) . . 1 (3) : (3)	43	2	(LB) 4HR	54	115			13	17
23	"	12			. : 1 (5 E1) . 1 (3)	121		1 (8)	44			55	118		23	14	
27	(12-5-24-0)		"	21	. ⊙ (E1) . : . 6 .	128					(NB) NB11	56	119				18
32	CAPEL	7			. 1 (8†)	130		. : 1 (8) :	48		† FOLLOW-ON AVERTED	57	121		24	15	
36			"	22	3 (1)	131		. : : 3 .	53			58	124		27		
41	"	8	(22-8-31-5)		: 1 (6)	133		. 2 . 1 (2LB 9)	57		(2LB) M19	59	130		28	18	20
47			DEFREITAS	14				. . . . . . E1†	63		† Dropped in slips (Athey & Emburey)	60					
50	"	9			LB :	134		x : . : . :	68		M20 (LB)	61	131				21
55			"	15	x : . . . : .	140					M21	62					
58	(10-2-32-0)	10	(15-4-31-0)			140	1	. : . : . .	74	2	M22	63	131	5	28	18	21
1.01	LUNCH										M22 NB11		LUNCH				

3RD DAY	BOWLERS (ALDRIDGE) CITY END		(WOODWARD) SOUTHERN END		BATSMEN SCOREBOARD LEFT			SCOREBOARD RIGHT			NOTES	NEW ZEALAND 1ST INNINGS END-OF-OVER TOTALS					
TIME	BOWLER	O.	BOWLER	O.	SCORING	BALLS	6s/4s	SCORING	BALLS	6s/4s		O.	RUNS	W.	'L' BAT	'R' BAT	EXTRAS
LUNCH					JJ CROWE	140	1	HADLEE	74	2	M22 NB11	63	131	5	28	18	21
1.40			DEFREITAS	16	. . . . . W (E1)	144	1					63^{2}	131	6	28	18	21
42					SMITH										0		
43			"	16	. . .	2					M23	64					
45	JARVIS	13			. . . . 6 . 4 4	8	2	① (4)	75		NB 12	65	140		8	19	
50			"	17				. . . . . 2 .	81			66	142			21	
54	"	14			. . ①	11		. 2 . .	85		NB 13 5HR	67	145		9	23	
59			"	18	. . . . LB	14		⊙ . . .	89		(LB) (NB) † Round wkt NB 14	68	147				23
2.03	"	15			. 4 . W (E1)	18	3					68^{4}	151	7	13	23	23
05					SNEDDEN		LHB								0		
07	"	15			. .	2						69					
08			"	19				. . . . ⊙ . .	96		(NB) NB 15	70	152				24
11	"	16			LB	6		. 1	98		(LB)	71	154			24	25
16			"	20	W	7	-	. . 1	101			71^{4}	155	8	0	25	25
18					MORRISON										0		
20			"	20	LB	1		.	102		(LB)	72	156				26
22	"	17			. . . W	4	-					72^{3}	156	9	0	25	26
24					CHATFIELD										0		
25	"	17			. 5	3					M24	73					
27			"	21				. . . . . .	108		M25	74					
31	"	18			. . . . . .	9					† Dropped 1st slip (GATTING) M26	75					
35			"	22	. . .	11		2 . . 1	112			76	159			28	
40	"	19	(22-6-39-2)		. .	13		. . . 1	116			77	160			29	
~~44~~ 47	DRINKS		DILLEY	23				. . . . . .	122		M27	78					
51	"	20			. . . . . .	19					M28	79					
55			"	24				 1	128		6HR	80	161			30	
3.00	"	21			. . . . .	23		. 1	130			81	162			31	
04	(21-8-43-2)		"	25		23	-	2 . . 4 W (E1)	135	3		81^{5}	168	10	0	37	26
3.07	ALL OUT		(24.5-9-38-6)								M28 NB15		ALL		OUT		
											506 balls						

3RD DAY	BOWLERS (WOODWARD) CITY END		(ALDRIDGE) SOUTHERN END		BATSMEN SCOREBOARD LEFT			SCOREBOARD RIGHT			NOTES	ENGLAND 2ND INNINGS END-OF-OVER TOTALS					
TIME	BOWLER	O.	BOWLER	O.	SCORING	BALLS	6s/4s	SCORING	BALLS	6s/4s		O.	RUNS	W.	'L' BAT	'R' BAT	EXTRAS
					BROAD		LHB	MOXON									
3.20			MORRISON	1	 1	6					† Hit on shoulder	1	1		1		
24	CHATFIELD	1			. x LB	10		L . .	2		(LB) M1	2	2				1
28			"	2	1 . . LB	14		. 4 . 1	4		(LB)	3	5		2	1	2
33	"	2			. . . . 2 4 .	20	1					4	11		8		
37	(2-1-6-0)		"	3	x 4 2 . . .	23	1	. 7 8 . 2 1	7	-		5	14	0	8	4	2
3.40	TEA		(3-0-6-0)								M1 NB -			T	E	A	
4.00	CHATFIELD	3						. . . . 2 . 1	13			6	17			7	
05			MORRISON	4				. . . . . .	19		M2	7					
10	"	4			 4	29	2					8	21		12		
14			"	5				4 x . . 2 .	25		M3	9					
18	"	5			. . 1	32		. . . .	28			10	22		13		
23			"	6	. 4 x . . 1	37	3	.	29			11	27		18		
27	"	6			G . . 1	40		. . .	32			12	28		19		
32			"	7	. (.) . 1	44		. . . .	35		(NB) NB1 1HR	13	30		20		3
37	"	7			P x	50					M4	14					
42			"	8				7F . . . . (2) . .	42		NB2	15	32			9	
46	"	8	(8-2-15-0)		. W	52	3					15[2]	32	1	20	9	3
47					ROBINSON										0		
49	"	8			. . . .	4					† Near sh. leg. M5	16					
52			SNEDDEN	1				. 2	48			17	34			11	
56	"	9			. . . x	10					M6	18					
5.00 / 04	DRINKS		"	2				 3	54		M7	19					
09	"	10			. 4 2	16						20	36		2		
11			"	3				. . . . 2 . .	60			21	38			13	
15	"	11			. . . W	19	-					21[3]	38	2	2	13	3
16					GATTING										0		
18	"	11			. . .	3					M8	22					
21			"	4	L . .	5		 1	64			23	39			14	
24	"	12						 1	70			24	40			15	
28			"	5	. . . .	9		. . 1	72			25	41			16	
32	"	13			. .	11		x 7 . . . 1	76			26	42			17	
35			"	6	3	12		1 4 . . 1	81	1	2HR	27	51		3	23	
39	"	14						. . . . . 2 1	87			28	54			26	
43			"	7	. . . .	17		1	88			29	55			27	
47	" (14-2-5-22-2)	15	(7-1-16-0)			17	-	. .	90	1		29[2]	55	2	3	27	3
5.48	BLSP										M8 NB2		S	T	U M	P S	

4TH DAY	BOWLERS (WOODWARD) CITY END		(ALDRIDGE) SOUTHERN END		BATSMEN SCOREBOARD LEFT			SCOREBOARD RIGHT			ENGLAND 2ND INNINGS	END-OF-OVER TOTALS					
TIME	BOWLER	O.	BOWLER	O.	SCORING	BALLS	6s/4s	SCORING	BALLS	6s/4s	NOTES	O.	RUNS	W.	'L' BAT	'R' BAT	EXTRAS
(RAIN DELAYED START)					GATTING	17	-	MOXON	90	1	M8 NB 2	29²	55	2	3	27	3
4.01	CHATFIELD	15						x 7 . . W	93	1		29⁵	55	3	3	27	3
02								ATHEY								0	
04	"	15						.	1		M9	30					
05			MORRISON	9	9 3 1 1	19		⊙ 7S 1 3 7/8F 4 . . .	6		(NB) NB 3	31	59		5	1	4
09	"	16			. : P P P .	25					M10	32					
14			"	10				8 . . 6 x 2	12			33	61			3	
18	"	17			. . . . . .	31					M11	34					
21			"	11				. ⊙ 2/3 2 . . L 4 5/6 23	19		(NB) NB 4	35	69			10	5
27	"	18						. . . . . .	25		M12	36					
30			"	12	. . x x . 6	37					M13	37					
35	"	19			. . 6	40		. . 6 1	28			38	70			11	
39			"	13				. † . 8 4 . 4 .	34	1	† Morrison fell.	39	74			15	
42	"	20			. P . 1E . . ⊙ . 2 .	47					(NB) NB 5	40	77		7		6
47			"	14	E1 3 7↑ . 4 . 4	51	2	7 2 . 1	36		3HR	41	86		15	16	
51	"	21	(14-3-42-0)					. 3 2	42			42	88			18	
55			SNEDDEN	8	. 3 4 . 7L .	57	3					43	92		19		
5.00	"	22			. . P	60		. . 7 1	45			44	93			19	
03			"	9				. 7	51		M14	45					
07	"	23			. 1E 2	66						46	95		21		
11			"	10				. . 7 E1 . . W	55	1		46⁴	95	4	21	19	6
13								CAPEL								0	
15			"	10				. .	2		M15	47					
16	"	24			. 2 1	68		2 6	6			48	96		22		
20			"	11	. . 7 3 2/3 F.	74					M16	49					
23	"	25						6 7 P . 6/7 . . . W	11	-		49⁵	96	5	22	0	6
26								EMBUREY								0	
28	"	25			. :	75					M17	50					
30			"	12	:	76		. . . . LB	5		(LB) M18	51	97				7
35	"	26			. 2 1	78		. 8 1 :	9			52	99		23	1	
39			"	13	7S . X . . . W	82	3					52⁴	99	6	23	1	7
41					FRENCH										0		
43			"	13	. .	2					M19	53					
44	"	27						. . . P .	15		M20	54					
48			"	14	. . . . . .	8					M21 4HR	55					
51	"	28			. P 2 2 . . . 1	12		9/8 1 .	17			56	101		1	2	
54			"	15	. 3 x . . 2 . 1	18						57	102		2		
59	"	29			. . . 3 7 .	24					M22	58					
6.04			"	16				. . . . . .	23		M23	59					
6.07	(30-13-36-4)	30	(16-8-21-2)		. . . 4 .	30	-		23	-	M24 NB 5	60	102	6	2	2	7

4TH DAY	BOWLERS (WOODWARD) CITY END		(ALDRIDGE) SOUTHERN END		BATSMEN SCOREBOARD LEFT			SCOREBOARD RIGHT			ENGLAND 2ND INNINGS NOTES	END-OF-OVER TOTALS					
TIME	BOWLER	O.	BOWLER	O.	SCORING	BALLS	6s/4s	SCORING	BALLS	6s/4s		O.	RUNS	W.	'L' BAT	'R' BAT	EXTRAS
					FRENCH	30	-	EMBUREY	23	-	M24 NB5	60	102	6	2	2	7
6.11			MORRISON	15				2LB	29		(2LB) 1+1 overthrow M25	61	104				9
15	SNEDDEN	17			2 1 x :	32		: 7 : 2 : : : 1	33		Chatfield off · sub LATHAM.	62	106		3	3	
21			"	16	: x : . .	35		†7 . 8 4 . 1	36	1		63	111			8	
25	"	18			2 . W	37	-	2 1 x 7 4 2 . 1	40	2		64	118	7	3	15	9
28					DE FREITAS										0		
30			"	17	1E 1	1		1 2 : : 8 1 : : : 1	45			65	121		1	17	
34	"	19			8 7 1 1	3		7 8 RO 1 1	47	2		65[4]	125	8	3	19	9
36								JARVIS								0	
38	"	19			2 . 1	5						66	126		4		
39			"	18	4 : 3/4 9 : : 2 1	9		P P : :	2			67	129		7		
43	"	20			: : : L . 8/7 : : : : : 2	15						68	131		9		
47			"	19	7 1	16		7 x 4 9 5 : : 3 2 .	7		5HR	69	137		10	5	
51	"	21			: 7† 3 . : 1 1	20		6 3 . 1	9		† Dropped mid-wkt (LATHAM)	70	140		12	6	
55			"	20	x 4 9 P 6 : : 1 . 1	25		6 1	10			71	143		14	7	
59	"	22			6 7S L 1 1 W	28	-	3 3 1 1	12			71[5]	147	9	16	9	9
7.01					DILLEY										0		
03	"	22			P .	1						72					
04			"	21	3 3 8 . . 1	4		3 . . 1	15			73	149		1	10	
08	"	23			7 LB 1 .	6		: LB 4 x . . : .	19		(LB) (LB)	74	152		2		11
11	(23-8-45-4)		"	22	4 W	7	-		19	-		74[1]	152	10	2	10	11
7.11	ALL OUT		(21.1-4.64-1)								M25 NB5		ALL		OUT		
											450 balls						

5TH DAY	BOWLERS (WOODWARD) CITY END		(ALDRIDGE) SOUTHERN END		BATSMEN SCOREBOARD LEFT			SCOREBOARD RIGHT			NEW ZEALAND 2ND INNINGS						
TIME	BOWLER	O.	BOWLER	O.	SCORING	BALLS	6s/4s	SCORING	BALLS	6s/4s	NOTES	END-OF-OVER TOTALS O.	RUNS	W.	'L' BAT	'R' BAT	EXTRAS
					WRIGHT		LHB	FRANKLIN									
11.00			DILLEY	1	· · · · P P	6					M1	1					
05	DEFREITAS	1						· · · · · ·	6		M2	2					
09			"	2	8 2 · x LB ·	10		x x · ·	8		(LB)	3	3		2		1
13	"	2			· x x · 8 1	15		·	9			4	4		3		
17			"	3	E2P · · P † ·	21					† Hit on chest M3	5					
21	"	3						1/2 2 · P · ·	15			6	6			2	
25			"	4	· · · 8 x x	27					M4	7					
29	"	4						· P · · · ·	21		M5	8					
32			"	5	P 7/8 F P 8 1	32		x ·	22			9	7		4		
37	"	5			x · † · P 3	38					† Round wkt (4 balls) M6	10					
41			"	6				· · · · † 1E	28		M7	11					
45	"	6			7/8 1 ·	40		· · · 7 1	32			12	9		5	3	
50	(6-3-5-0)		"	7				x · · 6 2 ·	38			13	11			5	
54	JARVIS	1			· · · · · 1E	46					M8 1HR	14					
58	"		"	8	† ·	47		x 2 · 2 · · 2/3 1	43			15	14			8	
12 02 05	DRINKS (2-2-0-0)	2	(8-4-8-0)			47	-	L · L · · ·	49	-	M9 NB -	16	14	0	5	8	1
12.09	BLSP										13 overs lost LUNCH at 1·00pm.		L	U	N	C	H
1.40			DEFREITAS	7	(·) · 2/3 1	50		2 · · · x	53		(NB) NB 1	17	16		6		2
44	EMBUREY	1			6 4 P · P · ·	56	1					18	20		10		
47			"	8				† · · · · ·	59		M10	19					
50	"	2			x 2 · 2 · · 1E 1	61		P ·	60			20	23		13		
53			"	9	† · 8 1	63		† (·) P 2 † ·	65		(NB) NB 2	21	25		14		3
57	"	3			· 2B · · P ·	69					(2B) M 11	22	27				5
59			"	10	· x · P† ·	74		9 1	66		† Nearly bowled off pad.	23	28			9	
2.03	"	4						4 · · · · ·	72		M 12	24					
06			"	11	9 1	75		G 4 · · ††	77		† Hit on helmet	25	29		15		
09	"	5			· · 7/6 4 · x ·	81	2					26	33		19		
11	(5-2-11-0)		"	12				· · 4 2 · ††	83		† Hit on arm	27	35			11	
15	JARVIS	3	(12-4-13-0)		· · · 3 1 ·	86		7 1	84			28	37		20	12	
20			DILLEY	9				L W	85	-		28[1]	37	1	20	12	5
21								JONES								0	
23			"	9	· ·	88		· · G (·) LB	4		(NB) (LB) NB3 2HR	29	39				7
28	"	4			· 2 3	90		7 1 x · 2	8			30	43		23	1	
33			"	10	· P · L W	94	2					30[4]	43	2	23	1	7
35					M.D. CROWE										0		
36			"	10	x ·	2					M13	31					
38	"	5						· · · · · ·	14		M14	32					
42			"	11	· · · · 3 1	7		(·) ·	16		(NB) NB 4	33	45		1		8
2.46	(6-3-7-0)	6	(11-5-11-2)		8 1	8	-	· · · · · ·	21	-	M14 NB 4	34	46	2	2	1	8

5TH DAY	BOWLERS (WOODWARD) CITY END		BOWLERS (ALDRIDGE) SOUTHERN END		BATSMEN SCOREBOARD LEFT			BATSMEN SCOREBOARD RIGHT			NOTES	NEW ZEALAND 2ND INNINGS END-OF-OVER TOTALS					
TIME	BOWLER	O.	BOWLER	O.	SCORING	BALLS	6s/4s	SCORING	BALLS	6s/4s		O.	RUNS	W.	'L' BAT	'R' BAT	EXTRAS
					MD CROWE	8	-	JONES	21	-	M14 NB4	34	46	2	2	1	8
2.50			DILLEY	12	↑ ↑ 7 1	11		· · ·	24		† Tableaux appeal ct cover (DeFreitas)	35	47		3		
54	JARVIS	7			· Y8 2 · · · ·	17						36	49		5		
58	(7-3-9-0)		"	13	· ·	19		4 ↑ L7 2 2 ⊙ · · 1	29		(NB) NB5	37	53			4	9
3.03	CAPEL	1			·	20		· · · · · LB	34		(LB) M15	38	54				10
08			"	14	· †	22		· · · 3 1	38		† Appeal c sh leg (Moxon) - DILLEY SWORE	39	55			5	
12	"	2			· ·	24		· · P 2 1	42			40	56			6	
16			"	15	·	25		· · · · 9 1	47			41	57			7	
20	"	3	(15-5-18-2)					· · · · · ·	53		M16	42					
24			JARVIS	8	↑ 1 · · · · ·	31					M17	43					
28	"	4						2 · 6G · · ·	59		M18 3HR	44					
31			"	9	· · · 9 1	35		6 2/3 · 1	61			45	59		6	8	
35	"	5						↑ · 2 2 · · 2	67			46	61			10	
38	(5-3-3-0)		"	10	2 · E1 W	38	-		67	-		46^3	61	3	6	10	10
3.40	TEA		(9.3-4-11-1)		JJ CROWE						M18 NB5			T	E	A	
4.00			JARVIS	10	· · ·	3					M19	47			0		
01	DEFREITAS	13						· · · · · ·	73		M20	48					
06			"	11	· 4B E2 · · ·	9					(4B) M21	49	65				14
09	"	14						69† · X · · 4 · · · ·	79	1	† inside edge	50	69			14	
13			"	12	· · E · · ·	15					M22	51					
17	"	15	(12-7-11-1)		·	16		↑ · 2 · 7 1	84			52	70			15	
21			DILLEY	16				4 · · 3 7/8 X 2 · · 4 2 ·	90	2		53	78			23	
25	"	16			↑†X L W	19	-				† Hit on back.	53^3	78	4	0	23	14
26					BRACEWELL										0		
28	"	16			· · ·	3					M23	54					
30			"	17	↑ ·	4		2 · · · · (2) 4 4 3	96		NB6	55	83			28	
35	"	17			· ↑ 8 · · 1	7		7 † · ·	99		† Round wkt	56	85		1	29	
40	(17-6-20-1)		"	18	↑ · 3 1	10		· · 2	102			57	86		2		
44	EMBUREY	6	(18-5-32-2)		· 8 2 · · · ·	16						58	88		4		
48			CAPEL	6				· 9E 3/2 3/2 EP 4 · · · ·	108	3	4HR	59	92			33	
52	"	7			· · P · · 3 1	22						60	93		5		
54			"	7	· · · · · ·	28					M24	61					
57	"	8						· · · 8P · ·	114		M25	62					
5.00 / 5.04	DRINKS		"	8	· · 3 1 ·	32		3 9 2 1	116		Drinks cart broke down. Then almost	63	97		6	36	
08	"	9	(8-4-11-0)					· · 9 2 · · ·	122		somersaulted. Drivers: Radford & Latham	64	99			38	
10			JARVIS	13	↑7 4 · 2 2 Y · · ·	38	1					65	105		12		
15	"	10						· 3 · · · · ·	128		M26	66					
16	(10-4-16-0)		"	14	2 2 · E1 · · ·	44						67	107		14		
20	CAPEL	9			· L · ·	47		· · 8 1	131			68	108			39	
5.24	(9-4-12-0)		" (15-7-20-1)	15	↑ 6 3 † · · · ·	51	1	3 8E · 1	133	3	† Round wkt M26 NB6	69	109	4	14	40	14

5TH DAY	BOWLERS (WOODWARD) CITY END		(ALDRIDGE) SOUTHERN END		BATSMEN SCOREBOARD LEFT			SCOREBOARD RIGHT			NEW ZEALAND 2ND INNINGS NOTES	END-OF-OVER TOTALS					
TIME	BOWLER	O.	BOWLER	O.	SCORING	BALLS	6s/4s	SCORING	BALLS	6s/4s		O.	RUNS	W.	'L' BAT	'R' BAT	EXTRAS
					BRACEWELL	51	1	JONES	133	3	M 26 NB 6	69	109	4	14	40	14
5·29	CAPEL	10			. 2 : . Y . : . .	56		8 1	134			70	110			41	
33			JARVIS	16	† . 7 1	58		7 . 4 2 . 1 3 .	138		† Round wkt	71	114		15	44	
36	"	11			LB . : ↑ . . .	62		: 8 1	140		(LB)	72	116			45	15
40			"	17	7 1	63		4 2 7 2 2 1 . L . .	145		JONES' 50: 179'	73	122		16	50	
45	"	12	(17-7-30-1)		. 7 . 1	68		9 1	146		SHR	74	124		17	51	
49			DE FREITAS	18	7 † 2	71		: x 1 : 3	149		† 1 overthrow. 50 p'ship: 83'	75	129		19	54	
53	"	13						: 4 4	155		M 27	76					
58	(13-5-16-0)		"	19	. 2 3 . . 1	74	1	. . 4	158	3		77	130	4	20	54	15
6·01	STUMPS		(19-6-26-1)								M 27 NB 6		STUMPS				
											468 balls		MATCH DRAWN				

Neal Radford upsets the cart but not fellow drinks waiter, Rod Latham (Canterbury) at Christchurch. His captain makes a mental note for the fines committee.

ENGLAND 1ST INNINGS v NEW ZEALAND (FIRST TEST) at LANCASTER PARK, CHRISTCHURCH on 12, 13, 14, 16, 17 FEBRUARY, 1988.

IN	OUT	MINS	No.	BATSMAN	HOW OUT	BOWLER	RUNS	WKT	TOTAL	6s	4s	BALLS	NOTES ON DISMISSAL — TOSS: NEW ZEALAND
11.00	5.38	341	1	B.C. BROAD	ct SMITH	SNEDDEN	114	4	219	·	11	244	Edged low to 'keeper's left.
11.00	11.24	24	2	M.D. MOXON	ct JONES	MORRISON	1	1	7	·	-	19	Defensive push to short-leg.
11.26	4.06	223	3	R.T. ROBINSON	ct SMITH	MORRISON	70	2	175	·	7	181	Edged leg-side flick.
4.08	4.31	23	4	M.W. GATTING *	ct SUB (MJ GREATBATCH)	MORRISON	8	3	187	·	1	19	Cut long-hop to cover.
4.33	12.00	114	5	C.W.J. ATHEY	ct SUB (MJ GREATBATCH)	MORRISON	22	6	241	·	1	79	Drove half-volley low to cover.
5.40	11.44	31	6	D.J. CAPEL	ct BRACEWELL	CHATFIELD	11	5	237	·	1	25	Edged low to 2nd slip.
11.46	2.30	124	7	J.E. EMBUREY	ct JONES	MORRISON	42	10	319	·	5	93	Drove low to cover.
12.02	12.12	10	8	B.N. FRENCH †	ct SMITH	CHATFIELD	7	7	248	·	1	4	Edged leg-cutter to 'keeper.
12.13	12.23	10	9	P.A.J. DeFREITAS	ct MORRISON	CHATFIELD	4	8	260	·	-	14	Skied hit to wide mid-on.
12.25	1.54	49	10	P.W. JARVIS	ct SMITH	CHATFIELD	14	9	285	·	1	37	Edged lifting away-seamer.
1.56	(2.30)	34	11	G.R. DILLEY	NOT OUT		7			·	-	14	
				EXTRAS	b - lb 11	w 1 nb 7	19			-6	28 4	729 balls (inc 8 no-balls)	
				TOTAL	(120.1 OVERS; 500 MINUTES)		319						ALL OUT at 2.30 pm on 2nd day.

* CAPTAIN † WICKET-KEEPER

14 OVERS 2 BALLS/HOUR
2.65 RUNS/OVER
43 RUNS/100 BALLS

UMPIRES: B.L. ALDRIDGE and S.J. WOODWARD.

BOWLER	O	M	R	W	W/NB
HADLEE	18	3	50	0	-/8
MORRISON	21.1	3	69	5	1/-
CHATFIELD	42	13	87	4	-
SNEDDEN	33	9	86	1	-
BRACEWELL	6	1	16	0	-
			11		
	120.1	29	319	10	

2ND NEW BALL taken after 85.1 overs at 5.50 pm 1st day - ENGLAND 223-4.

HRS	OVERS	RUNS
1	14	34
2	13	24
3	16	60
4	16	51
5	13	33
6	15	22
7	14	41
8	14	25

RUNS	MINS	OVERS	LAST 50 (in mins)
50	97	22.1	97
100	163	39.1	66
150	223	54.4	60
200	287	69.2	64
250	403	97.3	116
300	483	116.1	80

LUNCH: 66-1 [28 OVERS 123 MIN] BROAD 34* (123') ROBINSON 21* (97')

TEA: 171-1 [60 OVERS 243 MIN] BROAD 88* (243') ROBINSON 68* (217')

STUMPS (1ST DAY): 235-4 [90 OVERS 370 MIN] ATHEY 18* (94') CAPEL 10* (27')

2ND DAY - START DELAYED 40 MINUTES (RAIN)

LUNCH: 278-8 [108 OVERS 450 MIN] EMBUREY 11* (74') JARVIS 11* (35')

WKT	PARTNERSHIP		RUNS	MINS
1st	Broad	Moxon	7	24
2nd	Broad	Robinson	168	223
3rd	Broad	Gatting	12	23
4th	Broad	Athey	32	65
5th	Athey	Capel	18	31
6th	Athey	Emburey	4	14
7th	Emburey	French	7	10
8th	Emburey	DeFreitas	12	10
9th	Emburey	Jarvis	25	49
10th	Emburey	Dilley	34	34
			319	

NEW ZEALAND 1ST INNINGS (IN REPLY TO ENGLAND'S 319 ALL OUT)

IN	OUT	MINS	No.	BATSMAN	HOW OUT	BOWLER	RUNS	WKT	TOTAL	6s	4s	BALLS	NOTES ON DISMISSAL
2.41	3.26	45	1	J.G. WRIGHT	CT MOXON	DILLEY	10	1	20	·	·	37	Turned lifting ball to short-leg.
2.41	4.04	64	2	T.J. FRANKLIN	CT ATHEY	DILLEY	10	2	25	·	1	44	Edged lifter to 3rd slip.
3.28	4.13	26	3	A.H. JONES	CT FRENCH	DILLEY	8	3	32	·	1	14	Gloved fast lifter.
4.06	4.30	24	4	M.D. CROWE	CT MOXON	DILLEY	5	4	40	·	·	13	Fended lifting ball to short-leg.
4.14	1.42	207	5	J.J. CROWE *	CT FRENCH	DEFREITAS	28	6	131	·	1	144	Edged low to 'keeper's right.
4.32	11.23	89	6	J.G. BRACEWELL	CT FRENCH	DILLEY	31	5	96	·	4	67	Edged lifter to 'keeper.
11.25	3.07	183	7	R.J. HADLEE	CT FRENCH	DILLEY	37	10	168	·	3	135	(with MD Crowe as runner) Inside edge driving.
1.43	2.05	22	8	I.D.S. SMITH †	CT CAPEL	JARVIS	13	7	151	·	3	18	Edged cut to slip.
2.07	2.18	11	9	M.C. SNEDDEN	LBW	DEFREITAS	0	8	155	·	·	7	Late on inswinger.
2.20	2.24	4	10	D.K. MORRISON	BOWLED	JARVIS	0	9	156	·	·	4	Played outside ball of full length.
2.25	(3.07)	42	11	E.J. CHATFIELD	NOT OUT		0			·	·	23	
				EXTRAS	b 2 lb 12	w - nb 12	26				13 (4s)	506 balls (inc 15 no-balls)	
				TOTAL	(81.5 OVERS; 366 MINUTES)		168		ALL OUT at 3.07pm on 3rd day.				

* CAPTAIN † WICKET-KEEPER

13 OVERS 2 BALLS/HOUR
2.05 RUNS/OVER
33 RUNS/100 BALLS

BOWLER	O	M	R	W	nb
DEFREITAS	22	6	39	2	7
DILLEY	24.5	9	38	6	6
CAPEL	10	2	32	0	-
JARVIS	21	8	43	2	2
EMBUREY	4	3	2	0	-
			14		
	81.5	28	168	10	

HRS	OVERS	RUNS
1	13	25
2	13	38
3	15	33
4	13	19
5	13	30
6	13	16

RUNS	MINS	OVERS	LAST 50 (in mins)
50	104	22.2	104
100	194	43.5	90
150	303	68.2	109

TEA: 25-1 [13 OVERS, 60 MIN] FRANKLIN 10* (60') JONES 2* (13')

STUMPS (2ND DAY): 83-4 [37.1 OVERS, 163 MIN] JJ CROWE 15* (89') BRACEWELL 22* (71')

LUNCH: 131-5 [63 OVERS, 279 MIN] JJ CROWE 28* (205') HADLEE 18* (96')

151 BEHIND ON FIRST INNINGS

WKT	PARTNERSHIP		RUNS	MINS
1st	Wright	Franklin	20	45
2nd	Franklin	Jones	5	17
3rd	Jones	MD Crowe	7	7
4th	MD Crowe	JJ Crowe	8	16
5th	JJ Crowe	Bracewell	56	89
6th	JJ Crowe	Hadlee	35	98
7th	Hadlee	Smith	20	22
8th	Hadlee	Snedden	4	11
9th	Hadlee	Morrison	1	4
10th	Hadlee	Chatfield	12	42
			168	

ENGLAND 2ND INNINGS (151 RUNS AHEAD ON FIRST INNINGS)

IN	OUT	MINS	No.	BATSMAN	HOW OUT	BOWLER	RUNS	WKT	TOTAL	6s	4s	BALLS	NOTES ON DISMISSAL
3.20	4.47	67	1	B.C. BROAD	CT SUB (MJ GREATBATCH)	CHATFIELD	20	1	32	·	3	52	Ball 'stopped' – tucked-up, gentle catch to backward sq. leg.
3.20	4.02	129	2	M.D. MOXON	CT JONES	CHATFIELD	27	3	55	·	1	93	Mid-wicket – simple catch.
4.49	5.16	27	3	R.T. ROBINSON	CT WRIGHT	CHATFIELD	2	2	38	·	·	19	Mishmied turn to leg – leading edge to mid-on
5.18	5.41	130	4	M.W. GATTING *	BOWLED	SNEDDEN	23	6	99	·	3	82	Bowled through 'gate' by breakback which kept low.
4.04	5.13	69	5	C.W.J. ATHEY	CT SMITH	SNEDDEN	19	4	95	·	1	55	Edged breakback via thigh pad to 'keeper.
5.15	5.26	11	6	D.J. CAPEL	CT M.D. CROWE	CHATFIELD	0	5	96	·	·	11	Wide mid-on – skied mishit.
5.28	6.36	68	7	J.E. EMBUREY	RUN OUT (MORRISON / SNEDDEN)		19	8	125	·	2	47	DeFreitas attempted 2nd run to mid-wkt who returned to bowler.
5.43	6.28	45	8	B.N. FRENCH †	CT J.J. CROWE	SNEDDEN	3	7	118	·	·	37	Steered catch to 1st slip.
6.30	7.01	31	9	P.A.J. DeFREITAS	LBW	SNEDDEN	16	9	147	·	·	28	Low breakback.
6.38	(7.11)	33	10	P.W. JARVIS	NOT OUT		10			·	·	19	
7.03	7.11	8	11	G.R. DILLEY	CT JONES	MORRISON	2	10	152	·	·	7	Skied hit to extra-cover.
				EXTRAS	b - lb 7	w - nb 4	11			-6	10 4	450 balls (inc 5 no-balls)	

* CAPTAIN † WICKET-KEEPER

TOTAL (74.1 OVERS; 318 MINUTES) 152 ALL OUT at 7.11 pm on 4th day.

14 OVERS 0 BALLS/HOUR
2.04 RUNS/OVER
33 RUNS/100 BALLS

BOWLER	O	M	R	W	nb
MORRISON	21.1	4	64	1	4
CHATFIELD	30	13	36	4	1
SNEDDEN	23	8	45	4	-
			7	1	
	74.1	25	152	10	

HRS	OVERS	RUNS
1	13	30
2	14	21
3	14	35
4	14	13
5	14	38

RUNS	MINS	OVERS	LAST 50 (in mins)
50	117	26.3	117
100	238	55.1	121
150	315	73.1	77

TEA: 14-0 [5 OVERS 20 MIN] BROAD 8* MOXON 4*

STUMPS (3RD DAY): 55-2 [29.2 OVERS 128 MIN] MOXON 27* (128') GATTING 3* (30')

4th DAY: RAIN DELAYED START UNTIL 4.01 pm

ENGLAND LEAD BY 303 RUNS

WKT	PARTNERSHIP		RUNS	MINS
1st	Broad	Moxon	32	67
2nd	Moxon	Robinson	6	27
3rd	Moxon	Gatting	17	31
4th	Gatting	Athey	40	69
5th	Gatting	Capel	1	11
6th	Gatting	Emburey	3	13
7th	Emburey	French	19	45
8th	Emburey	DeFreitas	7	6
9th	DeFreitas	Jarvis	22	23
10th	Jarvis	Dilley	5	8
			152	

NEW ZEALAND 2ND INNINGS (REQUIRING 304 RUNS TO WIN @ 3.20 RUNS/OVER

IN	OUT	MINS	No.	BATSMAN	HOW OUT	BOWLER	RUNS	WKT	TOTAL	6s	4s	BALLS	NOTES ON DISMISSAL
11.00	2.35	124	1	J.G. WRIGHT	LBW	DILLEY	23	2	43	·	2	94	Beaten by breakback - delayed decision.
11.00	2.21	110	2	T.J. FRANKLIN	LBW	DILLEY	12	1	37	·	·	85	Late on fast breakback.
2.23	(6.01)	198	3	A.H. JONES	NOT OUT		54			·	3	158	
2.36	3.40	64	4	M.D. CROWE	CT FRENCH	JARVIS	6	3	61	·	·	38	Edged outswinger.
4.00	4.26	26	5	J.J. CROWE *	LBW	DEFREITAS	0	4	78	·	·	19	Played outside inswinger.
4.28	(6.01)	93	6	J.G. BRACEWELL	NOT OUT		20			·	1	74	
			7										
			8										
			9										
			10										
			11										
				EXTRAS	b 6 lb 4 w · nb 5		15			-6	6 4	468 balls (inc 6 no-balls)	
				TOTAL	(77 OVERS; 310 MINUTES)		130-4						

* CAPTAIN † WICKET-KEEPER

14 OVERS 5 BALLS/HOUR
1.68 RUNS/OVER
27 RUNS/100 BALLS

BOWLER	O	M	R	W	nb
DILLEY	18	5	32	2	4
DEFREITAS	19	6	26	1	2
JARVIS	17	7	30	1	-
EMBUREY	10	4	16	0	·
CAPEL	13	5	16	0	·
			10		
	77	27	130	4	

HRS	OVERS	RUNS
1	14	11
2	15	28
3	15	18
4	15	35
5	15	32

RUNS	MINS	OVERS	LAST 50 (in mins)
50	147	36.1	147
100	259	64.1	112

LUNCH: 14-0 [16 OVERS 69 MIN] WRIGHT 5* FRANKLIN 8*

TEA: 61-3 [46.3 OVERS 189 MIN] JONES 10* (77')

MATCH DRAWN

MATCH AWARD: E.J. CHATFIELD

TOTAL TIME LOST (NET): 4 HR 55 MIN

WKT	PARTNERSHIP		RUNS	MINS
1st	Wright	Franklin	37	110
2nd	Wright	Jones	6	12
3rd	Jones	MD Crowe	18	64
4th	Jones	JJ Crowe	17	26
5th	Jones	Bracewell	52*	93
			130	

AUCKLAND
THE SECOND TEST

Eden Park's origins and conversion · The Auckland Cricket Society · England's record at Auckland · Hammond's world records · Match report · Moxon's lost leg-byes · Jeff Crowe is sacked

Although Auckland's Eden Park began its sporting life as a cricket ground built over a reclaimed lake which had originally been formed within a volcano, it is now primarily yet another of New Zealand's rugby amphitheatres. Miraculously, its original wooden cricket pavilion has survived the ground's conversion to a soulless stadium and now houses the club rooms, library and trophies of the Auckland Cricket Society. It is a most convivial haven, recent alterations affording members excellent views of play, both on the Test arena and on the adjacent No. 2 Ground where Auckland play most of their first-class matches for the Shell Trophy.

In 1984 the latter ground provided the venue for a Leap Day match between my private touring team and an ACS side captained by Dave Crowe, father of Jeff and Martin. Dave had been a capable batsman, sufficiently handy to have represented both Wellington and Canterbury (not at the same time). His team that day included former Test starts Bert Sutcliffe and John Sparling; both had scored sixties, richly entertaining us with their strokeplay. The evening in the club rooms was one of the highlights of a superb tour.

The ACS in general and Graham Burgess in particular are most generous hosts. Graham's brother, Gordon, managed New Zealand's 1969 tour of England. His nephew, Mark, captained the Kiwis in ten Tests. Besides being a most active member of the ACS, Graham prepares the pitches at Cornwall Park, a delightful, tree-surrounded ground immediately beneath Auckland's famous One Tree Hill.

One look at Auckland's weather was sufficient to confirm that the most likely result of the Second Test was a draw. In 1984 the pitch had been so dead that each side only just completed its first innings before stumps on the final day. England's last victory at Eden Park was under Mike Denness in 1975, but the West Indies had managed to gain a 10-wicket win there in 1987.

Gatting's team were encouraged by the news that England have never been defeated in Auckland, eleven previous visits since 1930 having produced three victories by innings margins and eight draws. It was here, in 1955, that Len Hutton's triumphant Ashes team dismissed New Zealand for 26, still the lowest total in Test cricket. When I boasted about this feat to my oldest pen pal, my great aunt Marion in Manurewa, a major boost to my burgeoning stamp collection ceased abruptly.

Walter Hammond (to whom Fred Trueman refers on *Test Match Special* as 'the great Wally') set records galore at Eden Park in 1933 when he amassed 336 not out, the highest innings in Test matches until Hutton's 364 five and a half years later. He scored 295 on the second day (only Bradman with 309 at Headingley in 1930 has exceeded him), including 111 before lunch. His time of 288 minutes remains the fastest for scoring a triple century in Test cricket, while his 240-minute double century is the England record in terms of time rather than fewest balls received. In Test cricket no other batsman has come within three hits of Hammond's 10 sixes in that innings. He also stroked 34 fours, his tally of 196 in boundaries being second only to John Edrich's 238 during his 310 not out against New Zealand at Headingley in 1965. Three of his sixes came off consecutive balls from Jack Newman's left-arm seamers.

Sir Jack, who was knighted in 1978, was in sprightly form in the VIP enclosure alongside our press area during the first three days of the First Test at Lancaster Park. Not surprisingly Hammond's series average of 563.00 also remains a world record.

Richard Hadlee was reported to have had high hopes of playing in this Test. Desperate to take the wicket which would give him the mantle of the world's biggest Test match wicket-taker, he feared that if Ian Botham played in six Tests during the coming English summer he might never catch up with him again.

Luck deserted England from Graham Dilley's very first delivery of the match after Gatting had won the toss and decided to bowl. The vital ball took the edge of John Wright's reflex prod and flew chest-high between wicket-keeper and first slip. Neither Bruce French nor John Emburey appeared properly awake and both were slow to react.

It was French's catch and the cost was to prove exorbitant as Wright went on to compile his seventh hundred in Test cricket, his third against England and his third at Eden Park. He also completed 20,000 runs in first-class cricket. He also became the third New Zealander after Bert Sutcliffe and Bevan Congdon to score 1,000 runs against England.

Ironically Wright fell to the very same Dilley/French combination almost exactly 24 hours later off the first ball he received from Dilley on the second day. By then it was too late. Wright's partnerships with Trevor Franklin and a still-struggling Martin Crowe had paved the way for a total of 301 which was a guarantee against defeat unless England could score at a remarkable rate. On a slow, low pitch frequently immersed in murky light there was never much fear of that. Jeff Crowe described the surface as 'flatter than normal and it has lost the seam movement it used to have. Now it doesn't help the bowlers and it is too low and slow for the batsmen to time their shots.'

After Moxon, Robinson and Gatting had provided a marvellous platform, England again flattered to deceive before collapsing dramatically against the second new ball. At the end of the third day they led by a solitary run with just two first innings wickets intact. Inspired bowling by Chatfield and Morrison reduced England from 211 for 2 to 234 for 6 in 11.4 overs.

Dropped first ball, John Wright celebrates his escape with a century at Eden Park.

For the third Test in succession England had lost control of a match which appeared to be within their grasp. A chastened Micky Stewart commented: 'I had hoped to have a 100-run lead by tonight but there is still time to force a win'.

Moxon and Robinson carefully extended their second-wicket partnership to 108 on the third day before Robinson's lofted drive was plucked from the air by Morrison, leaping to his right at wide mid-off and clinging to the ball as he crashed to the ground, an astonishing catch. Robinson's 54 in 183 minutes from 151 balls included seven fours from cover drives and crisply timed pulls. Gatting exuded confidence from his first ball. His nimble footwork, surprising in such a bulky man, allowing him to advance and drive John Bracewell's off-spin. Moxon was the steadfast anchorman, contributing a single boundary among 30 of England's 70 pre-lunch runs from 32 overs.

It was plain fare, watched by a crowd more than double the strength of the 4,000 who had stoically shivered through each of the first two days. For the first time in Auckland's history club cricket was being played on the Saturday of an Eden Park Test. Did the Auckland Cricket Board make that decision after correctly predicting how boring the match was going to be? I must confess that there were many moments during that tedious afternoon when I envied those weekend cricketers at the Domain and Davenport, at Papatoetoe and Takapuna.

Ironically, the early cloud cleared to produce a sunny afternoon and easier batting conditions for England. Eden Park uses the No. 2 Ground as the main car park on big match days. The ACB member who controls it is Roger Seaton, an emigré from Leeds and former captain of the local Birkenhead City Cricket Club. During a barbecue at his house the previous evening he had promised me that he would arrange Saturday's cars in rows of red, white and blue to boost England's effort. Much to the confusion of their drivers and commentary teams he had achieved just this, causing quite a stir by segregating those three colours of the Union Jack in swathes across the adjacent ground.

Not that this bizarre operation provided any sort of talisman for the luckless Martyn Moxon. He did manage to exceed his previous highest Test score of 74 against New Zealand at Lord's in 1986. After five hours of stately progress that delighted his mentor, Geoffrey Boycott, who was searching for an intro to his *Daily Mail* observations, Moxon suddenly startled everyone by launching himself into two thunderous drives, straight and through the covers. It was as though a learner driver had suddenly discovered he had forgotten to disengage the handbrake.

Moxon had reached 98 out of 209 for 2 from 89.4 overs when Chatfield took the new ball. His first delivery moved late, took the edge, carried low to Bracewell at first slip and was dropped. The batsmen scurried a guilty run. Ignoring the fact that his partner was one run short of his maiden Test hundred, Gatting then turned the last ball of the over for a single to steal the strike. Those were the only two runs taken from Chatfield's bowling during his eight-over spell lasting 71 minutes.

Moxon was kept on 99 for 18 agonizing minutes which included two maidens by Morrison to Gatting and a lengthy drinks interval. Then the inevitable happened. Chatfield bowled an off-stump ball of perfect length. It cut away, clipped the edge of Moxon's bat and carried to Jeff Crowe at first slip. It was an honourable if tragic end to an innings of great tenacity. Mercifully there were no tantrums; to his eternal credit the Barnsley-born opener revealed none of his supreme disappointment and raised his bat to acknowledge a generous ovation.

The supreme irony was revealed later. Early in his innings a well-timed sweep for 3 runs off Bracewell had been signalled as leg-byes by umpire Rodger McHarg, standing in only his second Test. The bowler subsequently admit-

Martyn Moxon savages the Snedden analysis during his 99 at Auckland.

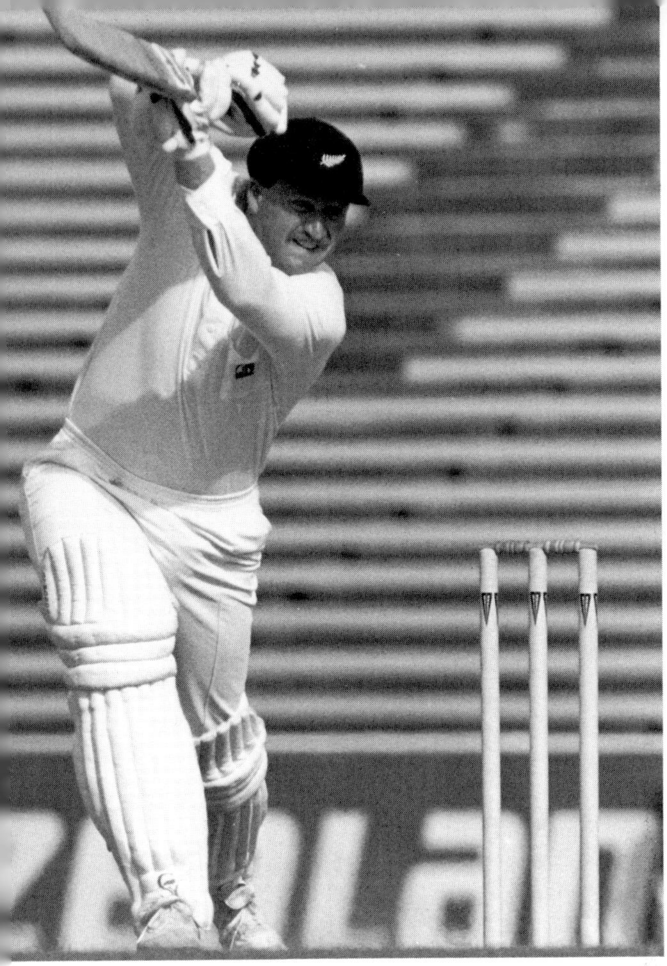

Mark Greatbatch joins New Zealand's elite band of left-handed debutant century-makers.

ted that the ball came off Moxon's bat. Moxon himself earned full marks for diplomacy when he said: 'I don't want to make a fuss about that and I'm not claiming those runs. I'm disappointed but the new ball made batting much more difficult. It was a good ball and perhaps I should have pushed forward more firmly.'

He is only the ninth England player (and fourth Yorkshireman) to perish on 99 in the course of 644 Tests. The most recent victim had been Graham Gooch; I saw him run himself out attempting a ridiculous single to mid-on to complete his maiden Test century at Melbourne in 1979-80. I can still recall the horror-stricken expression on the face of his wife Brenda when the TV cameras picked her out as Goochie began his desolate walk back.

One of the other three Yorkshiremen to perish on 99 in a Test was Geoffrey Boycott. I saw him in the ACS committee room after play.

'I were a bloody greyhound compared with this lot,' he growled at the assembled company, referring to England's scoring rate. Realizing that he had an audience and referring to an imaginative lbw decision which Roger McHarg had awarded against Martin Crowe, Boycott tested the piece he had just written: 'Visiting sides have been saying for years how atrocious your umpires are. It's only now they've sawn off your best player that you realize we're right!'

Once again it was Emburey and the tail who steered England into their nominal lead. He also removed Martin Crowe from the arena. He was squatting at silly-point when Emburey middled a firm-footed short-arm jab and appeared to inflict a fearful blow on Crowe's lower face. Mercifully there was no great damage; the ball grazed his chin and lower lip before severely bruising his shoulder. Hadlee's absence had left Crowe as the one player of undisputed world class on view in this series, and a long and commanding innings was desperately needed from New Zealand's master batsman if total tedium was to be avoided.

Soon after the start of the fourth morning, Bob Vance, Chairman of the New Zealand Cricket Council, came up to our press area to announce that Richard Hadlee would not be available for the final Test starting at Wellington in just four days' time. Bearing in mind Hadlee's hectic TV and radio broadcasting schedule during this match, I asked mischievously whether Hadlee's absence was due to injury or the pressure of other commitments. Vance wisely declined to answer.

Consecutive back-to-back Test matches without rest days are killers for the participants – and the media. Injured players, such as Andrew Jones who suffered wrist damage, have no time to recover.

The announcement of Hadlee's temporary retirement came as a boon that Sunday morning. The time difference of thirteen hours allowed London papers to carry a report of play up to 3 p.m. New Zealand time (1 a.m. in Britain). *The Mail on Sunday* could thus carry a full report of Saturday's play together with a 'runner' describing Sunday's proceedings during the pre-lunch session and for twenty minutes afterwards. This facility demanded that I virtually commentated live by telephone to a copy-taker on the London sports desk. I much prefer sending copy through a Tandy portable computer/word-processor linked to the phone, but Bidelia Corrigan, an emigré from Brisbane, eased my ordeal with her patience during a late night-shift at the other end of the ether.

As at Sydney and Christchurch, England began the final day with reasonable hopes of victory, but were unable to break through determined batting on an unresponsive surface. This time the hero was Mark Greatbatch, a comfortably-built blond who played the ball late. He had impressed at Christchurch as a substitute fielder, holding three dramatic catches. Now he dominated New Zealand's rearguard action, looking like a left-handed Trevor Bailey wearing a German helmet. After tea he became the fourth New Zealander after Jack Mills, Bruce Taylor and Rodney Redmond to score a century in his first Test, and the first to do so in the second innings of his debut match. Curiously all four are left-handers.

Greatbatch received excellent support from Martin Snedden, John Bracewell and Ian Smith, the latter taking advantage of the game's dying moments to score the 19 runs he needed to become the first New Zealander to complete the Test wicket-keepers' 'double' of 1,000 runs and 100 dismissals.

A slow pitch, dreary weather, the drab vastness of the mostly empty rugby stands and the absence of Richard Hadlee combined to ensure that this Auckland Test was guaranteed a place in most observers' lists of Most Unmemorable Matches. Its only claim to fame lay in the fact that out of ten Test matches scheduled to include play on 29 February, this was the first actually to end on a Leap Day!

England's chances of victory virtually disappeared when Bruce French was surprised by Wright's chance off the very first ball of the match. Run-making was never easy on a slow pitch that became increasingly uneven in bounce, and the average scoring rate seldom climbed above a miserly 2 runs an over. With Hadlee and Jones absent and their captain woefully out of form, New Zealand's ambitions did not seem to have risen above a holding operation in the hope that both would be fit for a decisive confrontation in Wellington.

The most dramatic event on that final day was the news of Jeff Crowe's removal from the captaincy because of his poor batting form. It was sad news for both camps; he is a friendly, popular character who communicates easily and had always handled press conferences with more enthusiasm and commonsense than most of his recent England counterparts. Ironically he is the first New Zealand captain to have been removed from office during a home series; three others – Harry Cave (1956), Murray Chapple (1966) and Barry Sinclair (1968) – stood down because of ill health or injury.

Don Neely, New Zealand's convenor of selectors, suggested that the players' dressing-room facilities might have had something to do with their mental approach to this match. Located in the bowels of a vast stand, they are dimly lit and not unlike those dingy interiors in PoW films featuring Colditz Castle. Certainly a re-run of that epic would have provided more entertainment. The highlight of one day's play was a fight on the outfield between two magpies. They stood side by side watching play, apparently secure in the knowledge that they were in absolutely no danger of being hit by the ball, until the TV cameras showed an interest in them. As soon as they were thrust into viewers' living rooms they started fighting like mad. It was a most dramatic scrap involving beak-sparring, jumping, diving, mid-air combat and chasing round tight circuits, all beautifully filmed in the style of a David Attenborough *Zoo Quest*. When the producer decided he had better get back to the cricket they stopped fighting immediately and resumed their dignified watch.

1ST DAY	BOWLERS (FR GOODALL) SANDRINGHAM RD END		(RL McHARG) DOMINION RD END		BATSMEN SCOREBOARD LEFT			SCOREBOARD RIGHT			NEW ZEALAND 1ST INNINGS	END-OF-OVER TOTALS					
TIME	BOWLER	O.	BOWLER	O.	SCORING	BALLS	6s/4s	SCORING	BALLS	6s/4s	NOTES	O.	RUNS	W.	'L' BAT	'R' BAT	EXTRAS
					WRIGHT		LHB	FRANKLIN									
11.00	DILLEY	1			1E† P 4 · · · · ·	6	1				† Low chance to FRENCH's right.	1	4		4		
04			JARVIS	1	· · 2 ·	9		3 6 · · 1	3			2	5			1	
08	"	2			· · · ·	13		1E · 1	5			3	6			2	
13			"	2	8 · 1	15		8 · 1 · ·	9			4	8		5	3	
17	"	3			x 3 P 6 · 4 · · · ·	21	2					5	12		9		
21			"	3	· · · · 3 ·	26		8/9 1	10			6	13			4	
25	"	4						x · · · 3 · · · · ·	16		M1	7					
29			"	4	4 · 4 † · · 1	29		· · † L	19		† RO chance (Fairbrother)	8	14		10		
33	"	5			3/2 ‡ † E‡ · · 2 · ·	35					† Hit on shoulder ‡ Dropped 3rd slip (Moxon)	9	16		12		
37			"	5	· · 4x	38		2 · EP8 · · 1	22			10	17			5	
41	"	6			E9 1	39		7 1 ⊙ 2 · · · ·	28		(NB) NB 1	11	20		13	6	1
46	(6-1-14-0)		"	6	3/2 · · · · · 2 · · ·	45						12	22		15		
50	RADFORD	1	(6-0-8-0)					P · · · E1 2/1 · · · 4 3	34	1		13	29			13	
55	(1-0-7-0)		CAPEL	1		45	2	· · · · · ·	40	1	M2	14	29	0	15	13	1
11.57	RAIN		(1-1-0-0)								M2 NB1 (7' lost)			R	S	P	
12.04	RADFORD	2			· · · · · ·	51					M3 1 HR	15					
08			CAPEL	2				4 · · x L 2 · · · ·	46			16	31			15	
12	"	3			2 · 3S · · 1	54		· ⊙ · PP	50		(NB) NB 2	17	33		16		2
16			"	3	EP x 7/8 · · · · · 2 ·	60						18	35		18		
20	"	4						E2 † 2 3 4 4 · · · · · ·	56		M4	19					
23			"	4	4 7 4 · 4 1	63	3	L 4 · ·	59			20	40		23		
27	" (5-2-10-0)	5	(4-1-9-0)		· · · † · 4 3/3	69	3		59	1	(W) † running.	21	41	0	23	15	3
12.31	RAIN										M4 NB 2 (9' lost)			R	S	P	
12.40			CAPEL	5				P 4/3 3 x · 2 · · · ·	65			22	43			17	
44	RADFORD	6			7 · · · · 6 4 · · · · ·	75	4					23	47		27		
48			"	6				· 6 · 8 · · · · · ·	71		M5	24					
52	"	7			· 4S · 1	77		3 † 4 · · · ·	75		† Appeal ct wk. (FRENCH hurled ball to ground).	25	48		28		
57	(7-2-15-0)		"	7	2 8 · 2 · · · ·	83	4		75	1	50 p'ship: 102'	26	50	0	30	17	3
1.00			(7-2-13-0)								M5 NB 2		L	U	N	CH	
1.38	RADFORD	8						4 · · · · 7S 2 ·	81			27	52			19	
42			JARVIS	7	2S 1	84		EP · · P · · · · ·	86			28	53		31		
46	"	9			3† 3 2 · · · ·	90					† 1 overthrow	29	55		33		
50			"	8				3 · 4 2 4 · · · 4 ·	92	3	2HR	30	63			27	
54	"	10			· · · · 3 ·	96					M6	31					
57			"	9				· · · · 66 · ·	98		M7	32					
2.01	"	11			2 2/3 · L 4 · 4 · · ,	102	6					33	71		41		
04			"	10				· † EP · · · · · ·	104		M8	34					
2.08	"	12	(10-2-17-0)		E1 † 5 4 7/8 · 2 · · 4 ·	108	7		104	3	† Round wkt (2 balls)	35	77	0	47	27	3
	(12-3-33-0)										M8 NB 2						

1ST DAY	BOWLERS (GOODALL) SANDRINGHAM ROAD END		(McHARG) DOMINION ROAD END		BATSMEN SCOREBOARD LEFT			SCOREBOARD RIGHT			NEW ZEALAND 1ST INNINGS	END-OF-OVER TOTALS					
TIME	BOWLER	O.	BOWLER	O.	SCORING	BALLS	6s/4s	SCORING	BALLS	6s/4s	NOTES	O.	RUNS	W.	'L' BAT	'R' BAT	EXTRAS
					WRIGHT	108	7	FRANKLIN	104	3	M 8 NB 2	35	77	0	47	27	3
2.12			JARVIS	11	}			: P X . . W	107	3		35[3]	77	1	47	27	3
13								JJ CROWE								0	
15			"	11				. x 8 . . 1	3			36	78			1	
18	RADFORD	13			P :	109		. . . . . 8 1	8			37	79			2	
21	(13-3-34-0)		"	12				3	14		M9	38					
25	DILLEY	7			4† . x 5(4) 4 . . 1 .	114	8	8 1	15		†Moxon 'torpedoed' WRIGHT'S 50: 151'	39	85		52	3	
29			"	13				. . . .	21		M10	40					
34	"	8	(13-4-18-1)		E8 L L . .	120					M 11	41					
38			CAPEL	8	:	121		. 5(6) . 8 . . 2 . 1	26			42	88			6	
42 44	DRINKS "	9						. . . . P .	32		M12	43					
49			"	9	: : 9 1	124		: : 6	35		3HR	44	89		53		
53	"	10			. 3 . . . 1 4	130	9					45	93		57		
56			"	10	: :	132		: : 6 8 4 1	39	1		46	98			11	
3.01	"	11	}					: : E2 W	42	1		46[3]	98	2	57	11	3
02								MD CROWE								0	
04	"	11			. 3 . 2	134		3 1	1			47	101		59	1	
06			"	11				. P . . . 4 1	7			48	102			2	
10	"	12	(11-2-23-0)		. . . .	138		: 8 1	9			49	103			3	
15			EMBUREY	1	:	139		. . . . 6 8 1	14			50	104			4	
17	"	13						. . . . L P . .	20		M13	51					
22	(13-4-28-1)		"	2	. . . . . .	145					M14	52					
24	CAPEL	12						L 3	26		M15	53					
28			"	3	. . . . . .	151					M16	54					
30	"	13			. 3 9 . 1	154		. 1/2 7/8 . 4 1	29	1		55	110		60	9	
35			"	4	P	160					M17	56					
37	(14-3-30-0)	14	(4-3-1-0)		: . :	163	9	. . 3 1	32	1		57	111	2	60	10	3
3.40	TEA										M17 NB 2			T	E	A	
4.00			RADFORD	14				7† . . 5(6) Y . . 1 . . 4 . .	38	2	† Ran 2 (1 short) (Wright)	58	116			15	
04	JARVIS	14			. . L 3 9 . . . 1	169						59	117		61		
07			"	15	. . 6 . . 6	175					M18	60					
11	"	15						2 . . P L 2	44		4HR	61	119			17	
15			"	16	3 . 3 x 4 . 2	181						62	121		63		
19	"	16						. . . .	50		M19	63					
22			"	17	7 . 2/1 5 . ⊙ . 4 . . .	188	10				(NB) NB 3	64	126		67		4
26	"	17			.	189		3 P . . 5 3	55			65	129			20	
30			"	18	7 . 5 2 4 . . 1	193	11	. 6 5 . 1	57			66	135		72	21	
34	"	18	(18-4-52-0)		. . . 7 P .	199					M20	67					
37			EMBUREY	5	. 2 . . 3	204		8 1	58			68	136			22	
4.40	(19-6-28-1)	19	(5-3-2-0)			204	11	5 4/5 . . 4 . . 4 . . .	64	3	M20 NB 3	69	140	2	72	26	4

1ST DAY	BOWLERS (GOODALL) SANDRINGHAM ROAD END		(McHARG) DOMINION ROAD END		BATSMEN SCOREBOARD LEFT			SCOREBOARD RIGHT			NEW ZEALAND 1ST INNINGS	END-OF-OVER TOTALS					
TIME	BOWLER	O.	BOWLER	O.	SCORING	BALLS	6s/4s	SCORING	BALLS	6s/4s	NOTES	O.	RUNS	W.	'L' BAT	'R' BAT	EXTRAS
					WRIGHT	204	11	MD CROWE	64	3	M 20 NB 3	69	140	2	72	26	4
4.44			EMBUREY	6	· · · 1 :	209		1	65			70	142		73	27	
47	CAPEL	15						· · · 2 · ·	71			71	144			29	
51			"	7	· · 44 · ·	215	13				50 p'ship: 89'	72	152		81		
55	"	16			· · ·	218		· · 1	74			73	153			30	
58			"	8	1	219		· 1 · · ·	79			74	155		82	31	
5.00 04	"	17			· 4 · · · 2	225	14					75	161		88		
08			"	9	· ·	227		· · · 1	83			76	162			32	
10	"	18			· · · · ·	232		1	84		5 HR	77	163			33	
14			"	10	· · · ·	236		· 3	86			78	166			36	
17	"	19			· 2 · ·	240		· LB	88		(LB)	79	169		90		5
21			"	11				· · · · · W	94	3	M 21	80	169	3	90	36	5
23								GREATBATCH		LHB						0	
24	"	20			· · · 1	244		· ·	2		† rain.	81	170		91		
29			"	12	4 · · · · ·	250	15					82	174		95		
31	"	21			· · · ·	255		1	3		Magpie fight on outfield.	83	175			1	
35	(21-3-44-0)		"	13				· 2 · · · ·	9			84	177			3	
38	DILLEY	14	(13-4-24-1)		· · 4 · 1	260	16	B	10		(B) WRIGHT'S 100: 327'	85	183		100		6
42			JARVIS	20				2 · · · · ·	16		† NEW BALL at 5.44 pm	86	185			5	
47	"	15			· 1	262		· · · L ·	20			87	186		101		
51			"	21	· · · · · ·	268					† Light appeal. M 22	88					
55	(16-5-34-1)	16	(21-7-30-1)			268	16	· · · · · ·	26	-	M 23	89	186	3	101	5	6
6.00	STUMPS										M 23 NB 3		STUMPS				
2ND DAY 11.00			RADFORD	19	(2) · · · · ·	275					NB 4	90	188		103		
04	DILLEY	17			W	276	16	· · · 3	30			90[5]	191	4	103	8	6
07					RUTHERFORD										0		
09	"	17			L ·	1						91					
11			"	20				· (·) · · · ·	37		(NB) NB 5 6 HR	92	192				7
15	"	18			4 · · 2 · ·	7	1					93	198		6		
19			"	21				· · · · · 2	43			94	200			10	
23	"	19			· · · · 4 1	13	2					95	205		11		
27			"	22	· · · · · 1	18		·	44			96	206		12		
31	"	20			· · · · · ·	24					M 24	97					
36			"	23	· · · ·	28		· 1	46			98	207			11	
40	"	21						· W	48	-		98[2]	207	5	12	11	7
41								BRACEWELL								0	
42	"	21			·	29		· · 1	3			99	208			1	
46			"	24	· (·) ·	32		· · · (·) 1	8		(NB) (NB) NB 7	100	211			2	9
50	"	22	(24-4-62-0)					· · · · · ·	14		M 25	101					
11.55	(22-7-49-3)		JARVIS (22-7-38-1)	22	· 1 · ·	36	2	4 3	16	1	M 25 NB 7	102	219	5	13	9	9

2ND DAY	BOWLERS (GOODALL) SANDRINGHAM ROAD END		(MCHARG) DOMINION ROAD END		BATSMEN SCOREBOARD LEFT			SCOREBOARD RIGHT			NEW ZEALAND 1ST INNINGS NOTES	END-OF-OVER TOTALS					
TIME	BOWLER	O.	BOWLER	O.	SCORING	BALLS	6s/4s	SCORING	BALLS	6s/4s	NOTES	O.	RUNS	W.	'L' BAT	'R' BAT	EXTRAS
					RUTHERFORD	36	2	BRACEWELL	16	1	M25 NB7	102	219	5	13	9	9
11.59	DILLEY	23						x · EP7 · · W	19	1		102^{3}	219	6	13	9	9
12.01	DRINKS							SMITH			Radford off for 9 balls.					0	
04	"	23						P · · ·	3		M26	103					
06			JARVIS	23	P 4 · x · 4 · · · 4 ·	42	3				(W) 7HR	104	224		17		10
11	"	24						x · · · ⊙ 2 2 ·	10		(NB) NB8	105	229			4	11
16	(24-8-54-4)		"	24	· · 3/4 1	45		· · ·	13		Dilley off for 20 min	106	230		18		
21	CAPEL	22			4 · · · · · ·	51					M27	107					
24			"	25				3 2 2 2 · · · 3 ·	19			108	234			8	
28	"	23			7/8 · 2 · · 4 8/7 4 ·	57	4					109	240		24		
32			"	26				· x 4 4/3 † 4 2 · · · 2 · 2	25		† sliding stop Fairbro'	110	244			12	
36	"	24			LB ·	58		6/5 7 † 8 7 7 4 · · · ·	30	1	(LB) † Moxon (sh.leg) hit on arm	111	249			16	12
42			"	27	1 P 2 4 · · 1	62	5	6 4 · ·	32			112	254		29		
47	"	25			x W	63	5					112^{1}	254	7	29	16	12
48					SNEDDEN		LHB								0		
50	"	25			· 3 1 · ·	4		8 1	33			113	256		1	17	
52			"	28				6 3 4 6 E1 2 · · 4 W	38	2		113^{5}	262	8	1	23	12
56								MORRISON								0	
57			"	28				:	1			114					
58	(26-4-57-1)	26	(28-7-63-2)		· P · · · 9 1	8	-	· · · ·	3	-		115	263	8	2	0	12
1.01	LUNCH										M27 NB8		L	U	N	CH	
1.40			RADFORD	25	· E1 · 2 · · · 4 8 · 1	14						116	266		5		
44	DILLEY	25			7 1	15		· · P · · ·	8			117	267		6		
49			"	26	5(4) 3	16		2 · · · · · ·	13		8 HR	118	270		9		
53	"	26			4 · · 4 · V2 4 · 3 ·	22	1					119	274		13		
57			"	27	· · 7 ⊙ 2 1	26		· · 7 3	16		(NB) NB9	120	279		14	3	13
2.01	"	27			· 14 · W	28	1					120^{2}	279	9	14	3	13
02					CHATFIELD										0		
04	"	27						· · · · 8 1	20			121	280			4	
07			"	28				· · · · ⊙ 8 2 · · · ·	27		(NB) NB10	122	283			6	14
11	"	28	(28-4-76-0)		· 2 · · · · · 7 ·	6					M28 Dilley off at 2.15 pm	123					
15	(28-9-60-5)		JARVIS	29				· · 2 2 · E1 † · · · · · 4	33	1	† chance to Gatting / Broad (slips)	124	287			10	
19	RADFORD	29			L 3 · 9 · · · 1	10		† · ·	35		† Dropped ct & b.	125	288		1		
23			"	30	· 2 · · · E1 3	15		:	36			126	291		4		
27	"	30	(30-7-70-2)		3 3 1 · · 2 · · ·	21						127	293		6		
30	(30-4-79-0)		EMBUREY	14				· · · · · ·	42		M29	128					
33	JARVIS	31			· · · · · ·	27					M30	129					
37			"	15				· · 4 † 4 · · ·	48	2	† Dropped extra-cover - Jarvis - diving	130	297			14	
40	"	32			4 · · · · ·	33	1					131	301		10		
43 46	DRINKS		"	16		33	1	· · · · · ·	54	2	M31	132					
48	"	33			· · E1 3 · · · · · · · ·	39					M32 9HR	133					
51	(33-9-74-2)		"	17				† P · · 5 · · · · · · · ·	60		† Round wkt M33	134					
54	CAPEL	27			· E1 · W	41	1		60	2	M33 NB10	134^{2}	301	10	10	14	14
2.55	(26.2-4-57-2) ALL OUT										816 balls						

2ND DAY TIME	BOWLERS (GOODALL) SANDRINGHAM ROAD END BOWLER	O.	(McHARG) DOMINION ROAD END BOWLER	O.	BATSMEN SCOREBOARD LEFT SCORING	BALLS	6s/4s	SCOREBOARD RIGHT SCORING	BALLS	6s/4s	ENGLAND 1ST INNINGS NOTES	END-OF-OVER TOTALS O.	RUNS	W.	'L' BAT	'R' BAT	EXTRAS
					BROAD		LHB	MOXON									
3.06	MORRISON	1			4/5 . . ①	3		. . 6 . .	4		NB 1	1	1		1		
11			CHATFIELD	1	. . . . . 6 .	9					M 1	2					
15	"	2			5/4 1	10		8 1E 1 . . ⊙ . .	10		(NB) NB2	3	4		2	1	1
20			"	2	8 1 8 1	12		72 21 6 . .	14			4	9		4	4	
24	"	3			LB . .	14		. . . 8 1	18		(LB)	5	11			5	2
28			"	3				. . . . . .	24		M2	6					
32	"	4			. . 6 1	17		6	27			7	12		5		
36	(4-0-6-0)		"	4	. P . . . P	23					M3	8					
39	BRACEWELL (1-0-4-0)	1	(4-3-5-0)			23	-	. . 2/1 . . 4 . PP .	33	1		9	16	0	5	9	2
3.41	TEA										M3 NB2			T	E	A	
4.01			CHATFIELD	5	7 7 7 . . 7 4	29	1					10	20		9		
04	BRACEWELL	2			.	30		. 6 . 5 7 1	38			11	21			10	
07			"	6				. . . E1L . .	44		M4	12					
11	"	3			P	36					M5	13					
13			"	7				3 1E . . P7 4 . . . 2	50	2		14	27			16	
17	"	4			L . P 4 EP . . . W	42	1				M6	15	27	1	9	16	2
19					ROBINSON										0		
20			"	8				. . . 5 . .	56		M7 1HR	16					
24	"	5			. . 3 1	3		. . .	59			17	28		1		
27			"	9	. LB .	5		. . . .	63		(LB) M8	18	29				3
30	"	6			. . . 6 1	9		. .	65			19	30		2		
33	(6-2-7-1)		"	10	. . 6S 1	12		x . .	68			20	31		3		
37	MORRISON	5			. . 7 4 . .	18	1					21	35		7		
42			"	11	. .	20		6 . . 7 1	72		Treatment on field to Moxon's wrist.	22	36			17	
47	"	6	(11-6-17-0)					. . 6 . . 9 1	78			23	37			18	
51			SNEDDEN	1	P . 9 . 4	23	2	. 5 7 1	81			24	42		11	19	
55	"	7			. 5 3 7/47 ⊙ . 4 4 3	29	4	7/8 1	82		(NB) † all-run. NB3	25	55		22	20	4
5.00 DRINKS 04			"	2	. . 7 . . .	35					M9	26					
08	"	8						7/8 . 6 . 4 2 . . . 1	88			27	58			23	
12	(8-0-27-0)		"	3				E1 4 . 4	94	3		28	62			27	
16	BRACEWELL	7			 4	41					M 10	29					
18			"	4				. . . E1/2 4 . 4 .	100	4		30	66			31	
22	"	8			. . 1	44		. 7 3	103		2HR	31	67		23		
25			"	5	4 . 4 . 8 3/3 . 4 . 2 1	50	5					32	74		30		
29	RUTHERFORD	1	(5-1-20-0)		4 . 7 4(5) . . 1	54		6 .	105			33	75		31		
32			BRACEWELL	9	. . . . 6 9 1	60					Hit by Moxon - bowler confirmed off bat	34	76		32		
35	"	2			. 8 1	62		L Y. 8/9 . 1	109		50 p'ship · 76'	35	78		33	32	
38	(2-0-3-0)		"	10				4 . 2LB 6 . 3LB	115		(2LB) (3LB) M 11	36	83				9
5.42	SNEDDEN (6-2-20-0)	6	(10-4-9-1)			62	5	. L . 5 . .	121	4	M12 NB3	37	83	1	33	32	9

2ND DAY	BOWLERS (GOODALL) SANDRINGHAM ROAD END		(McHARG) DOMINION ROAD END		BATSMEN SCOREBOARD LEFT			SCOREBOARD RIGHT			ENGLAND 1ST INNINGS NOTES	END-OF-OVER TOTALS					
TIME	BOWLER	O.	BOWLER	O.	SCORING	BALLS	6s/4s	SCORING	BALLS	6s/4s	NOTES	O.	RUNS	W.	'L' BAT	'R' BAT	EXTRAS
					ROBINSON	62	5	MOXON	121	4	M12 NB3	37	83	1	33	32	9
5.45			BRACEWELL	11	P P 9 · · 1	65		· · 6 · · 4	124	5		38	88		34	36	
48	SNEDDEN	7			· · 7 · · · 1 ·	70		1/2 1	125			39	90		35	37	
52			"	12	· P · ·	72		· · 5 8 · · · 1	129			40	91			38	
56	"	8						· · · · · 7 · · · · · 4	135	6		41	95			42	
59	(8-2-26-0)		"	13	· 2 · · P · 2 · · · ·	78	5		135	6		42	97	1	37	42	9
6.01	STUMPS		(13-4-17-1)								M12 NB3		STUMPS				
3RD DAY 11.00	MORRISON	9			· L · ·	80		· 1E 8 · · · 1	139			43	98			43	
05			CHATFIELD	12				7/8 2 · · · · · · ·	145			44	100			45	
09	"	10			· 4 · · · 4 · · · · · ·	86					M13	45					
13			"	13				· · · · · 7/8 · · · · · 2	151			46	102			47	
16	"	11			7 · · 1/2 · 4 · · ⊙ · 2	93	6				(NB) NB4	47	109		43		10
22			"	14				· · · 7 · 8 · · · · · 1	157		3HR	48	110			48	
26	"	12			· · · · 4	97		· 8 · 1	159			49	111			49	
30			"	15	8 1	98		4s · 3 1 · 4 · ·	164	7	MOXON'S 50: 185'	50	117		44	54	
34	"	13			· 4 3 6 5 7 · · 4 · · 1	104	7					51	122		49		
39			"	16	· · · · 3 · · · · · · ·	110					M14	52					
42	"	14						1E · · · EP 5 · · · · · ·	170		M15	53					
47	(14-2-41-0)		"	17	· · · · · 1	115		·	171		ROBINSON'S 50: 150'	54	123		50		
51	BRACEWELL	14			4 · 4 · · · · · · · · ·	121					M16	55					
54			"	18	· · · · · · · ·	126		8 1	172			56	124			55	
57	"	15			3 · · 5 · · · · ·	131		7 1	173			57	125			56	
59			"	19	· · · · · · · · · ·	136		3 1	174			58	126			57	
12 02 06	DRINKS "	16	(19-7-31-0)		· · ·	139		· 3 1E · 2 3	177		100 p'ship: 168'	59	131			62	
10			SNEDDEN	9				· · · P · · · · · · · ·	183		M17	60					
14	"	17			· · · 4 · · · 1	143		4 · · ·	185			61	132		51		
16			"	10	· · · 9 3/4 · · · 2 1	148		4 ·	186			62	135		54		
20	"	18			· · 4 · · W	151	7					62³	135	2	54	62	10
21					GATTING										0		
23	"	18			· · 9 · · 3	3					4HR	63	138		3		
25			"	11	· 5 · 8 · · · 1	7		· 6 · 2	188			64	141		4	64	
28	"	19			· · · · · 4B · · · · · ·	13					(4B) M18	65	145				14
31			"	12				· 6 · · · 6 · · · · · ·	194		M19	66					
34	"	20			3/2 · · · · · 2 · · · · ·	19						67	147		6		
37			"	13	· 6 · · · · 4 · · ·	24	1	8 1	195			68	152		10	65	
41	"	21			4 4 LB · 3 ·	27		4 1E 8 · 3 1	198		(LB)	69	160		13	69	15
45			"	14	· 5 2 · · 3/4 · · · · · 4	33	2					70	164		17		
49	"	22						· 7/8 · · L3 · 2 · · · ·	204			71	166			71	
51			"	15	5 X · · · · · · · · · ·	39					M20	72					
12.55	(23-6-39-2)	23	(15-5-41-0)		P ·	40	2	· · 3 · 8 · · · · 1	209	7	M20 NB4	73	167	2	17	72	15

3RD DAY	BOWLERS (GOODALL) SANDRINGHAM ROAD END		(McHARG) DOMINION ROAD END		BATSMEN SCOREBOARD LEFT			SCOREBOARD RIGHT			ENGLAND 1ST INNINGS	END-OF-OVER TOTALS					
TIME	BOWLER	O.	BOWLER	O.	SCORING	BALLS	6s/4s	SCORING	BALLS	6s/4s	NOTES	O.	RUNS	W.	'L' BAT	'R' BAT	EXTRAS
					GATTING	40	2	MOXON	209	7	M20 NB4	73	167	2	17	72	15
12.58			SNEDDEN	16		40	2	. : 4 : . :	215	7	M21	74	167	2	17	72	15
1.01	LUNCH		(16-6-41-0)								M21 NB4						
1.40	BRACEWELL	24			: . : 7 : :	46					M22	75					
42			SNEDDEN	17				: 4 . : 4 7	221		M23	76					
47	"	25			5 8 · 1 · P 9 · 1	51		4 1	222			77	170		19	73	
50			"	18	: · P : · :	57					M24	78					
53	"	26			8/7 · 1	59		4 1 · · ·	226			79	172		20	74	
56			"	19	4 · 2 · · 1	62		6 4 5 · · ·	229			80	173		21		
2.01	"	27			4 1	63		† 7/8 2 · 6 · · 1	234		† MOXON'S HS in Tests (prev 74) SHR	81	177		22	77	
04			"	20				· · 5(4) 4 · 4/3 4 ·	240	9	50 p'ship: 64'	82	185			85	
07	"	28	(20-8-50-0)		· : · 9 1 :	68		4 1	241			83	187		23	86	
11			RUTHERFORD	3	4 6 : 6 · ·	73		F7/8 1	242			84	188			87	
14	"	29			4 1 1	75		8 1 P · 8† 1 :	246		† bisected sh. legs.	85	192		25	89	
18			"	4	· : · P · P	81					M25	86					
20	"	30			· 1 2 · 4 4 P ·	86	3	3 1	247			87	199		31	90	
23			"	5				3 3 4 · · 4 4	253	10		88	203			94	
27	"	31	(5-1-8-0)		· 4 1 8 1	89		7 3 · 8 · 1	256			89	209		33	98	
30	(31-7-67-2)		CHATFIELD	20	8S 1	90		: · : · † 1E‡ 1	261		† NEW BALL (2.32pm) ‡ Dropped 2nd slip (low to BRACEWELL)	90	211		34	99	
35	MORRISON	15			: 6 P · · P	96					M26	91					
39			"	21				: 6 · X : :	267		M27	92					
42 DRINKS 46	"	16			· 3 : · · :	102					M28	93					
51			"	22				· 1E · W	269	10		93[2]	211	3	34	99	15
52								FAIRBROTHER		LHB						0	
54			"	22				: : : :	4		M29	94					
56	"	17			· · 2 4 · ⊙ 8 E1 4W	109	5				(NB) NB5	95	220	4	42	0	16
3.00					CAPEL						WRIGHT off (sub. 6HR PRINGLE)				0		
02			"	23				· · · · · ·	10		M30	96					
06	"	18			· 9/8 1	2		· · 3 · 9 1	14			97	222		1	1	
11			"	24				: 4 · : E1 W	19	-		97[5]	222	5	1	1	16
13								EMBUREY								0	
15			"	24				:	1		M31	98					
16	"	19			2 LB · ·	4		· · · 1 4	5	1	(LB)	99	227			4	17
21			"	25	: : : : : :	10					M32	100					
25	"	20			· 2LB Y · Y · · ·	14		· 9 1	7		(2LB)	101	230			5	19
30			"	26				· · · EP · · ·	13		M33	102					
34	"	21			: · 7 2 · 3 2 :	20						103	234		5		
38	(21-4-61-1)		"	27		20	-	: : : : : :	19	1	M34	104	234	5	5	5	19
3.41	TEA		(27-14-33-2)								M34 NB5			T	E	A	

3RD DAY	BOWLERS (GOODALL) SANDRINGHAM ROAD END		BOWLERS (McHARG) DOMINION ROAD END		BATSMEN SCOREBOARD LEFT			BATSMEN SCOREBOARD RIGHT			NOTES	ENGLAND 1ST INNINGS END-OF-OVER TOTALS					
TIME	BOWLER	O.	BOWLER	O.	SCORING	BALLS	6s/4s	SCORING	BALLS	6s/4s		O.	RUNS	W.	'L' BAT	'R' BAT	EXTRAS
					CAPEL	20	-	EMBUREY	19	1	M34 NB5	104	234	5	5	5	19
4.01	MORRISON	22			· · · · · E1 / · · · · · W	25	-					104⁵	234	6	5	5	19
04					FRENCH										0		
06	•	22			:	1					M35	105					
07			SNEDDEN	21	·	2		· · · 6 9 / · · · · 1	24			106	235			6	
11	•	23						· · · · · 3 / · · · · · ·	30		M36	107					
15			•	22	· · 3 · 1 3 / · · · · 4 ·	8	1					108	239		4		
19	•	24						3 4 4 5 ½ 4 / 4 · · · 2 ·	36	2	7HR	109	245			12	
25			•	23	· 6 2 / · · 1	11		· 6 · / · · ·	39			110	246		5		
28	•	25			EP 6 8 / · · 1	14		· 3 2 / · 4 ·	42	3		111	251		6	16	
32			•	24	· · P P · · / · · · · · ·	20					M37	112					
36	•	26			· · 3 · / · · 4 ·	24	2	⊙ · 8 / 1	45		(NB) NB 6	113	257		10	17	20
42			•	25	6 · E1 / · · · · · ·	29		8 / 1	46			114	258			18	
46	•	27			8 / 3 · · · · ·	33		1 1 / 1 1	48			115	263		13	20	
51	(27-6-83-2)		•	26				· · · · 8 8/7 / · · · · · ·	54		M38	116					
54	BRACEWELL	32			· · · 3 4B E1 / · · · · · W	39	2				(4B) M39	117	267	7	13	20	24
57	DRINKS				JARVIS										0		
5.01			•	27				· · · 1E · · / · · · · · ·	60		M40	118					
06	•	33			· 4 · · 4 · / · · · · 4 ·	6	1					119	271		4		
09			•	28	· · · 9 / · · · 1	10		3/4 / 1 ·	62			120	273		5	21	
13	•	34			· · · · 8 / · · · · 1	16						121	274		6		
16			•	29	· · P · · / · · · · · ·	22					M41	122					
20	•	35						8/9 3† 3 · / · 2 · · 2 ·	68		5.21pm. MD Crowe hit in face - off field.	123	278			25	
25			•	30	3 · 3 E1 / · · 4 W	26	2				8HR	123⁴	282	8	10	25	24
28					RADFORD										0		
30			•	30	· X / · ·	2						124					
32	•	36			5 P / · ·	4		L 2 6 / · · · 1	72			125	283			26	
35			•	31				3 · · · · · / · · · · · ·	78		M42	126					
39	•	37			8 / 1	5		· 7† · P / · · · · ·	83		† Near sh. leg.	127	284		1		
43			•	32	2 7 · · / 2 1 · · ·	10		2 / 1	84			128	288		4	27	
47	•	38						2 3 2 8/9 / · · 4 · · 1	90	4		129	293			32	
51			•	33				· · · E1 9 · / · · · · 4 ·	96	5		130	297			36	
55	•	39			· · 3 / · · 1	13		3 8†L / 2 2 ·	99		ENGLAND LEAD†	131	302		5	40	
58	(39-8-88-3)		•	34	· · · · · / · · · · · ·	19	-		99	5	M43 NB 6	132	302	8	5	40	24
6.01	STUMPS		(34-14-71-1)										STUMPS				

4TH DAY	BOWLERS (GOODALL) SANDRINGHAM ROAD END		(McHARG) DOMINION ROAD END		BATSMEN SCOREBOARD LEFT			SCOREBOARD RIGHT			ENGLAND 1ST INNINGS	END-OF-OVER TOTALS					
TIME	BOWLER	O.	BOWLER	O.	SCORING	BALLS	6s/4s	SCORING	BALLS	6s/4s	NOTES	O.	RUNS	W.	'L' BAT	'R' BAT	EXTRAS
					RADFORD	19	-	EMBUREY	99	5	M43 NB6	132	302	8	5	40	24
11.00	MORRISON	28			· · 3 · · 1	22		3 ① · × · · · ·	103		NB7	133	304		6	41	
06			CHATFIELD	28	LB ·	23		· · · · × · ·	108		(LB) M44	134	305				25
09	"	29			7 · · · · · × 8/7 2 ·	29						135	307		8		
14			"	29	× W	30	-	· 2 1	110			135³	308	9	8	42	25
15					DILLEY		LHB								0		
17			"	29	P · · · · ·	3						136					
19	"	30						· · · · P · · · ·	116		M45 9HR	137					
23			"	30	· P 8 · · · · 4 2	9						138	310		2		
28	"	31						· · · · · · · · 4B 2 1	122		(4B)	139	315			43	29
32			"	31				· · · · 3 · · 9 1	128			140	316			44	
36	"	32			3 1 2 4	11	1	· · · · 3 1	132			141	323		8	45	
41	(32-7-95-2)		"	32		11	1	2 W	133	5		141¹	323	10	8	45	29
11.41	ALL OUT		(31.1-15-37-4)								M45 NB 7		ALL OUT				
											854 balls						

4TH DAY	BOWLERS (McHARG) SANDRINGHAM ROAD END		(GOODALL) DOMINION ROAD END		BATSMEN SCOREBOARD LEFT			SCOREBOARD RIGHT			NEW ZEALAND 2ND INNINGS	END-OF-OVER TOTALS					
TIME	BOWLER	O.	BOWLER	O.	SCORING	BALLS	6s/4s	SCORING	BALLS	6s/4s	NOTES	O.	RUNS	W.	'L' BAT	'R' BAT	EXTRAS
					FRANKLIN			WRIGHT		LHB							
11.52	DILLEY	1			8 . : . 1	4		: :	2			1	1		1		
56			JARVIS	1	3 1	10						2	2		2		
12.00	"	2			LB . .	12		½† . 4 . .	6	1	(LB) † WRIGHT 1000 R v ENG.	3	7			4	1
04			"	2	. P . . : . . .	18					M1	4					
08	"	3						7/8 : 1	12			5	8			5	
13			"	3				: : : : : :	18		M2	6					
18	"	4			9 1 : : .	22		9 . 1	20			7	10		3	6	
22			"	4				L : : : : . .	26		M3	8					
26	"	5			7 4 2 : . . 3	27		1 1	27			9	16		8	7	
31	(5-0-14-0)		"	5				7 : : . : : 2	33			10	18			9	
35	RADFORD	1	(5-3-3-0)		5(6) 3	28		: . : : :	38			11	21		11		
39			EMBUREY	1	7 . : : : : :	34					M4	12					
41	"	2						5(4) . 4 : . . 2 . .	44			13	23			11	
45			"	2	. 4/5 2 : 4 3	37	1	: : :	47			14	30		18		
48	"	3			7 1	38		: : : : : :	52		1HR	15	31		19		
51			"	3	3 . 3	40		. . . .	56			16	34		22		
53	"	4			8 x 7 2 . 1	43		⊙ . . .	60		(NB) NB1	17	38		25		2
58	(4-0-10-0)		"	4	. P . . P : : : : : :	49	1		60	1	M5	18	38	0	25	11	2
1.00	LUNCH		(4-2-10-0)								M5 NB1		L	U	N	C	H
1.40	DILLEY	6						: : : : : :	66		M6	19					
43			EMBUREY	5	8 : 1	51		x 3 : : . .	70			20	39		26		
46	"	7			. . . . E1† . . . . . :	57					† Dropped 4th slip M7 (JARVIS)	21					
51			"	6				: . . . : . .	76		M8	22					
53	"	8			: 7 : 7 : . : 2 . .	63						23	41		28		
58			"	7				8 : . . : : 1	82			24	42			12	
2.00	"	9						S P : . : . 2 :	88			25	44			14	
03			"	8	: : : : : :	69					M9	26					
06	"	10						. 8 : 4 . : : .	94	2		27	48			18	
10	(10-2-22-0)		"	9	6 5 : : . : (4) .	76	2				NB2 5op'slip: 101'	28	52		32		
14	JARVIS	6			4 x 8 . 4 . 1	80	3	7 1 .	96			29	58		37	19	
18			"	10	4 S : . : : : :	86					M10	30					
21	"	7			P . :	88		L 2 LB : . 2 :	100		(LB)	31	61			21	3
25			"	11				6 . : : . : .	106		M11	32					
27	"	8			LB : . :	91		. . .	109		(LB) M12 2HR	33	62				4
31			"	12	4 1	92		. : : : :	114			34	63		38		
34	"	9			9 . 1	94		4 2 . : :	118			35	66		39	23	
38			"	13	P . . 4 : : : : : :	100					M13	36					
40 DRINKS 43	"	10						: : : . : :	124		M14	37					
2.48	(10-5-14-0)		(14-8-17-0)	14	. . . . . .	106	3		124	2	M15 NB 2	38	66	0	39	23	4

4TH DAY	BOWLERS (McHARG) SANDRINGHAM ROAD END		(GOODALL) DOMINION ROAD END		BATSMEN SCOREBOARD LEFT			SCOREBOARD RIGHT			NEW ZEALAND 2ND INNINGS	END-OF-OVER TOTALS					
TIME	BOWLER	O.	BOWLER	O.	SCORING	BALLS	6s/4s	SCORING	BALLS	6s/4s	NOTES	O.	RUNS	W.	'L' BAT	'R' BAT	EXTRAS
					FRANKLIN	106	3	WRIGHT	124	2	M15 NB2	38	66	0	39	23	4
2.50	JARVIS	11						· · · 1 / · · · · 4 ·	130	3	GATTING off (3 overs) sub ATHEY	39	70			27	
54			EMBUREY	15	8 4 6 P · / 2 · 4 · · ·	112	4					40	76		45	·	
56	"	12						· · 7 · 4 3 / · · 4 · 2 1	136	4		41	83			34	
3.01	(12-5-25-0)		"	16				· · · · · / · · · · · ·	142		M16	42					
03	CAPEL	1			· 4 · · · 6 / · · · · · ·	118					M17	43					
09			"	17				· 2 2 · · / · · · · · ·	148		M18	44					
12	"	2			6 9E† 7 · · / · · 4 · · ·	124	5				† chinese cut.	45	87		49		
16			"	18	· 9/8 · / · · 2 ·	128		· 1 / · 1	150		FRANKLIN'S 50: 166'	46	90		51	35	
19	"	3			2 / · 1	130		· · · LB / · · · ·	154		(LB)	47	92		52		5
24			"	19	4 · 4 4 / · · · 1	134		· · / · ·	156			48	93		53		
26	"	4			· · 5(4) · · / · · 4 · · ·	140	6				3HR	49	97		57		
30			"	20	5 / ·	141		· · · · 7 / · · · · · 1	161			50	98			36	
33	"	5	(20-10-28-0)		8 1 / 2 1	143		· · · 3† / · · · 1	165		† Dropped cover (Moxon) 100 p'ship: 185'	51	102		60	37	
39	(5-1-13-0)		GATTING	1	· 1 · 3 / · 2 · · · ·	149	6		165	4		52	104	0	62	37	5
3.41	TEA		(1-0-2-0)								M18 NB2			T	E	A	
4.01	DILLEY	11			6 · · / · · · · · ·	154		1/2 / 1	166			53	105			38	
06			RADFORD	5	· ·	156		7 · L 6 / 4 ⊙ · · 1	171	5	(NB) NB3	54	111			43	6
10	"	12						2 P 3 4 / · · · 4 · 1	177	6		55	116			48	
15			"	6				· 4 3 6 3 / · · · ⊙ · · ·	184		(NB) NB4	56	117				7
19	"	13			X / W	157	6					56'	117	1	62	48	7
					JJ CROWE										0		
21	"	13			· · · / · · · · · ·	5					M19	57					
24			"	7	· · 8 / · · 1	8		†8 · E1 / 1 · W	187	6		58	119	2	1	49	7
27								MD CROWE								0	
29	"	14			P · 1E · L / · · · · · W	14	–				M20	59	119	3	1	0	7
32					GREATBATCH		LHB								0		
34			"	8				6 · · · / · · · · · ·	6		M21	60					
38	"	15			· † / · · · · · ·	6					† Hit on box. M22	61					
43			"	9				L · · / · · · · · ·	12		M23	62					
46	"	16			1 / 1	7		3 P L · · / 4 · · · · ·	17	1	4HR	63	124		1	4	
51			"	10	· 8 / · 1	9		P · 5 / · · 4 ·	21	2		64	129		2	8	
55	"	17			· · · · / · · · · · ·	15					M24	65					
59	(17-6-33-2)		"	11				· · · · · 3 6/5 / · · · · · 4	27	3		66	133			12	
5.02 DRINKS 05	EMBUREY	21			P 4 6 5 · · / · · · · · ·	21					M25	67					
08			"	12				4 1 · · · · 8 / 4 (4) · · · · 1	34	5	NB5	68	142			21	
13	"	22			· · P / · · · ·	25		· 7 / · 1	36			69	143			22	
16	(22-11-29-0)		"	13				· · · 5 5 · / · · · · · ·	42		M26	70					
20	JARVIS	13	(13-3-37-1)		9 / 1 ·	27		3 · 4 / 2 · · 1	46			71	147		3	25	
5.25	(13-5-29-0)		EMBUREY (23-12-29-0)	23		27	–	· · · · · / · · · · · ·	52	5	M27 NB5	72	147	3	3	25	7

4TH DAY	BOWLERS (McHARG) SANDRINGHAM ROAD END		(GOODALL) DOMINION ROAD END		BATSMEN SCOREBOARD LEFT			SCOREBOARD RIGHT			NEW ZEALAND 2ND INNINGS	END-OF-OVER TOTALS					
TIME	BOWLER	O.	BOWLER	O.	SCORING	BALLS	6s/4s	SCORING	BALLS	6s/4s	NOTES	O.	RUNS	W.	'L' BAT	'R' BAT	EXTRAS
					GREATBATCH	27	-	MD CROWE	52	5	M27 NB5	72	147	3	3	25	7
5·27	JARVIS	14			9 1	28		. . 4 . LB	57		(LB)	73	149		4		8
31			EMBUREY	24	. . . . . .	33		7 1	58			74	150			26	
35	"	15						L W	59	5		74¹	150	4	4	26	8
35								RUTHERFORD								0	
37	"	15						. . 2 L	5		M28	75					
40			"	25	. . . . . P	39					M29	76					
43	"	16			. P 2 . . 1	42		. . 8 1	8			77	152		5	1	
46			"	26	P	48					M30	78					
49	"	17			. . . . .	51		. . 2 1	11		5HR	79	153			2	
52			"	27				. . . . x W	16	-		79⁵	153	5	5	2	8
54								SNEDDEN		LHB						0	
56			"	27				.	1		M31	80					
57	" (18-6-34-1)	18	(27-15-30-1)		. . . 2 1	54	-	. . .	4	-		81	154	5	6	0	8
6·00	STUMPS										M31 NB5		STUMPS				
5TH DAY 11·00			EMBUREY	28	. . . . . .	60					M32	82					
02	DILLEY	18						. . . . . .	10		M33	83					
07			"	29	. . . . . .	66					M34	84					
09	"	19						x . . 8	16		M35	85					
13			"	30	. . . 1 2 . .	72						86	156		8		
16	"	20	(30-17-32-1)		. 9/8 1	74		† LB . . 9 . 4	20	1	† NEW BALL (LB)	87	162		9	4	9
21			JARVIS	19	. 7 1	77		. . 4(5) . . 1	23			88	164		10	5	
25	"	21						. . L 1	29		M36	89					
29			"	20	. 7 . 1	79		L	33			90	165		11		
33	"	22			. . . . 9 1	84		.	34			91	166		12		
37			"	21	. 7 . 2 . EP L	90						92	168		14		
41	"	23			6 4 3 4 . .	93	1	9 . 8 1	37			93	173		18	6	
45	(23-9-44-2)		"	22				. . . . . .	43		M37 6HR	94					
50	RADFORD	14	(22-7-39-1)		4	99					M38	95					
54			EMBUREY	31				P . . P . P	49		M39	96					
56	"	15			⊙ 1 . . .	104		x 3 . 1	51		(NB) NB6	97	176		19	7	10
12·00 03	DRINKS		"	32				P	57		M40	98					
06	"	16			7 2 . P . . .	110						99	178		21		
09			"	33	. . . P	113		L P 8 . . 1	60			100	179			8	
13	"	17			. . 7 1	116		. . 3 . . 1	63			101	181		22	9	
17			"	34	5 4 . . x . . .	122	2					102	185		26		
19	"	18			. . 2 . . 1	125		. . 2/3 . . 1	66			103	187		27	10	
22			"	35	. 4 . . . 7/6 4⊙ .	132	3				(NB) NB7	104	192		31		11
25	"	19	(35-19-42-1)					7 . . . 6 (2) . .	73		NB8	105	194			12	
12·30	(19-4-48-1)		JARVIS	23	4 5 8 4 . 1	135	4	. 3 . . .	76	1	M40 NB8	106	199	5	36	12	11

5TH DAY	BOWLERS (McHARG) SANDRINGHAM ROAD END		(GOODALL) DOMINION ROAD END		BATSMEN SCOREBOARD LEFT			SCOREBOARD RIGHT			NEW ZEALAND 2ND INNINGS	END-OF-OVER TOTALS					
TIME	BOWLER	O.	BOWLER	O.	SCORING	BALLS	6s/4s	SCORING	BALLS	6s/4s	NOTES	O.	RUNS	W.	'L' BAT	'R' BAT	EXTRAS
					GREATBATCH	135	4	SNEDDEN	76	1	M40 NB8	106	199	5	36	12	11
12.34	RADFORD	20			: 1 (6)	137		: : . 4 (3 x E1)	80	2	50 p'ship: 102'	107	204		37	16	
38	(20-4-53-1)		JARVIS	24	2 : . . . : (7 P)	143						108	206		39		
42	EMBUREY	36			. 1 (P 6)	145		. : . 1 (E1 : 7)	84			109	208		40	17	
45			"	25	: . . . . 1 (2B . 4 1E)	150		:	85		(2B)	110	211		41		13
50	"	37			: : : . : 1 (P 8)	156					7HR	111	212		42		
52			"	26	4 : : : . : (4 7 5†)	162	5				† Ro appeal (Jarvis)	112	216		46		
57	"	38			: : : : : :	167		1 (7)	86			113	217			18	
59	(38-19-46-1)		"	27	. 2 : : : (7 6 4)	172	5	1 (9)	87	2		114	220	5	48	19	13
1.02	LUNCH		(27-7-54-1)								M40 NB8		L	U	N	CH	
1.41	CAPEL	6						: : . : . : (P)	93		M41	115					
46			EMBUREY	39	: : . . : : (4)	178					M42	116					
48	"	7			1 (8)	179		: . . . 1 (8)	98			117	222		49	20	
52			"	40	: : : : : : (x)	185					M43	118					
54	"	8						: . : . : : (L)	104		M44	119					
58			"	41	: 1 (7)	187		. : : .	108		GREATBATCH'S 50: 226'	120	223		50		
2.01	"	9			: : . : . 1 (P 7 8)	193						121	224		51		
05			"	42	: . 1 (6)	196		: : :	111			122	225		52		
08	"	10			4 : : . 1 (6 7†)	201	6	:	112		† Ro attempt (JARVIS)	123	230		57		
12			"	43	: : : : 2 . (6 4)	207						124	232		59		
14	"	11						: . W (E1)	115	2		124 (3)	232	6	59	20	13
16								BRACEWELL								0	
17	"	11						: . (X L)	3		M45	125					
20			"	44	: 4 1 (6 6)	210	7	(.) 2 . : (2)	7		(NB) NB9	126	240		64	2	14
24	"	12			: : : . (LB)	214		2 . (2)	9		(LB)	127	243			4	15
29			"	45	: : : . : : (x)	220					M46 8HR	128					
31	"	13			:	221		. : : . 1 (6 7)	14			129	244			5	
35			"	46	: : .	224		: . 1 (3)	17			130	245			6	
38	"	14			: 1 (5)	226		: 1 . 1 (7 5)	21			131	248		65	8	
43			"	47				2 : . : . : (2 6)	27			132	250			10	
49	"	15	(47-22-61-1)		. 1 . : (1/7 2B)	230		. 1 (8)	29		(2B)	133	254		66	11	17
54			GATTING	2				: . . 4 . : (P 1)	35	1		134	258			15	
58	"	16			: 1 (2)	232		. : : 1 (8)	39			135	260		67	16	
3.03			"	3				. : : . : . (P)	45		M47	136					
06	"	17			: : . 2 : . (2/3 x)	238						137	262		69		
09			"	4				. : . : . : (L P)	51		M48	138					
12	"	18			1 (7)	239		. : . . : :	56			139	263		70		
17			"	5	: : . 1 (6 8)	243		: :	58			140	264		71		
20	"	19			4 . : . . : (1† 7 L)	249	8				† Dropped 1st slip (EMBUREY)	141	268		75		
3.24	(19-4-38-1)		(6-2-10-0)	6	: : . : . :	254	8	: (3)	60	1	NB 10 M48	142	271	6	75	19	17

5TH DAY	BOWLERS (McHARG) SANDRINGHAM ROAD END		(GOODALL) DOMINION ROAD END		BATSMEN SCOREBOARD LEFT			SCOREBOARD RIGHT			NOTES	NEW ZEALAND 2ND INNINGS END-OF-OVER TOTALS					
TIME	BOWLER	O.	BOWLER	O.	SCORING	BALLS	6s/4s	SCORING	BALLS	6s/4s		O.	RUNS	W.	'L' BAT	'R' BAT	EXTRAS
					GREATBATCH	254	8	BRACEWELL	60	1	M48 NB 10	142	271	6	75	19	17
3.28	CAPEL	20						: : : : · 1 (2)	66		9HR	143	272			20	
32			GATTING	7	: : · :	258		· 3 (6)	68			144	275			23	
36	(21-4-40-1)	21	(7-2-13-0)		· (x)	259	8	2 : · · · 1 (2)	73	1		145	276	6	75	24	17
3.40	TEA										M48 NB 10			T	E	A	
4.01			GATTING	8				· 2 (7) · : (6) : :	79			146	278			26	
05	EMBUREY	48			: · : · : · (6)	265					M 49	147					
07			"	9				2 (9) : (4) · · : :	85			148	280			28	
10	"	49			: : · 1 (7/8) : (7)	269		: 1 (2)	87		50 p'ship: 94'	149	282		76	29	
13			"	10				: : : : 2 (7) :	93			150	284			31	
16	"	50			1 (6) · : :	273		: 1 (2/3)	95			151	286		77	32	
19			"	11	· 1 (4)	275		: 1 (3) (x) : :	99			152	288		78	33	
23	"	51			(7) : · : (4) · : ·	281					M50	153					
25			"	12	2 (5)	282		: · 2 (3) : 1 (4)	104			154	293		80	36	
29	"	52				283		: : · · 1 (7/8)	109			155	294			37	
31			"	13	1 (4)	284		1 (2/3) · W (L)	112	1		155 (4)	296	7	81	38	17
33								SMITH								0	
35			"	13				· 4 (4)	2	1		156	300			4	
36	"	53			: : : (7) · : 4 (6)	290	9					157	304		85		
39			"	14				(L) : · : 2 · 2 :	8		M 51	158					
42	"	54			1 (6)	291		2 : : L : :	13			159	305		86		
44			"	15	P 7 · LB : : :	295		: (2) :	15		(LB) M52	160	306				18
48	"	55			2 (1) : · 4 (3) 1 (6) ·	301	10	(3)	16		NB 11 10HR	161	316		93	7	
52			"	16				: · 4 (4) : (2) : :	22	2		162	320			11	
55	"	56			: : 4 (8) : : :	307	11					163	324		97		
58			"	17				4 (7) · : (2) : : :	28	3		164	328			15	
5.01 / 05	DRINKS "	57	(17-4-40-1)		: : 4 (7 7) · 2 (8) :	313	12				GREATBATCH'S 100: 392 min	165	334		103		
07	(57-24-91-1)		FAIRBROTHER	1				2 : · 4 (4/3†) 4 (7) : :	34	5	† 1000 R for NZ (WK DOUBLE)	166	342			23	
11	MOXON	1			(7) : · : (2) · 1 (2)	319						167	343		104		
15			"	2	1 (8)	320		(2) : · (4B) : (3) :	39		(4B) 50 p'ship: 42'	168	348		105		22
18	(2-0-3-0)	2	(2-0-9-0)		(2) : · · 2 (2/3) : :	326	12		39	5		169	350	7	107	23	22
5.21	DECLARATION										M52 NB 11		DECLARED				
											1025 balls		MATCH DRAWN				

NEW ZEALAND 1ST INNINGS v ENGLAND (SECOND TEST) at EDEN PARK, AUCKLAND on 25, 26, 27, 28, 29 FEBRUARY, 1988

IN	OUT	MINS	No.	BATSMAN	HOW OUT	BOWLER	RUNS	WKT	TOTAL	6s	4s	BALLS	NOTES ON DISMISSAL TOSS: ENGLAND.
11.00	11.07	353	1	J.G. WRIGHT	CT FRENCH	DILLEY	103	4	191	·	16	276	Edged low to 'keeper's left.
11.00	2.13	139	2	T.J. FRANKLIN	BOWLED	JARVIS	27	1	77	·	3	107	Off stump – bowled through 'gate'.
2.15	3.02	47	3	J.J. CROWE *	CT CAPEL	DILLEY	11	2	98	·	1	42	Edged to 4th slip. Ball lifted sharply.
3.04	5.23	119	4	M.D. CROWE	CT CAPEL	EMBUREY	36	3	169	·	3	94	Pulled ball from outside off stump to mid-wicket.
5.24	11.41	77	5	M.J. GREATBATCH	CT FRENCH	DILLEY	11	5	207	·	·	48	Involuntary edge – tried to remove bat.
11.09	12.48	99	6	K.R. RUTHERFORD	BOWLED	CAPEL	29	7	254	·	5	63	Misjudged line.
11.42	12.01	19	7	J.G. BRACEWELL	CT MOXON	DILLEY	9	6	219	·	1	19	Bat/pad catch to short square-leg.
12.04	12.56	52	8	I.D.S. SMITH †	CT FRENCH	JARVIS	23	8	262	·	2	38	Edged push at widish ball.
12.50	2.02	33	9	M.C. SNEDDEN	CT MOXON	DILLEY	14	9	279	·	1	28	Miscued hook to mid-off.
12.57	(2.55)	79	10	D.K. MORRISON	NOT OUT		14			·	2	60	
2.04	2.55	51	11	E.J. CHATFIELD	CT FRENCH	CAPEL	10	10	301	·	1	41	Defensive edge – 'walked'.
				EXTRAS	b 1 lb 2	w 2 nb 9	14			-6	354	816 balls (inc 10 no-balls)	

* CAPTAIN † WICKET-KEEPER

TOTAL (134.2 OVERS; 542 MINUTES) 301 ALL OUT at 2.55 pm on 2nd day.

14 OVERS 5 BALLS/HOUR
2.24 RUNS/OVER
36 RUNS/100 BALLS

UMPIRES: F.R. GOODALL and R.L. McHARG.

BOWLER	O	M	R	W	nb/w
DILLEY	28	9	60	5	2/-
JARVIS	33	9	74	2	-/1
RADFORD	30	4	79	0	8/1
CAPEL	26.2	4	57	2	-
EMBUREY	17	7	28	1	-
			3		
	134.2	33	301	10	

2ND NEW BALL taken at 5.44 pm 1st day – NEW ZEALAND 185-3 after 85.1 overs

HRS	OVERS	RUNS
1	15	29
2	15	34
3	14	26
4	17	30
5	16	44
6	15	29
7	12	32
8	14	46
9	15	31

RUNS	MINS	OVERS	LAST 50 (in mins)
50	102	25.2	102
100	192	47	90
150	280	71.4	88
200	369	94	89
250	448	111.1	79
300	527	130.1	79

LUNCH:	50-0	[26 OVERS 104 MIN]	WRIGHT 30* FRANKLIN 17*
TEA:	111-2	[57 OVERS 226 MIN]	WRIGHT 60* (226') MD CROWE 10* (36')
STUMPS: (1ST DAY)	186-3	[89 OVERS 346 MIN]	WRIGHT 101* (346') GREATBATCH 5* (36')
LUNCH:	263-8	[115 OVERS 467 MIN]	SNEDDEN 2* (11') MORRISON 0* (4')

WKT	PARTNERSHIP		RUNS	MINS
1st	Wright	Franklin	77	139
2nd	Wright	JJ Crowe	21	47
3rd	Wright	MD Crowe	71	119
4th	Wright	Greatbatch	22	43
5th	Greatbatch	Rutherford	16	32
6th	Rutherford	Bracewell	12	19
7th	Rutherford	Smith	35	44
8th	Smith	Snedden	8	6
9th	Snedden	Morrison	17	26
10th	Morrison	Chatfield	22	51
			301	

ENGLAND 1ST INNINGS (IN REPLY TO NEW ZEALAND'S 301 ALL OUT)

IN	OUT	MINS	No.	BATSMAN	HOW OUT	BOWLER	RUNS	WKT	TOTAL	6s	4s	BALLS	NOTES ON DISMISSAL
3.06	4.19	53	1	B.C. BROAD	CT M.D. CROWE	BRACEWELL	9	1	27	·	1	42	Edged via pad to silly point.
3.06	2.52	348	2	M.D. MOXON	CT J.J. CROWE	CHATFIELD	99	3	211	·	10	269	Edged to 1st slip.
4.20	12.21	182	3	R.T. ROBINSON	CT MORRISON	BRACEWELL	54	2	135	·	7	151	Skied drive to mid-off.
12.23	3.00	118	4	M.W. GATTING*	CT SMITH	MORRISON	42	4	220	·	5	109	Edged lifting away-seamer.
2.54	3.13	19	5	N.H. FAIRBROTHER	CT SMITH	CHATFIELD	1	5	222	·	·	19	Edged away-seamer.
3.02	4.04	42	6	D.J. CAPEL	CT BRACEWELL	MORRISON	5	6	234	·	·	25	Edged to 2nd slip.
3.15	11.41	187	7	J.E. EMBUREY	CT SMITH	CHATFIELD	45	10	323	·	5	133	Edged offside swish.
4.06	4.57	51	8	B.N. FRENCH †	CT FRANKLIN	BRACEWELL	13	7	267	·	2	39	Edged off-break via pad to slip.
5.01	5.28	27	9	P.W. JARVIS	CT SMITH	SNEDDEN	10	8	282	·	2	26	Edged lifting ball.
5.30	11.15	46	10	N.V. RADFORD	BOWLED	CHATFIELD	8	9	308	·	·	30	Beaten by breakback.
11.17	(11.41)	24	11	G.R. DILLEY	NOT OUT		8			·	1	11	
				EXTRAS	b 12 lb 12 w - nb 5		29			-6	334	854 balls (inc 7 no-balls)	

* CAPTAIN † WICKET-KEEPER

TOTAL (141.1 OVERS; 558 MINUTES) 323 ALL OUT at 11.41 am on 4th day

15 OVERS 1 BALLS/HOUR
2.28 RUNS/OVER
37 RUNS/100 BALLS

BOWLER	O	M	R	W	nb
MORRISON	32	7	95	2	7
CHATFIELD	31.1	15	37	4	-
BRACEWELL	39	3	88	3	·
SNEDDEN	34	14	71	1	·
RUTHERFORD	5	1	8	0	·
			24		
	141.1	45	323	10	

2ND NEW BALL taken at 2.32pm 3rd day – ENGLAND 209-2 after 89.4 overs

HRS	OVERS	RUNS
1	16	27
2	15	40
3	17	43
4	15	28
5	18	39
6	14	43
7	14	25
8	14	33
9	14	30

RUNS	MINS	OVERS	LAST 50 (in mins)
50	93	24.5	93
100	160	43.1	67
150	254	67.3	94
200	323	88	69
250	427	110.5	104
300	513	130.4	86

TEA: 16-0	9 OVERS 35 MIN	BROAD 5* MOXON 9*	
STUMPS (2ND DAY): 97-1	42 OVERS 155 MIN	MOXON 42* (155') ROBINSON 37* (101')	
LUNCH: 167-2	74 OVERS 276 MIN	MOXON 72* (276') GATTING 17* (38')	
TEA: 234-5	104 OVERS 397 MIN	CAPEL 5* (39') EMBUREY 5* (26')	
STUMPS (3RD DAY): 302-8	132 OVERS 517 MIN	EMBUREY 40* (146') RADFORD 5* (31')	

ENGLAND LEAD BY 22 RUNS

WKT	PARTNERSHIP		RUNS	MINS
1st	Broad	Moxon	27	53
2nd	Moxon	Robinson	108	182
3rd	Moxon	Gatting	76	110
4th	Gatting	Fairbrother	9	6
5th	Fairbrother	Capel	2	11
6th	Capel	Emburey	12	29
7th	Emburey	French	33	51
8th	Emburey	Jarvis	15	27
9th	Emburey	Radford	26	46
10th	Emburey	Dilley	15	24
			323	

NEW ZEALAND 2ND INNINGS (22 RUNS BEHIND ON FIRST INNINGS)

IN	OUT	MINS	No.	BATSMAN	HOW OUT	BOWLER	RUNS	WKT	TOTAL	6s	4s	BALLS	NOTES ON DISMISSAL
11.52	4.19	207	1	T.J. FRANKLIN	BOWLED	DILLEY	62	1	117	·	6	157	Played across slower ball.
11.52	4.27	215	2	J.G. WRIGHT	CT FRENCH	RADFORD	49	2	119	·	6	187	Edged ball angled across him.
4.21	4.32	11	3	J.J. CROWE *	LBW	DILLEY	1	3	119	·	·	14	Offered no stroke to slower ball.
4.29	5.35	66	4	M.D. CROWE	LBW	JARVIS	26	4	150	·	5	59	Misjudged 'lbw' to ball missing leg stump.
4.34	(5.21)	407	5	M.J. GREATBATCH	NOT OUT		107			·	12	326	HUNDRED ON TEST DEBUT.
5.37	5.54	17	6	K.R. RUTHERFORD	BOWLED	EMBUREY	2	5	153	·	·	16	Misjudged 'arm' ball - off stump.
5.56	2.16	161	7	M.C. SNEDDEN	CT FRENCH	CAPEL	20	6	232	·	2	115	Edged push to 'keeper.
2.17	4.33	115	8	J.G. BRACEWELL	LBW	GATTING	38	7	296	·	1	112	Played across slower ball.
4.35	(5.21)	46	9	I.D.S. SMITH †	NOT OUT		23			·	5	39	
			10										
			11										
				EXTRAS	b 8 lb 8 w - nb 6		22			-6	37 4	1025 balls (inc 11 no-balls)	

* CAPTAIN † WICKET-KEEPER

TOTAL (169 OVERS; 629 MINUTES) 350-7 DECLARED at 5.21 pm on 5th day.

16 OVERS 1 BALLS/HOUR
2.07 RUNS/OVER
34 RUNS/100 BALLS

BOWLER	O	M	R	W	nb
DILLEY	23	9	44	2	-
JARVIS	27	7	54	1	-
RADFORD	20	4	53	1	6
EMBUREY	57	24	91	1	4
CAPEL	21	4	40	1	-
GATTING	17	4	40	1	1
FAIRBROTHER	2	0	9	0	-
MOXON	2	0	3	0	-
	169	52	350	7	16

2ND NEW BALL taken at 11.16 am on 5th day - NEW ZEALAND 156-5 after 86 overs.

HRS	OVERS	RUNS
1	15	31
2	18	31
3	16	35
4	14	27
5	16	29
6	15	20
7	17	39
8	17	31
9	15	29
10	18	44

RUNS	MINS	OVERS	LAST 50 (in mins)
50	101	27.5	101
100	185	50.5	84
150	279	73.1	94
200	403	106.2	124
250	492	131.1	89
300	584	156	92
350	628	168.4	44

LUNCH : 38-0	18 OVERS 68 MIN	FRANKLIN 25* WRIGHT 11*
TEA : 104-0	52 OVERS 189 MIN	FRANKLIN 62* WRIGHT 37*
STUMPS (4TH DAY) : 154-5	81 OVERS 308 MIN	GREATBATCH 6* (86) SNEDDEN 0* (4')
LUNCH : 220-5	114 OVERS 430 MIN	GREATBATCH 48* (208) SNEDDEN 19* (126)
TEA : 276-6	145 OVERS 549 MIN	GREATBATCH 75* (327) BRACEWELL 24* (83)

MATCH DRAWN

MATCH AWARD : J.G. WRIGHT

WKT	PARTNERSHIP		RUNS	MINS
1st	Franklin	Wright	117	207
2nd	Wright	JJ Crowe	2	6
3rd	JJ Crowe	MD Crowe	0	3
4th	MD Crowe	Greatbatch	31	61
5th	Greatbatch	Rutherford	3	17
6th	Greatbatch	Snedden	79	161
7th	Greatbatch	Bracewell	64	115
8th	Greatbatch	Smith	54*	46
			350	

WELLINGTON
THE THIRD TEST

Ian Walter · Wellington · The Basin Reserve, scene of England's first defeat by New Zealand · Anniversary of Durban's infamous Timeless Test · Match report · Welcome Cyclone Bola

It is impossible for me to visit New Zealand, particularly Wellington where I used to stay as his house guest, without remembering Ian Walter, a remarkable and humorous man with an abiding love for sport and for his country.

He was a qualified librarian with an MA degree, a regular contributor to the New Zealand *Listener*, a single-figure handicap golfer, an expert on hockey, and the author of a book on soccer. In between he ran several marathons, survived a shipwreck and revolutionized New Zealand's television coverage of cricket and golf.

Cricket was Ian's abiding passion and, as an off-spin bowler and left-handed batsman, he represented Canterbury and Wellington 'B' teams in addition to captaining New Zealand Universities on a tour of Australia. As New Zealand's official scorer in England in 1973 he played in a one-day game against Scotland, but was destined never to play first-class cricket, although Wellington once selected him shortly before he fractured a bone in his foot. During a net practice at Lord's before the start of that tour, Jim Laker had his first sight of the visitors and was immediately impressed with a youngster flighting his off-breaks to Glenn Turner. It was Ian. 'I should let someone else do the scoring,' Laker suggested laconically.

Ian Walter skippered a tyro called Richard Hadlee at Christchurch Boys' High School and led Jeremy Coney at the Wellington Club, Onslow. He had been Graham Dowling's opening partner in Christchurch.

Dowling's pads accompanied him aboard the *Wahine* when it sailed from Lyttelton harbour, Christchurch, bound for Wellington in 1968. In the early hours of 10 April, the 8,948-ton ferry, a steamer express and pride of the Union Steam Ship Company's fleet, battled her way northwards from Cook Strait into Chaffers Passage, the narrow entrance leading to Wellington Harbour. Suddenly the ship was struck by a storm of unprecedented ferocity; gales whipped the sea into steep waves and reduced visibility to zero. The radar system was put out of action and the ship struck Barrett Reef, a chain of rocks in the centre of the passage. By now her engines were out of action; severely holed, she drifted a few hundred yards before foundering off Fort Dorset.

In violent conditions, Ian swam two-thirds of a mile to the eastern shore. Only his exceptional stamina had enabled him to combat those mountainous seas and survive a disaster in which 51 people lost their lives. Describing the experience many years later, he said that the incident he recalled most vividly was of a baby being thrown from the ship to rescuers in a lifeboat, only for a large wave to lift the boat out of reach as the child was in mid-air.

He joined NZBC (now TVNZ) in 1974 as a sports researcher. By the 1979-80 season he was in charge of cricket. It was he who introduced the pitch microphones much maligned by England's management. Among his other innovations were camera cover from both ends and a system of computer scoring then far in advance of that used in Australia.

Perhaps his only misguided experiment was to invite me to join his commentary team for England's 1983-84 tour. When I photographed commentator Glenn Turner slumbering contentedly in the commentary box, Ian startled the victim by putting the shot on air while he was actually talking – several times. He also encouraged me to suggest to Turner that Jeremy Coney's mother had invented radio (Ma Coney).

Surprisingly, I was asked back two years later.

In 1984 Ian married Sally Guinness, who had been his PA during his early years as a producer. They enjoyed just one blissful year of marriage before he collapsed with cancer of the sinuses. Three weeks after brain surgery he won the match, top-scoring and taking 3 for 8, in an annual game between the TVNZ staff of Auckland and Wellington, a fixture which he had himself instituted five years earlier.

Later that year, after massive radiotherapy, he covered the Commonwealth Games in Edinburgh, scored an unbeaten century for my Maltamaniacs in Farnham's Cricket Week, and went hiking around the Swiss Alps with his wife and Glenn Turner's golfing brother, Greg. He returned to Wellington, relapsed, lost his sight and, nursed by Sally, bravely outlived his physician's predictions by six months.

The Ian Walter Memorial Trophy is now awarded by the New Zealand Sporting Journalists'Association for the sports writer of the year. It is a most fitting tribute. Few men have crammed half as many activities into 39 years, or contributed more to their nation's enjoyment of sport.

If I were to make my home in New Zealand, I would choose to live in Wellington. Tucked neatly away in a vast bay which is confusingly named Port Nicholson, it is situated in the very south of the North Island, a central location which has made it an obvious choice as New Zealand's capital city since 1865. Built on a fault line and subject to numerous infinitesimal earth tremors each year, Wellington is excitingly hilly and often alarmingly windy. Many of its third-of-a-million population live like troglodytes in houses burrowed into the hillside or perched precariously on vicious slopes. Owing to the risk of earthquakes, most domestic buildings are wooden, timber being more pliable than bricks and mortar. Hillside residences with access roads are in great demand and highly priced, the alternative being extremely steep footpaths up which all shopping and deliveries have to be carried. The city itself is a thriving commercial centre with a wide necklace of high-rise office blocks. Unlike

(Left) Ian Walter's last big match: the author's Celebrity XI celebrate the 1100th anniversary of Ripon's charter. L-r: back row – Don Taylor (chairman, Ripon CC), Russell Cass, David Cass, Jon Harris, Phil Gould, Ian Walter, Graeme Wright, author: front row – Richard Hutton, Farokh Engineer, David Morgan, Tony Clarkson, Norman McVicker and Harold Rhodes. *(Debbie Brown)*

(Right) John Wright turns to see his off bail safely back in position after playing on to David Capel at Wellington.

the haphazard monstrosities in Auckland, most of Wellington's new architecture is pleasing and many buildings share similar features, an arch motif being especially popular.

The aptly-named Beehive is the most striking of Wellington's parliament buildings, while the Government Building (1876) is thought to be the largest wooden structure in the world. The best vantage point is the summit of Mount Victoria, which commands a breathtaking view of the city, the harbour, the airport dramatically situated between two mountains, and the Basin Reserve itself. Originally a lake which was elevated into a swamp by the 1855 earthquake before being drained by prison labour, it is the only New Zealand Test ground where cricket does not have to play second fiddle to rugby. Completely surrounded by a one-way system, it could also claim to be the only venue where Test cricket is played on a traffic island. The press, radio and TV facilities are sited along a vast gondola in the roof of the R. A. Vance stand and provide a panoramic view of the ground, Mount Victoria and the approaches to the airport.

England returned to Wellington knowing that unless they gained their first victory at the Basin Reserve since 1962-63, they would extend their run of Tests without a win to thirteen since December 1986, a sequence which would equal the dismal record established under Bob Willis and David Gower between August 1983 and December 1984. New Zealand, on the other hand, could boast of not having been defeated at Wellington since March 1968, the Basin Reserve's last dozen Tests having produced five victories and seven draws.

It was in Wellington in 1978 that England suffered their first-ever defeat by New Zealand in the 48th match of this series. John Wright, about to become the 19th player to captain New Zealand in 189 Tests, and the recalled Stephen Boock both made their debuts in that historic match, and were its only surviving players from either side.

The final Test began on the 49th anniversary of the infamous Timeless Test between South Africa and England at Durban, a coincidence which seemed to influence the preparation of the pitch and New Zealand's whole approach. That match, which lasted 43 hours and 16 minutes, the longest game of first-class cricket ever played, began 3½ hours after my birth. When torrential rain terminated play in a draw more than eleven days later, England were a tantalizing 42 runs short of victory. The team then had to embark upon a two-day train journey to catch up with their ship, which had sailed on to Cape Town without them.

Certainly Wes Armstrong's grassless pitch of rolled mud could easily have staged an eleven-day contest. It was a very bad toss for Gatting to lose, not only because he needed to take control of the match by making a large total quickly, but because his players had just finished two-and-a-half days fielding in the pastures of Eden Park.

Wright's success with the coin virtually ensured that New Zealand would at least retain their record of not having lost a home series since 1979. But he threw away any chance of winning the match when he allowed England's attack to restrict New Zealand to a paltry 192 for 3 off 92 overs on the first day. On a good batting surface surrounded by a fast outfield and in perfect light this was a shameful effort. Wright himself managed only 36 runs from 117 balls in 193 minutes, in stark contrast with his performances in the subsequent Rothman's Cup one-day series. When he had made 22 he was extremely fortunate to survive a ball from David Capel which he edged hard on to his off stump. The bail lifted at one end of its socket before dropping back neatly into its original position. Owing to the strong winds, special heavy bails are used at the Basin; they deprived England of a valuable wicket just when it would have put extra pressure on Wright's Test debutant partner, Robert Vance. Son of the New Zealand Cricket Council chairman, he played with increasing confidence after an extremely nervous start before being the victim of a farcical run out in partnership with Martin Crowe.

Crowe and Mark Greatbatch added 155 for the 4th wicket, setting a new record for this series. Greatbatch, undoubtedly New Zealand's major discovery of the season, has looked an assured cricketer from the moment he started grabbing unlikely catches as a substitute at Christchurch. Crowe at last played the major innings he had always threatened, but was well below his best form. He did not relish being out to the gentle dobbers of the England captain. With a Test haul now including Martin Crowe (twice) and Zaheer Abbas, Gatting's gentle seamers have been elevated to a new status. Crowe was so furious with his dismissal that he smashed a sign in the players' tunnel with a swing of his bat. Wisely he did so out of public view.

Not until their sixth session at the crease did New Zealand remove the handbrake. Then Ken Rutherford and John Bracewell added 110 from 27 overs against an attack reduced by a knee injury to Dilley which was to prevent him from taking any further part in the tour. Rutherford's maiden Test century must be viewed in that context, but his 12 boundaries included some scintillating cover-drives. A nervy Randall look-alike, he grimaces and chats to himself as he awaits each ball. Appallingly treated by his selectors, he has taken two seasons to recover from his baptism of fire as an opener in the West Indies. He almost did a war dance of delight as he breached an immense mental barrier by reaching his century. This was only the third time he had scored 50 in 23 Test innings. Second only to Crowe among New Zealand's most elegant strokemakers, his undefeated 107 elevated his Test average from 11.20 to 16.55. His partnership of 134 with Bracewell, who recorded his third Test fifty, eclipsed New Zealand's previous record against England for the 6th wicket.

Wright surprised even his own supporters by batting more than an hour into the third day, thus leaving his bowlers less than seventeen hours in which to dismiss England twice. At the end of the third day England needed only 130 to avoid the follow-on and eliminate any hopes of an outright result. There was a little turn for Bracewell and Boock, but the surface was too slow for it to trouble competent batsmen.

At the start of the day Gatting's frown had deepened into a brutal furrow as his fielders fumbled; the last three hours of New Zealand's marathon innings produced some of the worst fielding I have seen at Test level. The captain frequently made the elementary mistake of following the ball with his field changes.

Watched by French, Athey and a sparse Basin reserve audience, Martin Crowe drives off the back foot during his long-awaited major innings.

For the third successive Saturday Moxon held centre stage, his 232-ball, 282-minute vigil providing the kingpin for England's brave fight back against the third-highest total they have conceded in 66 Tests against New Zealand. His ten boundaries came from leg glances and drives into the 'V' and his 81 not out took him to the top of the Test and first-class batting averages for England's marathon winter haul.

Broad took 14 runs from Morrison's first two overs and extended his aggregate from 20 innings in twelve overseas Tests to 1,034 runs, average 57.44, including six centuries. When he groped outside an off-break (to him) and was bowled through a substantial gate, it was the first time he had scored fifty in a Test outside England and not gone on to make a hundred.

Although the lengthy vigils by Broad and Moxon were perhaps slightly short on entertainment, they said a great deal for the stamina and dedication of the pair, who had spent more than four successive playing days in the field, including the Auckland Test.

With Gooch and Gower waiting in the wings, Robinson's dismissal will have done his career prospects irreparable harm. Once again his footwork betrayed him in negotiating a lifting ball outside his off stump, producing a sizeable gap

With key protagonist Richard Hadlee absent injured, the series seldom rose above the lethargic and lacklustre.

between bat and body. It was a fault cruelly exposed by the West Indian fast bowlers on his visit to the Caribbean. Against the calmer pace of Chatfield he achieved the same effect in slower motion. That was Chatfield's thirteenth wicket of the series (126.1-51-198-13) leaving him two short of the national record for a home series against England. Even on the best batting surface of the winter, no batsman could dominate him.

The loss of two wickets in ten minutes compelled Mike Gatting to subdue his normal robust inclinations. Well aware of the frailty of England's middle order, he confined himself to four boundaries from sweeps and square-cuts during 92 minutes of wary defence.

Mercifully, that proved to be the final phase of the match and the series. The tail-end of Cyclone Bola eliminated the last two days to provide spectators and players with a heaven-sent act of euthanasia. It was a fitting end to the first series in New Zealand which had failed to produce a single outright result since Mike Smith's England team toured in 1965-66.

Two undistinguished teams, exhausted mentally and physically, had indulged in three days of lethargic and lacklustre cricket. The fact that it began on the anniversary of the unfinished Timeless Test seemed to influence all those taking part. Certainly the pitch encouraged soporific play and once Wright had won the toss and ordained a no-risks approach to batting, stalemate was inevitable. Without Hadlee, he had no chance of dismissing England twice on such a surface. Had England either won the toss or held vital catches there would have been a very, very slight chance of a result.

Just 8 wickets fell in the course of 276 overs, and one of those was a run-out. Although it began to take a little turn during England's innings, the pitch was too slow and low to trouble competent batsmen merely intent upon survival. The only real hope of a finish was for one of Wellington's many earthquakes to open up rifts on a length at each end.

New Zealand seemed obsessed with safety-first tactics to protect their record of not having lost a home series in the 'eighties. England simply did not have the fire power to prevent them from achieving an aim which had a disastrous effect on the box office. The loss of Richard Hadlee, Martin Crowe's poor form and the absence of Botham, Gooch and Gower condemned the whole series to the rank of an eminently forgettable 'B' movie.

1ST DAY	BOWLERS (BL ALDRIDGE) VANCE STAND END		(S.J. WOODWARD) MT VICTORIA END		BATSMEN SCOREBOARD LEFT			SCOREBOARD RIGHT			NEW ZEALAND 1ST INNINGS NOTES	END-OF-OVER TOTALS					
TIME	BOWLER	O.	BOWLER	O.	SCORING	BALLS	6s/4s	SCORING	BALLS	6s/4s	NOTES	O.	RUNS	W.	'L' BAT	'R' BAT	EXTRAS
					WRIGHT		LHB	FRANKLIN									
10.31	DILLEY	1			·21	3		···	3			1	3		3		
36			DEFREITAS	1	·····x··	9					M1	2					
40	"	2						······	9		M2	3					
44			"	2	······	15					M3	4					
48	"	3						2····4	15	1		5	9			6	
52			"	3	·1	17		····	19			6	10		4		
56	"	4			·1	19		····	23			7	11		5		
11.01			"	4	······	25					M4	8					
05	"	5			·····	30		1	24			9	12			7	
09			"	5	·4·	33	1	··1	27			10	17		9	8	
13	"	6			2	34		·2··1	32		† Appeal ct wkt. Dilley not pleased	11	22		11	11	
18			"	6				·····2	38			12	24			13	
23	"	7	(6-3-8-0)		·····4	40	2					13	28		15		
28			CAPEL	1				······	44		M5 1HR	14					
31 DRINKS 35	"	8			1	41		·····1	49			15	30		16	14	
39			"	2				······	55		M6	16					
43	"	9			2···1	46		·	56			17	33		19		
48	(9-1-25-0)		"	3	······	52					Athey sub (DILLEY) M7	18					
52	DEFREITAS	7						·W	58	1		18²	33	1	19	14	-
53								VANCE			Test debut					0	
55	"	7						····	4		M8	19					
58			"	4	··1 ··	57		1	5			20	35		20	1	
12.04	"	8						······	11		M9	21					
07			"	5	2·····	63					† off bail disturbed	22	37		22		
12	"	9			··	65		····1	15			23	38			2	
16			"	6				2····1	21			24	41			5	
20	"	10			····	69		··	23		M10 (LB)	25	42				1
24			"	7	·2·	72		··1	26		† No appeal	26	45		24	6	
28	(11-7-9-1)	11	(7-3-10-0)				2	······	32	-	M11 NB- 2HR	27	45	1	24	6	1
12.31	LUNCH												LUNCH				
1.10			EMBUREY	1	······	78					M12	28					
13	DILLEY	10			··4	81	3	··3	35			29	52		28	9	
18			"	2	····	85		·1	37			30	53			10	
21	"	11						·2·2·	43		(LB)	31	58			14	2
26	(11-1-36-0)		"	3				······	49		M13	32					
29	DEFREITAS	12			······	91					M14	33					
32			"	4	·1 ·	94		1 ·1	52			34	61		29	16	
35	"	13						······	58		M15	35					
1.38	(13-9-9-1)		" (5-3-4-0)	5	·····4	100	3		58	-	M16 NB-	36	61	1	29	16	2

1ST DAY	BOWLERS (ALDRIDGE) VANCE STAND END		BOWLERS (WOODWARD) MT VICTORIA END		BATSMEN SCOREBOARD LEFT			BATSMEN SCOREBOARD RIGHT			NEW ZEALAND 1ST INNINGS	END-OF-OVER TOTALS					
TIME	BOWLER	O.	BOWLER	O.	SCORING	BALLS	6s/4s	SCORING	BALLS	6s/4s	NOTES	O.	RUNS	W.	'L' BAT	'R' BAT	EXTRAS
					WRIGHT	100	3	VANCE	58	-	M16 NB-	36	61	1	29	16	2
1.41	DE FREITAS	14						† · † · · 2 · (6, 3, 9, 6)	64		† Round wkt.	37	63			18	
46			EMBUREY	6	· · · · 1 (2)	103		· · · · ·	67			38	64		30		
49	"	15			·† · × · · 1 (7, 3)	107		· 3 (8)	69		† Moxon hit (knee) - Athey sub. ‡ sub hit.	39	68		31	21	
58			"	7	2 · 2 · · (2/3, 2/3)	112		1 (7)	70			40	73		35	22	
2.01	"	16	(7-3-10-0)		· 1 · (7)	115		1 · 1 (7, 6)	73			41	76		36	24	
06	(16-9-18-1)		CAPEL	8				· · · · · · · 1 (2)	79		3HR	42	77			25	
10	HEMMINGS	1						· L · · 2 · · (8/9)	85			43	79			27	
12 DRINKS 15			"	9	L · · W (18)	118	3		85			43[3]	79	2	36	27	2
17					CROWE										0		
19			"	9	· LB · ·	2		·	86		(LB) M17	44	80				3
24	·	2			1 1 (7/8, 8)	4		· P · 1 · (7)	90			45	83		2	28	
28			"	10	× · · · 2 · · (3)	10						46	85		4		
31	"	3	(10-4-13-1)					· · 4 P · · · (6/7)	96	1		47	89			32	
35	(3-0-9-0)		EMBUREY	8	· · · · · · 2 (8)	16						48	91		6		
37	CAPEL	11	(8-3-12-0)		1	17		· · · · · LB	101		(LB)	49	93		7		4
42			HEMMINGS	4	P · · · · L · 2 (8)	23						50	95		9		
45	"	12			· · 2 · (8)	26		· 2 1 (2, 3s)	104			51	100		11	35	
50			"	5				P · · L · · 1 (6)	110			52	101			36	
52	"	13			· † 2 (8)	29		2 · 1 (7/8, 3s)	113			53	106		13	39	
57			"	6				· P · P · ·	119		M18	54					
3.00	"	14			1 (3s)	30		· 4 · · · (2)	124	2		55	111		14	43	
04			"	7	· P · · · 2 (7, 7/8)	36						56	113		16		
07	" (15-4-31-1)	15	(7-1-14-0)			36	-	· 2 · · · · (3)	130	2	4HR	57	115	2	16	45	4
3.10	TEA													T	E	A	
3.32			HEMMINGS	8	· P 3 · 6 ·	42					M19	58					
35	DE FREITAS	17						· (S)	131		DeFreitas cramp	58'					
40	(16.1-9-18-1) EMBUREY	9						· · P P ·	136			59					
43			"	9	· 6 7 · ·	48					M 20	60					
45	"	10						· 6 · 6 · L	142		M 21	61					
48			"	10	· P 4 · ·	54					M 22	62					
50	"	11						· 6 · 7 P · 1 (6)	148			63	116			46	
52			"	11	4 4 · 4 1 (6, 6, 6†, 7/8)	59	3	1 (6)	149		† Moxon misfield 50 p'ship: 73'	64	130		29	47	
55	"	12			· · · · 2 (6, 7, 4)	64		(RO)	149	2		64[5]	132	3	31	47	4
57								GREATBATCH		LHB						0	
59	"	12						·	1			65					
4.00			"	12	2 · · 1 (3, 7)	68		· ·	3			66	135		34		
03	"	13			· 1 (6)	70		P · · · 1 (3/4)	7			67	137		35	1	
06			"	13	· † · · 1 (7, 5/6)	74		4 1 (5, 5)	9	1	† Robinson hit (shin)	68	143		36	6	
4.09	" (13.5-4-18-0)	14	(13-4-37-0)		· · 1 (6)	77	3	F · ·	12	1	M22 NB-	69	144	3	37	6	4

1ST DAY	BOWLERS (ALDRIDGE) VANCE STAND END		BOWLERS (WOODWARD) MT VICTORIA END		BATSMEN SCOREBOARD LEFT			BATSMEN SCOREBOARD RIGHT			NEW ZEALAND 1ST INNINGS	END-OF-OVER TOTALS					
TIME	BOWLER	O.	BOWLER	O.	SCORING	BALLS	6s/4s	SCORING	BALLS	6s/4s	NOTES	O.	RUNS	W.	'L' BAT	'R' BAT	EXTRAS
					CROWE	77	3	GREATBATCH	12	1	M 22 NB -	69	144	3	37	6	4
4.11			HEMMINGS	14	· · · · · ·	83					M 23	70					
14	DEFREITAS	18						· · · · · ·	18		M 24	71					
18			"	15	· · · · · ·	89					M 25	72					
20	"	19						· · · · · 4	24	2		73	148			10	
25			"	16	· · · · · ·	95					M 26	74					
27	"	20			1	96		· · · · 1	29		5 HR	75	150		38	11	
32 DRINKS 35			"	17	· · · · · 1	102						76	151		39		
37	"	21			· · · · 1	107		·	30			77	152		40		
41			"	18	3 · ·	110		· · 1	33			78	156		43	12	
45	"	22						2 4 · · · ·	39	3		79	162			18	
50	(21-1-10-31-1)		"	19	· · · · 4 ·	116	4					80	166		47		
53	CAPEL	16	(19-7-46-0)		4 · · ·	120	5	· 1	41		CROWE'S 50: 134'	81	171		51	19	
58			EMBUREY	15				· · · 4 · ·	47	4		82	175			23	
5.00	"	17			· · 1	123		· · ·	50			83	176		52		
04			"	16	· · · · · 1	128		·	51			84	177		53		
07	"	18			1	129		· · · · · ·	56			85	178		54		
10			"	17	2 · · · · ·	135						86	180		56		
14	"	19						· 4 · · · ·	62	5	50 p'ship: 76'	87	184			27	
17	(19-4-42-1)		"	18	· · · · · ·	141					M 27	88					
20	HEMMINGS	20						· · · · · ·	68		M 28	89					
23			"	19	1	142		· · · 4 ·	73	6		90	189		57	31	
25	"	21			· · · · · ·	148					M 29	91					
29	(21-9-46-0)		(19.5-5-33-0)	20	·	149	5	· · · · 3	78	6	6 HR	92	192	3	57	34	4
5.31	STUMPS										M 29 NB -		STUMPS (1ST DAY)				

2ND DAY	BOWLERS (ALDRIDGE) VANCE STAND END		(WOODWARD) MT VICTORIA END		BATSMEN SCOREBOARD LEFT			SCOREBOARD RIGHT			NOTES	NEW ZEALAND 1ST INNINGS END-OF-OVER TOTALS					
TIME	BOWLER	O.	BOWLER	O.	SCORING	BALLS	6s/4s	SCORING	BALLS	6s/4s		O.	RUNS	W.	'L' BAT	'R' BAT	EXTRAS
					CROWE	149	5	GREATBATCH	78	6	Strong breeze M29 NB-	92	192	3	57	34	4
10·30	DE FREITAS	23						† · · · · · ·	84		† NEW BALL. M30	93					
35			CAPEL	20	· 3 · · · 4 / · · · · · ·	155					M31	94					
38	"	24						· · · · x · ·	90		M32	95					
42			"	21	· · · · · ·	161					M33	96					
45	"	25						· P · · · ·	96		M34	97					
49			"	22	P · · 7 / · · · · 1	166		·	97			98	193		58		
53	"	26			· P · · · ·	172					M35	99					
57			"	23	·	173		x 7/8 6/7 / · · 2 · 3	102			100	198			39	
11·01	"	27						· · · · · ·	108		M36	101					
05			"	24	· 2 8 7/8 / · 4 2 2 · ·	179	6					102	206		66		
10	"	28	(24-6-56-1)					8 / 2 · · · · ·	114			103	208			41	
15			EMBUREY	21	· 1 P 7 / · · · 1	183		· 3 / · ·	116			104	209		67		
18	"	29			· · · · · ·	189					M37	105					
22			"	22	· · · 3 / · · · 3	193		· 2/3 / · 3	118			106	215		70	44	
26	"	30			1/2 · · 3 / · 4 · · · ·	199	7				7HR	107	219		74		
30	(29·1-16·37-1)		"	23				· · · · · ·	124		M38	108					
34 DRINKS 37	CAPEL	25			8 3 · · 1/2 / 2 · 4 · · 4	205	9					109	229		84		
41			"	24	8 · · / 2 · ·	208		· · 5s / · · 1	127		100 p'ship: 165'	110	232		86	45	
45	"	26			· 2 / · 1	210		· 6/7 / · · · 1	131			111	234		87	46	
50			"	25	· · 7/8 / · · 1	213		· · ·	134			112	235		88		
53	"	27			2 / 1	214		· · · · ·	139			113	236		89		
58			"	26	· 6 · 8 · 3 / · · · · · ·	220					M39	114					
12·02	"	28			8 4 / 2 1	222		7/8 6/7 / · 4 1 ·	143	7	GREATBATCH'S 50: 185'	115	244		92	51	
06	(28-6·77-1)		"	27	· 7 · · 8 4 / · · · · · ·	228					M40	116					
09	HEMMINGS	22			· L · P 7 / · · · · ·	233		6/7 / 1	144			117	245			52	
12			"	28				· 6 3 · L · / · · · · · ·	150		M41	118					
15	"	23			· 2 P · 3 3 / · 2 · · · 3	239						119	250		97	·	
17			"	29	· · 7 · LB / · · · · ·	244		4 / 4	151	8	(LB)	120	255			56	5
20	"	24			· 4 · · · 8 / · · · · · ·	250					M42	121					
23			"	30	8 · / · · ·	253		· 8 / · · 1	154			122	256			57	
25	"	25			8 · 7 / 4 · 1	256	10	· 9 / · 3 ·	157		CROWE'S 100: 287'	123	264		102	60	
29	(25-10-60-0)		"	31	5 · 4 5 6 / · · · · 2 ·	262	10		157	8	M42 NB - 8HR	124	266	3	104	60	5
12·31	LUNCH		(30·5-9-51-0)										L	U	N	C	H
1·11	HEMMINGS	26						· P 6 · / · · · · · ·	163		M43	125					
14			EMBUREY	32	5 7 / 1 1	264		8 · · 8 / 1 · · 1	167			126	270		106	62	
18	"	27						· 8 · 6 8 / · · · · · ·	173		M44	127					
20			"	33	LB / ·	265		4 7 8 / · · · · ·	178		(LB) M45	128	271				6
23	"	28			· 7 · · 5 6 / · · · · · 1	271						129	272		107		
1·26	(28-12-61-0)		" (33·5-10-56-0)	34	7 / · 1	273	10	· 7 · 8 / · · · ·	182	8	M45 NB -	130	273	3	108	62	6

2ND DAY	BOWLERS (ALDRIDGE) VANCE STAND END		BOWLERS (WOODWARD) MT VICTORIA END		BATSMEN SCOREBOARD LEFT			BATSMEN SCOREBOARD RIGHT			NEW ZEALAND 1ST INNINGS NOTES	END-OF-OVER TOTALS					
TIME	BOWLER	O.	BOWLER	O.	SCORING	BALLS	6s/4s	SCORING	BALLS	6s/4s	NOTES	O.	RUNS	W.	'L' BAT	'R' BAT	EXTRAS
					CROWE	273	10	GREATBATCH	182	8	M45 NB -	130	273	3	108	62	6
1.29	HEMMINGS	29			· · · · · ·	279					M46	131					
31			EMBUREY	35				2 · · · · 1	188			132	276			65	
34	"	30						· · · · · 1	194			133	277			66	
36			"	36				· 2 · · · ·	200			134	279			68	
40	"	31			1	280		· · · · ·	205			135	280		109		
43			"	37	4 · 1	283	11	· · ·	208		150 p'ship: 245'	136	285		114		
47	"	32			· 1	285		· · · ·	212			137	286		115		
50			"	38	1	286		W	213	8		137[2]	287	4	116	68	6
51								RUTHERFORD								0	
53			"	38				· · · ·	4			138					
55	"	33			· 2 1	289		· · ·	7			139	290		119		
58			"	39	· 1 · · ·	294		1	8			140	292		120	1	
2.01	"	34			·	295		· · · · 3	13		† Dropped mid-off (1) Athey.	141	295			4	
05			"	40				· · 4 · ·	19	1		142	299			8	
08	"	35			· · 1	298		· · ·	22		9HR	143	300		121		
12 15	DRINKS (35-13-71-0)			41	1 ·	300		· · · 1	26			144	302		122	9	
18	DE FREITAS	31						· · · · · ·	32		M47	145					
23			"	42	2 1	302		· · 4 ·	36			146	305		125		
25	"	32			4 · · · · 4	308	13					147	313		133		
30			"	43	· · 2	311		· 2 1	39			148	318		135	12	
34	"	33	(42.5-10-83-1)					· 2 · · · ·	45		† v. hard c & b chance	149	320			14	
37			HEMMINGS	36	· · · LB	315		· ·	47		(LB) M48	150	321				7
41	"	34			· 4 · · · 1	321	14					151	326		140		
45			"	37	1 · ·	324		· · 1	50			152	328		141	15	
49	"	35			· ·	326		· · · 3	54			153	331			18	
54			"	38	· 1	328		· · 2 1	58			154	335		142	21	
56	"	36	(38-14-77-0)		· 1	330		· · · ·	62			155	336		143		
3.00			GATTING	1	· · W	333	14					155[3]	336	5	143	21	7
03					BRACEWELL										0		
05			"	1	· 1	2		4	63	2		156	341		1	25	
08	(36.1-18-56-1)	37	(1-0-5-1)		· · · · · ·	8	-		63	2	M49 NB - 10HR	157	341	5	1	25	7
3.11	TEA													T	E	A	
3.32			GATTING	2	· · ·	11		4 · · LB	66	3	(LB)	158	346			29	8
37	DEFREITAS	38						· · L · · ·	72		M50	159					
41			"	3	· · · · · ·	17					M51	160					
44	"	39			· · · 1	21		1 ·	74			161	348		2	30	
49			"	4	· 2 · · · 1	27						162	351		5		
53	"	40			· · · · · L	33					M52	163					
3.58	(39.1-20-58-1)		(5-1-20-1)	5		33	-	· · · · 4 4	80	5	M52 NB -	164	359	5	5	38	8

2ND DAY	BOWLERS (ALDRIDGE) VANCE STAND END		BOWLERS (WOODWARD) MT VICTORIA END		BATSMEN SCOREBOARD LEFT			BATSMEN SCOREBOARD RIGHT			NEW ZEALAND 1ST INNINGS	END-OF-OVER TOTALS					
TIME	BOWLER	O.	BOWLER	O.	SCORING	BALLS	6s/4s	SCORING	BALLS	6s/4s	NOTES	O.	RUNS	W.	'L' BAT	'R' BAT	EXTRAS
					BRACEWELL	33	-	RUTHERFORD	80	5	M52 NB-	164	359	5	5	38	8
4.02	DEFREITAS	41			· 6†L · / · · · · · ·	39					M53 † Dropped 1st slip (Moxon)	165					
07			GATTING	6				· · · x 8 / · · · · · 1	86			166	360			39	
11	"	42	(6-1-21-1)					· · 2/3 2 / · · · · 4 1	92	6		167	365			44	
18	(41.1-21-63-1)		HEMMINGS	39	:	40		· · · 7 / · · · · 1	97			168	366			45	
22	EMBUREY	44						3 · 2 · · 6 / 4 · 2 · · 2	103	7	RUTHERFORD'S 50: 130'	169	374			53	
25			"	40	· · · P · · / · · · · · ·	46					M54	170					
29	"	45						· · 6 · 7 / · · 2 · · 1	109		11 HR	171	377			56	
32 DRINKS 35			"	41	8S : / · 1 :	49		8S 7/8 8 / 1 41	112	8		172	384		6	62	
40	"	46			7 / 1	50		7 7 8 / 1 · · 2 1	117		50 p'ship: 75'	173	389		7	66	
44	(45.5-10-99-1)		"	42	: : : :	54		: 2 / · 1	119			174	390			67	
48	CAPEL	29			· · 7 6 / · · · 4 1	59	1	5 / 1	120			175	396		12	68	
54			"	43	· 3 / · 3	61		· · · 7 / · · · 1	124			176	400		15	69	
57	"	30						1 7 · 4 · / 4 2 · 4 · ·	130	10		177	410			79	
5.03			"	44	7 · · 3 / 2 · · · 3	66		6 / 1	131			178	416		20	80	
05	"	31			4 †7 / 2 · 1	69		· 3/4 8 / · 4 1	134	11	† Dropped mid-wkt Robinson	179	424		23	85	
10	(31-6-101-1)		"	45	· · 4 4 3 / · · 4 2 1	74	2	3/4 / 4	135	12		180	435		30	89	
14	DE FREITAS	43	(45-15-107-0)		x x · · 7/6 / · · · · · 4	80	3				100 p'ship: 114'	181	439		34		
20			CAPEL	32	7 · / 4 ·	82	4	· · LB / · · · ·	139		(LB)	182	444		38		9
25	"	44			: · 7 / : · 1	85		4 · / · 1 ·	142		12 HR	183	446		39	90	
30	(43.1-21-69-1)		"	33	· 3 7 8 / · 1 2 1	89	4	· 2 / · 1	144	12		184	451	5	43	91	9
5.35	STUMPS		(33-6-110-1)								M 54 NB-	STUMPS (2ND DAY)					
3RD DAY 10.30	DEFREITAS	45			x 2 3 3 3 2† / · · · · · 2	95					Cool † CAPEL misfielded	185	453		45		
37			CAPEL	34	1 / 1	96		· P 2†1 · / · · 2 1 ·	149		† RECORD NZ 6th wkt stand v ENG.	186	457		46	94	
41	"	46			· L 8 · 3 / · · 2 · 1	101		3S / 1	150			187	461		49	95	
45			"	35	3 · 1 / · · · 2	105		E9 9 / · 1	152		BRACEWELL'S 50: 149'	188	464		51	96	
50	"	47			: 9 2 / · 2 1	108		7 4 7 / · · 3	155			189	470		54	99	
55			"	36	6 · 6/7 / · · W	111	4					189.3	470	6	54	99	9
57					SMITH										0		
59			"	36	9E 3 / 1 ·	2		1 / 1	156		RUTHERFORD'S 100: 233'	190	472		1	100	
11.03	"	48			7 1 · 2 / 4 4 · 4	6	3	· 3 / · 1	158			191	485		13	101	
07			"	37				· P · 2 8/7 3 / · · · · 2 ·	164			192	487			103	
12	"	49			7 4 6 / 2 · 3	9		· · · / · · ·	167			193	492		18		
16			"	38	3 4 2 9 7 / · 4 2 1 1	14	4	LB / ·	168		(LB)	194	501		26		10
20	"	50			6 6FY1 / 4 · 1	17	5	3 3/2 / · 2 1	171			195	509		31	106	
25			"	39				4 3 L · 2 2 / · · · · · ·	177		M 55 13 HR	196					
29	(50.1-21-110-1)	51	(39-7-129-2)		6 9 / 1 1	19	5	· · 4 1E / · · · 1	181	12		197	512	6	33	107	10
11.34	DECLARATION										M 55 NB-	DECLARED					
											1182 balls						

3RD DAY	BOWLERS (ALDRIDGE) VANCE STAND END		(WOODWARD) MT VICTORIA END		BATSMEN SCOREBOARD LEFT			SCOREBOARD RIGHT			ENGLAND 1ST INNINGS	END-OF-OVER TOTALS					
TIME	BOWLER	O.	BOWLER	O.	SCORING	BALLS	6s/4s	SCORING	BALLS	6s/4s	NOTES	O.	RUNS	W.	'L' BAT	'R' BAT	EXTRAS
					BROAD		LHB	MOXON									
11.46	MORRISON	1			· · · · ④ 4 ·	7	2				NB 1	1	8		8		
52			CHATFIELD	1				· · · · · ·	6		M1	2					
56	"	2			3 3	9		1 · · ⊙ ·	11		(NB) NB 2	3	16		14	1	1
12.03			"	2	· 1	11		· · · · ·	15			4	17		15		
06	"	3			· · · ⊙ · 2 ·	18					(NB) NB 3 † Hit on hip.	5	20		17		2
12			"	3	· · · 1	22		· 1	17			6	22		18	2	
16	"	4	(3-1-3-0)		· · · 4 · ·	28	3					7	26		22		
20	(4-0-23-0)		BRACEWELL	1	·	29		1 · · · ·	22		(LB)	8	28			3	3
25	BOOCK	1			· · 1 · ·	34		3	23			9	32		23	6	
28	(1-0-4-0)		"	2	· ·	36	3	· · · 1	27	-		10	33	0	23	7	3
12.30	LUNCH		(2-0-2-0)								M1 NB 3		LUNCH				
1.10	CHATFIELD	4						· · · · · · 1	33			11	34			8	
16			BRACEWELL	3				4 · · · · · ·	39	1	(2LB)	12	40			12	5
21	"	5			· · 1	39		2 · ·	42		1HR	13	43		24	14	
25			"	4	· · · · 4 ·	45	4					14	47		28		
28	"	6						· · · · · ·	48		M2	15					
31			"	5	· · · · · ·	51					M3	16					
34	"	7						· · · · · ·	54		M4	17					
37			"	6	4 · · · · 1	57	5					18	52		33		
40	"	8			· · · · · 4	63	6					19	56		37		
44			"	7	· ·	65		· · · ·	58		(LB) M5	20	57				6
46	"	9						· · · · · ·	64		M6	21					
50			"	8	· · · · · ·	71					M7	22					
53	"	10						· · · · · 4	70	2		23	61			18	
57	(10-4-15-0)		"	9	· · · · · ·	77					M8 † Crowd movement behind screen.	24					
2.01	BOOCK	2			· · · · · ·	82		1	71			25	62			19	
05			"	10				· · · · · 4	77	3		26	66			23	
08	"	3			· · · · · 1	88						27	67		38		
10 14	DRINKS		"	11	· 1	90		4 · · ·	81	4	† Crowe off (ankle) (T Ritchie sub)	28	72		39	27	
18	"	4			· · · · · ·	96					M9	29					
20			"	12				· · · · · ·	87		M10	30					
23	"	5			1 · ·	100		· 1	89		2HR	31	74		40	28	
25			"	13				· 2 · · 2 ·	95			32	78			32	
28	"	6			1	101		· 2 · · ·	100			33	81		41	34	
31			"	14	· · · · · ·	107					M11	34					
34	"	7						4 · · · · ·	106	5		35	85			38	
36			"	15	· · · · · ·	113					M12	36					
38	"	8			· ·	115		· · · 3	110			37	88			41	
2.41	(8-1-18-0)		(16-7-31-0)	16	· · · · 2	120	6	1	111	5	M12 NB 3	38	91	0	43	42	6

3RD DAY	BOWLERS (ALDRIDGE) VANCE STAND END		(WOODWARD) M^T VICTORIA END		BATSMEN SCOREBOARD LEFT			SCOREBOARD RIGHT			NOTES	ENGLAND 1ST INNINGS END-OF-OVER TOTALS					
TIME	BOWLER	O.	BOWLER	O.	SCORING	BALLS	6s/4s	SCORING	BALLS	6s/4s		O.	RUNS	W.	'L' BAT	'R' BAT	EXTRAS
					BROAD	120	6	MOXON	111	5	M 12 NB 3	38	91	0	43	42	6
2·44	BOOCK	9						· · · · · · 4 ·	117		M 13	39					
46	(9-2-18-0)		BRACEWELL	17	· · 4 · · 4 ·	126					M 14	40					
49	MORRISON	5	(17-8-31-0)		3 2 4 4 / 4 · · 3	130	7	7 9E / 1 4	119	6	BROAD'S 50:	41	103		50	47	
55			BOOCK	10	P · 8 / · · 1	133		· · · · · ·	122		100 p'ship:	42	104		51		
59	"	6			7 · · LB† / 2 · · ·	137		9 / · 4	124	7	(LB)–off shoulder MOXON'S 50:	43	111		53	51	7
3·03	(6-0-41-0)		"	11				7 · · · · / · · · · · ·	130		M 15	44					
07	BRACEWELL	18						8/7 · 4 4 · / 4 · · · · ·	136	8		45	115			55	
09	(18-8-35-0)		"	12	8 · · P · / 1 · · · ·	142	7	1 / 1	137	8		46	117	0	54	56	7
3·12	TEA		(12-3-21-0)								M15 NB 3			T	E	A	
3·34	CHATFIELD	11			· 8 / · 1	144		8 · · 8 / 2 · · 1	141			47	121		55	59	
37			BOOCK	13	9 P 8 / 2 · · 1	148		· · · ·	143			48	124		58		
40	"	12			· 7/8 7 7 / · 3 · ·	152		· 3/4 / · 1	145			49	128		61	60	
44			"	14	· · x / · · W	155	7	3 7 7 / · · 1	148			50	129	1	61	61	7
46					ROBINSON						3HR				0		
48	"	13						· · · · / · · · · · ·	154		M16	51					
51			"	15	· · · · · x / · · · · · ·	6					M17	52					
54	"	14			E1 / W	7	-	7 · 2 / · · 3	157			52^4	132	2	0	64	7
56					GATTING										0		
58	"	14			· · ·	2						53					
4·00			"	16				x 7 / · · · · · ·	163		M18	54					
03	"	15			· · · LB / · · · · ·	6		· · · ·	165		M 19 (LB)	55	133				8
07			"	17	· · · x 3 · / · · · · 4 ·	12	1					56	137		4		
10	"	16						· · · · · · / · · · · · ·	171		M 20	57					
14			"	18	· · · · · · · ·	18					M 21	58					
16	"	17						2 · · · · / · · · · · ·	177		M 22	59					
20			"	19	· · · · · · · · · ·	24					M 23	60					
22	"	18						· · · · · · / · · · · · ·	183		M 24	61					
26			"	20	3 4/3 / 1 · 4	27	2	5 8 / · · 1	186			62	143		9	65	
29	"	19						8 · · 4 / 2 · · · · ·	192			63	145			67	
33 35	DRINKS		"	21	9 / · 3	29		6 · · · / · · · ·	196			64	148		12		
39	"	20			6 9 / · 1	31		4 · 7 · / · · · ·	200			65	149		13		
43			"	22	· · 9 8 / · · 1 1	35		6F †6 / 1 ·	202		† over wkt. 4HR	66	152		15	68	
46	"	21			· · · · 3 / · · · · 1	40		6 / ·	203			67	153		16		
50			"	23	· · · · · · / · · · · · ·	46					M 25	68					
53	"	22	(23-8-41-1)					6 · 4 4 · · / · · · · · ·	209		M 26	69					
57			BRACEWELL	19	· 6 3 · 6 · / · · · · · ·	52					M 27	70					
5·00	"	23						4†4 5/4 · · / 4 · 4 · · ·	215	10	† Franklin 'torpedoed'	71	161			76	
04	(23-10-38-1)		"	20	7 · 9E† / 1 · 1	55		· 8 · / · 1 ·	218		† Inside edge	72	164		18	77	
5·07	BOOCK (24-9-41-1)	24	(20-9-38-0)		· · / · · · · · ·	61	2		218	10	M 28 NB 3	73	164	2	18	77	8

3RD DAY	BOWLERS (ALDRIDGE) VANCE STAND END		(WOODWARD) MT VICTORIA END		BATSMEN SCOREBOARD LEFT			SCOREBOARD RIGHT			ENGLAND 1ST INNINGS NOTES	END-OF-OVER TOTALS					
TIME	BOWLER	O.	BOWLER	O.	SCORING	BALLS	6s/4s	SCORING	BALLS	6s/4s	NOTES	O.	RUNS	W.	'L' BAT	'R' BAT	EXTRAS
					GATTING	61	2	MOXON	218	10	M 28 NB 3	73	164	2	18	77	8
5.10			BRACEWELL	21				: : : ·(5) 2(8) ·(8)	224			74	166			79	
14	BOOCK	25	"		·(3) 4 ·(·) ·(4) 3(9)	66	3	:	225			75	173		25		
17			"	22	1(8)	67		·(4) ·(6) · ·(·) ·(7†) :	230		† Near short-leg	76	174		26		
20	"	26			4(9) : : : 1(9)	72	4	:	231			77	179		31		
24	(26-9-53-1)		"	23	: · · : 1(8)	76		: 2(7)	233			78	182		32	81	
26	RUTHERFORD	1	(23-9-44-0)		1(9)	77	4	· · · · · ·	238	10		79	183	2	33	81	8
5.30	1-0-1-0 STUMPS										M 28 NB 3		S	T	U	MP	S
4TH DAY	NO PLAY	–	RAIN								477 balls						
5TH DAY	NO PLAY	·	GROUND WATERLOGGED										MAT	CH	D	RAW	N

NEW ZEALAND 1ST INNINGS v ENGLAND (THIRD TEST) at BASIN RESERVE, WELLINGTON on 3, 4, 5, ~~6~~, ~~7~~ March, 1988

IN	OUT	MINS	No.	BATSMAN	HOW OUT	BOWLER	RUNS	WKT	TOTAL	6s	4s	BALLS	NOTES ON DISMISSAL Toss: NEW ZEALAND.
10.31	2.17	187	1	J.G. WRIGHT *	ct FAIRBROTHER	CAPEL	36	2	79	·	3	118	Hooked short ball to deep backward square-leg.
10.31	11.53	82	2	T.J. FRANKLIN	LBW	DeFREITAS	14	1	33	·	1	58	Played across late inswinger.
11.55	3.57	181	3	R.H. VANCE	RUN OUT [BROAD EMBUREY FRENCH]		47	3	132	·	2	149	Late responding to Crowe's call for third run to long-off.
2.19	3.03	403	4	M.D. CROWE	LBW	GATTING	143	5	336	·	14	333	Played across straight ball.
3.59	1.51	253	5	M.J. GREATBATCH	ct DeFREITAS	EMBUREY	68	4	287	·	8	213	Mistimed pull - mid-wicket.
1.53	(11.34)	265	6	K.R. RUTHERFORD	NOT OUT		107			·	12	181	
3.05	10.57	156	7	J.G. BRACEWELL	ct FAIRBROTHER	CAPEL	54	6	470	·	4	111	Mistimed pull - wide mid-on.
10.59	(11.34)	35	8	I.D.S. SMITH †	NOT OUT		33			·	5	19	
			9	D.K. MORRISON	Did not bat								
			10	S.L. BOOCK	Did not bat								
			11	E.J. CHATFIELD	Did not bat								
				EXTRAS	b - lb 10 w - nb -		10			-6	49 4	1182 balls (0 no-balls)	

* CAPTAIN † WICKET-KEEPER

TOTAL (197 OVERS; 787 MINUTES) 512-6 DECLARED at 11.34 am on 3rd day.

15 OVERS 0 BALLS/HOUR
2.59 RUNS/OVER
43 RUNS/100 BALLS

UMPIRES: B.L. ALDRIDGE and S.J. WOODWARD.

BOWLER	O	M	R	W
DILLEY	11	1	36	0
DeFREITAS	50.1	21	110	1
CAPEL	39	7	129	2
EMBUREY	45.5	10	99	1
HEMMINGS	45	15	107	0
GATTING	6	1	21	1
			10	1
	197	55	512	6

2ND NEW BALL taken 10.30 am on 2nd day - NEW ZEALAND 192-3 after 92 overs.

HRS	OVERS	RUNS
1	14	28
2	13	17
3	15	32
4	15	38
5	18	35
6	17	42
7	15	27
8	17	47
9	19	34
10	14	41
11	14	36
12	12	69
13	13	63

RUNS	MINS	OVERS	LAST 50 (in mins)
50	128	29	128
100	219	50.5	91
150	300	75	81
200	395	101.2	95
250	466	119	71
300	539	142.3	73
350	618	161.2	79
400	685	176	67
450	722	183.5	37
500	772	193.5	50

LUNCH:	45-1	27 OVERS 120 MIN	WRIGHT 24* (120') VANCE 6* (36')
TEA:	115-2	57 OVERS 240 MIN	VANCE 45* (156') CROWE 16* (51')
STUMPS (1ST DAY):	192-3	92 OVERS 359 MIN	CROWE 57* (170') GREATBATCH 34* (92')
LUNCH:	266-3	124 OVERS 480 MIN	CROWE 104* (291') GREATBATCH 60* (213')
TEA:	341-5	157 OVERS 600 MIN	RUTHERFORD 25* (78') BRACEWELL 1* (6')
STUMPS (2ND DAY):	451-5	184 OVERS 723 MIN	RUTHERFORD 91* (201') BRACEWELL 43* (129')

WKT	PARTNERSHIP		RUNS	MINS
1st	Wright	Franklin	33	82
2nd	Wright	Vance	46	103
3rd	Vance	Crowe	53	76
4th	Crowe	Greatbatch	155	253
5th	Crowe	Rutherford	49	70
6th	Rutherford	Bracewell	134	156
7th	Rutherford	Smith	42*	35
			512	

ENGLAND 1st INNINGS (IN REPLY TO NEW ZEALAND'S 512 - 6 DECLARED)

IN	OUT	MINS	No.	BATSMAN	HOW OUT	BOWLER	RUNS	WKT	TOTAL	6s	4s	BALLS	NOTES ON DISMISSAL
11.46	3.46	178	1	B.C. BROAD	BOWLED	BOOCK	61	1	129	·	7	155	Checked sweep – off-break to left-hander.
11.46	(5.30)	282	2	M.D. MOXON	NOT OUT		81			·	10	238	
3.48	3.56	8	3	R.T. ROBINSON	c SMITH	CHATFIELD	0	2	132	·	·	7	Edged defensive push at ball outside off stump.
3.58	(5.30)	92	4	M.W. GATTING *	NOT OUT		33			·	4	77	
			5	N.H. FAIRBROTHER	Did not bat								
			6	D.J. CAPEL									
			7	J.E. EMBUREY									
			8	B.N. FRENCH †									
			9	P.A.J. DeFREITAS									
			10	E.E. HEMMINGS									
			11	G.R. DILLEY									
				EXTRAS	b - lb 6 w - nb 2		8			-	21	477 balls (inc 3 no-balls)	
				TOTAL	(79 OVERS; 282 MINUTES)		183-2						

* CAPTAIN † WICKET-KEEPER

16 OVERS 5 BALLS/HOUR
2.31 RUNS/OVER
38 RUNS/100 BALLS

BOWLER	O	M	R	W	nb
MORRISON	6	0	41	0	3
CHATFIELD	23	10	38	1	-
BRACEWELL	23	9	44	0	-
BOOCK	26	9	53	1	-
RUTHERFORD	1	0	1	0	-
			6		
	79	28	183	2	

HRS	OVERS	RUNS
1	13	43
2	18	31
3	19	55
4	16	23

RUNS	MINS	OVERS	LAST 50 (in mins)
50	71	17.1	71
100	149	41	78
150	236	65.3	87

LUNCH	33-0	[10 OVERS 44 MIN]	BROAD 23*, MOXON 7*
TEA	117-0	[46 OVERS 166 MIN]	BROAD 54*, MOXON 56*
STUMPS (3RD DAY)	183-2	[79 OVERS 282 MIN]	MOXON 81* (282'), GATTING 33* (92')

NO PLAY 4th or 5th DAYS (RAIN)

MATCH and SERIES DRAWN

MATCH AWARD: K.R. RUTHERFORD

WKT	PARTNERSHIP		RUNS	MINS
1st	Broad	Moxon	129	178
2nd	Moxon	Robinson	3	8
3rd	Moxon	Gatting	51*	92
			183	

POST TOUR REFLECTIONS

Micky Stewart's end-of-tour report on the England team · His solution to the umpiring problem · New Zealand look to the future · The Shell Trophy ends in total confusion · A treadmill awaits

England's interminable winter schedule, which began just a fortnight after the end of the long English season and allowed only a three-week break during six months of travel, was always going to be a killer, taking grievous physical and mental toll of our best cricketers. Gower chose his sabbatical wisely.

Nevertheless, Micky Stewart was convinced that most of England's tourists had benefited from their winter's exertions. At Napier, with its famous art deco buildings separated from Hawkes Bay by a beach-side avenue of Norfolk pines, the team manager generously fitted a private interview into his demanding schedule.

Stewart is England's first salaried team manager. Appointed on a three-year contract on 1 April 1987, he has made permanent the position pioneered by the late Ken Barrington. Like his former Surrey and England colleague, Stewart is responsible for the playing side of the tour. In the main he organizes and supervises net practices and chairs team selection meetings. His fitness belies his 55 years; in appearance he has changed little since 1972 when he ended a nineteen-season career as an opening batsman and brilliant close catcher. A meticulous man, he carefully monitors his charges' progress and consulted his neatly kept files in giving this end-of-term assessment of the winter's cricket. He began by paying a warm tribute to Graham Gooch and Allan Lamb, who had dominated England's fine showing in the World Cup, before giving his verdict on the players who had been picked for Australia and New Zealand.

> There have been a lot of plusses. Chris Broad, after finding it difficult to adjust to restrictive-overs cricket and not being in the side for the second half of the World Cup, applied himself and has performed well at both levels of the game in New Zealand.
>
> Moxon is a big plus. A solid opening batsman, he has an anchorman's technique and application.
>
> After his innings of 166 against Northern Districts, Tim Robinson has played with much more aggressive intent. He shows a lot more confidence and looks to dominate more.

Stewart attributed the captain's shortage of runs (247 in his last eleven Test innings) to 'the pressures of a very, very demanding chain of events. Mentally and emotionally Gatt is completely and utterly drained.'

On the bowling side, Stewart admitted that Graham Dilley's latest injury was a worry:

> He has worked very hard and responded well to leading the attack.
>
> It has been good that Phillip DeFreitas has continued his one-day bowling form and has also brought his consistency and rhythm up to Test match standard.
>
> Paul Jarvis has also gained from the experience and is a better bowler for it. He now knows what is required and has done well.
>
> Neal Radford has improved on his other international appearances. Both he and DeFreitas have overcome their no-ball problems and this will help their county performances this summer.
>
> John Emburey won't be happy with the number of wickets he has taken (11 at 58.36 from 325.5 overs in the winter's seven Tests), but his consistency with the bat (336 runs at 48.00) has been a valuable bonus.
>
> The biggest minus of the tour from a cricket

(Opposite above) England team manager Micky Stewart (becapped centre) gives a press conference in Pakistan.

(Opposite below) 'The biggest minus of the tour from a cricket point of view has been the slip catching' – Emburey and Athey justify Micky Stewart's criticism.

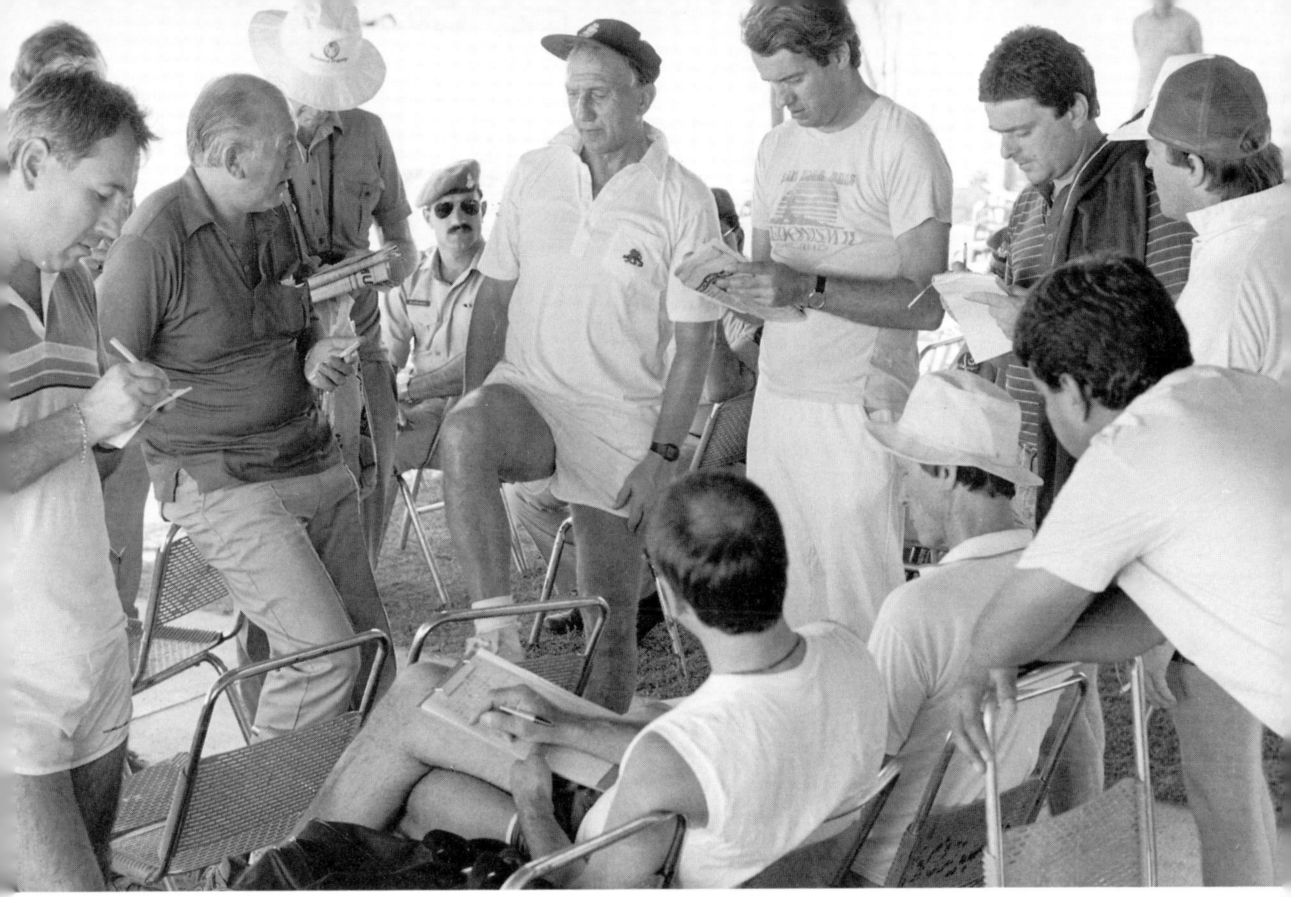

point of view has been the slip catching. This was a major strength last year in Australia. But having a younger, more athletic side out here we did improve the throwing and outfielding to an outstanding level during the Christchurch international.

Stewart's experience of overseas umpires during the last six months has left him in no doubt about the solution.

After the Pakistan thing, and having seen the limited experience of umpires in New Zealand, I would say that the game would benefit from having an international panel. I really feel that it is necessary, but it is a tragedy that we should lose one of the traditional and unique qualities of the game whereby the host country has always supplied the umpires. But such importance is placed on the commercial aspect of the game these days that you cannot afford incidents to occur in a match which are detrimental to the image of the game.

I think the panel should contain the best umpires, no matter where they come from. If you selected ten I would expect there to be six Englishmen and four from overseas.

Tony Crafter of Australia and the Indians Gupte and Ramaswamy were among those who had impressed Stewart during the World Cup.

New Zealand hope to host their first-ever five-match Test series when England pay their next visit early in 1992. During the Christchurch Test, Bob Vance, chairman of the New Zealand Cricket Council, and Raman Subba Row, his TCCB counterpart, had informal discussions about the next tour. Provided that such an extended tour is financially viable the major problem would seem to be fitting it into a winter when England is also provisionally scheduled to visit Pakistan. There would be no prize for guessing the players' solution to that particular problem.

By the time England next arrive in New Zealand they are likely to find that Chris Cairns has taken over Richard Hadlee's role as the team's key all-rounder. Cairns is the seventeen-year-old son of former Test all-rounder Lance, the 10-wicket hero of New Zealand's first victory in England at Headingley in 1983, and the wielder of the 'Excalibur' blade that smote vast sixes off Dennis Lillee's bowling in a one-day international at Melbourne.

A vast chip off a massive block, Cairns minor made a major name for himself in early weeks of 1988. First he featured heavily as opening bowler and middle-order batsman in New Zealand under-19s' victory against an Indian under-19 team which included Narendra Hirwani, the little leg-spinning wizard who had soared to stardom with a match-winning 16-wicket haul on his Test debut against West Indies a few weeks earlier. Then, playing in Lance Cairns' benefit match at Wanganui, Chris reduced a New Zealand XI to 114 for 5 before torrential rain ended his mayhem. In eight overs he yorked Trevor Franklin second ball and accounted for John Wright, Mark Greatbatch and Martin Crowe at a cost of 21 runs. He also had a slip catch dropped – by his father!

Chris Cairns is clearly a star player in the making, but such Kiwis are in very short supply. Replacements for Glenn Turner, Bruce Edgar, Geoff Howarth, John Reid and Jeremy Coney have been extremely hard to find. After their showing in the Lancaster Park Test, Turner assessed the batting line-up as 'the weakest ever to represent New Zealand'.

Hadlee (36) and Chatfield (37) have carried the bowling throughout the most successful era in the history of New Zealand's international cricket, but neither is likely to be available for the 1990 tour of England. From the evidence of this visit their most probable replacements will be Danny Morrison and Willie Watson, two Aucklanders who, at present, inspire hope rather than fear in opposing batsmen. Morrison, with his erratic run-up commencing on the wrong side of the pitch, has made some progress, but Watson looks a very ordinary medium-pacer who would struggle to get into a county side. Still, such bowlers often develop quickly and may well surprise their detractors; Hadlee and Chatfield looked anything but world-beaters when they began their international careers.

A major problem for New Zealand cricket is the tremendous gulf between the playing standard of their 20 currently available Test cricketers and the remaining 70 first-class players representing the 6 Shell Trophy teams. The absence of the national team in Australia for more than half the 1987-88 domestic programme devalued the two competitions.

Martin Crowe summed up the situation

when he said: 'I believe it would be better for the development of the game here for all the leading players to be available for the full domestic first-class programme than be playing one-day internationals in Australia.'

Auckland were bottom of the Shell Trophy table and without a single point when their Test stars returned from Australia at the end of January. They eventually finished equal top with Otago. Rather absurdly, the rules of the competition dictate that the Trophy cannot be shared when sides finish level on points and victories. The tie-breaker was a mathematical equation so complex that it took the New Zealand Cricket Council four days to calculate that Otago had won by some infinitesimal fraction. Auckland, who had come off for bad light in their final match when they had calculated that by so doing they had just won the title, had unfortunately based their sums on a misprinted score in the local paper. Otago, who also won the one-day Shell Cup, ended up with the champagne. Auckland and the NZCC took some time to remove the egg.

Mike Gatting and Co. returned home on 23 March, their flight delayed a day because of industrial action by firemen at Auckland Airport. Most of the players were due to report to their counties on 5 April before tackling another vast treadmill, one of the longest English first-class seasons – 16 April to 16 September inclusive. Meanwhile Isaac Vivian Alexander Richards was probably drooling at the prospect of extending West Indies' run of ten successive victories against England.

TRENT BRIDGE
THE FIRST TEST

West Indies faltering start to the tour · Texaco Trophy whitewash · David Gower returns · Trent Bridge celebrates · Match report · Gatting loses captaincy

The West Indies arrived at Trent Bridge for the First Cornhill Test in some disarray. They had won only one of their four first-class matches against the counties and been white-washed 3-0 in the Texaco Trophy series of one-day internationals. Viv Richards was struggling to lift their morale, and he had lost one of his reserve opening batsmen, Phil Simmons, to a horrific head injury which had required brain surgery; fortunately the victim made a complete recovery. His bowling strength was a major problem; he did not have the luxury of a single left-handed bowler and the action of his lone specialist spinner, Roger Harper, was in such disorder that, at the moment of delivery, he resembled a badly-programmed robot attempting to climb a rope ladder. To add to his problems, his key fast bowler, Malcolm Marshall, was still carrying a rib injury. If England were to slay the dragon this was always going to be their best opportunity. Once the tourists had gelled together as a cohesive unit and become properly acclimatized, they were going to take an awful lot of holding.

One-day thrashes are no guide to Test match form, as Pakistan had discovered a few weeks earlier in the Caribbean. Having lost the one-dayers 5-0, they came close to winning the Test rubber. Since 1985 England have achieved an excellent record at one-day level and a most unimpressive one in the five-day matches. Their performance in the Texaco Trophy was not totally unexpected, although the selectors' choices evoked widespread ridicule from press, public and the majority of county cricketers. The squad was: Gatting (captain), Athey, Broad, DeFreitas, Dilley, Downton, Emburey, Gooch, Lamb, Lynch, Pringle, Radford, and Small. If Athey, Downton and Pringle were all astonishing selections after their World Cup performances, the choice of Monte Lynch seemed to be a computer error. Mike Selvey of *The Guardian* suggested that someone had suggested 'lunch', Gatting, ever eager for food, had agreed and the list had been misread.

In the event Athey did not play a match, Lynch scored 0 (run out), 2 and 6, Pringle won the match award at Leeds, and Downton scored 30 in his only innings and kept wicket well. It was very much a case of the score in the national war against Peter and Co. reading: Selectors 3, The Rest of Britain 0.

When they met to choose the team for the First Test, the selectors found that, because of England's success in the Texaco trophy, they had made one or two rods for their own backs. By taking 5 for 83 and conceding only 2.51 runs per over, Derek Pringle had restored his confidence at international level and produced a virtually incontestable claim for inclusion. And yet, to be consistent with their policy for last winter, David Capel should have been given the all-rounder's berth at Nottingham. It also proved impossible to omit Paul Downton, especially, according to one selector, when the captain insisted on his inclusion. I have always been adamant that, for Test cricket, wicket-keepers should be chosen for that specialist ability alone, unlike the requirement for limited-overs matches where their batsmanship assumes greater importance. On that basis, Gloucestershire's 'Jack' Russell, by common consent the finest 'keeper in county cricket, should have been the first choice. Incidentally, Bruce French, Ian Botham and Neil Foster were all unavailable through injury, the first two for the whole series.

A vital factor in Downton's favour was the nature of the opposition. Even this touring side, with its six newcomers to English first-class cricket, boasted a wealth of battle-hardened Test cricketers; although short of their former batting depth, they still possessed four outstanding fast bowlers. In the light of previous experience, the selectors wisely took the view that a West Indies series was not the best place to blood Test cricketers. For this very reason I expected them to recall David Gower rather than experiment with a younger, inexperienced batsman like Northamptonshire's Robert Bailey or Glamorgan's Matthew Maynard.

David Gower had struggled to find any sort of form with Leicestershire and been omitted from the one-day internationals. His absence was a major shock for his many admirers and deprived the tournament of our most graceful stroke-maker. Apart from one brief hiatus in 1980, he had been an automatic England selection since his first appearance in 1978. Among current players, only Ian Botham approached his tallies of 96 Tests and 102 limited-overs internationals. His aggregates of 2,905 runs and seven centuries remain England one-day records, as does his highest score of 158.

No contemporary batsman can match his effortless timing or delight with such casual elegance. He is a class player with a special flair; a rare talent that can lift a drab innings into the highest dimension of batsmanship. Gower is an intelligent individual with a dry sense of humour and many interests outside cricket. Jaded and drained after nine successive winters of overseas tours and the demands of last season's benefit, he decided to exchange England's convoluted winter's touring schedule for a well-earned sabbatical.

Not that he idled the time away in front of the hearth: 'I've spent the winter relaxing with friendly people – a few days in Barbados shepherding a Fred Rumsey cricket tour, a fortnight in Antigua, two skiing visits to the Alps, a week at the Winter Olympics, and three weeks in Africa revisiting the scene of my childhood. I'm delighted I took the time off. It was the right thing to do in terms of cricket. I feel motivated again and I'm keener than I was this time last year. I'm even catching balls at slip!'

David Gower, a class player with a special flair.

Sadly the break and all his enthusiastic pre-season net practice did not produce the big innings expected of him. Selectors publicly committed to choosing players on current form rather than on reputation had little alternative to omitting him after he had amassed 26, 14, 7 and 1 in first-class matches, and 5, 14, 14 and 53 in one-day competitions.

This policy had its opponents. Basil D'Oliveira, Worcestershire's popular and astute coach, would have picked Gower and Botham amongst his first choices for any England team to take on the West Indies: 'Those guys are animals on the field and you need your toughest

and most experienced players to handle them.'

Gower's reaction to being left out of England's Texaco squad was philosophical: 'I can see why. I suppose I haven't been in great nick. But the pitches at Leicester have not been ideal for batsmen trying to find form. One-dayers don't turn me on as much as Test matches,' he admits, 'but I would have liked to have been chosen. The atmosphere of any big match can build you up a bit more. I shall carry on regardless. The runs will come. Someone will pay!'

I was one of his many admirers who fervently hoped that it would be Viv Richards who had to pick up the tab – and soon.

In the light of the Texaco Trophy performances, my predicted England twelve in the *Mail on Sunday* was: Gooch, Broad, Gatting, Gower, Lamb, Pringle, Downton, Emburey, DeFreitas, Small, Dilley and Hemmings.

The selectors chose thirteen players, adding Paul Jarvis and Greg Thomas to my list and omitting Gladstone Small, who developed a thigh injury after my piece had gone to press.

Trent Bridge is one of my favourite English grounds and has the best BBC commentary box, with windows that fold away completely to allow maximum ventilation for the dreaded Trueman pipe and provide a view of the entire playing area without the need to lean out of the window with a colleague holding your ankles. Even with some modernization it has retained its charm and looked in great shape as it celebrated its 150th anniversary by staging its 37th Test.

Only five of those contests had featured West Indies and none has resulted in an England win. (The home side suffered defeats in 1950, 1966 and 1980; there were draws in 1957 and 1976.) Even a draw would be acceptable after a run of ten consecutive West Indies wins in this series. This rubber marked the Diamond Jubilee of matches between the two sides. Beaten by an innings in each of the three Tests played on that inaugural 1928 visit, the tourists have gained some measure of revenge by not losing in England for nineteen years.

Malcolm Marshall, the jubilant destroyer, high-fives with Richie Robinson (hat).

England omitted Thomas and Hemmings, won the toss, and bravely opted to take on the calypso fast-bowling quartet on a pitch of dubious quality. A few overs were sufficient to show that it was so devoid of pace and bounce that groundsman and ace pitch doctor Ron Allsopp might have imported it direct from Eden Park or the Basin Reserve.

Graham Gooch and Chris Broad saw the innings off to a magnificent start with England's 16th century opening partnership in 91 Tests against West Indies. The crowd, deprived for security reasons of banners, staves, drums and horns, were eerily silent as though the prospect of England ending the absolute West Indian domination of these encounters since 1974 was too great a shock to bear. Normality did not return until mid-afternoon, the dismissal of Broad, playing-on in the final pre-tea over, heralding a collapse which saw all 10 wickets fall for 120 runs.

The brownish, damp pitch was too slow for bowlers reliant solely upon speed, although every so often the ball did something unexpected. Not until after lunch, when the outer lacquer had worn away to permit polishing of its actual leather, did the ball start to swing. Then Malcolm Marshall, assessing conditions with total accuracy, reduced his pace and, repeatedly varying his angle of attack from over to around the stumps, took 6 of the first 7 wickets to fall. This haul was his sixteenth of five or more in a Test innings (his fourth instance against England), and took him beyond Joel Garner (259) on the list of leading West Indies wicket-takers and into second place behind Lance Gibbs (309).

Marshall and Curtly Elconn Lynwall Ambrose, a six-foot seven-inch Antiguan beanpole, required only 13 overs to polish off England's last 5 wickets for 25 runs on the second morning. Using the yorker to devastating effect, Ambrose returned a final spell of 7-4-5-3 to end with 4 for 53, his best return of a four-Test career.

Rain and poor light docked more than five hours from the next two days but, by the third day's close, the tourists were 19 runs ahead with 6 wickets in hand and comfortably in control.

As so often happens on Test match Saturdays, a capacity crowd of 13,000 was deprived of nearly four hours of play. Fortunately their frustration was eased by an awesome display of batting by Viv Richards.

Relegated to league cricket with Rishton throughout last summer, Richards celebrated his return to the centre stage with a 135-minute exhibition of his genius. Blending dismissive power with delicate timing he gave England's bowlers a painful lesson, none more so than John Emburey, upon whom he launched a premeditated assault which produced 37 runs from three overs. His partner in this mayhem was Carl Hooper, a 21-year-old Guyanan who matched his captain in as memorable a display of stroke-making as can ever have graced William Clarke's famous ground during its entire 150-year history. Hooper, who launched his first-class career with a century, revealed a mature calm and temperament which bodes ill for opponent bowlers of the next decade.

Richards took only 60 balls (80 minutes) to reach his 54th fifty in 142 Test innings and soon afterwards overtook Greg Chappell's aggregate of 7,110 to become the eighth-highest run-getter in Test cricket. He fell to a fierce head-high second-slip chance, the impact of which flattened the catcher, Gooch. He faced 97 balls, hit a six and 12 fours and was just 20 runs short of his 99th first-class hundred.

A belligerent 8th-wicket stand of 91 in 96 minutes between Marshall (72) and Ambrose (43) allowed Richards to declare 203 ahead and leave himself with 126 overs in which to seal England's fate.

The final morning began with England 67 for 1 and 95 overs to survive. Their rearguard action was considerably eased by a rib-muscle injury to Marshall. Although he removed Gatting with a beauty which swung away late to uproot the off stump, he could manage only five painful overs at half pace before trudging sadly from the field. Few quarrelled with Ray Illingworth's decision to grant Marshall the Cornhill Match Award for his 72 runs and 7 wickets.

Gooch led the resistance with a 410-minute vigil which was rewarded by an eighth Test match hundred, while Gower treated us to glimpses of his sublime genius interwoven with several hazardous edges and off-side wafts.

With the aid of Marshall's injury, the net loss of five hours and nine minutes of play, and a sunny final afternoon, England earned a comfortable draw. In relative terms this result represented a major success, ending as it did a sequence of ten successive defeats in this series, even if it could not prevent England registering a record fourteenth Test without victory.

Fears that the drawing of the Trent Bridge Test might well prove to be the zenith of England's achievement in the current West Indies campaign were strengthened by the dramatic series of events which immediately followed. As a result of allegations in three daily tabloids about Mike Gatting's sexual escapades with a barmaid during the weekend of the Nottingham Test, he lost the captaincy and asked not to be considered for the following Test at Lord's.

Viv Richards, the eighth-highest scorer in Test cricket and with power to add.

1ST DAY	BOWLERS (J. BIRKENSHAW) PAVILION END		BOWLERS (H.D. BIRD) RADCLIFFE RD END		BATSMEN SCOREBOARD LEFT			BATSMEN SCOREBOARD RIGHT			NOTES	ENGLAND 1ST INNINGS END-OF-OVER TOTALS					
TIME	BOWLER	O.	BOWLER	O.	SCORING	BALLS	6s/4s	SCORING	BALLS	6s/4s		O.	RUNS	W.	'L' BAT	'R' BAT	EXTRAS
					GOOCH			BROAD		LHB	Warm. overcast. Slow pitch – outfield						
11.00			MARSHALL	1	2① 1	3		:3 2.	4		NB 1	1	9		4	5	
06	PATTERSON	1			+.2 ::::	9					(W)	2	12		6		1
11			"	2				.: :.⊙..	11		(NB) NB 2	3	13				2
15	"	2			3 1	11		:.1 .	15			4	18		10	6	
20			"	3	...41	16	1	1	16			5	24		15	7	
25	"	3			:....	20		..	18		(LB) off his back M1 • driving slip (MARSHALL)	6	25				3
30			"	4	...	23		:.1	21			7	26			8	
34	"	4						:.2:.	27			8	28			10	
39			"	5	:::1	29						9	29		16		
43	"	5	(5-0-18-0)		4 : :④:	36	3				NB3	10	37		24		
49			AMBROSE	1				3 : : :4 :	33	1		11	41			14	
53	"	6			1	37		: : :01	39		(NB) NB 4 1HR	12	44		25	15	4
59			"	2				2 : : : :	45		Arthurton sub (mid sh) (1 over)	13	46			17	
12.03	"	7			1 .	39		: : :①	50		NB 5	14	48		26	18	
08	(7-1-23-0)		"	3	: :2 . .	44		1	51		Dark cloud 50 p'ship: 70'	15	51		28	19	
12	WALSH	1						2⊙. : : :	58		(NB) NB 6	16	54			21	5
18			"	4	: : . .1	49		1	59			17	56		29	22	
22	"	2			4	50	4	⊙2 : . .1	65		Sunny (NB) NB 7	18	64		33	25	6
27	(2-0-11-0)		"	5				: : : : :	71		M 2	19					
32	HOOPER	1			2 : : : :	56					• Turned (OB)	20	66		35		
34			WALSH	3				. . . . . .	77		M3	21					
39	"	2			4 : 1	59	5	: :	80			22	71		40		
42			"	4	. : : :⊙1	66					(NB) NB 8	23	73		41		7
47	"	3			:1	68		.2 . .	84			24	76		42	27	
50			"	5	:1	70		: : :	88			25	77		43		
54	"	4	(5-1-14-0)		: 1	73		:3 :	91		• 8th leg (LOGIE) his on leg	26	78		44		
57	(4-0-11-0)		RICHARDS	1	: : :1	77	5	:1	93	1	2HR	27	80	0	45	28	7
1.00	LUNCH		(1-0-2-0)								M3 NB 8		LUNCH				
1.40	MARSHALL	6			: .2 . .	82		1	94		overcast	28	83		47	29	
44			AMBROSE	6				: : : : . .	100		M4	29					
48	"	7			: . . :1	87		:	101			30	84		48		
51			"	7	: . . .421	93	6				GOOCH'S 50: 133'	31	91		55		
55	"	8			:41	96	7	. .	104			32	96		60		
2.00			"	8	3 : . .	100		.3	106		100 p'ship: 142'	33	102		63	32	
04	"	9			. . : :1	105		1	107			34	104		64	33	
08			"	9	: .41	109	8	.4	109	2		35	113		69	37	
12	"	10	(9-2-33-0)		: : : : : :	115					• Dr 2nd slip (Greenidge) M5	36					
17			PATTERSON	8	. .	117		+: . .1	113		(W)	37	115			38	8
2.22	(11-1-31-0)	11	(8-1-25-0)		:1	119	8	: : :	117	2	Sunny M5 NB 8	38	117	0	70	39	8

1st DAY	BOWLERS (BIRKENSHAW) PAVILION END		(BIRD) RADCLIFFE RD END		BATSMEN SCOREBOARD LEFT			SCOREBOARD RIGHT			ENGLAND 1st INNINGS NOTES	END-OF-OVER TOTALS					
TIME	BOWLER	O.	BOWLER	O.	SCORING	BALLS	6s/4s	SCORING	BALLS	6s/4s	NOTES	O.	RUNS	W.	'L' BAT	'R' BAT	EXTRAS
					GOOCH	119	8	BROAD	117	2	M5 NB8	38	117	0	70	39	8
2.26			PATTERSON	9	· P ⊙ : · 4LB 8 · 1	125		:	118		(NB) (4LB) NB 9	39	123		71		13
32	MARSHALL	12			· x : 3 8 2 · x W	131	8				cloudy 3HR	40	125	1	73	39	13
35					GATTING										0		
37			"	10	8 1	1		P P ⊙ 5 4 · 1 x : :	124		(NB) NB 10	41	128		1	40	14
43	"	13			6 · 8 3 : 6 6 · ·	6		4 1	125		Sunny (NB) NB 11	42	132		4	41	
48			"	11				4 P x ⊙ † 4 2P · · · ·	132		• 'bowled' - played on. • ducked - hit on shoulder	43	133				15
53	"	14			EP7 1	7		8/7 4 · 4 : 4 · 2 ·	137	3	• Walsh misfielded	44	140		5	47	
58			"	12	: LB	9		P · · 4	141		(LB) M6	45	141				16
3.02	"	15			x : : · · EP7 W	15	-				M7	46	141	2	5	47	16
06					GOWER		LHB								0		
08			"	13	2 1	1		4 · 3/4 2 L · E1/2 1 P ·	146		• Tried to avoid ball. BROAD's 50: 210'	47	145		1	50	
13	"	16			3 : · · † 3 7 · 1	7					† Round wkt (1 ball)	48	146		2		
18			"	14	8/7 4 · 3/4 1 8s 1	11	1	4 ⊙ 3s 1	149		(NB) NB 12	49	154		8	51	17
24	"	17	(14-2-43-0)		· · · 4 1	15		5 :	151			50	155		9		
29			HOOPER	5	· 8 1 3 : ·	19		1 8 2 1	153			51	159		10	54	
33	"	18						: · · · · : † :	159		† Round wkt. M 8	52					
36			"	6	EP8 1	20		· x : · :	164		4HR	53	160		11		
39	(18.4-3-47-3)	19	(6-0-16-0)		2 1	21	1	† · : x W	167	3	† Round wkt.	53.4	161	3	12	54	17
3.41	TEA							LAMB			M8 NB 12			T	E	A	
4.00	MARSHALL	19						P L · W	2	-	Sunny	54	161	4	12	0	17
01								PRINGLE								0	
02			WALSH	6	· LB : EP	25		: 7 1	2		(LB)	55	163			1	18
07	"	20						P : : 6 2 ·	8			56	165			3	
11			"	7	7 1	26		2 : : x 7 ·	13			57	166		13		
16	"	21			† T · · · · · x	32					† Round wkt. M9	58					
19			"	8				: ⊙ 6/5 E1 E9 4 : 6	20	1	(NB) • Edged dab NBB past off stump.	59	171			7	19
24	"	22			† 7 1 · · 2 ·	37		8 1	21		† Round wkt. to LHB overcast	60	173		14	8	
28			"	9				2 · 2 †8E 6 · 2 4 · ·	27	2		61	179			14	
33	"	23			† · 4s : 1	39		· · P ‡ ·	31		† Round wkt. to LHB ‡ Round wkt.	62	180		15		
38			"	10	9 1 : :	42		x : 9 · 1	34		Poor light	63	182		16	15	
41	(24-4-54-4)	24				42	1	: † · + ‡ : · · † 7 1	40	2	† Round wkt (2 balls) (W) ‡ Light discussed	64	184	4	16	16	20
4.47	BLSP										5 min (1 over) lost		BAD		LIGHT		
4.52			"	11				: · : · · · :	46		M10	65					
56	AMBROSE	10			4 · · · · · E10 1	48					• Hard chance to left of 2nd slip (Greenidge)	66	185		17		
5.00			"	12	4 L x 3 P :	54					M11 5HR	67					
04	"	11						: · : · · x	52		M12	68					
07			"	13	7 1	55		: · · 4 :	57		Sunny	69	186		18		
11	"	12	(13-3-30-0)		E1 W	56	1		57	2	M12 NB 13	69.1	186	5	18	16	20
5.11	(12-3-35-1)																

1ST DAY	BOWLERS (BIRKENSHAW) PAVILION END		(BIRD) RADCLIFFE RD END		BATSMEN SCOREBOARD LEFT			SCOREBOARD RIGHT			ENGLAND 1ST INNINGS NOTES	END-OF-OVER TOTALS					
TIME	BOWLER	O.	BOWLER	O.	SCORING	BALLS	6s/4s	SCORING	BALLS	6s/4s		O.	RUNS	W.	'L' BAT	'R' BAT	EXTRAS
					DOWNTON		-	PRINGLE	57	2	M12 NB 13	69^1	186	5	0	16	20
5.13	AMBROSE	12			6 ½ · 1	2		: · x	60			70	187		1		
17			WALSH	14	: LB E1	5		· · EP 8E 1	63		(LB)	71	189			17	21
21	"	13			7 1	6		1 1 6 E1 · 5(4) 1	68			72	192		2	19	
24			"	15				x x P · · 2 1	74			73	193			20	
27	"	14			7 1 ·	8		: E1 1 · 8 1	78		Cloudy	74	196		3	22	
31			"	16				· : x 6 · E1	84		M 13	75					
34	"	15			EP · · · Y ·	14					Light poor M 14	76					
38			"	17				2/3 P · · 2 3 1	90			77	197			23	
42	"	16			: ↑ ↑ Y9 3 4 :	19	1	2 1	91			78	202		7	24	
46	(16-4-46-1)		"	18		19	1	· P 3	95	2	M14 NB 13	78^4	202	5	7	24	21
5.48	BLSP		(17.4-4-33-0)								8 min (1 over) lost		BAD		LIGHT		
5.56			"	18	:	20		6½ 1	96			79	203			25	
58	"	17			(·) · E7 7 :	25		· 8/7 1	98		(NB) NB 14	80	205			26	22
6.02			"	19	:	26		E1 · P · 1	103			81	206			27	
06	"	18						· · : · : 4	109		M15	82					
09			"	20	4 : : 9 1	30		5/6 1 2 1	111		6HR	83	210		8	30	
13	"	19	(20-4-39-0)					G1 Y : : :	117		M16	84					
17	(19-6-48-1)		PATTERSON	15	: 3 8 1	33		6/7 · : 2 ·	120			85	213		9	32	
22	HOOPER	7			· P · 2 7 :	39					M17	86					
24			"	16				1E P 2 ↑ 4 6s 2 · 1	126			87	216			35	
28	" (8-1-20-0)	8	(16-2-49-0)			39	1	: 3 4† 4 : : EP.	132	3	† off s. point's leg (Richardson)	88	220	5	9	39	22
6.30	STUMPS	(1ST	DAY)								M17 NB 14		STUMPS				
2ND DAY 11.00			AMBROSE	20	8 ·	40	1		132	3		88^1	220	5	9	39	22
11.01	RSP		-								9 min (2 overs) lost		R	A	IN		
11.10			"	20	9 1	41		: · · ·	136			89	221		10		
14	MARSHALL	25			+ · : : · · :	47					(W)	90	222				23
18			"	21				7 8 : : 4 :	142		M18	91					
22	"	26			3S 1	48		Yx W	143	3		91^2	223	6	11	39	23
23								EMBUREY								0	
25	"	26						: : † · E1 W	4	-	† Round wkt	92	223	7	11	0	23
27								DEFREITAS								0	
29			"	22	: : 2/3 : : XY	54					M19	93					
32	"	27			P	55		: x : : 2 1	5			94	224			1	
37			"	23	EP 6 · + PLB · ·	59		: Y£8 1	7		(W) (LB)	95	227			2	25
41	"	28			7† 8‡4 2 2 · · 1	63		4LB 4/5 · 1	9		† 1 overthrow (Patterson) ‡ over wkt (4LB)	96	235		14	3	29
46			"	24				x W	10	-		96^1	235	8	14	3	29
								JARVIS								0	
48			"	24				3/4 · 2 P YE	5		M 20 7HR	97					
52	"	29			6 · · P 4 1	67	1	4 ½E · 4	7	1		98	240	8	15	4	
56			"	25	4 3/4 x 8 P	73					M21	99					
12.00	"	30			7 P 1 ·	75		P · †3S 5. · · 1 1	11		† Round wkt (1 ball) • = b (low to rt)	100	243		16	6	
05	(30-4-69-6)		"	26				↑ ↑ · · Yx W	15	1		100^4	243	9	16	6	29
07								DILLEY		LHB						0	
09			" (26-10-53-4)	26		75	1	E2 x 2 W	2	-	M21 NB 14	101	245	10	16	2	29
12.10	ALL OUT										620 balls		ALL		OUT		

2ND DAY	BOWLERS (BIRKENSHAW) PAVILION END		(BIRD) RADCLIFFE RD END		BATSMEN SCOREBOARD LEFT			SCOREBOARD RIGHT			WEST INDIES 1ST INNINGS	END-OF-OVER TOTALS					
TIME	BOWLER	O.	BOWLER	O.	SCORING	BALLS	6s/4s	SCORING	BALLS	6s/4s	NOTES	O.	RUNS	W.	L BAT	R BAT	EXTRAS
					GREENIDGE			HAYNES			Restart delayed by rain - 14 min (3 overs) lost						
12.34			DILLEY	1	5 EP8 P	6					sunny M1	1					
39	DEFREITAS	1						2 8 P 4	6	1		2	4			4	
43			"	2	⊙ P ⊙ x	14					(NB)(NB) NB 2	3	6				2
48	"	2				17		8 1	9			4	7			5	
52			"	3	8 4 2	21		LB	11		(LB) M 2	5	8				3
57	(3-1-5-0)	3	(3-2-2-0)			21	–	L 8/7 EPP	17	1	M3 NB 2	6	8	0	0	5	3
1.00	LUNCH												LUNCH				
1.40	RSP		DILLEY	4										RAIN			
3.40	TEA										33 overs lost			TEA			
4.00	RAIN										31 overs to bowl			RAIN			
4.15			DILLEY	4	P ⊙ 8 1	28					(NB) GREENIDGE 31' on 0 NB3	7	10		1		4
20	DEFREITAS	4			3 ⊙ T 9 1	33			19		(NB) NB 4	8	12		2		5
25			"	5	3 P 6 ⊙	40					(NB) NB 5	9	13				6
30	"	5			EP	43		1E 4/3 4 ①	23	2	NB 6	10	18			10	
34			"	6	7/8 1	45		P 8 1	27			11	20		3	11	
39	"	6			L	51					M4	12					
43			"	7	6/7 1	53		YE1 2 7 7/83 1 1	31		1 HR	13	23		4	13	
48	"	7							37		M5	14					
52			"	8	4 6/7 8 4 1	58	1	8	38			15	28		9		
57	"	8	(8-2-15-0)		7 E1 E1 6 4 2	64	2					16	34		15		
5.02			JARVIS	1	L 8 2	67		4 3	41		sunny	17	39		17	16	
06	"	9	(1-0-5-0)		2/3 ⊙	73		4S 1	42		(NB) NB7	18	41			17	7
11			PRINGLE	1				x G 1 3	48		G - lifter hit bottom hand	19	44			20	
15	"	10						T G8 1	54			20	45			21	
21			"	2				L x	60		M6	21					
24	"	11			⊙ P Y 2/3 P 6 4 4	80	4				(NB) NB 8. 50 D/ship: 99	22	54		25		8
29	(11-3-30-0)		"	3				L 2/3 8	66		M7	23					
33	JARVIS	2			•1E 1E W	86	4				• dropped EMBUREY 1st slip (knee high) · M8	24	54	1	25	21	8
36					RICHARDSON										0		
38			"	4				x P	72		x lost grip on bat M 9	25					
42	"	3			x 1 P T 4	6	1					26	58		4		
46			"	5	3	10		P 7 1	74		2 HR	27	59			22	
50	"	4			4 5(6) 3	12		x 2/3 B	78		(B)	28	63		7		9
54			"	6	7 S P	18					M10	29					
57	"	5						6/5 L 2	84			30	65			24	
6.01			"	7	EP	24					M11	31					
04	"	6	(7-5-4-0)					8 4 x 2 4	90	3		32	71			30	
08			DILLEY	9	3 1 8/9 1	29		3S 1	91			33	74		9	31	
6.13	(7-1-24-1)	7	(9-2-18-0)		5 7 6/7 2 1	32	1	3S 1	94	3	M11 NB8	34	78	1	12	32	9

2ND DAY	BOWLERS (BIRKENSHAW) PAVILION END		BOWLERS (BIRD) RADCLIFFE RD END		BATSMEN SCOREBOARD LEFT			BATSMEN SCOREBOARD RIGHT			WEST INDIES 1ST INNINGS	END-OF-OVER TOTALS					
TIME	BOWLER	O.	BOWLER	O.	SCORING	BALLS	6s/4s	SCORING	BALLS	6s/4s	NOTES	O.	RUNS	W.	'L' BAT	'R' BAT	EXTRAS
					RICHARDSON	32	1	HAYNES	94	3	M11 NB8	34	78	1	12	32	9
6.18			DILLEY	10	: 4/3 3	34		8 1 : . P	98			35	82		15	33	
23	EMBUREY	1			2 P : 3 2 · 7 W	40	1					36	84	2	17	33	9
25					RICHARDS										0		
27			"	11	. . : :	4		2 : 7 3	100			37	87			36	
32	"	2			5 :	5		•2 6/5 : 4 · 6 4 2 1	105	5	• Diving stop (Broad)	38	96			45	
36			"	12	7 2 x : 4• 4 x :	9	1	3 : 9 1	107		• Jarvis misfielded	39	103		6	46	
41	"	3			8/7 4 P 6 P 7 · · · 4	14	3	3 3	108			40	114		14	49	
44			"	13	· 5(6) 4 · †7/8 4 ·	19	5	8 1	109		Light poor, 3HR, HAYNES' 50: 177'	41	123		22	50	
49	"	4	(13-2-41-0)		6 7 6 : · · ·	23		: 1 3	111			42	126			53	
53	(4-0-25-1)		PRINGLE	8		23	5	:	112	5	Light discussed	42'	126	2	22	53	9
6.54	BLSP		(7.1-5-4-0)								M11 NB 8	STUMPS					
3RD DAY 11.00			PRINGLE	8	x : 1 4	25	6	6 P 8 · · 1	115			43	131		26	54	
04	JARVIS	8				25	6	:	116	5		43'	131	2	26	54	9
11.04½	(7.1-1-24-1) RSP											RAIN					
1.00	LUNCH											LUNCH					
2.00	JARVIS	8			2† P 8 · · 1	28		7 1 2E ·	118		† Lamp spoof catch	44	133		27	55	
04			"	9	LB · 1 6 4 3	31	7	2 · 9 · · 1	121		(LB) 50 p'ship: 35'	45	142		34	56	10
09	"	9			2LB 3 †3/4 7 · 4 · 4 2 ·	37	9				(2LB)	46	154		44		12
13			"	10	x : :	39		P† : : 1/2 3	125		† Almost played on.	47	157			59	
17	"	10			EP · . . . : .	44		1E 1	126			48	158			60	
22			"	11				. : : x . :	132		M12	49					
25		11			: L LB · ·	47		E1 W	133	5	(LB)	49⁴	159	3	44	60	13
28								HOOPER								0	
30	"	11						L 9 · 1	2			50	160			1	
32			"	12	7/8 1	48		7 : 8 1 2 : :	7			51	162		45	2	
36	"	12			: : 7 1	51		: : :	10			52	163		46		
40			"	13	2 : : 3S 1 : 7S 1	56		4 3	11			53	168		48	5	
44	"	13			: 1/2 1	58		: : : 8 2	15		4HR	54	171		49	7	
48			"	14	6 : 9 1 7 : 2 1	62		7 1 :	17		RICHARDS'S 50: 80' out of 88	55	174		51	8	
53	"	14	(14-6-30-0)		E1 · P · 2 1	65		3 · · ·	20		Edged short of wk.	56	175		52		
57			DEFREITAS	12	P · EP · LB ·	68		: 2 2 :	23		(LB)	57	178			10	14
3.02	"	15			4 1	69		: 5 4 P : 5(6) 4	28	2		58	187		53	18	
06	(15-1-52-2)		"	13	2/3 ⊙ : : : 1 1	75		:	29		(NB) NB 9	59	189		54		15
13	EMBUREY	5			5(6) 4 1 3	77	10	4 4 4 4 · † 4 1	33	4		60	205		61	27	
17			"	14				: : 6 ⊙ · · 7 1	40		(NB) NB 10	61	206				16
21	"	6			: 2/3 4 3 4 P · P · 3 3	83	12				50 p'ship: 52'	62	217		72		
25			"	15	G · . : 1 1	87		: :	42		G left hand (treatment)	63	218		73		
30	"	7			: 6 6 4 1 :	91	1/12	6 · 9 3	44			64	228		80	30	
3.34	(7-0-62-1)		" (15.2-3-38-0)	16		91	1/12	8/7 2 :	46	4	M12 NB10 off at 3.35pm	64²	230	3	80	32	16

3RD DAY	BOWLERS (BIRKENSHAW) PAVILION END		(BIRD) RADCLIFFE RD END		BATSMEN SCOREBOARD LEFT			SCOREBOARD RIGHT			WEST INDIES 1ST INNINGS NOTES	END-OF-OVER TOTALS					
TIME	BOWLER	O.	BOWLER	O.	SCORING	BALLS	6s/4s	SCORING	BALLS	6s/4s		O.	RUNS	W.	'L' BAT	'R' BAT	EXTRAS
TEA					RICHARDS	91	1/12	HOOPER	46	4	M12 NB10	64²	230	3	80	32	16
4.03			DEFREITAS	16	: : :	94		½ 1	47			65	231			33	
07	PRINGLE	15						: : . : : 2	53		M13	66					
10			"	17	. P E2 W	97	1/12					66²	231	4	80	33	16
12					LOGIE										0		
14			"	17	: . .	3					M14	67					
16	"	16						: : : . . 1E 1	59		NB 11 5HR	68	232			34	
20			"	18	. . ⊙ 2/3 4 . 4 4	9	2	3(6) ② 3	61		(NB) NB 12	69	246		8	39	17
24	"	17			: : . 3 4 .	14	3	6 3	62			70	253		12	42	
28			"	19	. 6† 1 . .	18		4 1 6 3	64		† Broad misfielded	71	258		13	46	
32	"	18	(19-4-58-1)					. . . . . .	70		M15	72					
36	(18-8-38-0)		DILLEY	14	9 6 4 1	20	4	7 1	71	4		72³	264	4	18	47	17
4.41	BLSP		(13.3-2-47-0)								M15 NB12			B	L S	P	
6.05	PLAY ABANDONED										Gatting's 31st birthday		S	T	UM	PS	
4TH DAY 11.00			DILLEY	14	4 x x : : :	23						73					
03	PRINGLE	19			• 8 2 7 . 6 2 : : : :	28		7/8 1	72		• Ro chance (Gower)	74	267		20	48	
07			"	15				5(6) 4 : : 2 : .	78	5	HOOPER'S 50: 110'	75	271			52	
12	"	20			2/3 : : . 2/3 . G1 W	34	4				M16	76	271	5	20	52	17
14					DUJON										0		
16			"	16	. 3 3	2		: 4 1E 1 2 1	82			77	276		3	54	
21	"	21			. . 2 : . P .	7		2 1	83			78	277			55	
24			"	17				: . . 7 P . 3 ⊙ . 4 .	90	6	(NB) NB 13	79	282			59	18
29	"	22			. x : 6/7S 1	11		3 : :	92			80	283		4		
32			"	18	4 x : . : 1 1	16		:	93		6HR	81	284		5		
37	"	23			: . . P 6 . :	22					M17	82					
40			"	19	2 1	23		2 : . 1/2 1 : 4 :	98			83	286		6	60	
45	"	24			L 4 : . : . LB	29					(LB) M18	84	287				19
48			"	20	3 : 3 : 2/3 : 3	34		7E .	99			85	290		9		
53	"	25			. : 1 1	37		: 5 :	102			86	291		10		
57			"	21	L 4 x LB : : : . :	42		2 1	103		(LB)	87	293			61	20
12.01	"	26			.	43		: L . . 7S 1	108			88	294			62	
05			"	22	: x . .	47		: 1E• 3	110		• Low to Gooch's right (2nd slip)	89	297			65	
09	"	27			P . : x :	52		2 1	111			90	298			66	
13			"	23	x 3 2/3 3 2 :	56		x 2 : 1	113			91	301		12	67	
17	"	28			3 7/6 . 2	58		G . . 1S : . . 1	117			92	304		14	68	
22			"	24	8 5 2 W	60	-	x : 5(6) 3	120		cloud	92⁵	309	6	16	71	20
25					MARSHALL										0		
27			"	24	x :	1						93					
28	"	29			8 1	2		: 4/3 2 7 8 . 1 :	125			94	313		1	74	
12.32	(29-11-53-1)		(25-2-81-1)	25	: : 1E 1 : :	7	-	8S 1	126	6	M18 NB13 7HR	95	315	6	2	75	20

4TH DAY	BOWLERS (BIRKENSHAW) PAVILION END		(BIRD) RADCLIFFE RD END		BATSMEN SCOREBOARD LEFT			SCOREBOARD RIGHT			WEST INDIES 1ST INNINGS NOTES	END-OF-OVER TOTALS					
TIME	BOWLER	O.	BOWLER	O.	SCORING	BALLS	6s/4s	SCORING	BALLS	6s/4s		O.	RUNS	W.	'L' BAT	'R' BAT	EXTRAS
					MARSHALL	7	-	HOOPER	126	6	M18 NB 13 7HR	95	315	6	2	75	20
12.37	JARVIS	16			4 × 3 . . . 4	11	1	EP 2 . 1	128			96	320		6	76	
41			DEFREITAS	20				. 3 8† 8 9 4 . . 2 . 4 .	134	7	† NEW BALL at 12.43	97	326			82	
46	"	17			3/4 4 . 4† . 4G 4	17	2				† tumbling stop (PRINGLE)	98	330		10		
50			"	21				. 6 . 7 2/3 ×	140		M19	99					
53	"	18			6 6 EP8 4 7E . . 1 . .	22		8/9 1	141			100	332		11	83	
57	(18-1-63-2)		"	22	1/2 1	23	2	L 8 . 1 . . 2	146	7		101	334	6	12	84	20
1.00	LUNCH		(22-5-66-1)								M19 NB 13		LUNCH				
1.40	DILLEY	26			. . 7 . . 7	29					occ. cloud – humid. M20	102					
45			DEFREITAS	23				S G1 . W	148	7		102²	334	7	12	84	20
46								AMBROSE		LHB						0	
48			"	23				. P . 3† 2	4		† 1 overthrow via stumps	103	336			2	
51	"	27			3 × 2 . . 1	32		3	7			104	337		13		
56			"	24	. 7 4 3 3 ×4 2 ⊙	39					(NB) NB 14	105	340		15		21
2.00	"	28			× .	40		4 × . † B	12		(B) † ball changed M21	106	341				22
06			"	25	. 3 L . . .	43		× . 2 . . 3	15			107	344			5	
10	"	29						7 5 † 7 × 2 . . 4 . .	21	1	LEAD: 100+	108	350			11	
14			"	26	3/2 1E 7 4 4 1	46	4	× 3 2 . . 1	24		8HR	109	360		24	12	
19	"	30						P . × 6	30		M22	110					
23			"	27	3 8/9 4 1	48	5	P 6 Y . 4 . .	34	2		111	369		29	16	
28	"	31	(27-5-93-2)		6 5(4) . . 1	51		6• † . ⊙ . .	38		• "ct" Pringle - mid-on (NB) NB 15	112	371		30		23
33			EMBUREY	8	P . P . 7	57					M23	113					
38	"	32			St 3 . 1E . . . 1	61		3 2 1 1	40		† Hit bowler's wkt.	114	374		31	18	
43			"	9				. . × × . 8	46		Round wkt to LHB. M24	115					
47	"	33			4 7 7 . 1 . .	65		8 8/9 2 1	48			116	378		32	21	
52			"	10				9 . 2 . . . 4	54	3	Hardie sub (Gooch) (2 overs)	117	382			25	
56	"	34			3 7 7/8 2 . 1	68		. 4 2 . . 1	57		50 pship: 69'	118	386		35	26	
3.01	(34-5-101-1)		"	11				4 . . 3 . †	63		† over wkt M25	119					
04	PRINGLE	30			P 3E 8 4 . . 2 1	72		4 . . .	65			120	389		38		
08			"	12	4 6/7 4 3 1 6 6 1	76	2/5	7• 1 .	67		• leaping attempt at catch (Gower)	121	404		52	27	
12	"	31			4 3 7 2 6 1 4 2	80	3/6	8 . 1	69		MARSHALL'S 50: 123'	122	418		65	28	
16			"	13				P . 4 6P	75		M26 9HR	123					
19	"	32			. 4 4 3 . . 2 1	84		† × × . .	77		† Round wkt.	124	421		68		
23			"	14	4F 7 5 × 2 2 . W	88	3/6					124⁴	425	8	72	28	23
24					WALSH										0		
27			"	14	. .	2					Rd wkt.	125					
28	"	33						4 . 6 7• 4 † . . . . 2 . ⊙ .	84		• Dr DeFreitas w/w running in. (NB) NB16	126	428			30	24
32			"	15	6 4 . 1 .	5		7 5 3S . 6 1	87	1/3		127	436			37	
36	" (34-11-82-1)	34	(15-4-93-2)		4 1	6	-	9E 9E × × . 4 1 . . .	92	1/4	Rd wkt (5 balls)	128	442	8	2	42	24
3.40	TEA										M26 NB16			TEA			
4.00			EMBUREY	16	6 1	7		4B . 6 6 6 1	97		(4B) LEAD 200+	129	448		3	43	28
03	JARVIS	19	(16-4-95-2)			7	-	6 RO	98	1/4	M26 NB 16	129¹	448	9	3	43	28
4.04	(18-1-1-63-2) DECLARATION										791 balls		DECLARED				

4TH DAY	BOWLERS (BIRD) PAVILION END		BOWLERS (BIRKENSHAW) RADCLIFFE RD END		BATSMEN SCOREBOARD LEFT			BATSMEN SCOREBOARD RIGHT			ENGLAND 2ND INNINGS	END-OF-OVER TOTALS					
TIME	BOWLER	O.	BOWLER	O.	SCORING	BALLS	6s/4s	SCORING	BALLS	6s/4s	NOTES	O.	RUNS	W.	L BAT	R BAT	EXTRAS
					GOOCH			BROAD		LHB							
4.17	MARSHALL	1			· · · · · 2	6						1	2		2		
21			PATTERSON	1				· · · · · ·	6		M1	2					
25	"	2			4 · · · · ·	12					M2	3					
28			"	2	· · · 4 ·	17	1	1	7			4	7		6	1	
33	"	3			· · · 1	21		LB ·	9		(LB)	5	9		7		1
37			"	3	1	22		2 · · · ·	14			6	12		8	3	
42	"	4			· · · · · ·	28					M3	7					
46	(4-2-3-0)		"	4				· · · · · 1	20			8	13			4	
52	AMBROSE	1						· 4 · · · ·	26	1		9	17			8	
56			"	5	· · · · · ·	34					M4	10					
5.00	"	2			3 · ·	37		1 · ·	29		† Ducked - hit in ribs. (LB)	11	22		11	9	2
05			"	6	· · 2 ·	41		· 1	31			12	25		13	10	
09	"	3						· · · · · ·	37		M5	13					
13			"	7	· 1	43		· · 4 ·	41	2	1 HR	14	30		14	14	
18	"	4	(7-2-17-0)		· 1	46		· 2 ·	44		† Hit bowler's stumps	15	33		15	16	
22			WALSH	1	· · · · 1	51		·	45			16	34		16		
27	"	5			· · · · · ·	57					M6	17					
30			"	2	4 ·	59	2	· · ·	49		(LB)	18	39		20		3
35	"	6						· · · · · W	55	2	† Hit bowler's stumps M7	19	39	1	20	16	3
38								GATTING								0	
40			"	3	3	60		· ⊙ · · ·	6		(NB) (LB) NB 1	20	44		23		5
46	"	7			· · ·	63		· · 1	9			21	45			1	
50			"	4				· · 2 · · 1	15			22	48			4	
54	"	8			· ·	65		· · · 1	19			23	49			5	
58	(8-3-13-1)		"	5				· · · · · ·	25		M8	24					
6.02	MARSHALL	5			· 2 · · · 1	71						25	52		26		
06			"	6	· · · · · 1	77						26	53		27		
10	"	6			· · · · · 2	83					† MARSHALL warned.	27	55		29		
14			"	7	3	84		· · 1 · ·	30		2 HR	28	59		32	6	
18	"	7			· 2 · · · ·	90					† Round wkt.	29	61		34		
23			"	8				· · · · 2 ·	36			30	63			8	
27	(8-2-14-0)	8	(8-1-19-0)		· · 4 · · ·	96	3		36	-	Round wkt	31	67	1	38	8	5
6.30	STUMPS										M8 NB 1		STUMPS				

5TH DAY	BOWLERS (BIRD) PAVILION END		(BIRKENSHAW) RADCLIFFE RD END		BATSMEN SCOREBOARD LEFT			SCOREBOARD RIGHT			ENGLAND 2ND INNINGS	END-OF-OVER TOTALS					
TIME	BOWLER	O.	BOWLER	O.	SCORING	BALLS	6s/4s	SCORING	BALLS	6s/4s	NOTES	O.	RUNS	W.	'L' BAT	'R' BAT	EXTRAS
					GOOCH	96	3	GATTING	36	-	Pitch - quicker. Sunny. M8 NB 1	31	67	1	38	8	5
11.02			AMBROSE	9				. . . . ↑ x	42		Marshall r.b injury M9 [illegible]	32					
06	PATTERSON	8			. : 3E : . 7 2	102						33	69		40		
11			"	10				3/2 3 5(4) ↑ P T 2	48			34	71			10	
15	"	9			L : 2 6 7/8 4 .	108	4					35	75		44		
19			"	11				↓ T ↓ 1E ↑ : 2 . .	54		• Hook - under edge - Ar Dujon in front 1st slip	36	77			12	
23	"	10			4 : ↑ 7 1	112		. :	56			37	78		45		
27			"	12	: 3 1	114		: : : 9 1	60			38	80		46	13	
31	"	11			LB : 8 3	117		7 ↑ 9SF 1 . 1	63		(LB)	39	86		49	15	6
36			"	13	: : ↑ : F 4/3S 1	123					GOOCH's 2nd 50: 171'	40	87		50		
40	"	12	(13-4-20-1)		P 2 6/5 1	126		P fx :	66		3HR	41	88		51		
45			WALSH	9	9 1 : T	129		P 8 1 2 3	69		50 p'ship: 93 min.	42	94		52	20	
50 52	"	13						† 3 . L	75		† ball changed. M10	43					
57			"	10	. . 6 3 7 4 . . 4	135	6					44	102		60		
12.03	"	14			1E* 4	136	7	: 6P P 69 1	80		• Bisected slips 2-3	45	107		64	21	
08			"	11				. : 6/7 : .	86		M 11	46					
12	"	15			: : : 7 : .	142					M12	47					
16	(15-4-35-0)		"	12				L : . . : 7 4	92	1		48	111			25	
21	MARSHALL	9			. : 7 P P	148					Round wkt (1 over). M13	49					
25			"	13				: : . : 6P 1/2 4	98	2		50	115			29	
29	"	10			: : LB	151		: x W	101	2	(LB) M14	51	116	2	64	29	7
32								GOWER		LHB						0	
35			"	14	: : : 7 2 :	157					M15	52					
39	"	11						4 8 6P : 2 . . :	6		Round wkt (balls 1-3, 6)	53	118			2	
44			"	15	3 3	158		4 7 ↑ 2 : 2 .	11		Gooch on 64 for 36' 4HR	54	125		67	6	
49	"	12			: 2 9E 1	161		. : 7 4	14	1	Round wkt to LHB (2b)	55	130		68	10	
53			"	16	7 ↑ T 7 7/6 . 2 . 4 1	167	8					56	137		75		
56	(13-4-23-1)	13	(16-3-55-0)		. 7 8 2	173	8		14	1		57	139	2	77	10	7
1.00	LUNCH										M15 NB 1		LUNCH				
1.42			AMBROSE	14	7 LB	175		1/2 9P 6 2 1	18		(LB)	58	143			13	8
47	RICHARDS	1			8/7 7 3/2 4	181	9					59	147		81		
50			"	15				3 2† ↑ P 3 1E Y (4)	25	2	† Gully stop (Haynes) NB 2	60	151			17	
54	"	2			7/8 1	183		7 ^ :	29			61	152		82		
58			"	16	: 2 3	185		↑ : 6 P	33			62	155		85		
2.03	"	3			4 4 4	191	10				ARTHURTON sub for MARSHALL	63	159		89		
06	(3-0-9-0)		"	17				7 2 F x P 2 4	39	3		64	165			23	
10	HOOPER	1			: 6 6 1	196		3	40		50 p'ship: 55'	65	166		90		
13			"	18	4 8 6F 4 2	202						66	168		92		
17	"	2			6 1	203		: 1E : 3 1	45			67	170		93	24	
2.20	(2-0-3-0)		(19-4-47-1)	19	x 1 1/2 8 4 1	208	11	1 4	46	4	M15 NB 2	68	179	2	98	28	8

5TH DAY	BOWLERS (BIRD) PAVILION END		(BIRKENSHAW) RADCLIFFE RD END		BATSMEN SCOREBOARD LEFT			SCOREBOARD RIGHT			ENGLAND 2ND INNINGS	END-OF-OVER TOTALS					
TIME	BOWLER	O.	BOWLER	O.	SCORING	BALLS	6s/4s	SCORING	BALLS	6s/4s	NOTES	O.	RUNS	W.	'L' BAT	'R' BAT	EXTRAS
					GOOCH	208	11	GOWER	46	4	M15 NB2	68	179	2	98	28	8
2.24	HOOPER	3			: 6 1	210		1 EP 2 : 4 . .	50	5	Sunny	69	184		99	32	
27			AMBROSE	20	x• 1 4 6 6 8 1	216					• Appeal c wk. 5HR GOOCH'S 100: 300'	70	185		100		
31	"	4			P . . 4 P P	222					M16	71					
33			"	21	. LB	224		. 7 1 : FG	54		(LB)	72	187			33	9
37	"	5	(21-4-49-1)		EP8 1 7 6 : :	227		: : 8 1	57			73	189		101	34	
41			PATTERSON	16				4 : 4 F : .	63		M17	74					
45	"	6			7 8 : 1	229		: : : 2† 2	67		† over gully (Richards)	75	192		102	36	
48			"	17	4/3 1 7/8 1	231		⊙ . . 2/1 1 4 :	72		(NB) NB3	76	196		104	37	10
54	"	7			3F 4 1E . : 7/S 1	235	12	: :	74			77	201		109		
57			"	18	7 1 . ⊙ : T3 3	241		2† 1	75		† ENGLAND LEVEL at 2.58 pm. (NB) NB4	78	207		113	38	11
3.03	"	8	(18-5-45-0)		9/8 1 6 6 : 1	244		†: 7/8 1 :	78		† Round wkt to LHB	79	210		115	39	
0			RICHARDS	4	8 1 5(6) 1	246		: 3 : 8 1	82		HARPER sub (HAYNES) Round wkt to LHB	80	213		117	40	
11	"	9			6 1	247		P . EP 2LB 9 . . . 2	87		100 p'ship: 117 min	81	218		118	42	13
15			"	5	3 4† 1 . 2 1	250		: 7 :	90		† Harper torpedoed	82	221		121		
17	"	10			: 6 7 1 : :	255		7 1	91			83	223		122	43	
20			"	6				4 3 . 4 : :	97		M18	84					
22	"	11			6 8 P 6 . 4F 1	261						85	224		123		
25			"	7	8/9 1	262		6/7 P 3 . . . : :	102			86	225		124		
27	"	12			: 9 1	264		: . . 4 1	106		6HR	87	227		125	44	
29			"	8	: 8 1	266		7F 3 8 . 2 4 1	110	6	GOWER'S 50:	88	235		126	51	
32	"	13			6 1	267		: . : . .	115			89	236		127		
34			"	9	: 6 1 : :	271		7 8 : 1	117			90	238		128	52	
38	(14-1-33-0)	14	(9-1-26-0)			271	12	: : 3 . : 3 8 2 1	123	6		91	241	2	128	55	13
3.40	TEA										M18 NB4			T	E A		
4.03			WALSH	17				†1/6E 4° ⊙ . . 7 3† 2 . .	130	7	† NEW BALL (NB) NB5 • Inside edge via body to wk	92	248			61	14
08	PATTERSON	19			: † 4 6 : :	277					M19	93					
14			"	18	3 4 . 4/3 8† . . . 2 4	282	13	3 1	131		Haynes back.	94	255		134	62	
19	"	20			: 4 8/7 3 : 4 .	286	14	6 †8 . 1	133		150 p'ship: 166'	95	260		138	63	
23			"	19	8/7F 6 7 4• 4 . : .	290	15	2 2 2 1	135		• low, hard chance to Haynes (m-off)	96	267		142	66	
29	"	21			8 1	291		4 : 7 2/3 5• . . 4 1	140	8	• Just over bowler's reach.	97	273		143	71	
33			"	20	. 2 EP 5 6 2 1	297						98	274		144		
40	"	22			. 2/3 4 6F† E1 : 2 ⊙ . 5 W	303	15				(NB) NB6	98 5	277	3	146	71	15
43					LAMB										0		
46	"	22			2 2	1						99	279		2		
48			"	21				: : . 7 P 2 : :	146		7HR	100	281			73	
52	"	23			x 7/8 : † 3 . F8 : ⊙ : . . . 1	8					(NB) NB7	101	283		3		16
57			"	22	: : : 4 . : . . : .	14					M 20	102					
5.02	"	24						5 . . 3/4 2 . . . 4 2 .	152	9		103	289			79	
07	(24-6-69-1)		"	23	. 7/8 . L . : . . : .	20	–		152	9	M 21	104	289	3			
11	AMBROSE	22						7 4 . †+ † L 7	158	10	† Hit on shoulder	105	293			83	
17			"	24	: †8/9 1 4F . : . .	24		: 2• 1	160		• Low chance to diving gully (Hooper)	106	295		4	84	
21	"	23			: 7F 2 . 2 L : . .	29		3/4 1	161		20 OVERS MIN.	107	298		6	85	
25	(23-4-56-1)		" (25-5-84-0)	25	: : :	32	–	L 8/7 7 . 2 1	164	10	M21 NB7	108	301	3	6	88	16
5.30	MATCH	DRAWN									655 balls		STUMPS				

ENGLAND 1ST INNINGS v. WEST INDIES (FIRST TEST) at TRENT BRIDGE, NOTTINGHAM on 2,3,4,6,7 JUNE, 1988.

IN	OUT	MINS	No.	BATSMAN	HOW OUT	BOWLER	RUNS	WKT	TOTAL	6s	4s	BALLS	NOTES ON DISMISSAL Toss: ENGLAND.
11·00	2·35	175	1	G.A. GOOCH	BOWLED	MARSHALL	73	1	125	·	8	131	Played on – inside edge into leg-stump (off-driving).
11·00	3·41	241	2	B.C. BROAD	BOWLED	MARSHALL	54	3	161	·	3	167	Played on - edged offside push in last pre-tea over.
2·37	3·06	29	3	M.W. GATTING*	Ct LOGIE	MARSHALL	5	2	141	·	·	15	Firm bat/pad catch to short leg.
3·08	5·11	99	4	D.I. GOWER	Ct DUJON	AMBROSE	18	5	186	·	1	56	Top-edged cut to keeper's left.
4·00	4·01	1	5	A.J. LAMB	LBW	MARSHALL	0	4	161	·	·	2	Adjudged LBW to vast inswinger – pushing forward.
4·02	11·23	149	6	D.R. PRINGLE	BOWLED	MARSHALL	39	6	223	·	3	143	Yorked by late inswinger.
5·13	(12·10)	130	7	P.R. DOWNTON†	NOT OUT		16			·	1	75	
11·25	11·27	2	8	J.E. EMBUREY	Ct DUJON	MARSHALL	0	7	223	·	·	4	Edged ball slanted across him from round the wicket.
11·29	11·46	17	9	P.A.J. DeFREITAS	BOWLED	AMBROSE	3	8	235	·	·	10	Played inside ball that 'straightened'.
11·48	12·07	19	10	P.W. JARVIS	BOWLED	AMBROSE	6	9	243	·	1	15	Yorked.
12·09	12·10	1	11	G.R. DILLEY	BOWLED	AMBROSE	2	10	245	·	·	2	Yorked off stump.
				EXTRAS	b - lb 13	w 5 nb 11	29			0	17	620 balls (including 14 no-balls)	

* CAPTAIN † WICKET-KEEPER

TOTAL (101 OVERS; 439 MINUTES) 245 ALL OUT at 12·10 on 2nd day.

13 OVERS 5 BALLS/HOUR
2·42 RUNS/OVER
39 RUNS/100 BALLS

UMPIRES: H.D. BIRD & J. BIRKENSHAW.

BOWLER	O	M	R	W	nb/w
MARSHALL	30	4	69	6	2/2
PATTERSON	16	2	49	0	7/2
AMBROSE	26	10	53	4	1/1
WALSH	20	4	39	0	4/-
HOOPER	8	1	20	0	-
RICHARDS	1	0	2	0	-
			13		
	101	21	245	10	

2ND NEW BALL NOT TAKEN.

HRS	OVERS	RUNS
1	12	44
2	15	36
3	13	45
4	13	35
5	14	25
6	16	25
7	14	25

RUNS	MINS	OVERS	LAST 50 (in mins)
50	70	14·4	70
100	142	32·3	72
150	218	48·1	76
200	341	77·5	123

LUNCH: 80-0 [27 OVERS, 120 MIN] GOOCH 45*, BROAD 28*

TEA: 161-3 [53.4 OVERS, 241 MIN] GOWER 12* (33')

STUMPS (1ST DAY): 220-5 [88 OVERS, 378 MIN] PRINGLE 39* (135'), DOWNTON 9* (69')

MARSHALL 5 wkts in innings × 16 (4th instance v. England) (261 TEST WKTS)

AMBROSE CAREER BEST IN TESTS

ENGLAND added 25-5 off 13 overs in 71 min (MARSHALL 6-0-15-2, AMBROSE 7-4-5-3)

WKT	PARTNERSHIP		RUNS	MINS
1st	Gooch	Broad	125	175
2nd	Broad	Gatting	16	29
3rd	Broad	Gower	20	33
4th	Gower	Lamb	0	1
5th	Gower	Pringle	25	64
6th	Pringle	Downton	37	83
7th	Downton	Emburey	0	2
8th	Downton	DeFreitas	12	17
9th	Downton	Jarvis	8	19
10th	Downton	Dilley	2	1
			245	

WEST INDIES 1ST INNINGS — IN REPLY TO ENGLAND'S 245 ALL OUT

IN	OUT	MINS	No.	BATSMAN	HOW OUT	BOWLER	RUNS	WKT	TOTAL	6s	4s	BALLS	NOTES ON DISMISSAL
12·34	5·36	108	1	C.G. GREENIDGE	Ct DOWNTON	JARVIS	25	1	54	·	4	86	Edged off-side force to 'keeper.
12·34	2·28	217	2	D.L. HAYNES	Ct DOWNTON	JARVIS	60	3	159	·	5	133	Lifting ball took bat shoulder - caught diving forward.
5·38	6·25	47	3	R.B. RICHARDSON	Ct GATTING	EMBUREY	17	2	84	·	1	40	Fended lifting off-break to short-leg (diving forward, one-handed)
6·27	4·12	135	4	I.V.A. RICHARDS*	Ct GOOCH	DeFREITAS	80	4	231	1	12	97	Egged cover-drive to 2nd slip.
2·30	1·46	229	5	C.L. HOOPER	Ct DOWNTON	DeFREITAS	84	7	334	·	7	148	Gloved lifter low to keeper's right.
4·14	11·14	41	6	A.L. LOGIE	Ct GOOCH	PRINGLE	20	5	271	·	4	34	Gloved lifter to 2nd slip - taken at second attempt.
11·16	12·25	69	7	P.J.L. DUJON†	Ct AND BOWLED	DILLEY	16	6	309	·	·	60	Mistimed bounce - attempted pull - simple return catch.
12·27	3·24	137	8	M.D. MARSHALL	BOWLED	EMBUREY	72	8	425	3	6	88	Made room for flat-batted drive - missed.
1·48	4·04	116	9	C.E.L. AMBROSE	RUN OUT [GOOCH]		43	9	448	1	4	98	Attempted quick run to mid-on - direct hit on bowler's wkt.
3·27	(4·04)	17	10	C.A. WALSH	NOT OUT		3			·	·	7	
			11	B.P. PATTERSON									
				EXTRAS	b 6 lb 8	w - nb 14	28			5[6]	43[4]	791 balls (including 16 no-balls)	

*CAPTAIN †WICKET-KEEPER

TOTAL (129.1 OVERS; 566 MINUTES) 448-9 DECLARED at 4.04 pm on 4th day. LEAD: 203

13 OVERS 4 BALLS/HOUR
3.46 RUNS/OVER
56 RUNS/100 BALLS

BOWLER	O	M	R	W	nb
DILLEY	34	5	101	1	6
DeFREITAS	27	5	93	2	9
JARVIS	18·1	1	63	2	-
PRINGLE	34	11	82	1	1
EMBUREY	16	4	95	2	-
			14	1	
	129·1	26	448	9	

2nd NEW BALL taken at 12.43pm on 4th day. WEST INDIES 322-6 after 96.3 overs

HRS	OVERS	RUNS
1	13	23
2	14	36
3	14	64
4	13	48
5	14	61
6	13	52
7	14	31
8	14	45
9	14	58

RUNS	MINS	OVERS	LAST 50 (in mins)
50	99	21·4	99
100	171	38·5	72
150	201	45·4	30
200	265	59·3	64
250	308	69·5	43
300	397	90·4	89
350	474	107·4	77
400	532	120·4	58

LUNCH: (TEA at 3.40) RAIN 1.40 - 4.15.	8-0	6 OVERS 26 MIN	HAYNES 5* GREENIDGE 0*
STUMPS (2ND DAY):	126-2	42.1 OVERS 185 MIN	HAYNES 53* (185') RICHARDS 22* (27')
RSP at 11.04 after 6 balls: LUNCH:	131-2	43.1 OVERS 189 MIN	HAYNES 54* (189') RICHARDS 26* (31')
TEA:	230-3	64.2 OVERS 284 MIN	RICHARDS 80* (126') HOOPER 32* (65')
STUMPS (3RD DAY):	264-4	72.3 OVERS 322 MIN	HOOPER 37* (103') LOGIE* 18* (27')
LUNCH:	334-6	101 OVERS 442 MIN	HOOPER 84* (223') MARSHALL 12* (33')
TEA:	442-8	128 OVERS 562 MIN	AMBROSE 42* (112') WALSH 2* (13')

WKT	PARTNERSHIP		RUNS	MINS
1st	Greenidge	Haynes	54	108
2nd	Haynes	Richardson	30	47
3rd	Haynes	Richards	75	59
4th	Richards	Hooper	72	74
5th	Hooper	Logie	40	41
6th	Hooper	Dujon	38	69
7th	Hooper	Marshall	25	39
8th	Marshall	Ambrose	91	96
9th	Ambrose	Walsh	23	17
10th			448	

ENGLAND 2ND INNINGS — 203 RUNS BEHIND ON FIRST INNINGS

IN	OUT	MINS	No.	BATSMAN	HOW OUT	BOWLER	RUNS	WKT	TOTAL	6s	4s	BALLS	NOTES ON DISMISSAL
4.17	4.43	410	1	G.A. GOOCH	C^t DUJON	PATTERSON	146	3	277	·	15	303	(8th in Tests, (4th v WI, (63rd F.C. Edged ball that lifted and left him.
4.17	5.38	81	2	B.C. BROAD	C^t DUJON	AMBROSE	16	1	39	·	2	55	Edged ball angled across him.
5.40	12.32	140	3	M.W. GATTING *	BOWLED	MARSHALL	29	2	116	·	2	101	Pushed inside line of outswinger which uprooted off stump.
12.35	(5.30)	230	4	D.I. GOWER	NOT OUT		88			·	10	164	His HS (first-class) of 1988 to date.
4.46	(5.30)	44	5	A.J. LAMB	NOT OUT		6			·	·	32	
			6										
			7										
			8										
			9										
			10										
			11										
				EXTRAS	b - lb 10 w - nb 6		16			·	29	655 balls (inc 7 no-balls)	
				TOTAL	(108 OVERS; 457 MINUTES)		301-3.						

* CAPTAIN † WICKET-KEEPER

14 OVERS 1 BALLS/HOUR
2.78 RUNS/OVER
45 RUNS/100 BALLS

BOWLER	O	M	R	W	nb
MARSHALL	13	4	23	1	-
PATTERSON	24	6	69	1	4
AMBROSE	23	4	56	1	1
WALSH	25	5	84	0	2
RICHARDS	9	1	26	0	-
HOOPER	14	1	33	0	-
			10		
	108	21	301	3	

2ND NEW BALL taken at 4.03pm on 5th day - ENGLAND 241-2 after 91 overs.

HRS	OVERS	RUNS
1	14	30
2	14	29
3	13	29
4	13	37
5	16	60
6	17	42
7	13	54

RUNS	MINS	OVERS	LAST 50 (in mins)
50	107	24.2	107
100	194	44.0	87
150	263	59.5	69
200	324	76.1	61
250	384	93.5	60
300	453	107.2	69

STUMPS (4th DAY): 67-1 (136 BEHIND) [31 OVERS, 133 MIN] GOOCH 38* (133') GATTING 8* (50')

LUNCH: 139-2 [57 OVERS, 252 MIN] GOOCH 77* (252') GOWER 10* (25')

TEA: 241-2 [91 OVERS, 370 MIN] GOOCH 128* (370') GOWER 55* (143')

MATCH DRAWN

ENGLAND'S 14th SUCCESSIVE MATCH WITHOUT VICTORY (ENGLAND RECORD) - END OF WI SEQUENCE OF 10 WINS.

MATCH AWARD: M.D. MARSHALL (Adjudicator: R. ILLINGWORTH)

WKT	PARTNERSHIP		RUNS	MINS
1st	Gooch	Broad	39	81
2nd	Gooch	Gatting	77	140
3rd	Gooch	Gower	161	184
4th	Gower	Lamb	24*	44
5th				
6th				
7th				
8th				
9th				
10th			301	

LORD'S

THE SECOND TEST

Gatting assessed · Emburey's task · England's team predicted · Lord's extends record · Match report · Marshall's dominance

The eight-day period between the first two Tests was one of the saddest for the game of cricket that I can remember; appallingly handled on all sides, it was bungling and humbug at its best. At the end of it England were left with a makeshift captain and the West Indian morale must have been sky-high.

Gatting deserved to be defrocked and dethroned, not for inviting a handmaiden to share his cheese and pickle or a game of Scrabble, but for thoughtlessly creating a compromising situation which enabled the comic scribes to humiliate cricket. He was definitely on borrowed time after the Shakoor Rana affair and his churlish bickering in New Zealand. More relevantly, his record of just two wins in 23 Tests, allied to his obstinate abuse of his tour contract were factors which seemed certain to force the selectors to end his reign before the end of this series.

Mike Gatting has always been honest, straightforward, and pugnacious. He is also extremely cussed and obstinate. These can be admirable qualities, and they certainly enabled him to return to the fray more quickly than most after having his features rearranged by a Malcolm Marshall bouncer. They are not qualities which have helped his role as England cricket captain, and he has frequently been inflexible in his strategy and assessment of players. I doubt if he ever really coveted the role, and he seems to have had grave doubts about it even after his successful mission in Australia. When the dust has cleared, he will probably be relieved to be back as one of the boys. I hope so, because he was a much happier soul before his appointment and he is far too good a batsman to be missing from this England team.

My choice of captain would have been Gower but, having sacked him in 1986 in favour of Gatting, Peter May was unlikely seriously to consider reversing the procedure. As a senior member of the team and its vice-captain, John Emburey was an obvious successor. Sadly, he was in no sort of bowling form and had been taken apart by Richards and Hooper at Trent Bridge. I suspect that the selectors always saw him as a temporary prince regent rather than as the new king. At 35 he was four years Gatting's senior. Ironically, he would probably already have captained both Middlesex and his country but for his rebel South African interlude.

Emburey had little time in which to restore the deflated morale of his players, most of whom had been shattered by the edicts from Lord's, before becoming England's 66th captain in official Tests and the eleventh – four more than any other county – to be given that honour while playing for Middlesex. He was fortunate that fate provided him with the considerable bonus of making his first appearance as England's Test captain on his home ground at Lord's. Playing in familiar surroundings must have given him a vital psychological boost; no current bowler has more intimate knowledge of the ground's peculiar slope and shape when it comes to bowling changes and field-placing.

I expected the selectors to reduce England's party to twelve (Thomas having been added merely as cover for Dilley) and, in addition to Gatting who had made himself unavailable, to omit Hemmings. A second spinner would have been something of a luxury at Lord's where, at that stage of the season, no Middlesex slow bowler had taken a single first-class wicket. His obvious replacement would be Small, who had proved his fitness with a career-best 7 for 15.

I would have recalled Moxon to replace Gatting at number three. He has a sound technique against fast bowling and proved in New Zealand that he could play a long innings. His last two Test innings had been 99 and 81 not out.

A possible third change would have involved Allan Lamb, whose on-side bias had been speedily undermined by Marshall's late swing. With Gatting unavailable, Lamb's experience was likely to earn him a final chance. In view of the urgent need to groom Emburey's successor, I would have given a first cap to Derbyshire's successful young captain, Kim Barnett, whose career average of 34.75 and bold approach to fast bowling certainly merited a showing at Test level.

My *Mail on Sunday* predicted eleven was: Gooch, Broad, Moxon, Gower, Barnett, Pringle, Downton, Emburey, Jarvis, Small, Dilley. Twelfth man: DeFreitas.

Apart from the selectors preferring Lamb to Barnett, my predictions were for once correct, even down to the twelfth man.

Lord's extended its world record by staging its 82nd Test match, two more than its nearest rival, the Melbourne Cricket Ground. In the past decade it had been anything but a happy home hunting ground for England, who had won only two out of the fourteen Tests played there since 1978. Six matches since their last victory at headquarters (against New Zealand in 1983) had produced defeats by West Indies, Australia and India, and three draws. West Indies could claim five victories in their last seven encounters at Lord's with no defeat since 1957.

For the *Test Match Special* commentary team, Test matches at Lord's have a special atmosphere. Our box is within the nerve centre of cricket's headquarters, inside one of the twin turrets on the pavilion roof. To reach it we travel up four flights of stairs and pass the Long Room, the visitors' dressing room and Nancy's dining rooms. The latter, situated immediately below us, provide the best lunches on the first-class circuit and are a source of the most delicious aromas. Our view from a roomy, well-aired box is not directly behind the bowler's arm, but it is considerably better than the one afforded to

A rampant Dilley during his pre-lunch Lord's spell of 4 for 35, with prospective victim Viv Richards in anxious attendance.

the press box in the adjacent Warner stand.

Living just half a dozen miles away, I have covered more matches at Thomas Lord's third ground than anywhere else. Having the largest seating capacity of our major grounds and being in London it frequently stages two Test matches a season and always stages the finals of the two major one-day county tournaments.

Lord's has a very special significance for cricketers, and is the ground upon which every visiting Test player yearns to play. It celebrated the bicentenary of the Marylebone Cricket Club in 1987 with a five-day match against the Rest of the World which, played in a benign atmosphere, recaptured the true spirit of cricket.

One visitor to our box during this match had special reason to remember Lord's with affection. He was Wes Hall, now Minister of Tourism in the Barbados Government, who had almost bowled West Indies to victory in that epic nail-biting finish in 1963.

Having endured one of cricket's more catastrophic weeks, England were entitled to a change of fortune. It occurred soon after Viv Richards had opted to bat after agonizing several minutes during his walk back to the pavilion. Almost as he revealed his decision, hot sunlight gave way to the heavy cloud which endured throughout an action-packed first day.

Emburey must have enjoyed a reflective lunch wondering how anyone found captaincy difficult. West Indies, who fielded an unchanged team, were 66 for 5 and Graham Dilley had bowled unchanged to earn figures of 13-4-35-4. Such was his accuracy of line and degree of outswing that the West Indies batsmen, although compelled to play, frequently missed altogether. It was a classic piece of old-fashioned bowling supported by brave field placing. At one point Emburey set a six-strong slip cordon and positioned only one man on the leg side.

After the interval Gus Logie and Jeff Dujon engaged in the first of their match-winning partnerships. Neither had been in any sort of form so far on the tour. The diminutive Logie almost played on to his second ball and was given lives by Pringle at 10 (a vital miss) and by Downton when 55. Looking very much like a mirror image of Alvin Kallicharran, he seized mercilessly on any errors of length or line and was at his most brutal against Small, who conceded nine of the twelve boundaries in Logie's 65-ball fifty. Dujon is a most elegant batsman whose wicket-keeping duties have rather overshadowed the talent which originally earned him a Test place in Australia in 1981-82.

Their partnership of 130 in 150 minutes enabled West Indies, assisted by two other dropped catches, to total 209. It appeared a modest score until England began their innings and quickly lost Chris Broad. Late on a ball which moved down the slope, the Nottinghamshire left-hander mouthed his own captions to the TV close-up of his departure, a display of displeasure which, added to a certain amount of 'previous', was to earn him a final 'final warning' about his future conduct.

England's luck ran out completely on the

Martyn Moxon's swift reactions earn Dilley the wicket of Desmond Haynes at Lord's.

second day. Having reached 112 for 2, the last 8 wickets were clinically removed for 53 runs, Malcolm Marshall taking 5 or more wickets for the seventeenth time in 55 Tests and putting himself in line for a hat-trick for the second innings. He received excellent support from the beanpole, Ambrose, and also from Courtney Walsh who recaptured his rhythm and bowled particularly well against Gooch.

For once the Saturday crowd of a Lord's Test was treated to a fine day and some exhilarating cricket. They saw a vintage display of batting by Greenidge and Richards, followed by another century stand between Logie and Dujon which carried West Indies to a lead of 398.

Greenidge dominated the pre-lunch session, contributing 55 of the 88 runs by which West Indies extended their overnight lead of 60. Favoured by the best batting conditions of the match, he treated a capacity crowd to an object lesson in technique. No current player cuts with greater power or dabs late more delicately. He began in company with Desmond Haynes; it was their 118th partnership at this level, by a vast distance the most enduring opening partnership Test cricket has known. Although Dilley quickly removed Haynes, the surviving half dispatched with great aplomb any ball remotely unworthy of a defensive response.

Partnered by his captain, who reminded Emburey of his Trent Bridge mauling by hoisting his new opposite number's third ball into the Tavern Stand, Greenidge reached his 15th century in 143 Test innings off 177 balls with his fourteenth boundary. It was his sixth hundred against England and it enabled him to become the fifth West Indian to score 6,000 runs in Tests.

Although Paul Jarvis returned his best analysis and Dilley achieved his best match figures (9 for 128) as West Indies lost their last 5 wickets for 43 runs off 11 overs on the Monday, England were left with the impossible target of 442. Thanks to a gritty innings by Allan Lamb they took the match into the final day, the last 5 wickets producing 202 runs.

Lamb's eighth Test hundred was his fourth against West Indies and a record second against them at Lord's. Marooned on 99 overnight, he took 24 minutes to find the essential run, his hundred taking 172 balls, 277 minutes and including 14 fours. It was his first Test hundred since he scored four in the 1984 season and undoubtedly rescued his Test career. So much for thoughts of dropping him!

Jarvis and Dilley celebrated their bowling feats with a last wicket thrash worth 53 runs and kept the tourists waiting until 1.59 p.m. for their well-merited 134-run victory. Marshall's latest act of destruction was rewarded by his third ten-wicket analysis in Tests and his first against England. Restored to fitness after his painful rib-cage problem, he had already established himself as the dominant force of the series. In just two games, one played when he was barely half fit, he had taken 17 wickets at a cost of 10.82 runs apiece and at a frequency of one every 30 balls. His colleagues had contributed 14 dismissals each costing 55.71 runs and they had occurred only once every 115 balls.

Trevor Bailey awarded the Cornhill Match Award to Gus Logie, a worthy tribute to two memorable innings, the first played when conditions were at their most difficult.

The Gatting affair had effectively wrecked England's fine start and helped restore the West Indies juggernaut to its full strength. This result extended England's abysmal record at Headquarters to two wins in their last fifteen matches, their last victory in 1983 being succeeded by four defeats and three draws.

The mighty Marshall – a wicket every 30 balls.

CAFE

1ST DAY	BOWLERS (DR SHEPHERD) PAVILION END		(KE PALMER) NURSERY END		BATSMEN SCOREBOARD LEFT			SCOREBOARD RIGHT			WEST INDIES 1ST INNINGS	END-OF-OVER TOTALS					
TIME	BOWLER	O.	BOWLER	O.	SCORING	BALLS	6s/4s	SCORING	BALLS	6s/4s	NOTES	O.	RUNS	W.	'L' BAT	'R' BAT	EXTRAS
					GREENIDGE			HAYNES			Bright sunshine						
11.00			DILLEY	1	F2 3/4 2 · · 4 · · ·	6	1					1	4		4		
05	JARVIS	1						4 x · · · · · ·	6		M1	2					
09			"	2	2 9 YP · · 4 · · ·	12	2					3	8		8		
13	"	2						7 · EP 7 · · · · · 2	12			4	10			2	
17			"	3	· · · · P X	18					M2	5					
22	"	3			LB ·	19		4E 9 7 4 1 · · 1	17	1	(LB) overcast	6	17			8	1
26			"	4				x · P 3 · · · · 4 · ·	23	2		7	21			12	
31	"	4			2 EP 3 · · · · · ·	25					M3	8					
35			"	5				x x x 7 · · · W	27	2		8^{4}	21	1	8	12	1
38								RICHARDSON								0	
40			"	5				3 · ·	2		M4	9					
42	"	5			7 8E 4 1°	27	3	· · 5 4 P · · · ·	6		• Almost played on.	10	26		13		
46	(5-2-13-0)		"	6	· 4 · P 3 5(6) · · · · 4	33	4					11	30		17		
51	SMALL	1						2 1E 3 P LB · · 4 · · ·	12	1	(LB)	12	35			4	2
56			"	7				· · 2 x 3 P · · · ·	18		M5 1HR	13					
12.00	"	2			8 1	34		6 P EP · 2/3 · · · · ·	23			14	36		18		
05			"	8	2E P E1 (4) · · · W	39	5				NB1	14^{4}	40	2	22	4	2
08					RICHARDS										0		
10			"	8	· · ·	2						15					
12	"	3			1/2 8 4 · · 1	6	1	· 8 1	25			16	46		5	5	
17			"	9	3/4 1	7		1 W	26	1		16^{2}	47	3	6	5	2
18								HOOPER								0	
20			"	9	·	8		· · 3 3	3			17	50			3	
24	"	4						E1 W	4	-		17^{1}	50	4	6	3	2
24								LOGIE								0	
26	"	4						x 9E 4E 4 P · 4° · · ·	5	1	• Almost played on	18	54			4	
30			"	10	1E W	9	1					18^{1}	54	5	6	4	2
					DUJON										0		
32			"	10	8/7 · · · · ·	5					M6	19					
36	"	5			x Y · · · · · ·	10		3 1	6			20	55			5	
40			"	11	·	11		4 7/8 · 3 4 · · · 1	11	2	5 slips + 1 gully - 1/8 field	21	60			10	
45	"	6						8/7 EP · 5 · · · · · · ·	17		M7	22					
49			"	12	· 3 1	13		1 1E 6 · · 4 · ·	21	3	• ch to Pringle's rt.	23	65		1	14	
53	"	7			x · · · · · ·	19					M8	24					
57	(7-2-16-1)		"	13	·	20	-	x x 1E 2/3 · · · · 1	26	3	2HR	25	66	5	1	15	2
1.01	LUNCH		(13-4-35-4)								M8 NB1		LUNCH				
1.40	SMALL	8						3 2 · EP 6 · · · · · ·	32		M9	26					
44			DILLEY	14	· 2 3	22		3 4 7 · · · ·	36			27	69		4		
1.48	(9-3-20-1)	9	(14-4-38-4)		· LB · ·	24	-	7/6 · 2 3 4 · · ·	40	4	(LB) M9 NB1	28	74	5	4	19	3

1st DAY	BOWLERS (SHEPHERD) PAVILION END		(PALMER) NURSERY END		BATSMEN SCOREBOARD LEFT			SCOREBOARD RIGHT			WEST INDIES 1st INNINGS	END-OF-OVER TOTALS					
TIME	BOWLER	O.	BOWLER	O.	SCORING	BALLS	6s/4s	SCORING	BALLS	6s/4s	NOTES	O.	RUNS	W.	'L' BAT	'R' BAT	EXTRAS
					DUJON	24	-	LOGIE	40	4	M9 NB1	28	74	5	4	19	3
1.53			DILLEY	15	2 3 x : : 4 2	30						29	76		6		
57	SMALL	10						: P 2/3 L 7 4 4 : 4	46	6		30	84			27	
2.02			"	16	. 4 . EP 3 3	35		5 .	47		DeFreitas sub (Pringle) (2 overs)	31	87		9		
06	"	11			P . x P . L	41					M10	32					
10			"	17				3 7 4 : 6 8 4 2	53	7		33	93			33	
15	"	12	(17-4-49-4)		3 1	42		: 8/7 8/7 4 3 4 4	58	9		34	102		10	41	
20			PRINGLE	1	: : x . . P	48					M11	35					
23	"	13						9 P 2 6(6) : 4 . . ④ . 4	65	12	Sop'ship: 73 min. NB2 Logie's 50: 83'	36	114			53	
29	(13-4-49-1)		"	2	. x . : : :	54					DeFreitas sub (Lamb) M12 (2 overs)	37					
32	JARVIS	6			2 1E 2 P . 4 . :	58	1	: 6/7 1	67			38	119		14	54	
36			"	3	9 4 : 1E 6	62	2	3 8 . 1	69		3HR	39	124		18	55	
40	"	7			. 3 :	65		7/8 1E 2 4 1	72	13	• Dr Downton (top edge)	40	129			60	
44			"	4				: : : : : 9E	78		• Almost played on M13	41					
48	"	8			: . : 2 1	69		. :	80			42	130		19		
52			"	5	3 4 : : : 7 2	75	3					43	136		25		
56	"	9			2 . 1	77		2LB 9/8 2/1 4 . 2 1 :	84		(2LB)	44	142		26	63	5
3.00	(9-2-28-0)		"	6	9 2 : 3 4 . :	83	4					45	146		30		
05	EMBUREY	1			4 8/9 P 8 . 1 . 1	87		8 8 1 1	86			46	150		32	65	
08			"	7	. : : ⊙ 3 4 .	94	5				(NB) 100p'ship: 120' NB3	47	155		36		6
12	"	2	(7-3-20-0)					: : P : : :	92		M14	48					
15			JARVIS	10	5 4 1E 3 4 : . 4 . :	100	6					49	159		40		
19	"	3			8 : 7 7 8	105		7 1	93			50	160			66	
21			"	11	3† . x 2 :	108		6 6† 7 . 2 3	96		† Misfields.	51	167		42	71	
26	"	4						8 8 : : : 8	102		M15	52					
28			"	12	: : E1 3 3 2 4 :	114	7				• Dropped Gooch (x3)	53	171		46		
32	"	5			P 8 1	116		6 1 : : :	106			54	173		47	72	
35			"	13	4 L . 6 . 3 : : : : 4	122	8				Dujon's 50: 147' 4HR	55	177		51		
39	(5.5-2-14-1)	6	(13-2-47-0)		7/8 XE 2W	124	8	7 5(6) 6 4 : 1	109	14		55[5]	184	6	53	77	6
3.41	TEA				MARSHALL						M15 NB3			T	E	A	
4.01	EMBUREY	6			1/2 3	1						56	187		3		
03	(6-2-17-1)		DILLEY	18	x x 9E . 1	4		7 7 2 : 1	112			57	189		4	78	
08	SMALL	14			:	5		3 : : . 1E 1	117			58	190			79	
13			"	19	2 : . x	10		2 1	118			59	191			80	
17	"	15			8 3 . 2 4	13	1	: . 7 1	121			60	198		10	81	
22			"	20				: : : . : :	127		M16	61					
26	"	16			2 1	14		L 2/3 . W	129	14		61[3]	199	7	11	81	6
28								AMBROSE LHB								0	
30	"	16						P : 8 : :	3			62					
4.33	(16-4-58-2)		(21-6-52-5)	21	x E1 - W	16	1		3	-	Out at 4.34 pm M16 NB3	62[2]	199	8	11	0	6

1st DAY	BOWLERS (SHEPHERD) PAVILION END		(PALMER) NURSERY END		BATSMEN SCOREBOARD LEFT			SCOREBOARD RIGHT			WEST INDIES 1st INNINGS NOTES Misty	END-OF-OVER TOTALS					
TIME	BOWLER	O.	BOWLER	O.	SCORING	BALLS	6s/4s	SCORING	BALLS	6s/4s		O.	RUNS	W.	'L' BAT	'R' BAT	EXTRAS
					WALSH	.	.	AMBROSE	3	-	M16 NB3	62²	199	8	0	0	6
4.36			DILLEY	21	x 1E Y. x	4					M17	63					
39	SMALL	17						x x 8 . . W	6	-	walsh changed bat	63³	199	9	0	0	6
41								PATTERSON								0	
43	"	17						8/T Y 2 . . .	3		M18	64					
45			"	22	x x 2 LB . . 2 .	8		x x . .	5		(LB)	65	202		2		7
50	"	18			. . P . 6/5 2 . 2 1	14						66	205		5		
54			"	23	x x x x 2/1 1	19		x .	6		5HR	67	206		6		
59	(18.5-5-64-4)	19	(23-6-55-5)		7 3 : 2 1	22	-	x x . W	8	.	• Skier dr LAMB - vast height.	67⁵	209	10	9	0	7
5.02	ALL OUT										M18 NB 3		ALL		OUT		
											410 balls						

Century-maker Allan Lamb contemplates the swift procession of his early partners at Lord's.

1st DAY	BOWLERS (SHEPHERD) PAVILION END		(PALMER) NURSERY END		BATSMEN SCOREBOARD LEFT			SCOREBOARD RIGHT			ENGLAND 1st INNINGS	END-OF-OVER TOTALS					
TIME	BOWLER	O.	BOWLER	O.	SCORING	BALLS	6s/4s	SCORING	BALLS	6s/4s	NOTES	O.	RUNS	W.	'L' BAT	'R' BAT	EXTRAS
					GOOCH			BROAD		LHB							
5.15			MARSHALL	1	· P · 1E 8 · · 4 1	5	1	† ·	1			1	5		5		
20	PATTERSON	1			3 8/7 8/7 · 4 · 1	10	2	:	2			2	10		10		
25			"	2	: 3 · x 2 · · · ·	16						3	12		12		
30	"	2						· · : · x 5	8		M1	4					
34			"	3	3/2 1	17		L W	9	-		4[2]	13	1	13	0	-
35								MOXON								0	
37			"	3				8 · L 2 · ·	4			5	15			2	
41	"	3			3 : FS(6) 4 · · :	23	3					6	19		17		
45	(3-1-9-0)		"	4		23	3	L · 8/7 · · 1	8	-	M1 NB-	6[4]	20	1	17	3	-
5.49	BAD LIGHT		(3.4-0-11-1)										B	L	S	P	
6.20	ABANDONED												STUMPS				
2ND DAY 11.00			MARSHALL	4	EP 1E · ·	25					overcast. Light poor cool.	7					
02	PATTERSON	4			P · ·	28		Y · 5(6)3 · · 1	11		v. light drizzle.	8	21			4	
07			"	5				†† · · · · †	17		M2	9					
11	"	5			7 8 4 1 2 · 4 ·	33	4	3/2 1	18			10	29		24	5	
16			"	6				· · · · · 3/4 1	24			11	30			6	
20	"	6						3 · †1 1E · · 2 · 4	30	1	1HR	12	36			12	
25			"	7	† P 8/9 · · · 1	38		1 4	31	2		13	41		25	16	
30	"	7			3 x · · · · ·	44					M3	14					
35			"	8	8/7 1	45		† 6 P · 1 · · ·	36			15	43		26	17	
39	"	8	(8-1-19-1)		5(4) · 3	47		7 · 1E ⊙4 · · 4	41	4	(NB) NB1	16	55		29	25	1
46	(8-2-36-0)		AMBROSE	1	· x† 3 8/7 · 1 ·	52		8 1	42		† appeal ct wk.	17	57		30	26	
51	WALSH	1			· ·	54		· · † LB†	46		(LB) off arm M4	18	58				2
55			"	2				· P E1 · · W	49	4		18[3]	58	2	30	26	2
56								GOWER		LHB						0	
58			"	2	· ·	56		8 1	1			19	59			1	
12.01	"	2			L ·	58		1/2E 6 7/8 · 4 · 3	5	1		20	66			8	
06			"	3				7 1E 4 x 4 · 4 · · ·	11	3		21	74			16	
10	"	3			8 1	59		7 †8 L T 2 2 · ·	16			22	79		31	20	
15			"	4	8 8 1 1	61		2/3 4 · · 1 ·	20			23	82		33	21	
20	"	4			3 x x 6 · · · · · · · ·	67					M5 2HR	24					
25			"	5	†	68		8/7 x 4 4 4 · · 1	25	4		25	87			26	
29	(5-2-13-0)	5	(5-0-19-1)		·	69	4	3 x P L 6/7 · · · · 1	30	4		26	88	2	33	27	2
12.33	BAD LIGHT							†			† Light discussed. M5 NB1		B	L	S	P	
12.50	LUNCH												LUNCH				
1.30			AMBROSE	6	·	70		3 † · 4 · · · 1	35		Benjamin subs (G'midge)	27	89			28	
34	WALSH	6			2 2	71		· · · · x† LB	40		† Appeal ct wkt (? pad) (LB)	28	92		35		3
39			"	7				· · † 2/3 · 9 4 · (4)	47	6	NB2	29	100			36	
1.45	(7-3-15-0)	7	(7-0-28-1)		· · · · · ·	77	4		47	6	M6 NB2	30	100	2	35	36	3

2ND DAY	BOWLERS (SHEPHERD) PAVILION END		(PALMER) NURSERY END		BATSMEN SCOREBOARD LEFT			SCOREBOARD RIGHT			ENGLAND 1ST INNINGS NOTES	END-OF-OVER TOTALS					
TIME	BOWLER	O.	BOWLER	O.	SCORING	BALLS	6s/4s	SCORING	BALLS	6s/4s	NOTES	O.	RUNS	W.	'L' BAT	'R' BAT	EXTRAS
					GOOCH	77	4	GOWER	47	6	M6 NB2	30	100	2	35	36	3
1.50			AMBROSE	8	↑.	82		7 4 4 ①	49	7	Arthurton sub (nee Benjamin) NB3	31	105			41	
54	WALSH	8			ˣ.⊙ 7 1 . ˣ:	87		↑1E 1 3/2 1	51		(NB) 50 pship: 62' NB4	32	109		36	43	4
2.00			"	9	2 3 : :	89		. T 7 9 : . . 1	55			33	110			44	
04	"	9						5(4) P 7 3 ↑7 . . 2 . W	60	7		33[5]	112	3	36	46	4
07								LAMB								0	
09	"	9			4 :	90						34					
10			"	10				. . 3 4 . . .	6	1		35	116			4	
14	"	10			: ˣ↑ P 4 6 ˣ	96					† over stumps M7	36					
19			"	11				. : . : . ↑	12		M8 3HR	37					
23	"	11			6 . 2/1 8 5(6) . . 4 . 2 2	102	5				GOOCH 98' in 30s	38	124		44		
28			"	12	. :	104		† 4LB 1/2 . . . 1	16		† round wkt. (4LB)	39	129			5	8
33	"	12	(12-1-39-1)					: : : 3 : :	22		M9	40					
38			MARSHALL	9	ˣ ˣ . W	106	5				Greenidge back Haynes off (hay fever)	40[2]	129	4	44	5	8
40					PRINGLE										0		
42			"	9	2/3 1	1		2/3 : . :	25			41	130		1		
45	"	13			: : . : : :	7					M10	42					
50			"	10	: ˣ . ˣ :	11		4/3 . 1	27			43	131			6	
54	"	14			E1 . 3	16		7S 1	28			44	132			7	
58			"	11				. 8 . 4 EP . . 2	34			45	134			9	
3.02	"	15			↑G9 W	17	-					45[1]	134	5	1	9	8
					DOWNTON										0		
04	"	15			. 8/7 6 : : . 2 . . .	5						46	136		2		
09			"	12				. 3† : . : . . .	40		† superb stop (sub) M11	47					
13	"	16			9 3 6 8/7 Y 1 . . 2 :	10		3 1	41			48	140		5	10	
17	(16-6-36-2)		"	13				3 L : . . W	45	1	Haynes back	48[4]	140	6	5	10	8
19								EMBUREY								0	
22			"	13				↑H : . :	2		H - hit on helmet ear flap. M12 4HR	49					
25	PATTERSON	9			2 8 . 1E . 4 . 1	14	1	. 2 . 1	4			50	146		10	1	
29			"	14	6 8 7 . . . 1	18		8 1 .	6			51	148		11	2	
34	(10-3-42-0)	10	(14-3-25-3)		. : ˣ ˣ . :	24	1		6	-	M13	52	148	6	11	2	8
3.38	TEA										M13 NB4			T	E	A	
4.00			MARSHALL	15				ˣ P T 2 : 1 1	12			53	149			3	
03	PATTERSON	11						2 : ˣ 9† ˣ . . 4 : :	18	1	† over stumps	54	153			7	
08			"	16	↑ . : : . :	30					M14	55					
12	"	12						: 1E ˣ . . W	21	1		55[3]	153	7	11	7	8
13								SMALL								0	
16	"	12						9 4 . ˣ:	3	1		56	157			4	
19	(12-3-50-1)		"	17	L . W	32	1		3	1		56[2]	157	8	11	4	8
4.20			(17-4-32-4)								M14 NB4						

2ND DAY	BOWLERS (SHEPHERD) PAVILION END		(PALMER) NURSERY END		BATSMEN SCOREBOARD LEFT			SCOREBOARD RIGHT			ENGLAND 1ST INNINGS NOTES	END-OF-OVER TOTALS					
TIME	BOWLER	O.	BOWLER	O.	SCORING	BALLS	6s/4s	SCORING	BALLS	6s/4s		O.	RUNS	W.	'L' BAT	'R' BAT	EXTRAS
					JARVIS	-	-	SMALL	3	1	M14 NB4	56²	157	8	0	4	8
4.22			MARSHALL	17	4 ↑H · · 2	4	1				H - helmet (ducking)	57	163		6		
26	PATTERSON	13			↑4 · 2 · · · · 1	8		L 2 · 1	5			58	165		7	5	
31	(13-3-52-1)		"	18	· · · · · · · · W	13	1					58⁵	165	9	7	5	8
34					DILLEY		LHB								0		
36			" (18-5-32-6)	18	W	1	-		5	1	M15	59	165	10	0	5	8
4.37	ALL OUT										M15 NB4		ALL		OUT		
											358 balls						

England's new captain John Emburey is bowled off his thumb by a throat ball from Curtly Ambrose.

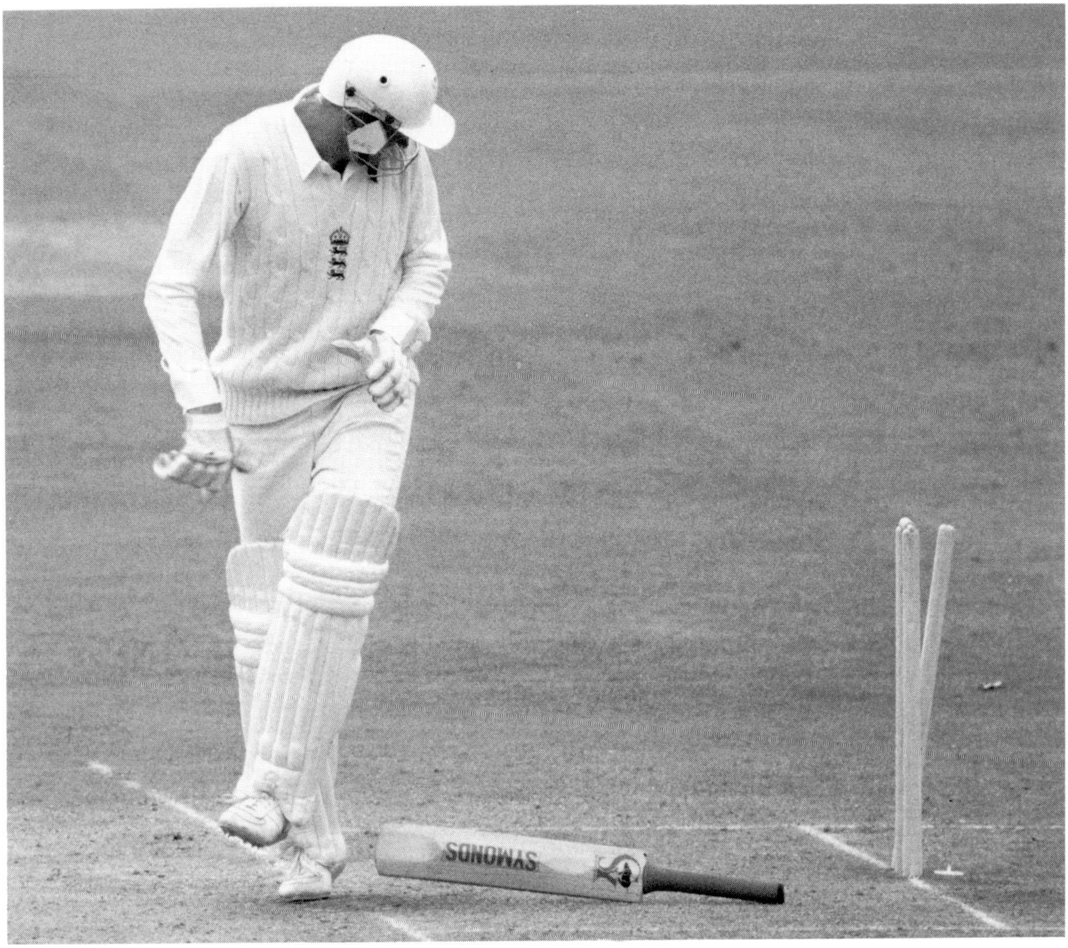

2ND DAY	BOWLERS (PALMER) PAVILION END		(SHEPHERD) NURSERY END		BATSMEN SCOREBOARD LEFT			SCOREBOARD RIGHT			WEST INDIES 2ND INNINGS	END-OF-OVER TOTALS					
TIME	BOWLER	O.	BOWLER	O.	SCORING	BALLS	6s/4s	SCORING	BALLS	6s/4s	NOTES	O.	RUNS	W.	'L' BAT	'R' BAT	EXTRAS
					GREENIDGE			HAYNES									
4.50			DILLEY	1	8/9 1	1		× × 6	5			1	1		1		
55	SMALL	1			: P P . 1E . . . : 1	7						2	2		2		
59			"	2	T 2 9E† . . 2 . 4 .	13	1				† Almost played on	3	8		8		
5.04	"	2						. . . . × G . 8/9 1	11			4	9			1	
08	(2-0-2-0)		"	3		13	1	. . †	13	–	† light discussed	4²	9	–	8	1	–
5.10	BAD LIGHT		(2.2-0-7-0)								7 overs lost (28')		B	L	S	P	
5.38			"	3	. . 3 4	16	2	1E 1	14			5	14		12	2	
41	SMALL (3-0-3-0)	3	(3-0-12-0)		•7E × P P	21	2	3 1	15	–	• nr sh leg (MOXON)	6	15	–	12	3	–
5.46	BAD LIGHT										6 overs lost (22')		B	L	S	P	
6.08			"	4		21	2	3 2 . 1	17	–		6²	16	–	12	4	–
6.10	BAD LIGHT		(3.2-0-13-0)								M – NB –		B	L	S	P	
6.30	ABANDONED												S	T	UM	PS	
3RD DAY 11.00			DILLEY	4	. . . × 1/2 1	25						7	17		13		
04	SMALL	4			2 . . . P P	31					M1	8					
08			"	5	. 6 2 2 .	35		. 1E 1	19			9	20		15	5	
13	"	5						4 . . . . P :	25		(W)	10	21				1
17			"	6	8 2 6 . 2 . . 2 .	41						11	25		19		
22	"	6			3/4 3/2 . × . 4 2 : :	46	3	LB .	26		(LB) 1HR	12	32		25		2
27			"	7				EI W	27	–		12¹	32	1	25	5	2
								RICHARDSON								0	
29			"	7	2 . .	48		2 : LB	3		(LB) M2	13	33				3
33	"	7						. P P 3 4 . 4 :	9	1		14	37			4	
37	(7-1-14-0)		"	8	. 4 . LB	52		: :	11		(LB) M3	15	38				4
42	JARVIS	1			5 1 4 P : 2 . . 4 :	58	4					16	44		31		
46			"	9				. : 46 × . × 4 :	17	2		17	48			8	
51	"	2			: : 2 : . 2 . 2	64						18	50		33		
55			"	10	. . 3S 1	67		: LB :	20		(LB)	19	52		34		5
12.00	"	3			2 . 5(6) . 1 : 4 . . 2	73	5					20	58		40		
04			"	11	4 . 6 1	76		L : 9 1	23			21	59			9	
09	"	4			1 . L . 1 1 : 1	80		PE6 2 1 •1	25		• Dr Lamb gully (low to left) (b pt.)	22	63		42	11	
14			"	12	: × 1/2 1	83		P : :	28			23	64		43		
19	"	5	(12-2-28-1)		. . × . : P	89					M4	24					
24			SMALL	8	4 . 4 P 1/2	94	6	LB	29		(LB) 2HR	25	70		48		6
28	"	6			P† 7 . 4/5 1 . 2 . 4 1	99	7	†9 4	30	3	† Appeal c sh leg. 50: 120' (GREENIDGE)	26	81		55	15	
34			"	9	. P T : 3S : 1	105					50 p'ship: 69'	27	82		56		
39	"	7			3 3/3 1 4	108	8	: 5(6) 2	33		Greenidge pad (left) reinforcement.	28	87		61		
43	(7-1-34-0)		"	10	3 P 1 . : 1 . :	113		3 1	34			29	89		62	16	
47	EMBUREY	1						9 8 P 4 . . : : :	40	4		30	93			20	
12.50	(1-0-4-0)		" (11-1-26-0)	11	3 6 4 . . . : .	119	9		40	4	M4 NB –	31	97	1	66	20	6

3RD DAY	BOWLERS (PALMER) PAVILION END		(SHEPHERD) NURSERY END		BATSMEN SCOREBOARD LEFT			SCOREBOARD RIGHT			WEST INDIES 2ND INNINGS NOTES	END-OF-OVER TOTALS					
TIME	BOWLER	O.	BOWLER	O.	SCORING	BALLS	6s/4s	SCORING	BALLS	6s/4s	NOTES	O.	RUNS	W.	'L' BAT	'R' BAT	EXTRAS
					GREENIDGE	119	9	RICHARDSON	40	4	M4 NB-	31	97	1	66	20	6
12.54	EMBUREY	2						6 : : : : :	46		M5	32					
56	(2-1-4-0)		SMALL	12	· 1	121	9	8 3 1E 2 · 4 :	50	5		33	104	1	67	26	6
1.00	LUNCH		(12-1-33-0)								M5 NB+		L	U	N C	H	
1.42	EMBUREY	3			7 3/4 P · LB : 4 : ⊙ ·	126	10	E! : · ·	52		(LB) (NB) NB 1 *dr wk.	34	110		71		8
46			PRINGLE	1	: : P : 1	131		:	53			35	111		72		
50	"	4			: 8 : 9 4 : :	137	11					36	115		76		
52			"	2				: L W	55	5		36[2]	115	2	76	26	8
53								RICHARDS								0	
55			"	2				P · · G · · · 1	4			37	116			1	
58	"	5						7 7 P 7 2 · ⊙ 6 · · ·	11	1/-	(NB) NB2 Tavern Stand.	38	125			9	9
2.02			"	3	: 7 ⊙ · : 8 1	143		1	12		(NB) NB 3	39	128		77	10	10
06	"	6			P P 1 · · 1	146		8 8 4 · · 1	15		3HR	40	130		78	11	
09			"	4	· x : 7 3 ⊙ ·	152		3S 1	16		(NB) NB 4	41	135		81	12	11
13	"	7			: P P 7 2	156		6 · 1	18			42	138		83	13	
17			"	5				2 3 : : : 9E 4	24	1/1	*Almost bowled.	43	142			17	
21	"	8			4 1 4 :	158		7 P : P 7/8 4 : · ①	29	1/2	NB5	44	148		84	22	
24			"	6				7 P · · T 2 · 4 ⊙ : : : ·	36	1/3	T - hit on box. (NB) NB6	45	153			26	12
30	"	9			: : 1 4 P 8 2 4 · 4	164	13					46	163		94		
33	(9-1-43-0)		"	7	: : 8 1 1	168		8 1 2 1	38		50 p'ship: 41 min.	47	167		96	28	
38	SMALL	13	(7-0-23-1)		· · · 1/2 1 8 2	173		1/2 1	39			48	171		99	29	
43			DILLEY	13	4 :	175		3 7 P LB	43		(LB) M6	49	172				13
48	"	14			4 4 50 · 4 : :	179	14	3 1E · 1	45		100 at 2.50 *arb GREENIDGE'S 100: 218'	50	177		103	30	
53			"	14	: 6 · ·	182		1E · 7 · · 1	48			51	178			31	
57	"	15						5/4) · : P 6) 4 · · · ·	54	1/4		52	182			35	
3.02			"	15	: : P 6 3 :	188					M7	53					
07	"	16						2 P 7 4 4 7/8 · · 4 4 4 4	60	1/8	RICHARDS 50: 76' 4HR	54	198			51	
12	(16-1-62-0)		"	16	: 7 : E! W	192	14					54[4]	198	3	103	51	13
14					HOOPER										0		
16			"	16	1/2 1	1		·	61			55	199		1		
18	PRINGLE	8			: : : · : ·	7					M8	56					
22			"	17				: · 8/7 · 3/4 : 4 · 4 ·	67	1/10		57	207			59	
27	"	9			7 : : : P :	13					M9	58					
31			"	18	LB	14		2 4/3 1 4 · · ·	72	1/11	(LB)	59	213			64	14
36	(10-2-29-1)	10	(18-4-43-2)		: 4 1 : : 6 4	19	1	6S 1	73	1/11		60	219	3	6	65	14
3.40	TEA										M9 NB6			T	E	A	

3RD DAY	BOWLERS (PALMER) PAVILION END		(SHEPHERD) NURSERY END		BATSMEN SCOREBOARD LEFT			SCOREBOARD RIGHT			WEST INDIES 2ND INNINGS	END-OF-OVER TOTALS					
TIME	BOWLER	O.	BOWLER	O.	SCORING	BALLS	6s/4s	SCORING	BALLS	6s/4s	NOTES	O.	RUNS	W.	'L' BAT	'R' BAT	EXTRAS
TEA					HOOPER	19	1	RICHARDS	73	1/11	M9 NB 6	60	219	3	6	65	14
4.01			JARVIS	8				..2.41	79	1/12		61	226			72	
06	PRINGLE	11						.W	81	1/12		61²	226	4	6	72	14
07								LOGIE								0	
09	"	11						x	4		M10	62					
12			"	9	4.....	25	2					63	230		10		
16	"	12						..42..	10	1		64	236			6	
19			"	10	......	31					M11	65					
23	"	13			1	32		1...1	15			66	239		11	8	
27			"	11	.W	34	2	.1	17			66⁴	240	5	11	9	14
29					DUJON										0		
31			"	11	:4	2	1				5HR	67	244		4		
33	"	14			..	4		.4.3	21	2		68	251			16	
38			"	12	......	9		1	22			69	252			17	
42	"	15			..4..	14	2	1	23			70	257		8	18	
46	(15-3-50-2)		"	13	...3	18		..	25		• Hit on elbow. (LB)	71	261		11		15
51	EMBUREY	10			....4.	24	3					72	265		15		
53			"	14				4	31	3		73	269			22	
59	"	11			::1	27		...	34			74	270		16		
5.02			"	15	....2.	33						75	272		18		
06	"	12						..4..	40	4		76	276			26	
09			"	16	1	34		4.......	45		• Ro ch (MOXON)	77	277		19		
13	"	13	(16-2-61-1)		...1	38		.1	47			78	279		20	27	
16			PRINGLE	16				2	53			79	281			29	
20	"	14			...1	42		..	55			80	282		21		
22			"	17	4.....LB	48					(LB) M12	81	283				16
26	"	15			..1	51		42.	58	5	Sop'ship: 57'	82	290		22	35	
28	(15-1-62-0)		"	18	:4....	57	4				6HR	83	294		26		
32	SMALL	17	(18-4-56-2)		......	62		5	59	5	4 o/t off stumps (MOXON)	84	299			40	
37			DILLEY	19				4..4..	65	7		85	307			48	
43	"	18			†P : F2LB .4.	68	5				† 2ND NEW BALL (2LB)	86	313		30		18
47			"	20				......	71		M13	87					
52	"	19			x..1	72		.4	73	1/8	LOGIE'S 50: 106'	88	318		31	52	
57	(19-1-76-0)		"	21	.x1	75		.4.	76	1/9	Small off (sub LYNCH)	89	323		32	56	
6.02	JARVIS	17			.4...1	81	6					90	328		37		
06			"	22	4...1	86		:	77			91	329		38		
10	"	18	(22-5-57-2)		6434..	92					M14	92					
15			PRINGLE	19	:	93		1	82			93	330			57	
18	"	19			..24	97	7	.1	84			94	337		44	58	
6.22	(19-3-73-1)		(20-4-59-2)	20	..LB.	100	7	4LB 1 1	87	1/9	100 p'ship in 111' (LB) (4LB) M14 NB6	95	344	5	44	60	23

3RD DAY	BOWLERS (PALMER) PAVILION END		(SHEPHERD) NURSERY END		BATSMEN SCOREBOARD LEFT			SCOREBOARD RIGHT			WEST INDIES 2ND INNINGS NOTES	END-OF-OVER TOTALS					
TIME	BOWLER	O.	BOWLER	O.	SCORING	BALLS	6s/4s	SCORING	BALLS	6s/4s		O.	RUNS	W.	'L' BAT	'R' BAT	EXTRAS
					DUJON	100	7	LOGIE	87	1/9	M14 NB 6	95	344	5	44	60	23
6·26	JARVIS	20			· · 3 · · 1	103		2 8 7 4 1 3	90	1/10		96	353		45	68	
30	(20-3-82-1)		PRINGLE	21	x : : 4 : · · · · ·	108	7	6 1	91	1/10	7HR	97	354	5	45	69	23
6·33	STUMPS		(21-4-60-2)								M14 NB 6		S	T	UM	PS	
4TH DAY 11.00	JARVIS	21			. 4† 6E · L · · · ·	113		9 1	92		† ball examined. LYNCH sub for SMALL	98	355			70	
06			DILLEY	23	: 7/8 3 · 4 3	116	8	: 6 9 · 1 1	95		DUJON'S 50: 132'	99	364		52	72	
11	"	22			Ex W	117	8	8 3/4 3 24 1	98	1/11		99 (4)	371	6	52	79	23
13					MARSHALL										0		
16	"	22			3 4 :	2	1					100	375		4		
17			"	24	P ·	3		: 3 · 3/2 4 : · · · 1	103			101	376			80	
22	"	23			x 3 4/3 Y · · 2 W	7	1	8 1	104			101 (5)	379	7	6	81	23
25					AMBROSE		LHB								0		
27	"	23			:	1						102					
28			"	25	4 4 4 x · · · W	5	-	L : LB	106		(LB) M15	103	380	8	0	81	24
32					WALSH										0		
34	"	24			: x · ·	2		4P · 3 3S 2 · · 1	110			104	383			84	
38			"	26	x W	3	-	6† · x 2 · · · 1	114		† run refused.	104 (5)	384	9	0	85	24
41					PATTERSON										0		
43			"	26	P ·	1						105					
45	"	25			6 †LB · ·	3		7/8 F6 · 3S 1 4 · 1	118	1/12	(LB) - elbow	106	391			91	25
49			"	27	9 1/2 7 1 1 ·	6		6 6 2 1 1 1	121			107	396		2	94	
55	" (26-3-107-4)	26	(27-6-73-4)		3 E1 · · W	9	-	2 ↑ 2 · · 1	124	1/12		108	397	10	2	95	25
11·58	ALL OUT										M15 NB6		AL	L	OU	T	
											654 balls						

4TH DAY	BOWLERS (PALMER) PAVILION END		(SHEPHERD) NURSERY END		BATSMEN SCOREBOARD LEFT			SCOREBOARD RIGHT			ENGLAND 2ND INNINGS NOTES	END-OF-OVER TOTALS					
TIME	BOWLER	O.	BOWLER	O.	SCORING	BALLS	6s/4s	SCORING	BALLS	6s/4s	77 overs	O.	RUNS	W.	'L' BAT	'R' BAT	EXTRAS
					GOOCH			BROAD		LHB	Pitch quicker. overcast. Humid.						
12.11			MARSHALL	1	↑↑ : . 4+1 3/4	4		↑ 2/2 : .	2		(W)(W)	1	3		1		2
18	PATTERSON	1			× 1/2 6 1 7 3 : 4 · (4) · 2 ·	11	2				• dr sh leg (LoGie) NB1	2	13		11		
24	(1-0-10-0)		"	2	6 EP 2/3 : . 1	15	2	: 9E • 1	4	–	• Nc played on.	3	14	–	11	1	2
12.28	BAD LIGHT		(2-0-4-0)								5 overs lost	B	LSP				
12.50	LUNCH												L	U	N	CH	
1.31	PATTERSON	2			E1 3 (4) 1	17	3	. 4LB P(LB) : .	10		bisected wk - Richard (4LB)(NLB) NB 3	4	24		16		7
37			MARSHALL	3	↑ : 2LB . 2 4 : : .	23					(2LB) M1	5	26				9
42	"	3						⊙ 3 : : : : :	17		(NB) NB4	6	27				10
47			"	4	. : × L W	26	3					6³	27	1	16	1	10
49					MOXON										0		
52			"	4	: ↑ LB : :	3					(LB) M2	7	28				11
54	"	4			× 3 2 : . ⊙ . .	10					(NB) NB 5	8	29				12
2.01			"	5				E1 · W	19	–		8²	29	2	0	1	12
02								GOWER		LHB						0	
04			"	5	P :	11		4 : 9 : 1	3			9	30			1	
08	"	5						· ⊙ · · · E1 W	9	–	(NB) NB 6	9⁵	31	3	0	1	13
13								LAMB								0	
15	"	5						·	1		1HR	10					
16			"	6	× : : P Y : :	17					M 3	11					
20	"	6						P × 4 P 3 . . . 4 .	7	1		12	35			4	
25			"	7	: L 9 : 1 :	21		: 8 3/2 (2) 1	10		MOXON 35' on O. NB 7	13	39		1	7	
30	"	7						: 2 × 3 1 2× 4 ⊙ · 4 2 ·	17	3	(NB) NB 8	14	50			17	14
38	(7-0-34-1)		"	8	↑ P 2 : . . 1	25		3 · 1	19		Arthurton sub (Patterson)	15	52		2	18	
43	WALSH	1			7 :	27		× L 3 7 : : : 1	23			16	53			19	
48			"	9	↑ : .	30		. : 3/2 1	26		† Round wkt	17	54			20	
53	"	2	(9-3-12-2)					9E 1 EP3 T 4 : : 4 :	32	5		18	62			28	
59			AMBROSE	1	. : . ↑2 2 .	36					Patterson back. (21') M4	19					
3.03	"	3			× 8 1	38		P 6 EP7 E1 . . 1 4	36	6	Sun through. • torch to 1st's (G'ridge)	20	68		3	33	
08			"	2	5(6)5	39		3 5(4) 8 ↑ · 4 2 ·	41	7	2HR	21	75		4	39	
12	"	4			P : ↑ A ↑ 1 4	45	1					22	79		8		
17			"	3	:	46		5 · 5 4 3S : : : : 1	46			23	80			40	
21	"	5			:	47		: : : : 1/2 3	51		50 p'ship: 70 min	24	83			43	
26			"	4				: : : : : ↑	57		M5	25					
30	"	6			LB .	48		3 · 4 3 3 2 · · · 1	62		(LB)	26	87			46	15
35	(6-0-25-0)		"	5	Y · 3 : : 1	51	1	: 8/7 1 :	65	7		27	89	3	9	47	15
3.38	TEA		(5-2-10-0)								M5 NB8			T	E	A	
4.00	RAIN										45 overs left.			R	A I	N	
4.50	WALSH	7			6 1 ⊙ 8 : 4 : :	56		3 ⊙ 2 1	68		13 overs lost (NB)(NB) NB 10	28	93		10	48	17
4.57	(7-0-29-0)		AMBROSE	6	:	57	1	L P 2 7 : : : 1	73	7	M5 NB10	29	94	3	10	49	17

4TH DAY	BOWLERS (PALMER) PAVILION END		(SHEPHERD) NURSERY END		BATSMEN SCOREBOARD LEFT			SCOREBOARD RIGHT			NOTES	ENGLAND 2ND INNINGS END-OF-OVER TOTALS					
TIME	BOWLER	O.	BOWLER	O.	SCORING	BALLS	6s/4s	SCORING	BALLS	6s/4s		O.	RUNS	W.	'L' BAT	'R' BAT	EXTRAS
					MOXON	57	1	LAMB	73	7	M5 NB 10	29	94	3	10	49	17
5.01	WALSH	8			: : 2 . (LB) ⊙	62		B . :	75		(B) (NB) NB 11	30	96				19
06			AMBROSE	7	: : T 3S . 1	66		PE P . .	77			31	97		11		
10	"	9			4 3	67		P 7. 3 8/7. : : 4 :	82	8	• Ch to sh leg (LOGIE) LAMB'S 50: 107'	32	104		14	53	
15			"	8	RO : 7	69	1					32[2]	104	4	14	53	19
17					PRINGLE										0		
19			"	8	: . : 6	4					M6 3HR	33					
22	"	10			L W	5	-	: 5† 3 7 . . 1	86		† Hit bowler's stumps.	33[5]	105	5	0	54	19
25					DOWNTON										0		
28	"	10			:	1						34					
29			"	9	5(6) EP ÷ 8/7 . . 2	6		9 1	87		• Dr sh. leg (LOGIE)	35	108		2	55	
33	"	11			LB .	7		1 x x 2/3 : 1 : : /	92		(LB)	36	110			56	20
37			"	10	. . ↑ . : 3	13					M7	37					
41	"	12						7 8 . x . 3S . 2 . . . 1	98			38	113			59	
45			"	11	: : 7. : EP	18		1/2 1	99		• LOGIE hit on knee (chance)	39	114			60	
51	"	13			7 4B : 2 ①	21		. EP 1 : . . 1 .	103		NB 12	40	118		5	61	
57			"	12	2 7 7 . 3 : 4 . 2 : :	27	1					41	124		11		
6.01	"	14	(12-4-22-0)					: 7F P† EP : : 4	109	9	† Light discussed	42	128			65	
07	(14-0-50-1)		MARSHALL	10	. : : E1/2 8• 2 . 2	33					• Ro chance (Patterson)	43	132		15		
12	PATTERSON	8						. 2 8/7 . ↑. . ⊙ 4 4 . . .	116	11	(NB) NB 13	44	141			73	21
18			"	11	† . : : : : 2	39					† Light discussed M8 4HR	45					
23	"	9			3 9F . 1 1	42		3 2/3 8 1 1	119			46	145		17	75	
29			"	12	↑8/9 : 1E 1 : .	46		↑ 3/4 . 1	121			47	147		18	76	
34	"	10			9E . 4B/S ④ . 1	49	2	6† ↑ 2 3S 4 . : 1	125	12	† All run NB 14 50 p'ship: 70'	48	157		23	81	
40			"	13	49 L 4 W	51	3					48[2]	161	6	27	81	21
42					EMBUREY										0		
45			"	13	•9E 1	1		3 5(6) . : .	128		• Nr played on.	49	162		1		
48	"	11			2 T ↑. : ↑ : 4	7	1					50	166		5		
54			"	14				: 9 4B x : LB 2 . : . .	134		(4B) (LB)	51	173			83	26
59	"	12			8 3Y ↑. 3 1E1 . 2 . 4 ④ 4	13	4	2 1	135		NB 15	52	188		19	84	
7.05	(12-0-76-1)		"	15	x 1E x . . .	16		8/7 x 4 2 . 1	138			53	191			87	
11	AMBROSE	13			↑ 2 . 1	18		4 : 6 T 1 . .	142			54	193		20	88	
15			"	16	: 2/3† 1/2 . 4 . : :	24	5				† Good stop (HAYNES)	55	197		24		
19	"	14			Y. 3 8/9 . . 1	27		2/1 4 1 . .	145		4HR	56	199		25	89	
24			"	17	1/2 1	28		1 : † 4 5/6 2 . . . 4 4	150	14	† Round wkt.	57	208		26	97	
29	"	15			7 3 Y. 6xF 4 . . W	32	6				50 p'ship: 45 min	57[4]	212	7	30	97	26
32					SMALL										0		
34	"	15			3 : . :	2					Sunny	58					
36	(15-4-30-1)		"	18		2	-	x . . 8 1E† . 2 . :	156	14	Round wkt † Short of 1st slip	59	214	7	0	99	26
7.41	STUMPS		(18-4-43-3)								M8 NB 15		STUMPS				

5TH DAY	BOWLERS (PALMER) PAVILION END		(SHEPHERD) NURSERY END		BATSMEN SCOREBOARD LEFT			SCOREBOARD RIGHT			ENGLAND 2ND INNINGS	END-OF-OVER TOTALS					
TIME	BOWLER	O.	BOWLER	O.	SCORING	BALLS	6s/4s	SCORING	BALLS	6s/4s	NOTES overcast. Humid	O.	RUNS	W.	'L' BAT	'R' BAT	EXTRAS
STUMPS					SMALL	2	-	LAMB	156	14	M8 NB 15	59	214	7	0	99	26
11.01	PATTERSON	13			1E 4LB 3 T · (2) · · · · · ·	9					(4LB) NB 16	60	220		2		30
07			MARSHALL	19				4 x · 4LB 5 · · · · · ·	162		Round wkt (4LB) M9	61	224				34
11	"	14			2 4 · 1	11		8 · · · ·	166			62	225		3		
16			"	20	1 x P ‡ 4 · · · · ·	17	1				over wkt	63	229		7		
21	"	15						· 3 2 2 7/8 4s · · · · 1	172		LAMB'S 100: 277' 100 at 11·24	64	230			100	
26			"	21	† E1 ⊙ W	19	1	· · 6 4 1	176		Round wkt (NB) NB 17	64[5]	232	8	7	101	35
30					JARVIS										0		
32			"	21	† ·	1						65					
33	"	16			1 † · † · · · ·	6		7 1	177			66	233			102	
38			"	22	3 EP 1/2 · · 1	9		2 4 2 1 3 ·	180		sunny	67	237		1	105	
43	"	17			· † G 5 · · · · · ·	15					M 10 6HR	68					
47			"	23	‡2/1 4	16	1	†3(4) 4†3 · · · · · 1	185		† runs refused. ‡ over wkt (1 ball)	69	242		5	106	
53	"	18			6 2	17		G † · 9/7† LB · · · · ·	190		† run refused (LB)	70	245		7		36
58			"	24	‡ · ·	18		4† 4† 4† 2 3 · · · · 1	195		† runs refused ‡ over wkt	71	246			107	
12.02	"	19						x 8/7† ‡x 3 L 1E T · · ⊙ · · 4 ·	202	15	† run refused (NB) NB 18	72	251			111	37
08			"	25	3 · 8 · · 1	21		3† · · · ·	205		over wkt † run refused	73	252		8		
13	"	20	(25-5-60-4)		2 L YP EP 3†4 · · · · · ·	27					† run refused M 11	74					
18	(20-2-88-1)		AMBROSE	16	Y · ·	28		· · 2 · 3/25 · · · · 1	210			75	253			112	
22	WALSH	15						L · 4 · · 1	213	15		75[3]	254	9	8	113	37
25								DILLEY		LHB						0	
27	"	15			8/7 6 1/2 · · 1	31						76	255		9		
29			"	17	Y · 8E 7 · 2 1	34		P 4F 9 · · 4	3	1		77	262		12	4	
34	"	16			4 7 T · 1 ·	37		5(4) 4F † x8 4 ⊙ · ⊙	8	2	(NB) NB 20	78	269		13	9	38
40			"	18	5 · 4 8 4 · · · 2 ·	42		9E 1	9		7HR	79	272		15	10	
44	"	17						x 5(6) 4 2x · · ⊙ 4 2 · ·	16	3	(NB) NB 21	80	279			16	39
50			"	19	3 P · 2 3 · · · · 2 ·	48						81	281		17		
53	"	18						3 x · 1E · · · · · · · ·	22		M12	82					
57	(18-1-66-1)		"	20	3 P 4 · · · · ·	54	2		22	3		83	285	9	21	16	39
1.01	LUNCH		(20-4-47-1)								M 12 NB 21	LUNCH					
1.40	WALSH	19			· 4 P · · 4 ⊙ ·	58	3	4 x LB · · ·	25		(LB) (NB) NB 22	84	291		25		41
46			PATTERSON	21				F · 4 Y · 5 1E · · 4 · · 4	31	5		85	299			24	
51	"	20			· P P 3 4/7 4 · · · 4 ·	64	4					86	303		29		
56	(20-1-75-1)		"	22		64	4	6 6 · 1E 2E · 4 · · W	36	6	50 p'ship: 51 min	86[5]	307	10	29	28	41
1.59	ALL OUT		(21.5-2-100-2)								M12 NB 22	ALL OUT					
											543 balls						

WEST INDIES 1st INNINGS v ENGLAND (SECOND TEST) at LORD'S, LONDON on 16, 17, 18, 20, 21 JUNE, 1988

IN	OUT	MINS	No.	BATSMAN	HOW OUT	BOWLER	RUNS	WKT	TOTAL	6s	4s	BALLS	NOTES ON DISMISSAL — TOSS: WEST INDIES
11.00	12.08	68	1	C.G. GREENIDGE	Ct DOWNTON	DILLEY	22	2	40	·	5	39	Edged defensive push at outswinger - 2-handed in front of 1st slip.
11.00	11.38	38	2	D.L. HAYNES	Ct MOXON	DILLEY	12	1	21	·	2	27	Superb short-leg catch - diving forward, taken low off bat only
11.40	12.18	38	3	R.B. RICHARDSON	Ct EMBUREY	DILLEY	5	3	47	·	1	26	Steered low catch to third slip.
12.10	12.30	20	4	I.V.A. RICHARDS *	Ct DOWNTON	DILLEY	6	5	54	·	1	9	Edged flourish at outswinger.
12.20	12.24	4	5	C.L. HOOPER	Ct DOWNTON	SMALL	3	4	50	·	·	4	Edged push at ball outside off stump.
12.26	4.28	183	6	A.L. LOGIE	Ct EMBUREY	SMALL	81	7	199	·	14	129	Square-cut hard to backward point's left.
12.32	3.41	150	7	P.J.L. DUJON †	BOWLED	EMBUREY	53	6	184	·	8	124	Played on - off-break squeezed between bat and pad.
4.01	4.34	33	8	M.D. MARSHALL	Ct GOOCH	DILLEY	11	8	199	·	1	16	Edged push to second slip's left.
4.30	4.41	11	9	C.E.L. AMBROSE	Ct GOWER	SMALL	0	9	199	·	·	6	Backward square-leg - diving to his left.
4.36	(5.02)	26	10	C.A. WALSH	NOT OUT		9			·	·	22	
4.43	5.02	19	11	B.P. PATTERSON	BOWLED	SMALL	0	10	209	·	·	8	Beaten by inswinger.
				EXTRAS	b - lb 6	w - nb 1	7			-6	32 4	410 balls (inc 3 no-balls)	

* CAPTAIN † WICKET-KEEPER

TOTAL (67.5 OVERS; 303 MINUTES) 209 ALL OUT at 5.02 pm on 1st day.

UMPIRES: K.E. PALMER and D.R. SHEPHERD

13 OVERS 2 BALLS/HOUR
3.08 RUNS/OVER
50 RUNS/100 BALLS

BOWLER	O	M	R	W	nb	HRS	OVERS	RUNS
DILLEY	23	6	55	5	1	1	13	35
JARVIS	13	2	47	0	-	2	12	31
SMALL	18.5	5	64	4	1	3	14	58
PRINGLE	7	3	20	0	1	4	16	53
EMBUREY	6	2	17	1	-	5	12	29
			6					
	67.5	18	209	10				

RUNS	MINS	OVERS	LAST 50 (in mins)
50	82	16.5	82
100	159	34.0	77
150	208	46.0	49
200	288	64.3	80

LUNCH: 66-5 [25 OVERS, 121 MINUTES] LOGIE 15*(35') DUJON 1*(29')

TEA: 184-6 [55.5 OVERS, 242 MINUTES] LOGIE 77*(156')

WKT	PARTNERSHIP		RUNS	MINS
1st	Greenidge	Haynes	21	38
2nd	Greenidge	Richardson	19	28
3rd	Richardson	Richards	7	8
4th	Richards	Hooper	3	4
5th	Richards	Logie	4	4
6th	Logie	Dujon	130	150
7th	Logie	Marshall	15	27
8th	Marshall	Ambrose	0	4
9th	Ambrose	Walsh	0	5
10th	Walsh	Patterson	10	19
			209	

ENGLAND 1ST INNINGS — IN REPLY TO WEST INDIES' 209 ALL OUT

IN	OUT	MINS	No.	BATSMAN	HOW OUT	BOWLER	RUNS	WKT	TOTAL	6s	4s	BALLS	NOTES ON DISMISSAL
5.15	2.40	197	1	G.A. GOOCH	BOWLED	MARSHALL	44	4	129	.	5	106	Beaten by breakback. Ended sequence of 6 successive F.C. fifties.
5.15	5.35	20	2	B.C. BROAD	LBW	MARSHALL	0	1	13	.	.	9	Late on ball that broke back down slope.
5.37	11.56	68	3	M.D. MOXON	CT RICHARDS	AMBROSE	26	2	58	.	4	49	Edged forward push waist-high to 1st slip.
11.58	2.07	72	4	D.I. GOWER	CT SUB (ARTHURTON)	WALSH	46	3	112	.	7	60	Pulled short ball to deep backward square-leg.
2.09	3.19	70	5	A.J. LAMB	LBW	MARSHALL	10	6	140	.	1	45	Beaten by breakback/inswing.
2.42	3.02	20	6	D.R. PRINGLE	C DUJON	WALSH	1	5	134	.	.	17	Gloved pull at leg-side short-pitched ball.
3.04	4.20	54	7	P.R. DOWNTON †	LBW	MARSHALL	11	8	157	.	1	32	Played back - ball kept low.
3.22	4.13	30	8	J.E. EMBUREY *	BOWLED	PATTERSON	7	7	153	.	1	21	Off stump - missed pull.
4.16	(4.37)	21	9	G.C. SMALL	NOT OUT		5			.	1	5	
4.22	4.34	12	10	P.W. JARVIS	CT HAYNES	MARSHALL	7	9	165	.	1	13	Mistimed drive at slower inswinger - simple mid-on catch.
4.36	4.37	1	11	G.R. DILLEY	BOWLED	MARSHALL	0	10	165	.	.	1	Off-stump - beaten by fast, straight ball.
				EXTRAS	b - lb 6	w - nb 2	8			- 6	21 4	358 balls (inc 4 no-balls)	

* CAPTAIN † WICKET-KEEPER

TOTAL (59 OVERS; 292 MINUTES) 165. ALL OUT at 4.37 pm on second day.

12 OVERS 0 BALLS/HOUR
2.79 RUNS/OVER
46 RUNS/100 BALLS

BOWLER	O	M	R	W	nb
MARSHALL	18	5	32	6	-
PATTERSON	13	3	52	1	1
AMBROSE	12	1	39	1	2
WALSH	16	6	36	2	1
			6		
	59	15	165	10	

HRS	OVERS	RUNS
1	12	36
2	12	46
3	13	34
4	12	24

RUNS	MINS	OVERS	LAST 50 (in mins)
50	76	15.3	76
100	140	28.5	64
150	262	53.4	122

STUMPS (1ST DAY): 20-1 [6.4 OVERS, 34 MINUTES] GOOCH 17* (34') MOXON 3* (12')

LUNCH: 88-2 [26 OVERS, 127 MINUTES] GOOCH 33* (127') GOWER 27* (35')

TEA: 148-6 [52 OVERS, 255 MINUTES] DOWNTON 11* (34') EMBUREY 2* (16')

ENGLAND LOST LAST 8 WICKETS FOR 53 RUNS

MARSHALL 5 or more wickets for 17th time in TESTS (on a hat-trick for second innings)

WEST INDIES LEAD: 44

WKT	PARTNERSHIP		RUNS	MINS
1st	Gooch	Broad	13	20
2nd	Gooch	Moxon	45	68
3rd	Gooch	Gower	54	72
4th	Gooch	Lamb	17	31
5th	Lamb	Pringle	5	20
6th	Lamb	Downton	6	15
7th	Downton	Emburey	13	30
8th	Downton	Small	4	4
9th	Small	Jarvis	8	12
10th	Small	Dilley	0	1
			165	

WEST INDIES 2ND INNINGS (44 RUNS AHEAD ON FIRST INNINGS)

IN	OUT	MINS	No.	BATSMAN	HOW OUT	BOWLER	RUNS	WKT	TOTAL	6s	4s	BALLS	NOTES ON DISMISSAL
4.50	3.14	242	1	C.G. GREENIDGE	C^T EMBUREY	DILLEY	103	3	198	·	14	192	Edged outswinger to 1st slip. (15th in TESTS. (6th v ENG (all in Eng))
4.50	11.27	57	2	D.L. HAYNES	C^T DOWNTON	DILLEY	5	1	32	·	·	27	Edged full-length ball low to 'keeper's right.
11.29	1.53	102	3	R.B. RICHARDSON	LBW	PRINGLE	26	2	115	·	5	55	Played across straight ball.
1.55	4.07	111	4	I.V.A. RICHARDS*	BOWLED	PRINGLE	72	4	226	1	12	81	Played on – under-edged cut.
3.16	4.29	52	5	C.L. HOOPER	C^T DOWNTON	JARVIS	11	5	240	·	2	34	Edged ball leaving him off seam.
4.09	(11.58	202	6	A.L. LOGIE	NOT OUT		95			5s · 1	12	124	
4.31	11.13	135	7	P.J.L. DUJON †	BOWLED	JARVIS	52	6	371	·	8	117	Played on – inside edge – off-driving.
11.16	11.25	9	8	M.D. MARSHALL	BOWLED	JARVIS	6	7	379	·	1	7	Drove over yorker – middle and leg stumps flattened.
11.27	11.32	5	9	C.E.L. AMBROSE	BOWLED	DILLEY	0	8	380	·	·	5	Off stump removed – through 'gate' – 'PAIR'.
11.34	11.41	7	10	C.A. WALSH	BOWLED	DILLEY	0	9	384	·	·	3	Off stump – missed straight ball.
11.43	11.58	15	11	B.P. PATTERSON	C^T DOWNTON	JARVIS	2	10	397	·	·	9	Outside edge to 'keeper.
				EXTRAS	b - lb 19	w 1 nb 5	25			$1^{6}\,1^{5}$	54^{4}	654 balls (inc 6 no-balls)	

* CAPTAIN † WICKET-KEEPER

TOTAL (108 OVERS; 478 MINUTES) 397 ALL OUT at 11.58 pm on 4th day.

13 OVERS 3 BALLS/HOUR
3.67 RUNS/OVER
60 RUNS/100 BALLS

BOWLER	O	M	R	W	nb
DILLEY	27	6	73	4	-
SMALL	19	1	76	0	-
JARVIS	26	3	107	4	-
EMBUREY	15	1	62	0	3
PRINGLE	21	4	60	2	3
			19		
	108	15	397	10	

2ND NEW BALL taken at 5.43 pm 3rd day – WEST INDIES 307-5 after 85 overs.

HRS	OVERS	RUNS
1	12	32
2	13	38
3	15	60
4	14	68
5	13	46
6	16	50
7	14	60

RUNS	MINS	OVERS	LAST 50 (in mins)
50	85	18.0	85
100	148	32.3	63
150	193	44.1	45
200	252	56.3	59
250	304	67.4	52
300	365	84.1	61
350	415	95.5	50

STUMPS (2ND DAY)	16-0	6.2 OVERS 30 MINUTES	GREENIDGE 12* HAYNES 4*
LUNCH	104-1	33 OVERS 150 MIN	GREENIDGE 67* RICHARDSON 26* (91)
TEA	219-3	60 OVERS 268 MIN	RICHARDS 65* (105) HOOPER 6* (24)
STUMPS (3RD DAY)	354-5 LEAD: 398	97 OVERS 420 MIN	LOGIE 69* (144) DUJON 45* (122)

WEST INDIES lost last 5 wickets for 43 runs off 11 overs in 58 minutes

WKT	PARTNERSHIP		RUNS	MINS
1st	Greenidge	Haynes	32	57
2nd	Greenidge	Richardson	83	102
3rd	Greenidge	Richards	83	80
4th	Richards	Hooper	28	30
5th	Hooper	Logie	14	20
6th	Logie	Dujon	131	135
7th	Logie	Marshall	8	9
8th	Logie	Ambrose	1	5
9th	Logie	Walsh	4	7
10th	Logie	Patterson	13	15
			397	

ENGLAND 2ND INNINGS — REQUIRING 442 RUNS TO WIN OFF A MINIMUM OF 172 OVERS (2·56 per over)

IN	OUT	MINS	No.	BATSMAN	HOW OUT	BOWLER	RUNS	WKT	TOTAL	6s	4s	BALLS	NOTES ON DISMISSAL
12·11	1·49	35	1	G.A. GOOCH	LBW	MARSHALL	16	1	27	·	3	26	Beaten by late inswing.
12·11	2·02	48	2	B.C. BROAD	Ct DUJON	MARSHALL	1	2	29	·	·	19	Edged late outswinger low to keepers left.
1·52	5·17	133	3	M.D. MOXON	RUN OUT (PATTERSON)		14	4	104	·	1	69	Called Lamb for run to mid-wicket. Sent back. Beaten by direct throw.
2·04	2·13	9	4	D.I. GOWER	Ct RICHARDSON	PATTERSON	1	3	31	·	·	9	Sliced short ball very low to 3rd slip (umpires conferred).
2·15	12·25	338	5	A.J. LAMB	RUN OUT (HOOPER/WALSH)		113	9	254	·	15	213	Abandoned attempt to take second run to deep extra-cover.
5·19	5·25	6	6	D.R. PRINGLE	LBW	WALSH	0	5	105	·	·	5	Played back - plumb.
5·28	6·42	74	7	P.R. DOWNTON†	LBW	MARSHALL	27	6	161	·	3	51	Beaten by breakback.
6·45	7·32	47	8	J.E. EMBUREY*	BOWLED	AMBROSE	30	7	212	·	6	32	Played on - full toss struck right glove and hit off stump.
7·34	11·30	36	9	G.C. SMALL	Ct RICHARDS	MARSHALL	7	8	232	·	1	19	Edged outswinger to 1st slip.
11·32	(1·59)	108	10	P.W. JARVIS	NOT OUT		29			·	4	64	
12·27	1·59	53	11	G.R. DILLEY	Ct RICHARDSON	PATTERSON	28	10	307	·	6	36	Sliced drive to 3rd slip.
				EXTRAS	b 5 lb 20	w 2 nb 14	41			-6	39 4	543 balls (22 no-balls)	

* CAPTAIN † WICKET-KEEPER

TOTAL (86·5 OVERS; 454 MINUTES) 307. ALL OUT at 1·59 pm on 5th day.

11 OVERS 3 BALLS/HOUR
3·53 RUNS/OVER
56 RUNS/100 BALLS

BOWLER	O	M	R	W	w/nb
MARSHALL	25	5	60	4	2/2
PATTERSON	21·5	2	100	2	-/12
WALSH	20	1	75	1	-/8
AMBROSE	20	4	47	1	-
			26	2	
	86·5	12	307	10	

2ND NEW BALL NOT TAKEN.

HRS	OVERS	RUNS
1	10	31
2	11	44
3	12	29
4	12	37
5	11	58
6	12	38
7	11	35

RUNS	MINS	OVERS	LAST 50 (in mins)
50	83	13·5	83
100	164	31·1	81
150	248	47·1	84
200	297	56·1	49
250	380	71·5	83
300	449	85·5	69

LUNCH: 14-0	3 OVERS 17 MIN	GOOCH 11* (17') BROAD 1* (17')
TEA: 89-3	27 OVERS 144 MIN	MOXON 9* (106') LAMB 47* (83')
STUMPS (4TH DAY): 214-7 228 NEEDED	59 OVERS 315 MIN	LAMB 99* (254') SMALL 0* (7')
LUNCH: 285-9	83 OVERS 435 MIN	JARVIS 21* (89') DILLEY 16* (34')

WEST INDIES WON BY 134 RUNS

MAN OF THE MATCH: A.L. LOGIE
(Adjudicator: T.E. BAILEY)

WKT	PARTNERSHIP		RUNS	MINS
1st	Gooch	Broad	27	35
2nd	Broad	Moxon	2	10
3rd	Moxon	Gower	2	9
4th	Moxon	Lamb	73	110
5th	Lamb	Pringle	1	6
6th	Lamb	Downton	56	74
7th	Lamb	Emburey	51	47
8th	Lamb	Small	20	36
9th	Lamb	Jarvis	22	53
10th	Jarvis	Dilley	53	53
			307	

Old Trafford
The Third Test

Peter May and the selectorial system under pressure · Analysis of England's dismal record · Old Trafford · John Arlott's kindness · Match report · Marshall's rate of devastation

Defeat at Lord's after the Texaco victories and an honourable draw at Trent Bridge was a bitter pill. It was made more unpalatable by the selectors' handling of the Gatting affair, which affected team morale and removed a key player.

Chairman Peter May came under special fire. An outstanding batsman, probably the best England has produced since the Second World War, he does not rank high on the lists of great communicators, man-managers or wits. He was not without his critics when he was England captain and, despite having been educated at Charterhouse and at that time a prospective Cambridge undergraduate, he never advanced beyond the lowly rank of Writer during his national service in the Royal Navy.

At an early-season press conference May had said that everyone smiled when we won. Someone suggested that he must have an exceptional memory since England's last victory in his presence had been achieved against an extremely weak Australian team almost three years ago. He also declared that everyone, including the selectors, was currently on trial. If so, they were in danger of being found guilty of hypocrisy in their reasons for Mike Gatting's sacking and of sheer woolly-minded folly in their lack of forward-planning with regard to the captaincy.

I analysed England's results since May succeeded Alec Bedser in 1982; Tests played – 68; wins – 14 (20.6 per cent); defeats – 25 (36.8 per cent); draws – 29. Apart from Sri Lanka, who were yet to be fully integrated into the system, only India (10.9 per cent) had won fewer matches during that period and no country had suffered a higher proportion of defeats.

England's performance since regaining the Ashes in 1985 had been even more disastrous: the team had played 30 matches, won 2 (in Australia in 1986-87), lost 12 and drawn 16. Five series out of seven had been lost, two more than any other country had managed during that time. By some distance England's record was the worst of all the seven Test-playing countries, including the novice Sri Lankans.

The appointment of Micky Stewart as England Team Manager in 1987 had rendered Peter May's position as Chairman at least awkward, if not incongruous or possibly obsolete. The TCCB were anxious to retain control over a traditional panel of selectors rather than move towards the soccer-style system of a supremo. Ray Illingworth and David Brown had both declined the job because they realized that their powers of selection and control were still to be limited by a system incorporating amateur, part-time selectors which, with the appointment of a permanent team manager, seemed to be both unprofessional and outmoded.

A team manager, plus possibly an assistant, together with a captain appointed for the whole series, would be able to co-ordinate reports on players from county captains, managers and coaches, and the first-class umpires, just as efficiently as the 1988 quartet of selectors, three of whom were based in the home counties.

Trevor Bailey is always worth listening to. He thought a supremo would be dangerous because he would inevitably have his favourite and not-so-favourite players and the latter would never gain selection. 'The Boil' was reasonably happy with the current system but thought it essential that at least two of the quartet were senior current county cricketers. In that category Fletcher would have been a perfect candidate – and not just because of his association with Essex!

The subject was a favourite for discussion between the Second and Fifth Tests, when English morale reached its nadir. Everyone had a different solution but most recommended the fastest possible exit for the unfortunate Peter May. His attitude was that he and his committee had been entrusted with a task by the Board and they would fulfil that commitment.

Just three days after the Lord's defeat the selectors had to convene to pick the team for Old Trafford. One down with three to play was not the end of the world, but it could easily degenerate into the beginning of the end. After an astonishingly good start we had missed vital catches and then copped the worst of the second-innings batting conditions.

The crucial role in England's destruction had been played by Gus Logie who, batting at number six, had played two key innings. That was the position from which Garfield Sobers and Clive Lloyd used to control events. It was also Ian Botham's position in England's line-up. At Lord's, if not earlier, it became painfully obvious that the latest incumbent, Derek Pringle, was at least two places too high there. Well as the Essex all-rounder had bowled at international level, his batting continued to disappoint.

Another all-rounder was needed for that vital number six slot but the cupboard was not exactly overflowing. The only obvious contenders were David Capel and Chris Cowdrey. At that stage of the season their first-class records were remarkably similar: Capel had scored 536 runs at 41.23 and taken 25 wickets at 27.44, while Cowdrey had made 545 runs at 41.92 and taken 29 wickets at 22.65.

I hoped Cowdrey would be chosen. He is a positive cricketer who had just led Kent to six consecutive championship wins. Now in his fourth season as county skipper, this popular player had

John Childs – England's oldest debutant since 1947 – watched by fellow new-boy, Nigel Plews.

the experience of the 1984-85 series in India, and could have solved captaincy problems.

Gatting's expected return at number three after his self-imposed exile put pressure on Chris Broad's place. Besides having a nightmare game at Lord's, the Nottinghamshire left-hander's 'expressions of disappointment' which followed his first innings dismissal, when added to a certain amount of 'previous', could well excuse the selection of Martyn Moxon to open as a just reward for his brave second-innings vigil.

Neil Foster's jubilant return to the Essex side was too premature, and his swollen knee did not recover in time for him to replace the injured Small. Fortunately Paul Jarvis, who enjoyed an excellent match at Lord's, was a handy deputy.

As for the captaincy, Emburey had led the side well at Lord's and deserved another match, particularly at Old Trafford where the pitch was usually a slow turner. Its character made a second spinner essential. If another off-spinner was required, Vic Marks would strengthen the batting, but Eddie Hemmings had bowled well during the winter tours. A left-armer would give more balance to the attack, but none had enjoyed earth-shattering success during the season to date. Nick Cook (27 wickets at 25.96 from 339 overs) and David Graveney (17 wickets at 23.82 from 212 overs) were the obvious candidates.

Inevitably the final decision concerned the 'keeper. Downton's batting at Lord's had not compensated for his mistakes behind the wicket. His obvious challenger was 'Jack' Russell who, apart from being the country's outstanding specialist with the gloves, was a capable left-handed batsman with a sound technique and a first-class average for the season of 46.00.

My *Mail on Sunday* twelve for Old Trafford (chosen when Foster was expected to be available and reports promised a pitch to favour seam rather than spin) was: Gooch, Moxon, Gatting, Gower, Lamb, Cowdrey, Russell, Pringle, Emburey, Foster, Dilley, Jarvis.

I had only nine correct, but none of my colleagues fared any better. The selectors again chose thirteen players, retaining Broad and Downton, recalling DeFreitas and Gatting, dropping Pringle, Small and Hemmings, preferring Capel to Cowdrey, and bringing in Nick Cook as the second spinner. Cook withdrew after turning his ankle on a boundary rope and, after Graveney had decided that his back problems would not stand up to a five-day match, and Lancashire had advised that Ian Folley was in no sort of form, the selectors turned to the Essex left-arm spinner, John Childs. Greg Thomas received another call when Jarvis strained his back in a Sunday League game.

I have a special affection for old Trafford. it was the ground on which I made my *Test Match Special* debut in 1966 and I shall always be grateful to John Arlott for his consideration and kindness that first morning. He had been my passenger on the previous day's drive from London, and we were staying at the same hotel close to the city centre. Knowing that I would be especially nervous that first morning, he arranged for me to see a special collection of cricket books at Gibbs' Book Shop. The 'secret' storeroom was a treasure-house for a cricket-book collector, and we set off for the ground with a complete set

Gus Logie – two key innings and the Cornhill match award at Lord's.

The vultures claim another victim at Old Trafford: David Capel caught sub (Keith Arthurton at silly mid-off) bowled Marshall for 0.

of *Scores and Biographies*, a forerunner of *Wisden Cricketers' Almanack*.

It must have been a sad day for the commentary team because my predecessor Arthur Wrigley had been the first radio Test match scorer, and had missed very few broadcasts since the post was instituted at Howard Marshall's request after Hedley Verity had demolished the Australians at Lord's in 1934. Wrigley had been on the groundstaff at Old Trafford and his accountancy training had led to the Lancashire secretary's recommendation.

The first ball I scored in a Test match was described by John Arlott, bowled by Glamorgan's left-armer, Jeff Jones, and cut very hard to the point boundary by Conrad Hunte. England lost by an innings in three days and Mike (M. J. K.) Smith got the sack. I suppose that nothing much changes in cricket.

Manchester has the most consistent climate in Britain – it always seems to be raining. As we reached the outskirts on my first journey there, John Arlott remarked: 'Ah, Manchester! Where they teach lifeboat drill on the buses!' Beset by injuries and indecision, England were always likely to find the local weather their most reliable ally during the Third Test. Rain had washed out two of Old Trafford's previous 57 scheduled Tests and caused the loss of 27 complete days of Test cricket there, more than twice the tally suffered by any other English venue.

This was the eleventh West Indies Test on this ground, the tourists having previously won four encounters to England's three, the last being in 1969. England's most recent success at Old Trafford had been against the 1981 Australians.

England omitted Broad and Thomas from their revised thirteen, thus giving a first cap to John Henry Childs. At the age of 36 years and 320 days, he was the oldest English debutant since Dick Howorth of Worcestershire had first appeared in 1947, when he was two years older. Plymouth-born, Childs brought to four the number of Devonian England Test cricketers, following E. G. Arnold (Exmouth), L. J. Coldwell (Newton Abbot) and R. W. Tolchard (Torquay).

Childs also became the 55th player to represent England in Test matches since 1982, when Peter May became chairman of selectors, and the 35th to make his debut during that period. Of those 35 debutants, only fifteen had enjoyed careers spanning more than five matches. Excluding Childs, nine had played in only one or two: M. R. Benson, I. A. Greig, T. A. Lloyd, A. C. S. Pigott, A. Sidebottom, D. M. Smith, L. B. Taylor, V. P. Terry and J. J. Whitaker.

With Viv Richards and his Merry Men moving into top gear during the Lord's Test, it was inevitable that England would be under increased pressure at Old Trafford. The saga of one of England's most humiliating defeats is simply told. Electing to bat on a slow pitch of even bounce but likely to take spin, they were bundled out for 135 on the first day. Hindered by considerable interruptions for light and rain, West Indies eventually declared at 4 p.m. on the fourth day and took just over three hours to complete their demolition work a second time. Two up with two to play in the rubber, West Indies had made sure of retaining the Wisden Trophy, thus achieving their seventh consecutive successful defence of the prize they had regained in 1973.

On a turning pitch the two England spinners considered to be the best available took precisely one wicket in 65 overs at a cost of 145 runs. Taking into account the loss of 125 overs during the first four days, West Indies achieved their victory in under three days of actual play.

Thanks to the weather, England were still in

Jeff Dujon – a touch player and a most elegant stroke-maker.

How many times have we shuddered as Gatting has padded up to a break-back?

with a chance of averting defeat on the third day, which began with West Indies 242 for 5, a lead of 107. Although the rain eventually returned to limit the day to 50 overs, that Saturday provided some of the best cricket of the season. The day's play began like a dream sequence with two slow bowlers operating in sparkling sunshine. It was the first time in the series that spin bowlers had appeared in tandem – very rarely had they even appeared as a solo act – and it provided a fascinating and merciful relief from the usual diet of pace and seam.

While Emburey probed and tested from the Stretford End, Childs, sleeves buttoned *à la* Tony Lock, twirled his left-arm leg-breaks with the City behind him. It was vintage Test cricket, a marvellously subtle contest between bat and ball. Although the slowness of the pitch minimized the danger of balls which turned sharply, Jeff Dujon and Roger Harper were frequently asked some intriguing questions. Their 6th-wicket partnership of 94, not to mention its successor between Harper and Marshall worth 92, demonstrated the massive depth of talent in this West Indies team.

Dujon is a most elegant stroke-maker, a touch player who, at the peak of his form, is second only to his captain as an entertainer. He has the added bonus of being a wicket-keeper of the highest class. Harper is no slouch with the bat either. Although primarily an off-spinner, he has amassed two double-centuries in first-class cricket and boasted a tour average of 187.50 before this match.

England's first innings was a shambles all too familiar to those who had seen their early order commit suicide by demonstrating their shortcomings in basic footwork against swing bowling. How many times have we shuddered as Gatting has padded up to a breakback, as Gower, feet anchored, has flailed outside the off stump, as Gooch has driven at balls he should have ignored or as Lamb has cut uppishly to gully?

Enough of England's abject display. Even allowing for the quality of Malcolm Marshall's bowling, a remarkable demonstration of controlled movement of swing and seam, it was one of the most spineless exhibitions I have seen in 147 Test matches. How one longed for a Dexter, Barrington, Edrich, Cowdrey or Close; for a fleeting glimpse of basic technique, particularly footwork, against the moving ball. In fairness to the selectors, there were no obviously superior players waiting in the wings, apart from the phenomenal but unqualified Graeme Hick and the inexperienced Michael Atherton. But, in view of the malaise of defeatism which appeared to have pervaded this England side, the time had obviously come for a totally fresh approach involving players who had not become conditioned to losing, even if their county record was not superior to those they were replacing. Of those on view at Old Trafford only Gooch, Lamb and Dilley deserved to retain their places.

My criticism is in no way intended to detract from the magnificent bowling performance by Malcolm Marshall. His figures of 7 for 22 were his best in Tests and he was an obvious choice for Tom Graveney's Cornhill Match Award.

Marshall had taken his 281 wickets more cheaply (20.29 runs apiece) and at a greater frequency (every 44.5 balls) than any of the nine bowlers ranged above him on the list of leading Test wicket-takers. Since returning to Test cricket after missing the World Cup and the West Indies tour of India, Marshall averaged 8 wickets per Test. If he maintained that rate he would overhaul the record of 373 (jointly held by Botham and Hadlee) during the final Test against India in the Caribbean in early 1989 when he anticipates ending his international career.

At the end of this particular piece of devastation, Marshall needed just five more victims in the current series to become the third West Indian after Sir Garfield Sobers and Lance Gibbs to take 100 wickets against England. With 26 wickets at the remarkably low cost of 8.65 runs apiece, he was only 7 short of the West Indies series record.

1st DAY	BOWLERS (D.J. CONSTANT STRETFORD END		N.T. PLEWS) WARWICK RD END		BATSMEN SCOREBOARD LEFT			SCOREBOARD RIGHT			ENGLAND 1st INNINGS NOTES	END-OF-OVER TOTALS					
TIME	BOWLER	O.	BOWLER	O.	SCORING	BALLS	6s/4s	SCORING	BALLS	6s/4s		O.	RUNS	W.	'L' BAT	'R' BAT	EXTRAS
					GOOCH			MOXON			overcast, humid						
11·01	MARSHALL	1			? . 9 4 . 7 :	6	1					1	4		4		
06			AMBROSE	1				. . : . : .	6		M1	2					
10	"	2			x LB : .	8		: . EP 7 .	10		(LB) M2	3	5				1
14			"	2	. : 1E 4 . : :	14	2					4	9		8		
18	"	3						† : : 5 . :	16		M3	5					
22			"	3	P x : : 2E 1	19		⊙ :	18		(NB) NB1	6	11		9		2
25	"	4			7 x . P 8/9 1	24		.	19		Light brighter.	7	12		10		
30			"	4	6 : . 3 : :	30					M4	8					
34	"	5						: : x W	22	-		8³	12	1	10	0	2
36								GATTING								0	
38	"	5						5 6 ? :	3		• Nr. played on M5	9					
40			"	5	4 2 4 5(6) 5 : : : 2 : .	36						10	14		12		
44	"	6						L W	4	-		10¹	14	2	12	0	2
								GOWER		LHB						0	
46	"	6						4 . : 1/2 7 4 :	5	1		11	18			4	
51			"	6	: 8/7 2 x 7 3 4s . . . 1	42						12	21		15		
54	"	7			: : . : 6 .	48					M6	13					
58	(7-4-9-2)		"	7	4 5(6) . 1	50		3 : 6 1 :	9		1HR	14	23		16	5	
12·02	WALSH	1	(7-2-13-0)		8/9 1	51		. : . . 2 1 ⊙4	15	2	(NB) • over slips NB 2	15	29		17	9	3
08			BENJAMIN	1	: 1E 4 : : 3 .	57	3					16	33		21		
12	"	2						: . : 3E1 W	20	2		16⁵	33	3	21	9	3
15								LAMB								0	
17	"	2						2 1	1			17	34			1	
18			"	2				: . 2 : .	7		M7	18					
22	"	3			P L 1E . x P	63					M8	19					
26			"	3	: 6 1	65		T 3 1 3 :	11			20	36		22	2	
29	"	4			: P P 9 1	69		pt 3‡ 1	13		† Appeal ct wkt. ‡ Diving stop (Hooper)	21	38		23	3	
33			"	4	: 8 2	71		: : . 1E 1	17			22	41		25	4	
37	"	5			6 .	72		7 2 . 4 . : 3/4 1	22			23	44			7	
41			"	5				8 . 4/5 4 . 4/5 4 3	28	2		24	52			15	
45	"	6			P . 8/7 1 3 9E . 1	77		• 8 1	29		• Ro chance (LOGIE) ‡ Nr. played on.	25	55		27	16	
49			"	6	7 P . . E1 W	81	3					25⁴	55	4	27	16	3
51					CAPEL										0		
53			"	6	: !	2					M9	26					
55	"	7						: P : 6 . †	35		M10	27					
58	(7-2-15-1)		"	7	: : EP P : :	8	-		35	2	M11 NB2 2HR	28	55	4	0	16	3
1·02	LUNCH		(7-3-17-1)										L	U	N	CH	

1ST DAY	BOWLERS (CONSTANT) STRETFORD END		(PLEWS) WARWICK RD END		BATSMEN SCOREBOARD LEFT			SCOREBOARD RIGHT			ENGLAND 1ST INNINGS	END-OF-OVER TOTALS					
TIME	BOWLER	O.	BOWLER	O.	SCORING	BALLS	6s/4s	SCORING	BALLS	6s/4s	NOTES	O.	RUNS	W.	'L' BAT	'R' BAT	EXTRAS
LUNCH					CAPEL	8	-	LAMB	35	2	Sun. M11 NB2 2HR	28	55	4	0	16	3
1.41	MARSHALL	8			P .	9		2 : LB	40		(LB) M12	29	56				4
45			BENJAMIN	8	: : ↑ ↑	13		8 . 1	42			30	57			17	
49	"	9						: P . . 4/5 4 : 2 1	48			31	60			20	
55			"	9				: : x 7 : :	54		M13	32					
59	"	10			: : . 7 1	17		7 L : :	56			33	61		1		
2.03			"	10	x W	18	-					33^{1}	61	5	1	20	4
					DOWNTON										0		
05			"	10	x 3 : . . 6/5 1	5						34	62		1		
09	"	11			4 2 1 .	7		x 3 P 9 . 2 . 1	60			35	66		2	23	
14			"	11	. 3 . . EP	11		: 9 1	62			36	67			24	
17	"	12						7/E 3 . 4 3 : 2	68			37	69			26	
21	(12-5-19-2)		"	12	7 3 6 1 . . . 3	15		2 :	70			38	72		5		
25	WALSH	8			P 2 6 P 2/3 :	21					M14	39					
29			"	13	3/4 8/7 4 2 3 1	24		9 1 49 1 :	73			40	80		11	28	
34	"	9	(13-4-31-2)		2 4 . P E1† 2 :	30	1				Arthurton sub (Hooper) † Nr played on. 3HR	41	84		15		
38			AMBROSE	8	: 4 2/3 6†46 :	35	2	3/4 1	74		† ball examined. overcast	42	89		19	29	
43	"	10						L P : 4/3 4 2 . .	80			43	91			31	
47			"	9	3 7/8 Y9 . . 1	38		8 2 2W	82	2		43^{5}	94	6	20	33	4
49								EMBUREY								0	
51			"	9				Y .	1			44					
52	"	11			P 4 . . 1	42		L P . .	3		† Nr played on	45	95		21		
56			"	10	3 1 3 :	45		: . E1 1	6			46	97		22	1	
3.00	"	12						P : ↑ . P :	12		M15	47					
03	(12-4-22-1)		"	11	6 P : : . .	51	2		12	-	Light poor. M16 NB 2	48	97	6	22	1	4
3.07	RAIN/TEA		(11-3-23-1)								137' lost (34 overs)		R	S	P/	TE	A
5.44	WALSH	13						P : x ⊙ : E1 W	17	-	(NB) NB3	48^{4}	98	7	22	1	5
47								DEFREITAS								0	
49	"	13			:	52		LB .	1		(LB)	49	99				6
51			AMBROSE	12	:	53		3 1 4 3 . 4 . : 1	6	1		50	104			5	
54	"	14			3 7 : 2 :	57		x 5(6) . 1	8			51	107		24	6	
58			"	13	P :	58		8 3 4 4f 2 . . . 1	13			52	110			9	
6.02	"	15			7 8/7 : 4	62		EP† 9 . 1	15		† Nr played on.	53	111			10	
06			"	14				x : 4 3 : 8 2	21			54	113			12	
10	"	16			2 W	63	2					54^{1}	113	8	24	12	6
					DILLEY		LHB								0		
12	"	16			. 4 1E LB . 3/4 2	4		2 3	22		(LB) 4HR	55	123		6	15	7
17			"	15				6 4 L . x 4 W	28	1	M17	56	123	9	6	15	7
19								CHILDS		LHB						0	
21	"	17			: x E1 ④ P : PB 3 ⊙ .	12	1				(NB) NB5	57	128		10		8
27			"	16				3 . . . 4 2 3 2 .	6			58	130			2	
31	"	18			: 4 3 F3 ⊙ x 1E4 4 .	19	2				(NB) NB6	59	135		14		9
36			"	17				x 3 x x 6 1	12		M18	60					
6.39	(18.2-4-46-4)	19	(17-5-35-2)		: E1 W	21	2		12	-	M18 NB6 368b. ovr at 6.40	60^{2}	135	10	14	2	9

1st DAY	BOWLERS (CONSTANT) STRETFORD END		BOWLERS (PLEWS) WARWICK RD END		BATSMEN SCOREBOARD LEFT			BATSMEN SCOREBOARD RIGHT			WEST INDIES 1st INNINGS	END-OF-OVER TOTALS					
TIME	BOWLER	O.	BOWLER	O.	SCORING	BALLS	6s/4s	SCORING	BALLS	6s/4s	NOTES	O.	RUNS	W.	'L' BAT	'R' BAT	EXTRAS
					GREENIDGE			RICHARDSON									
6.52			DILLEY	1	. 4	6	1				+ Good stop	1	4		4		
57	EMBUREY	1						. . . . . .	6		• legside ch (wk) M1	2					
59	(1-1-0-0)		(2-1-4-0)	2	. . . . . .	12	1		6	–	• Dr Gooch (2nd slip) M2 NB –	3	4	–	4	0	–
7.03	STUMPS	(1st	DAY)										STUMPS				
2nd DAY 11.23	EMBUREY	2			. . .	15		2 . 1	9		START DELAYED by rain • bad light – 6 overs lost	4	7			3	
27			DILLEY	3	3	16		4 . 3 . .	14	1		5	17		7	10	
32	〃	3			. . 4 . . .	22	2					6	21		11		
35			〃	4	. . .	25		. . 3	17			7	24			13	
39	〃	4			1	26		. 1 . . 1	22			8	27		12	15	
43			〃	5				. 4 4 . W	27	3		8⁵	35	1	12	23	–
46								HOOPER								0	
48			〃	5				.	1			9					
49	〃	5	(5-1-25-1)		. . . 1	30		2 .	3			10	38		13	2	
53	(5-1-13-0)		DEFREITAS	1	 3	36						11	41		16		
56	DILLEY	6			 1	41		.	4			12	42		17		
12.02			〃	2	3	42		. . . 2 .	9			13	47		20	4	
06	〃	7			. 4	48	3				1HR	14	51		24		
11			〃	3	. .	50		. . . 1	13			15	52			5	
15	〃	8						. . . . . .	19		M3	16					
20			〃	4	. . . . . .	56					M4	17					
23	〃	9			. . . 1	60		1 .	21			18	54		25	6	
28	(9-2-32-1)		〃	5	. . . . . .	66					M5	19					
32	CAPEL	1			. . .	69		1 . .	24		(LB)	20	56			7	1
36			〃	6	. . (4)	76	4				NB1	21	60		29		
41	〃	2			. . .	79		. . 1	27			22	61			8	
46			〃	7	. . . .	83		. 1	29			23	62			9	
50	〃	3	(7-2-14-0)		1	84		. . . 1 .	34			24	64		30	10	
55			CHILDS	1	. . . 1	88		2 .	36		Round wkt	25	67		31	12	
58	(4-0-10-0)	4	(1-0-3-0)		. 1 4 . .	93	5	1	37	–		26	73	1	36	13	1
1.02	LUNCH										M5 NB1		LUNCH				
1.40			CHILDS	2				. . 2 . . .	43		Round wkt. light rain. poor light.	27	75			15	
43	CAPEL	5			. . . .	97		.	45		(LB)(LB) M6 2HR	28	77				3
47			〃	3				. W	47	–		28²	77	2	36	15	3
48								RICHARDS								0	
50			〃	3				. 2 . .	4		+ Turned – lifted	29	79			2	
53	〃	6			. . . 1	101		. .	6			30	80		37		
57			〃	4	. . 2 . . .	107					(2LB)	31	84		39		5
2.00	〃	7			. 4 .	110	6	. . 1	9			32	89		43	3	
2.05	(7-1-16-0)		(5-0-11-1)	5		110	6	. 2	15	–	(2LB) M6 NB1	33	93	2	43	5	7

2ND DAY	BOWLERS (CONSTANT) STRETFORD END		(PLEWS) WARWICK RD END		BATSMEN SCOREBOARD LEFT			SCOREBOARD RIGHT			WEST INDIES 1ST INNINGS NOTES	END-OF-OVER TOTALS					
TIME	BOWLER	O.	BOWLER	O.	SCORING	BALLS	6s/4s	SCORING	BALLS	6s/4s	NOTES	O.	RUNS	W.	'L' BAT	'R' BAT	EXTRAS
					GREENIDGE	110	6	RICHARDS	15	-	M6 NB1	33	93	2	43	5	7
2.08	CAPEL	8			3 3 6	116					M7	34					
12	(8-2-16-0)		CHILDS	6	: P P . . .	120		x LB . .	17		(LB) M8	35	94				8
16	DEFREITAS	8			: 7 1	122		7 L LB . . . 1 4	21	1	(LB)	36	100		44	9	9
20			"	7	: L : . 6 1	127		P .	22			37	101		45		
23	"	9			: L W	129	6					37[2]	101	3	45	9	9
24					LOGIE										0		
26	"	9			. 9 1	2		2 : :	24			38	102		1		
30			"	8	6 : : . 2 1	6		3 4 2 4	26	2		39	109		2	15	
33	"	10			4 . 9/8 . . 1	9		2 2 LB 2 . .	29		(LB)	40	113		3	17	10
38			"	9	: : 9 1	12		L 3 . 1 6 4	32	3		41	119		4	22	
42	"	11			: : 4 3 1E 8/7 . 2 : .	18					sunshine	42	121		6		
46			"	10				: : LP 3 x P	38		M9 3HR	43					
49	"	12			7 1	19		P x P L :	43			44	122		7		
53			"	11	7F 3 . 2 . 6/5 4 : : : . 4	25	2					45	130		15		
56	"	13			4 2 . 2	27		: . L LB . .	47		(LB)	46	133		17		11
3.01			"	12				7 P : 3 4 P 2 . : 4 6 .	53	1/4		47	145			34	
06	"	14	(12-2-45-1)		2 1 : 2 2	30		3(4) P 8/7 2 . 1	56		50 p'ship: 45 min. Treatment to rt. wrist	48	151		20	37	
11	(14-2-34-1)		CAPEL	9	4 : 7 . 3	33		4 4 4 1 3 .	59	1/5		49	159		23	42	
16	EMBUREY	6			: 7/8 2 : : P 2 . 2	39						50	163		27		
19			"	10	3 3	40		7S 1 P . . . 2 2	64			51	169		30	45	
23	"	7			7 : : : : : 7	46					M 10	52					
27			"	11	6 8 : .	48		. 6 P FP2 . . . 1	68		Thomas sub (Dilley)	53	170			46	
31	"	8			P . . 6 . . . 4	52	3	. 6 . 1	70			54	175		34	47	
34	(8-2-22-0)		"	12				EX W	71	1/5		54[1]	175	4	34	47	11
								DUJON								0	
36			"	12		52	3	4 : 3 4 : 3 3	5	1		55	182	4	34	7	11
3.39	TEA		(12-2-38-1)								M10 NB1			T	E	A	
4.00	DILLEY	10						: 4 7 6 : : . . .	11		M 11	56					
05			EMBUREY	9	4 . . . 8 4 : : : 1	57	4	L .	12		4HR	57	187		39		
08	"	11			7 L . W	59	4					57[2]	187	5	39	7	11
09					HARPER										0		
11	"	11			: 3 1	2		2 : 2	14			58	190		1	9	
15			"	10	P : T : : :	8					M12	59					
17	"	12						: . . 8/7 4 . .	20	2		60	194			13	
21			"	11	2LB : : P : :	14					(2LB) M13	61	196				13
24	"	13						: : 2 : : (.) .	27		(NB) NB 2	62	197				14
29	(13-3-40-2)		"	12	x 2 . 3	16	-		27	2		62[2]	200	5	4	13	14
4.31	RAIN		(11.2-4-30-0)								M13 NB2		R	S	P		

2ND DAY	BOWLERS (CONSTANT) STRETFORD END		(PLEWS) WARWICK RD END		BATSMEN SCOREBOARD LEFT			SCOREBOARD RIGHT			WEST INDIES 1ST INNINGS NOTES	END-OF-OVER TOTALS					
TIME	BOWLER	O.	BOWLER	O.	SCORING	BALLS	6s/4s	SCORING	BALLS	6s/4s	NOTES	O.	RUNS	W.	'L' BAT	'R' BAT	EXTRAS
					HARPER	16	-	DUJON	27	2	min (4 overs) lost M13 NB2	62²	200	5	4	13	14
4.45			EMBUREY	12	: 1	18		5(4) 1 5 :	29			63	202		5	14	
47	DILLEY	14			: x 8 2 4 :	22	-		29	2	M13 NB2	63⁴	204	5	7	14	14
50	(13.4-3-42-2) RAIN													R	S	P	
5.02	DILLEY	14			: 9 1	24					sunny	64	205		8		
04			"	13	P 3/2 4 : 7 : :	30	1					65	209		12		
08	"	15						: : 3 7 2 4 4+4 2/3 · 1	35	3	† All run.	66	216			21	
12	(15-3-50-2)		"	14	3 3	31		7 6 1 : 7 6 1	40			67	221		15	23	
15	DEFREITAS	15	(14-4-41-0)		x† x x	34		4 : 16† 1	43		† Appeal ct wk.	68	222			24	
19			CHILDS	13				: : : 4 : :	49		M14	69					
23	"	16			LB : 3 1	37		: 2 1 :	52		(LB)	70	225		16	25	15
26			"	14	P : : P : P	43					M15	71					
30	"	17						: 8/7 4 2 7 8 1	58			72	226			26	
34			"	15	7 6 1	45		: 4 1 : :	62		5HR	73	228		17	27	
36	"	18			4 6 P P 2 :	51					light poor	74	230		19		
40	(18-2-40-1)		"	16		51	1	4 8 1	64	3	M15 NB2	74²	231	5	19	28	15
5.41	BAD LIGHT		(15.2-4-48-1)										B	L	S	P	
6.35			"	16	: : : 7	55					sunny	75					
37	DEFREITAS	19			7 1	56		5 7 4 3 4 :	69			76	235		20	31	
42			"	17	: : L x : 7 2	62					50 p'ship: 73 min	77	237		22		
45	"	20			T† 3 5(6) 1	65		5 4 9 1	72		† Round wkt	78	239		23	32	
50			"	18	: 3 P P : P	71					M16	79					
53	"	21			: 4 P	74		4 : 6† 3	75		† Childs misfield.	80	242			35	
58	(21-2-49-1)		"	19		74	1	: x 4 : :	81	3	M17 NB2	81	242	5	23	35	15
7.01	STUMPS		(19-6-50-1)										S	T	UM	PS	
3RD DAY 11.00	EMBUREY	15			: : : : : :	80					M18	82					
02			CHILDS	20				: : : P : :	87		M19	83					
05	"	16			: : 8 1	83		: 4 P	90			84	243		24		
07			"	21	. . 4 : P P	89					M20	85					
10	"	17			: P 6	92		: : 4 1	93			86	244			36	
13			"	22				2 4 : : : :	99	4		87	248			40	
16	"	18			2 : : P P	98					M21	88					
18			"	23				3 3 P 6 5	105		M22	89					
21	"	19			P† 5(4) 1	100		P : : LB	109		† Round wkt (to Harper) (LB)	90	250		25		16
25			"	24	: P : :	105		2 1	110		6HR	91	251			41	
28	"	20						P 7 2 x : 6 2	116			92	255			45	
32			"	25	: P : 2 P :	111					over wkt M23	93					
34	"	21			: P :	114		P : 4 3	119			94	258			48	
37			"	26	P : : : P	119		4 1	120			95	259			49	
11.40	" (22-6-52-0)	22	(26-10-56-1)		P P	121	1	: : 7†8/7 1	124	4	† Moxon hit on shin. 50: 147' M23 NB2	96	260	5	25	50	16

3RD DAY	BOWLERS				BATSMEN						WEST INDIES 1ST INNINGS						
	(CONSTANT) STRETFORD END		(PLEWS) WARWICK RD END		SCOREBOARD LEFT			SCOREBOARD RIGHT			NOTES	END-OF-OVER TOTALS					
TIME	BOWLER	O.	BOWLER	O.	SCORING	BALLS	6s/4s	SCORING	BALLS	6s/4s		O.	RUNS	W.	'L' BAT	'R' BAT	EXTRAS
					HARPER	121	1	DUJON	124	4	M23 NB2	96	260	5	25	50	16
11.44			CHILDS	27				8 × 4 8/7 2 · : · : 1	130		rain	97	263			53	
47	EMBUREY	23	(27-10-59-1)		P ·	122	1	7/8 1	131	4	M23 NB2	97²	264	5	25	54	16
11.48	(22.2-6-53-0) RAIN										56 min lost (13 overs)			R	S	P	
12.44	EMBUREY	23			: P · P	126						98					
46			″	28				2 2 : : : : :	137			99	266			56	
49	″	24			: : P P : P	132					M24	100					
51			″	29				8 4† P E1 3LB 2 2 · · · ·	143		† 1 overthrow (DeFreitas) (3LB)	101	273			60	19
55	″	25			: ·	134		: 7 6 1 · · 1	147			102	274			61	
57	(25-7-54-0)		″	30	P P P : · · · :	138	1	× 2 · 3	149	4		103	277	5	25	64	19
1.00	LUNCH		(30-10-68-1)								M24 NB2		L	U	NC	H	
1.40	DILLEY	16			4 × × × P · · · · ·	143		76† 3	150		† NEW BALL late outswingers	104	280			67	
45			DEFREITAS	22				: : 4 4 : 4	156		M25	105					
48	″	17			1 1	144		: 3 · 6b. W	159	4	HARPER 51' on 25.	105⁴	281	6	26	67	19
51								MARSHALL								0	
53	″	17						: ×	2			106					
55			″	23	⊙4 5 : 3 : 8/7b 2 ·	151	2				(NB) NB3	107	288		32		20
2.00	″	18						6†4 × 2 2 × · · · 2 2 ·	8		† dropped ball. 7HR	108	292			4	
05			″	24	⊙ 3 × · 4LB · · ·	156		4 :	10		(NB) (LB) - off chest NB4	109	294				22
10	″	19			5(6) 1	157		5 4 3 7 × · 4 · · ·	15	1		110	299		33	8	
15			″	25	EP 4 × P 3 P · (2) · · · · ·	164					NB5	111	301		35		
19	″	20	(25-3-59-1)		: 3 6 · · 1	167		1/2 1 : P	18			112	303		36	9	
25			CHILDS	31	× × 3 3S · · · 1	171		P P · ·	20			113	304		37		
29	″	21			4 7 8 4 · 1 2 1	175		2/3 3 3 4	22	2		114	315		41	16	
34	(21-3-76-3)		″	32	3† · P ·	178	2		22	2	Very poor light. † Moxon hit on leg.	114³	315	6	41	16	22
2.38	RAIN		(31.3-10-69-1)								M25 NB5		R	S	P		
3.40	TEA												T	E	A		
4.50			CHILDS	32	3E 1	179		: :	24			115	316		42		
52	DILLEY	22			· 6 7 · 1	182		7 7 4 2 · ·	27			116	319		43	18	
58			″	33	P P 8/7 · · 1	185		4 2 × · · ·	30			117	320		44		
5.01	″	23			7/8 7/6 7/6 1 · · · · ·	191					M26	118					
05 08			″	34	· 1E · 1	193		2 7 2 × 3 4 · ·	34	3	Sawdust for wet patches no trench.	119	328		45	25	
14	″	24			7 6† · 3	195		: 5 : :	38		† spectacular sliding stop (DeFreitas). 8HR	120	331		48		
19	(24-4-82-3)		″	35	6 1	196		: : 2 2 2 · · 3	43		'50 p'ship: 70'	121	335		49	28	
24	DEFREITAS	26						L 3 · 4 Y. × · · · · · ·	49		M27	122					
27			″	36	· 9 3	198		4 : 2 EP · · ·	53		50: 250'	123	338		52		
31	″	27			2 × 7 LB 9 2 · · · 1	203		2 1	54		(LB)	124	343		55	29	23
35			″	37	P 8 P P · P · 2 · · · ·	209						125	345		57		
38	″	28			6 · 8 · · 3	212		× 4 1 · · 1	57			126	349		60	30	
5.43	(28-4-67-1)		(38-11-88-1)	38	L · · · P P	218	2		57	3	M28 NB5	127	349	6	60	30	23

3RD DAY	BOWLERS (CONSTANT) STRETFORD END		BOWLERS (PLEWS) WARWICK RD END		BATSMEN SCOREBOARD LEFT			BATSMEN SCOREBOARD RIGHT			WEST INDIES 1ST INNINGS	END-OF-OVER TOTALS					
TIME	BOWLER	O.	BOWLER	O.	SCORING	BALLS	6s/4s	SCORING	BALLS	6s/4s	NOTES	O.	RUNS	W.	'L' BAT	'R' BAT	EXTRAS
					HARPER	218	2	MARSHALL	57	3	M28 NB 5	127	349	6	60	30	23
5.46	DEFREITAS	29			2 6 1	221		EP 3 1	60			128	350			31	
50			CHILDS	39				3 P 4 P	66		M29	129					
54	•	30			4 1	222		8E 4 +L7 2 1	71		HARPER'S HS (Tests) † Light offered	130	354		61	34	
59	(30-4-72-1)		•	40	F P P	225	2	P 9 3	74	3		131	357	6	61	37	23
6.02	RAIN		(40-12-91-1)								M29 NB 5			R	S	P	
6.12	PLAY ABANDONED												S	T	UMPS		
4TH DAY	NO PLAY BEFORE LUNCH				(OVERNIGHT RAIN)						(30 OVERS LOST)						
1.41	DEFREITAS	31						3	80		Light poor M30	132					
45			DILLEY	25	X 6 6 6 7 2/3 3	231						133	360		64		
50	•	32			3 7/8 6 X ↓X8 2	237					9HR	134	362		66		
54			•	26	7 3 4 1	239	3	4X 4 LB 2/3	84		(LB)	135	368		71		24
59	•	33			3 6S X 2 1 1	243		L 4S 1	86			136	371		73	38	
2.03			•	27	3 1 4X W	245	3	3 1	87			136.3	373	7	74	39	24
04					AMBROSE		LHB								0		
06			•	27	5 8(A) 4	3	1					137	377		4		
09	•	34						3S 7/8 4 3 1	93		rain.	138	378			40	
13			•	28	IF AT 2	6		3 3 1	96			139	381		6	41	
18	•	35			9 1 +8S	8		↓ 6(S) 6 8/7 1 1	100		† Round wkt	140	384		7	43	
22	(35-5-81-1)		•	29		8	1	:	101	3		140.1	384	7	7	43	24
2.23	RAIN		(28.1-4-99-4)								M30 NB 5		R	S	P		
4.00	DECLARATION										846 balls		DECLARED				

4TH DAY	BOWLERS (PLEWS) STRETFORD END		(CONSTANT) WARWICK RD END		BATSMEN SCOREBOARD LEFT			SCOREBOARD RIGHT			ENGLAND 2ND INNINGS	END-OF-OVER TOTALS					
TIME	BOWLER	O.	BOWLER	O.	SCORING	BALLS	6s/4s	SCORING	BALLS	6s/4s	NOTES	O.	RUNS	W.	'L' BAT	'R' BAT	EXTRAS
					GOOCH			MOXON			41 overs left.						
4.15	MARSHALL	1			4LB . . . : 7 1	5		3 1	1		(4LB)	1	6		1	1	4
20	(1-0-2-0)		AMBROSE	1		5	-	. : 3 : . .	7	-	M1 NB-	2	6	-	1	1	4
4.24	BLSP		(1-1-0-0)								19 MINS		B	L	S P		
4.43	"	2	}		7E : 3 L . . . W	9	-					2^4	6	1	1	1	4
45					GATTING										0		
47	"	2			.	1					M1 NB-	2^5	6	1	0	1	4
4.48	(1.5-0-2-1) BLSP												B	L	S	P	
5.18	MARSHALL	2			:	2					M2	3					
19			"	2	. P 4 x†x	7		LB .	8		(LB) M3 † over middle stump	4	7				5
23	"	3						x x 4 . . . 2	14			5	9			3	
27			"	3	P8 4LB 8 . 1 .	12		4 3	15		(4LB)	6	17		1	6	9
31	"	4			. : † . x :	17		7 1	16		† MARSHALL 1st warning	7	18			7	
35			"	4	4 4 † . 8 3	21		†9 . 1	18		† hit on shoulder	8	22		4	8	
39	"	5	}		L : x EI . . . W	25	-					8^4	22	2	4	8	9
41					GOWER		LHB								0		
43	"	5			3 1	1		:	19			9	23		1		
45			"	5	: 1E 3 1	4		† † 2 1	22		† Hit on rt arm.	10	25		2	9	
49	"	6						: : . . 4 2/3 P 2	28			11	27			11	
54			"	6	†G 4 1	6		. . EL 4 9 1	32		• Dropped 3rd slip (RICHARDSON)	12	29		3	12	
57	"	7						. 6 . 2/3 6 7 .	38		M4	13					
6.01			"	7	3 3 E EI 3 3 2	12					• Dropped 4th slip (MARSHALL) 1HR	14	31		5		
05	"	8						: : : . 6/7 2 .	44			15	33			14	
09			"	8	: † 3 1	15		T : 7 1	47			16	35		6	15	
13	"	9						. T . L P† 1E	53		† MARSHALL 2nd warning M5	17					
18	(9-3-10-2)		"	9	6 1	16		: P † . PY	58			18	36		7		
22	WALSH	1	(9-2-17-0)		. . . x : 1E	22					M6	19					
26			BENJAMIN	1	}			1E W	59	-		19^1	36	3	7	15	9
27								LAMB								0	
29			"	1				9 Gt x . 3 4 . . .	5	1	† Treatment.	20	40			4	
35	"	2			7 8 2 . 1 2 . .	27		7 1	6			21	44		10	5	
39			"	2				3 x x . P	12		M7	22					
43	"	3			: 2 4 x 9E : 4 . . 1	33	1					23	49		15		
47			"	3	3 1	34		3 6 4 : †	17			24	50		16		
51	"	4			: ↓ : : 4 8E 1	40						25	51		17		
54	(4-1-10-0)		"	4	8 1	41		: 3 3 : L	22			26	52		18		
58	HARPER	1	(4-1-6-1)		: 8 (1) 7/8	44		8 P PPP 1 (.) . .	27		(NB) NB2 2HR	27	56		20	6	10
7.05			HOOPER	1	4 2 : 8† 4	50	2				† Walsh 'torpedoed'!	28	60		24		
07	(2-1-4*-0)	2	(1-0-4-0)			50	2	: P . P : :	33	1	M8	29	60	3	24	6	10
7.09	STUMPS										M8 NB2		STUMPS				

5TH DAY TIME	BOWLERS (PLEWS) STRETFORD END BOWLER	O.	(CONSTANT) WARWICK RD END BOWLER	O.	BATSMEN SCOREBOARD LEFT SCORING	BALLS	6s/4s	SCOREBOARD RIGHT SCORING	BALLS	6s/4s	ENGLAND 2ND INNINGS NOTES	END-OF-OVER TOTALS O.	RUNS	W.	'L' BAT	'R' BAT	EXTRAS
					GOWER	50	2	LAMB	33	1	Arthurton sub (Greenidge) M8 NB2	29	60	3	24	6	10
11.00			AMBROSE	10	7 6 3 1	52		2 4 2/3 1 . . 2	37		sunny - warmer	30	67		28	9	
04	MARSHALL	10			8 7 9 . 4 . 2 . .	58	3					31	73		34		
08			"	11				. : : : L .	43		overcast M9	32					
12	"	11			E1 . W	60	3					32^{2}	73	4	34	9	10
13					CAPEL						Williams sub (Rich'son) chipped finger				0		
15	"	11			3 : L :	4					M10	33					
18			"	12				. : : x : 1x	49		M11	34					
21	"	12			. P EP3 W	7	-					34^{3}	73	5	0	9	10
23					DOWNTON										0		
25	"	12			. x . .	3					M12	35					
27			"	13				P T 3 G7 . . . W	53	1		35^{4}	73	6	0	9	10
29								EMBUREY								0	
31			"	13				T 8 . 2	2			36	75			2	
32	"	13			. : 2 1 2 . 3	8		LB .	3		(LB)	37	80		4		11
37			"	14	x 2 4 : . 1 8E 1	12		2 B 4 .	5	1	(B)	38	87		6	6	12
41	"	14			E1 W	13	-					38^{1}	87	7	6	6	12
41					DEFREITAS										0		
42	"	14			4 E1 . W	2	-					38^{3}	87	8	0	6	12
44					DILLEY		LHB								0		
46	(14-5-21-6)	14			T 8 . 1	2		L .	6			39	88		1		
49			"	15	8 1	3	-	P . . :	9	1	Heavy cloud	39^{4}	89	8	2	6	12
52	BLSP		(14-4-4-33-1)								RAIN at 11.53 M12 NB2		B	L	S	P	
12.07			"	15				9E x . .	11		5 overs lost	40					
08	"	15			x x 3 8 . . . 1	7		. :	13		3HR	41	90		3		
11			"	16	: 2 1	9		8 P . 7 2 . . W	17	1		42	93	9	4	8	12
14			(16-4-36-2)					CHILDS		LHB						0	
16	" (15.4-5-22-7)	16			. : x x W	13	-		-	-		42^{4}	93	10	4	0	12
12.18	ALL OUT										M12 NB2		ALL		OUT		
											258 balls						

ENGLAND 1ST INNINGS v. WEST INDIES at OLD TRAFFORD, MANCHESTER (THIRD TEST) on 30 JUNE, 1, 2, 4, 5 JULY, 1988.

IN	OUT	MINS	No.	BATSMAN	HOW OUT	BOWLER	RUNS	WKT	TOTAL	6s	4s	BALLS	NOTES ON DISMISSAL TOSS: ENGLAND
11.01	12.51	110	1	G.A. GOOCH	Ct DUJON	BENJAMIN	27	4	55	·	3	81	Edged firm-footed drive at offside ball.
11.01	11.36	35	2	M.D. MOXON	BOWLED	MARSHALL	0	1	12	·	·	22	Bowled off pads by late inswinger.
11.38	11.44	6	3	M.W. GATTING	LBW	MARSHALL	0	2	14	·	·	4	Padded up to inswinger.
11.46	12.15	29	4	D.I. GOWER	Ct HARPER	WALSH	9	3	33	·	2	20	Edged offside slash to 4th slip.
12.17	2.49	112	5	A.J. LAMB	Ct GREENIDGE	AMBROSE	33	6	94	·	2	82	Cut chest-high to gully.
12.53	2.03	30	6	D.J. CAPEL	BOWLED	BENJAMIN	1	5	61	·	·	18	Bowled off stump by breakback – 'half-cock' stroke
2.05	6.10	88	7	P.R. DOWNTON †	Ct GREENIDGE	WALSH	24	8	113	·	2	63	Cut waist-high to gully.
2.51	5.47	19	8	J.E. EMBUREY *	Ct DUJON	WALSH	1	7	98	·	·	17	Followed lifting ball outside off stump.
5.49	6.19	30	9	P.A.J. DeFREITAS	Ct GREENIDGE	AMBROSE	15	9	123	·	1	28	Silly mid-off intercepted lofted off-drive - head-high, 2nd attempt
6.12	6.40	28	10	G.R. DILLEY	Ct HARPER	WALSH	14	10	135	·	2	21	Top-edged slash to 2nd slip - 2nd attempt catch.
6.21	(6.40)	19	11	J.H. CHILDS	NOT OUT		2			·	·	12	TEST DEBUT
				EXTRAS	b - lb 4	w - nb 5	9			·6	12 4	368 balls (6 no-balls)	

* CAPTAIN † WICKET-KEEPER

TOTAL (60.2 OVERS; 263 MINUTES) 135. ALL OUT at 6.40pm on 1st day

13 OVERS 4 BALLS/HOUR
2.23 RUNS/OVER
36 RUNS/100 BALLS

UMPIRES: D.J. CONSTANT and N.T. PLEWS

BOWLER	O	M	R	W	nb
MARSHALL	12	5	19	2	-
AMBROSE	17	5	35	2	1
WALSH	18.2	4	46	4	5
BENJAMIN	13	4	31	2	-
			4		
	60.2	18	135	10	

HRS	OVERS	RUNS
1	14	23
2	14	32
3	13	29
4	14	39

RUNS	MINS	OVERS	LAST 50 (in mins)
50	102	23.5	102
100	215	49.2	113

LUNCH: 55-4 [28 OVERS 121 MIN] LAMB 16* (44') CAPEL 0* (8')

TEA: 97-6 [48 OVERS 207 MIN] DOWNTON 22* (62') EMBUREY 1* (16')

WKT	PARTNERSHIP		RUNS	MINS
1st	Gooch	Moxon	12	35
2nd	Gooch	Gatting	2	6
3rd	Gooch	Gower	19	29
4th	Gooch	Lamb	22	34
5th	Lamb	Capel	6	30
6th	Lamb	Downton	33	44
7th	Downton	Emburey	4	19
8th	Downton	DeFreitas	15	21
9th	DeFreitas	Dilley	10	7
10th	Dilley	Childs	12	19
			135	

WEST INDIES 1ST INNINGS — IN REPLY TO ENGLAND'S 135 ALL OUT

IN	OUT	MINS	No.	BATSMAN	HOW OUT	BOWLER	RUNS	WKT	TOTAL	6s	4s	BALLS	NOTES ON DISMISSAL
6.52	2.24	154	1	C.G. GREENIDGE	LBW	DeFREITAS	45	3	101	·	6	129	Late on breakback that kept low.
6.52	11.46	34	2	R.B. RICHARDSON	BOWLED	DILLEY	23	1	35	·	3	27	Bottom-edged hook at bouncer.
11.48	1.48	82	3	C.L. HOOPER	LBW	CHILDS	15	2	77	·	·	47	Changed mind – played back without offering stroke. CHILD'S 14th b.
1.50	3.34	104	4	I.V.A. RICHARDS*	BOWLED	CAPEL	47	4	175	1	5	71	Played on – under-edged cut. 7250 Test runs (overtook HAMMOND)
2.26	4.09	82	5	A.L. LOGIE	LBW	DILLEY	39	5	187	·	4	59	Straddled crease – hit on back leg by low breakback.
3.36	1.51	180	6	P.J.L. DUJON †	Ct CAPEL	DILLEY	67	6	281	·	4	159	Leading edge – knee-high catch to mid-on running in.
4.11	2.04	307	7	R.A. HARPER	BOWLED	DILLEY	74	7	373	·	3	245	Yorked. HIGHEST TEST SCORE.
1.53	(2.23)	159	8	M.D. MARSHALL	NOT OUT		43			·	3	101	
2.06	(2.23)	17	9	C.E.L. AMBROSE	NOT OUT		7			·	1	8	
			10	W.K.M. BENJAMIN	did not bat								
			11	C.A. WALSH	did not bat								
				EXTRAS	b - lb 21 w - nb 3		24			1	29	846 balls (inc 5 no-balls)	

* CAPTAIN † WICKET-KEEPER

TOTAL (140.1 OVERS; 566 MINUTES) 384-7 DECLARED at 4.00 pm on fourth day.

LEAD: 249

14 OVERS 5 BALLS/HOUR
2.73 RUNS/OVER
45 RUNS/100 BALLS

BOWLER	O	M	R	W	nb
DILLEY	28.1	4	99	4	1
EMBUREY	25	7	54	0	-
DeFREITAS	35	5	81	1	4
CAPEL	12	2	38	1	-
CHILDS	40	12	91	1	-
			21		
	140.1	30	384	7	

2ND NEW BALL taken at 1.41 pm third day – WEST INDIES 280-5 after 103.1 overs

HRS	OVERS	RUNS
1	14	51
2	14	26
3	15	44
4	14	66
5	16	41
6	18	23
7	17	41
8	12	39
9	14	31

RUNS	MINS	OVERS	LAST 50 (in mins)
50	55	13.2	55
100	149	36.0	94
150	199	48.0	50
200	260	62.2	61
250	355	90.0	95
300	430	110.1	75
350	510	127.3	80

STUMPS: 4-0 [3 OVERS, 11 MINUTES] GREENIDGE 4*, RICHARDSON 0*

2ND DAY: START DELAYED BY RAIN & BAD LIGHT (23 MIN - 6 OVERS)

LUNCH: 73-1 [26 OVERS, 110 MIN] GREENIDGE 36* (110'), HOOPER 13* (74')

TEA: 182-4 [55 OVERS, 229 MIN] LOGIE 34* (73'), DUJON 7* (3')

STUMPS (2ND DAY): 242-5 (107 LEAD) [81 OVERS, 330 MIN] DUJON 35* (104'), HARPER 23* (90')

LUNCH: 277-5 (142 LEAD) [103 OVERS, 394 MIN] DUJON 64* (168'), HARPER 25* (154')

TEA: 315-6 (180 LEAD) [114.3 OVERS, 452 MIN] HARPER 41* (212'), MARSHALL 16* (45')

STUMPS: 357-6 [131 OVERS, 524 MIN] HARPER 61* (284'), MARSHALL 37* (117')

WKT	PARTNERSHIP		RUNS	MINS
1st	Greenidge	Richardson	35	34
2nd	Greenidge	Hooper	42	82
3rd	Greenidge	Richards	24	34
4th	Richards	Logie	74	68
5th	Logie	Dujon	12	12
6th	Dujon	Harper	94	166
7th	Harper	Marshall	92	140
8th	Marshall	Ambrose	11*	17
9th				
10th			384	

ENGLAND 2ND INNINGS (249 RUNS BEHIND ON FIRST INNINGS)

IN	OUT	MINS	No.	BATSMAN	HOW OUT	BOWLER	RUNS	WKT	TOTAL	6s	4s	BALLS	NOTES ON DISMISSAL
4.15	4.45	11	1	G.A. GOOCH	LBW	MARSHALL	1	1	6	·	·	9	Beaten by breakback - shuffled across stumps.
4.15	6.27	83	2	M.D. MOXON	Ct RICHARDS	BENJAMIN	15	3	36	·	·	59	Edged Benjamin's first ball to first slip.
4.47	5.41	24	3	M.W. GATTING	Ct RICHARDSON	MARSHALL	4	2	22	·	·	25	Edged away-seamer to third slip.
5.43	11.13	99	4	D.I. GOWER	Ct RICHARDSON	MARSHALL	34	4	73	·	3	60	Edged slash at widish ball to second slip.
6.29	11.29	69	5	A.J. LAMB	Ct LOGIE	AMBROSE	9	6	73	·	1	53	Gloved lifting late inswinger to short-leg.
11.15	11.23	8	6	D.J. CAPEL	Ct SUB (ARTHURTON)	MARSHALL	0	5	73	·	·	7	Edged inswinger via pad to silly mid-off.
11.25	11.41	16	7	P.R. DOWNTON†	Ct HARPER	MARSHALL	6	7	87	·	·	13	Edged outswinger to third slip.
11.31	12.14	28	8	J.E. EMBUREY *	Ct LOGIE	AMBROSE	8	9	93	·	1	17	Fended lifting ball to short-leg.
11.42	11.44	2	9	P.A.J. DEFREITAS	Ct HARPER	MARSHALL	0	8	87	·	·	2	Edged outswinger to third slip.
11.46	12.18	17	10	G.R. DILLEY	BOWLED	MARSHALL	4	10	93	·	·	13	Late on defensive push at straight ball that removed off stump.
12.16	(12.18)	2	11	J.H. CHILDS	NOT OUT		0			·	·	-	
				EXTRAS	b 1 lb 10 w - nb 1		12			-6	5[4]	258 balls (including 2 no-balls)	

* CAPTAIN † WICKET-KEEPER

TOTAL (42.4 OVERS; 188 MINUTES) 93. All out at 12.18 pm on fifth day.

13 OVERS 4 BALLS/HOUR
2.17 RUNS/OVER
36 RUNS/100 BALLS

BOWLER	O	M	R	W	nb
MARSHALL	15.4	5	22	7	-
AMBROSE	16	4	36	2	-
WALSH	4	1	10	0	-
BENJAMIN	4	1	6	1	-
HARPER	2	1	4	0	2
HOOPER	1	0	4	0	-
			11		
	42.4	12	93	10	

HRS	OVERS	RUNS
1	14	31
2	13	25
3	14	34

RUNS	MINS	OVERS	LAST 50 (in mins)
50	103	23.1	103

STUMPS: 60-3 [29 OVERS / 125 MIN] GOWER 24*(86') LAMB 6*(40')
(4TH DAY) (189 BEHIND)

ENGLAND LOST LAST 7 WICKETS FOR 33 RUNS OFF 13.4 OVERS IN 63 MINUTES ON FIFTH MORNING.

WEST INDIES WON BY AN INNINGS & 156 RUNS

[ACTUAL PLAYING TIME: 16 HOURS 57 MIN]

MATCH AWARD: M.D. MARSHALL

(Adjudicator: T.W. GRAVENEY)

WKT	PARTNERSHIP		RUNS	MINS
1st	Gooch	Moxon	6	11
2nd	Moxon	Gatting	16	24
3rd	Moxon	Gower	14	44
4th	Gower	Lamb	37	53
5th	Lamb	Capel	0	8
6th	Lamb	Downton	0	4
7th	Downton	Emburey	14	10
8th	Emburey	DeFreitas	0	2
9th	Emburey	Dilley	6	13
10th	Dilley	Childs	0	2
			93	

HEADINGLEY
THE FOURTH TEST

Headingley's Test match highlights · A Churchillian remedy · Cowdrey is chosen · The Guildford Guillotine · Match report

The last century had only a few months of life remaining when Headingley staged its first Test match between Archie MacLaren's England side and Joe Darling's touring Australians. Some of cricket's most illustrious names were on view to launch the ground's international career: Monty Noble, Victor Trumper, Clem Hill, 'Ranji', Charles Fry, Tom Hayward and Stanley Jackson. That inaugural Leeds Test will be remembered for Jack Hearne's hat-trick, the first in a Test in England, and for the very sad demise of Lancashire's left-arm spinner, Johnny Briggs, the first bowler to take 100 wickets in Test cricket. Briggs suffered a violent epileptic fit on the first night of the match and ended his life in Cheadle Asylum. There he is said to have engaged upon imaginary bowling stints up and down the ward; at the end of each day he would proudly announce his full analysis.

Even poor Briggs would not have invented the world's best first-class analysis, achieved by another left-handed spinner, Hedley Verity, at Headingley in 1932. Bowling for Yorkshire against Nottinghamshire he returned the unbelievable figures of 10 for 10 off 19.4 overs, including 16 maidens.

In 1930 the 21-year-old Don Bradman marked his first series in England by scoring 334 (still the highest first-class score at Headingley), 309 of them on the first day; he made 105 before lunch, 115 between lunch and tea, but could muster a mere 89 in the final session. His double-century took 214 minutes and remains the fastest in Tests measured by time rather than by balls faced. Bradman rather enjoyed Leeds. In 1934 he contributed 304 to Australia's 584 (the highest Test innings on the ground) and shared a 4th-wicket partnership of 388 with Bill Ponsford, then the record for all Ashes Tests. Four years later he celebrated his first tour as captain with a match-winning innings of 103. In 1948, when Australia were set 404 runs in 344 minutes on a pitch taking spin, Bradman led an improbable quest with an undefeated 173. It was the last of his 29 Test hundreds, four of which came in just six innings at Headingley.

It was there in 1952 that a tyro tearaway called Fred Trueman donned his first England sweater and so terrorized the hapless Indians that the scoreboard read 0 for four wickets, still the worst start to any Test innings.

John Edrich played the innings of his life at Headingley against the 1965 New Zealanders. His 310 not out remains England's only triple century since 1938 and the highest score by an Englishman in all first-class cricket at Leeds. He hit five sixes and 52 fours – the highest number of boundaries in any Test innings.

The 1968 Ashes encounter saw Tom Graveney and Barry Jarman make their only appearances as Test captains when Colin Cowdrey and Bill Lawry were both forced to withdraw because of injuries.

Four years later Derek Underwood routed the Aussies in three days, returning match figures of 10 for 82 on a pitch that took spin from the first morning. Its grass had perished to an attack of *Fusarium oxysporum*; this fungus seems a fairly unlikely denizen of Leeds since it normally thrives in soil temperatures above 75 degrees Fahrenheit.

The 1975 pitch fell prey to a different form of pestilence when vandals, campaigning for the release of a convicted criminal, sabotaged it with knives and oil causing a delicately poised final day of an Ashes Test to be abandoned. Rain, which fell from noon until late afternoon, would probably have produced the same result.

In 1977 Geoffrey Boycott was batting on his native soil when he became the first batsman to score his hundredth first-class century during a Test match.

Of all Headingley's famous matches, none will be recalled more often than the sensational Ashes Test of 1981. Having followed on, England were 135 for 7 and still 92 behind when Graham Dilley joined Ian Botham. With further support from Chris Old and Bob Willis, Botham blasted an undefeated 149 and Australia were set a modest 130 to win. But Willis, bounding in from the Kirkstall Lane End, took 8 for 43, the best analysis in any Leeds Test, and Australia were beaten by 18 runs. It remains only the second instance in 1,100 Tests in which a side has won after following on.

Headingley has not been a happy hunting ground for England in recent years, defeats by New Zealand, West Indies, India and Pakistan being interrupted by a solitary success against Australia.

Test Match Results at Headingley (1899–1987)

	P	W	L	D
Australia	19	6	5	8
South Africa	8	5	1	2
West Indies	7	2	4	1
New Zealand	5	3	1	1
India	5	3	1	1
Pakistan	6	3	1	2
Totals	50	22	13	15

Curiously, West Indies did not play a Test in Yorkshire until their fifth full tour in 1957. England won that initial low-scoring contest by an innings, Peter Loader ending their first innings with the last hat-trick achieved by an England bowler. The tourists gained ample revenge in 1963, spurred by a century from Gary Sobers and a career-best analysis of 6 for 36 by Charlie Griffith. They won by an innings three years later with Sobers, now their captain, contributing 174 runs (including 103 in the post-lunch session) and 8 wickets. His innings, which remained his highest in England, took him past 5,000 runs in Tests, 2,000 against England, 500 in the rubber and 1,000 for the tour. His partnership of 265 with Seymour Nurse remains the West Indies fifth-wicket record in all Tests. England won the 1969 Headingley Test by just 30 runs and retained the Wisden Trophy for the last time. Ten years later West Indies won by 55 runs after amassing 437 for 9 off 83 overs on the first day. The 1980 match was ruined by rain, more than fourteen hours being lost. Four years later, Malcolm Marshall ignored a doubly-fractured, plaster-encased left thumb to bat left-handed and return his (then) career-best figures of 7 for 53. In the last of his 90 Test matches (easily the record for any fast bowler), Bob Willis extended his world record of 'not out' innings to 55 and his (then) record tally of wickets for England to 325.

After the *débâcle* of Old Trafford, it seemed that the entire cricket world was rife with solutions for restoring England's morale and improving their dismal record. Some suggestions, involving torture and loss of life, seemed a trifle extreme, but most cricket enthusiasts were sickened by the apparent lack of resolution amongst our batsmen as they surrendered so pathetically to Malcolm Marshall's guile and accuracy.

There could be no doubt that England were confronted by a team superior in every department. After enduring their worst session of the series on the first day at Lord's, West Indies had gone from strength to strength as touring teams so often do. What especially galled English supporters was the selectors' hesitant choice of a caretaker captain and safety-first selection tactics which had boosted the confidence of a relatively inexperienced visiting team.

In the short term, I would have had no hesitation in bringing in a new captain to install some Churchillian resolution. The new skipper could have introduced a team motto – perhaps 'Never Give In' – and have taken his charges to see *Winnie*, an inspiring musical play involving the wartime leader which was currently delighting audiences at the Victoria Palace.

I wrote the following piece for *The Mail on Sunday*:

> I would give the captaincy to Chris Cowdrey and I would boost his self-confidence by also appointing him for this winter's mission to India where he has successfully toured before.

England captains future, past and present appear resigned to their fate at Headingley. L-r : Gooch, Gower and Cowdrey.

No doubt the selectors will consider Graham Gooch but he found county captaincy too much and it would be criminal to load such responsibility on our best batsman. Gooch is alone amongst current players in having a higher average against West Indies than he does in his overall Test career.

I would also make wholesale changes to the side – no eleven could do worse than the shambles that wore England colours at Old Trafford. It might be an interesting departure from recent custom to pick players who are actually in form.

For Headingley, a seamer's paradise desperately in need of the heavy plough, it is important that we select batsmen of sound technique against the moving ball. It would also be a bonus if our best seam and swing bowlers were fit – Neil Foster, Richard Ellison and Gladstone Small would have been automatic selections throughout this series.

In the long term I should like to see counties penalized by having points deducted if they produce 'result' pitches. Their narrow-minded pursuit of local honours must give way to the national team's interest in grooming players who can perform in five-day conditions. Many county squares have been an absolute disgrace this season.

Whether or not the selectors read my suggestions, they did, after considerable dithering, appoint Christopher Cowdrey as captain for the remaining two Tests against West Indies. Moreover, by the autumn the TCCB was giving serious consideration to my penalty idea by proposing a deduction of 25 county championship points for any pitch found to be sub-standard.

At the time I regarded Chris Cowdrey's appointment as the most cheering news item of a fairly dismal summer for English cricket.

As one who had advocated his selection as a player for the Third Test and nominated him for the captaincy after the fiasco at Old Trafford, I was naturally delighted that he had been chosen. He had gained the reputation of being an inspired leader whose confidence and charisma had achieved wonders with a fairly mediocre Kent team. After losing their opening three games of the season, the White Horse County had won each of their next six, an astonishing sequence which established them at the head of the table until the final week of the season when Worcestershire pipped them by a solitary point. Cowdrey's elevation completed only the second father/son captaincy double for England after Frank and George Mann.

The Headingley pitch was very much an unknown quantity, the traditional Test match strip having been discarded after playing so badly during the Texaco Trophy international. The chosen surface had staged a rain-abbreviated Benson and Hedges Cup match in April and had proved anything but a terror track. In 37.2 overs Yorkshire had amassed 173 for 1, Martyn Moxon and Ashley Metcalfe sharing an opening partnership of 166. It was apparently unrecognizable from the fiery surfaces which had made such a farce of recent Leeds Tests. After England's 1987 defeat by Pakistan the pitch had been inspected by the chairman of the TCCB's pitches committee, Donald Carr, and the future of Headingley as a Test match venue appeared to be in some jeopardy.

Gatting having already made himself unavailable for international cricket until the 1989 season, my own selection would have retained only three of England's team at Old Trafford: Gooch, Lamb and Dilley. This would have meant the postponement, at least, of David Gower's one-hundredth Test appearance, but he had been in poor form and seemed quite unable to refrain from wafting firm-footedly at balls angled across him.

My own selections included Tim Curtis; he had impressed not only with consistently high aggregates for the past three seasons but by providing such a brave and steadfast foil for Graeme Hick when the two added 284 against the West Indies attack on a poor Worcester pitch. As opening batsmen are best equipped technically to face a barrage of fast bowlers, I opted for Surrey's David Smith and Derbyshire's captain Kim Barnett at three and four, the former being a superb left-handed player of fast bowling who had been totally ignored since he top-scored in both innings on his final Test outing during the last Caribbean mission.

If the new pitch warranted the inclusion of a spinner I would have preferred the off-breaks of Vic Marks to either Emburey or Childs on their Manchester form. A distinctly handy middle-order batsman, his last three innings in Test cricket had produced scores of 83, 74 and 55. With the Middlesex influence removed I expected 'Jack' Russell to gain at last the selection that was at least a year overdue. I also anticipated that Cowdrey would opt for Richard Ellison if he considered Kent's star swing bowler ready for a long-awaited return. If not, then Yorkshire supporters could be rewarded with a maiden appearance in a Leeds Test by Paul Jarvis.

My twelve was: Gooch, Curtis, David Smith, Barnett, Lamb, Cowdrey, Marks, Russell, Foster, Ellison (or Jarvis), Small and Dilley.

Like the permutations of my colleagues, my dozen bore scant resemblance to the official party, which showed six changes from the previous Test: Gooch, Curtis, Athey, Gower, Lamb, *Robin* Smith, Cowdrey, Richards, Pringle, Foster, Dilley and Childs. It was one of the most swingeing reshuffles of recent times. As the selectors had convened in the town where Cowdrey was leading Kent in a three-day match against Surrey, the result of their deliberations became known as 'The Guildford Guillotine'.

I found the choice of Bill Athey surprising. A prolific scorer in county cricket, he had failed frequently at Test level. Apart from a successful series opening the innings against a weak Australian attack in 1986-87 and a subsequent hundred against Pakistan at Lord's, he had only once reached fifty in 31 other Test innings.

With due respect to 'Jack' Richards, I was dismayed by his recall. Yet again the selectors, particularly the new captain, had preferred a useful all-rounder to a more talented specialist. It was a pathetic safety-first tactic to employ with West Indies dormy two in the rubber and I felt desperately sorry for 'Jack' Russell.

Derek Pringle's selection received most criticism, but at least his return was logical. He had

Debutant Robin Smith indulges in a favourite back-foot square-drive.

bowled well in the Leeds Texaco Trophy match and fully deserved his chance when neither Jarvis nor Ellison was considered fit for a five-day match. Gower kept his place partly because of the need to have a left-hander, partly because his experience was sorely needed with Gatting in self-imposed exile and two new caps in the first six, but mainly, I suspect, because it was to be his hundredth Test.

Smith was an interesting choice. The Durban-born and educated younger brother of Chris 'Kippy' Smith, Robin had been tipped for England honours in 1986 but had rather marked time in the interim. So far he had endured another indifferent season but I had seen him play a match-winning innings of 87 not out on an absolute pig of a pitch at Worcester in the quarter-final of the Benson and Hedges Cup. It turned out to be a trophy-winning innings too because without it Hampshire would not have gone on to reach their first-ever Lord's final and win the competition. Six feet tall and fourteen stone, he delights in hitting the ball hard and is one of the best square-cutters I have seen.

By omitting John Childs from their twelve, England made a seventh change to the side humiliated at Old Trafford, but the grand product of their revamping was merely to reduce the margin of defeat from an innings and plenty to one of 10 wickets. Despite being beaten in under 17 hours of actual playing time, the new-look England appeared more purposeful under Chris Cowdrey's guidance, and even enjoyed a scent of victory before their disastrous second innings.

West Indies had one last-minute change forced upon them when Gordon Greenidge withdrew because of a neck spasm and Keith Lloyd Thomas Arthurton, a gifted 23-year-old left-handed batsman and superb fielder from the tiny island of Nevis, was given his first cap.

Starting 50 minutes late because of overnight

Desmond Haynes congratulates David Gower on his 7000th run.

rain, Headingley's 51st Test was suspended until 2.30 p.m. after just two overs because of a mysterious water seepage into the bowler's approach at the Main Stand End. After his second over, Ambrose complained about his run up and there was lengthy inspection of the area by umpires and groundsman before the players solemnly trooped off. Various rumours were rife. Most involved complicated tales of certain drains being blocked to aid the pitch's preparation. The statement explaining the cause led to even greater confusion and mystery. It was all a frustrating but glorious cock-up which caused 27 overs to be lost – nearly one-third of the day's allotted span for which the Yorkshire public had paid handsomely and, in many cases, travelled far. For a ground determined to justify its continued international status it was a sad case of self-inflicted gunshot wounds to both feet. Perhaps the most astonishing aspect of the mini-saga was the great good humour with which the crowd watched the farcical proceedings in the middle. In many parts of the world riot police would have been sorely stretched.

When play eventually restarted at 2.30 p.m., the pitch lived up to most of groundsman Keith Boyce's expectations. There was still ample lateral movement but the bounce was reasonably true, even if the West Indian pace quartet still caused problems after Marshall had claimed the prize wicket of Gooch. Curtis excited memories of Boycott with his monumental patience and perished unexpectedly when he seemed on the verge of a significant score. Athey, warmly received by his native crowd, alas never conveyed much impression of permanency.

Gower, accorded a magnificent reception, responded with a hectic little cameo before inevitably nicking a ball angled across his bows. At least he could celebrate becoming the fifth player to appear in 100 Tests, following Colin Cowdrey (Edgbaston 1968), Geoffrey Boycott (Lord's 1981), Clive Lloyd (Edgbaston 1984) and Sunil Gavaskar (Faisalabad 1984). At 31, Gower was the youngest by four years to reach this landmark. It is an indication of the amount of Test cricket now played by England that Gower's century of Tests was the fastest by three-and-a-half years, just ten years and 50 days having elapsed since he struck his first ball to the boundary in the match that launched Cornhill's sponsorship. *Test Match Special* commentator Don Mosey, confused by several simultaneously delivered verbal and written messages, revealed that Gower had reached the landmark in *fewer* Tests than any of the others!

England struggled to 80 for 4 in nearly 34 overs before Allan Lamb and debutant Robin Smith produced some of the most memorable batting of the series. Their fifth-wicket partnership of 103 was ended only when Lamb tore a calf muscle when setting off for a quick single. That tragic injury ended England's first three-figure stand since Trent Bridge. As it heralded a collapse which saw 4 wickets fall for 2 runs, it also marked the game's turning point. From the affluence of 183 for 4, England toppled to

The giant Curtly Elconn Lynwall Ambrose during his Cornhill match award-winning performance at Headingley.

a sorry 201 all out in just 46 minutes.

West Indies were made to struggle for their runs, particularly after Curtis had held an amazing two-handed diving catch at square-leg to dismiss Viv Richards. Saturday crowds at Test matches have been notoriously unlucky in recent seasons and Headingley's have suffered as grievously as most. Perhaps it came as no surprise to early arrivals on the third day when they were greeted by a combination of drizzle, Stygian gloom, ominous public address warnings about the likelihood of play, and a damp rendering of the 'Thunder and Lightning Polka' by the local sauce works band.

Fortunately the warnings proved ill-founded and a near-capacity crowd, well-fortified by an extended lunch interval, had their patience rewarded by a mid-afternoon start. They were treated to one of England's best bowling displays of the summer. It was spearheaded by Derek Pringle, who silenced both criticism of his recall and his many tormentors in the crowd with a devastating spell of 3 for 11 in 16 balls. When bad light heralding further rain brought about a premature close West Indies were just 37 ahead with 2 wickets left.

When play resumed on Monday, Roger Harper shepherded the tail into a rally which produced a substantial lead of 74. Pringle's final analysis was only the fourth 5-wicket haul against West Indies at Leeds, following Peter Loader (1957), Bob Willis (1976) and Paul Allott (1984). His fine effort protected a threadbare attack consisting of just three specialist bowlers, two of them with suspect under-carriages.

England were still in with a slither of a chance but, after a brave opening partnership of 56 between Curtis, who survived for over 90 minutes in each innings, and Gooch, who scored his third half-century of the series, they managed to lose all 10 wickets for a paltry 82.

Gower did manage to score the 2 runs he needed to become the tenth batsman from all countries to complete 7,000 runs in Test cricket. Before he could add to them he perished to a tumbling catch off an attempted leg-glance.

To everyone's astonishment, Lamb, last seen hobbling painfully on crutches, walked gingerly out to bat at the fall of the 6th wicket with Smith as his runner. For 87 minutes he defied the pace attack on one leg, hitting three boundaries. The West Indies bowlers showed him no mercy and, despite the pain-killing injection administered just before his journey to the middle, he frequently winced in agony.

Well before noon on the fifth day, Curtly Elconn Lynwall Ambrose celebrated the successful conclusion of only his 20th first-class match by winning the Cornhill Award. A year earlier he could have boasted of just one appearance at first-class level.

And so England extended their dismal record in Yorkshire Tests, this being the fifth comprehensive defeat inside four days of actual play in the course of their last six matches there.

1ST DAY	BOWLERS (HD BIRD) MAIN STAND END		(DR SHEPHERD) KIRKSTALL LANE END		BATSMEN SCOREBOARD LEFT			SCOREBOARD RIGHT			ENGLAND 1ST INNINGS NOTES	END-OF-OVER TOTALS					
TIME	BOWLER	O.	BOWLER	O.	SCORING	BALLS	6s/4s	SCORING	BALLS	6s/4s		O.	RUNS	W.	'L' BAT	'R' BAT	EXTRAS
11.00	START DELAYED - OVERNIGHT RAIN.							PITCH CUT at 11.15 am			Toss at 11.25 am.						
					GOOCH			CURTIS			12 overs lost						
11.51			MARSHALL	1	6 2LB 6 . :.:..:	6					(2LB) M1	1	2				2
56	AMBROSE	1	1-1-0-0					2	6		M2	2					
12.03	1-1-0-0 PLAY SUSPENDED										Bowlers' run up dried (water hog)						
12.40	LUNCH										27 overs lost		LUNCH				
2.30			MARSHALL	2	: LB	8		T P 8 .	10		49 overs (LB) M3	3	3				3
34	AMBROSE	2			P 8 .. 1 .	12		† 7 . 1	12			4	5		1	1	
38			"	3				1E P .	18		M4	5					
41	"	3			: . : 7 : 8 4	18	1					6	9		5		
45			"	4	6/7 . 7 2 . 4 .	23	2	49 1	19			7	14		9	2	
49	"	4						3 3 . x P	25		M5	8					
53			"	5	† P . E1 W	27	2					8[4]	14	1	9	2	3
55					ATHEY										0		
57			"	5	6 7/8 . 2	2						9	16		2		
58	"	5						3 3 . : . ?	31		M6	10					
3.02			"	6	. : . : x :	8					M7	11					
06	"	6						3 P . 8 2	37			12	18			4	
09			"	7	: : : P 8† :	14					† Round wkt. M8	13					
13	"	7			Y. 8 . 1	16		† P P 49 P . 1	41		† Round wkt. 1HR	14	20		3	5	
18	(7-3-10-0)		"	8	P LB	18		3 3 8/7 1	45		(LB)	15	22			6	4
23	BENJAMIN	1	(8-5-8-1)					L : . : : .	51		M9	16					
27			WALSH	1	9x 7 (.) (1) . . E1 f8 4 x	26	1	9 (1)	52		(NB) NB 3	17	29		8	7	5
32	"	2						. 4LB . . P 2	58		(4LB) M10	18	33				9
37			"	2	8/7 3 7 1	28		P 48/7 . 8 . 4 . (1)	63	1	NB 4	19	42		12	12	
41	"	3			. P 8 1	31		: . :	66			20	43		13		
45			"	3	5/4 . 7 P 2 : :	37					• c&b (leading edge) M11	21					
50	"	4						: L L . L W	71	1		21[5]	43	2	13	12	9
52								GOWER		LHB	100th TEST.					0	
54	"	4						9 1	1			22	44			1	
56			"	4				•7 . 3 8 7/8 (.) : 2 . 1	8		• 'ct' sh. leg (Logie) (NB) NB 5	23	48			4	10
4.01	"	5			9 1	38		4/3 3 8/7 3 5(4) 2 4 2 . 1	13	1		24	58		14	13	
05			"	5	L . 6 . : .	44					M12	25					
09	(5-3-2-12-2)	6	(5-2-20-0)				1	: : E1 W	16	1		25[3]	58	3	14	13	10
4.10	TEA							LAMB			M12			T	E	A	
4.31	BENJAMIN	6						P 2 . 4 .	3	1		26	62			4	
34			WALSH	6	. P X . P L	50					M13 2HR	27					
37	"	7			: P . 3 4	55		3 1	4			28	63			5	
41			"	7	2 : . : . :	60		3S 1	5			29	64			6	
4.45	(8-2-23-2)	8	(7-3-21-0)		6s 1	61	1	P 8/9 . 1 : 4 4 :	10	2	M13 NB 5	30	70	3	15	11	

1st DAY	BOWLERS (BIRD) MAIN STAND END		(SHEPHERD) KIRKSTALL L. END		BATSMEN SCOREBOARD LEFT			SCOREBOARD RIGHT			ENGLAND 1st INNINGS	END-OF-OVER TOTALS					
TIME	BOWLER	O.	BOWLER	O.	SCORING	BALLS	6s/4s	SCORING	BALLS	6s/4s	NOTES	O.	RUNS	W.	'L' BAT	'R' BAT	EXTRAS
					ATHEY	61	1	LAMB	10	2	M 13 NB 5	30	70	3	15	11	10
4.49			WALSH	8	. 7 1E : : :	67					M 14	31					
53	BENJAMIN	9						: : : 5(6) 4 † :	16	3		32	74			15	
58	(9-2-27-2)		"	9	x LB ⊙ : 7 1	71		7 3 E1 : :	19		(NB) (LB) NB 6	33	80		16	18	12
5.03	AMBROSE	8			. x† : L W	75	1				† Appeal ct wk.	33⁴	80	4	16	18	12
05					RA SMITH										0		
07	"	8			3 .	2					M 15	34					
08			"	10				x . 3† . P48 : : 4 : : 2	25	4	† one-handed.	35	86			24	
12	"	9			8/7 . 6 7 . . 3 2	8					• Dr sh leg	36	88		2		
16			"	11				P 2 3 8 4 1E : : . 2 4 .	31	5		37	94			30	
20	"	10			3 P : : . 8 1	14						38	95		3		
24			"	12	x . : . 6 3/2 4	20	1					39	99		7		
28	"	11	(12-4-42-0)		T P P . 2 : : ✱	24		x LB	33		(LB) (4W)	40	104				17
33			MARSHALL	9				. . . 2 8E 3S 4 . 1	39	6	3 HR	41	109			35	
37	"	12			3/4S 1	25		. † P . 6 : : . 1	44		† Lamb - eye problems	42	111		8	36	
41			"	10	1/2 : 7 . 3 2 :	31						43	113		10		
45	"	13			6/7S 1	32		3/4 8 : 4 1 : :	49	7		44	119		11	41	
50			"	11	: : L P 2 4 4 :	38	2					45	123		15		
54	"	14						: : : x x ⊙ :	56		(NB) NB 7	46	124				18
59			"	12	. . 2 8 3S 4 1 1	43	3	4 1	57		50 p'ship: 57 min	47	131		21	42	
6.05	"	15			† 4 ⊙ . 3† 1 : .	49		3S 1	58		(NB) † Marshall slipped NB 8	48	134		22	43	19
10	(15-4-29-1)		"	13	8 1 : . .	53	3	8 1 3 1	60	7		49	137	4	23	45	19
6.17	BLSP		(13-5-29-1)								M 15 NB 8		B	L	SP		
6.45	PLAY ABANDONED												S	T	U M	P	S
2ND DAY 11.01	AMBROSE	16			:	54		: † . P 2 3	65			50	140			48	
07			MARSHALL	14				4 . : 4 . E1 4 .	71	8	(W) LAMB'S 50: 115'	51	145			52	20
11	"	17			: 2 : . 7/8 x	60					M 16	52					
15			"	15				: 4 8E 2 4LB B : 2 . .	77		(4LB) (B)	53	152			54	25
20	"	18			⊙ . . 3/8 8 E1 2 4	66	4	8 1	78		(NB) • Between 1st/2nd slip NB 9 4 HR	54	160		29	55	26
24			"	16	P P E1 LB : 2 .	71		3/3 1	79		(LB)	55	164		31	56	27
28	"	19			7S 1	72		7 3 4 4 8 4 2 . 4 .	84	9		56	171		32	62	
33			"	17	2 4 . 4 : † † !	78	5					57	175		36		
37	"	20			6/5 . 4	81		8/7 LB	87		(LB) M 17	58	176				28
41			"	18	† L 3 7 2 4 . : . 1	85		8E LB	89		(LB) (W)	59	179		37		30
46	"	21			8 • LB 1 .	87		3S 3 ⓘ 1	91	9	NB 10 (LB) • NB LB Bye	59³	183	4	38	64	31
53								COWDREY			100 p'ship 115'					0	
55	"	21			4 . :	90						60					
58			"	19				. L . : T 7	6		M 18	61					
12.02	"	22	(19-6-45-1)		E W	91	5		6	-		61¹	183	5	38	0	31
12.02	(22-7-50-2)										M 18 NB 10						

2ND DAY	BOWLERS (BIRD) MAIN STAND END		(SHEPHERD) KIRKSTALL LANE END		BATSMEN SCOREBOARD LEFT			SCOREBOARD RIGHT			ENGLAND 1ST INNINGS NOTES	END-OF-OVER TOTALS					
TIME	BOWLER	O.	BOWLER	O.	SCORING	BALLS	6s/4s	SCORING	BALLS	6s/4s		O.	RUNS	W.	'L' BAT	'R' BAT	EXTRAS
					RICHARDS	-	-	COWDREY	6	-	M18 NB 10	61^1	183	5	0	0	31
12.04	AMBROSE	22			P x ·:·:··	5					M19	62					
07			MARSHALL	20				x x P L ··:·:W	12	-	M20	63	183	6	0	0	31
10								PRINGLE								0	
12	"	23			EP ·:2·:·	11					• ct (off arm)	64	185		2		
16			"	21				·:W E1↑	3	-		64^3	185	7	2	0	31
17								FOSTER								0	
19			"	21				·:4	3		M21 5HR	65					
22	•	24			7 x ·W	13	-					65^2	185	8	2	0	31
22					DILLEY		LHB								0		
24	"	24			x x ··::	4					M22	66					
27			"	22	E1• ··4	7	1	::3 5(6)	6		• Low chance to WK's right.	67	192		4	3	
32	"	25			·1 4	9		8↑ 1 8↑ ④··· x 2Y	11	1	NB 11	68	198		5	8	
36			"	23	····:2 1 2 7	15						69	201		8		
41	" (25.1-8-58-4)	26	(23-8-55-3)		E1 W	16	1		11	1		69^1	201	9	8	8	31
12.41	ALL OUT										M22 NB 11						
											426 balls						

Derek Pringle silenced his tormentors with three wickets in 16 balls during his best analysis for England.

2ND DAY	BOWLERS (BIRD) MAIN STAND END		(SHEPHERD) KIRKSTALL L. END		BATSMEN SCOREBOARD LEFT			SCOREBOARD RIGHT			WEST INDIES 1ST INNINGS	END-OF-OVER TOTALS					
TIME	BOWLER	O.	BOWLER	O.	SCORING	BALLS	6s/4s	SCORING	BALLS	6s/4s	NOTES overcast. v. humid.	O.	RUNS	W.	'L' BAT	'R' BAT	EXTRAS
					HAYNES			DUJON			CHILDS sub (LAMB)						
12.52			DILLEY	1	LB ·	1		L : 3† 5(6) 4 : 4 ·	5	1	† fumbling stop (Smith) (LB)	1	5			4	1
58	FOSTER	1	(1-0-4-0)		8 1 : ·	4	-	6 : 4 : 3	8	1	M - NB -	2	9	-	1	7	1
1.01	(1-0-4-0) LUNCH												L	U	N	CH	
1.40			DILLEY	2				: ! 5(6) 4 2 2 · 3 W	14	2		3	15	1	1	13	1
43								HOOPER								0	
45	FOSTER	2			8 1	5		: 3 1E · 7E † 4 : :	5	1	• Bisected 2 + 3 slip.	4	20		2	4	
49			"	3	: · † : 7 2 22	11						5	24		6		
54	"	3						· 7 : · 2 :	11		M1	6					
57			"	4	· x · · : EP :	17					M2	7					
2.02	"	4						: : 3 : T :	17		M3	8					
04			"	5	: P 4† 1 8† 4	21	1	: 1	19		† Pringle misfielded	9	30		11	5	
09	"	5						3 : · 2 : :	25		M4	10					
12			"	6	· · 2 8E† 1	25		: x	27			11	31		12		
17	"	6			8 4 · L : † :	31	2					12	35		16		
20	(6-3-13-0)		"	7				x : 4 4 4 : · ·	33	2		13	39			9	
25	PRINGLE	1			P EP : 9 2 · ·	37					1 HR	14	41		18		
28			"	8				: P : · : 4	39		M5	15					
33	"	2	(8-2-25-1)		2 1 : G P ·	42		2 3	40			16	45		19	12	
37			FOSTER	7	: · · 7 7 41	47	3	8E 1	41			17	51		24	13	
40	"	3			7 : 7 P 6 :	53					M6	18					
44			"	8				: : · 2 : :	47		M7	19					
47	"	4			: : P 7 P ·	59					DILLEY off (sub:- Jeremy BATTY) M8	20					
51			"	9	LB · x 6 :	62		8 1 : 4 1	50		(LB)	21	54			15	2
54	"	5						· : T P 3 · 4	56	3	rain.	22	58			19	
58			"	10	· 6/7 3	64		L W	57	3	Dilley back.	22³	61	2	27	19	2
59								RICHARDS								0	
3.01			"	10				· · 1 4	3	1		23	65			4	
04	"	6			· : 5(6) 4 : 5(4) 2† 6 :	70	4				† slowed by sawdust	24	71		33		
08			"	11				4LB 19E 6 · · 4 · · 2 ·	9	2	(4LB)	25	79			8	6
12	"	7			· P : · : x	76					M9	26					
16			"	12				· 3 7/6 4 · 8 2 2 ·	15	3		27	85			14	
19	"	8			1E 4 4 : · : 4 8 4 :	82	6					28	93		41		
24	(8-3-24-0)		"	13				: P : 4†7/8 4 W	20	4	Dilley torpedoed.	28⁵	97	3	41	18	6
26								LOGIE								0	
28			"	13				:	1		2HR	29					
30	COWDREY	1			x · 4 2/3 4 · ·	88	7					30	101		45		
33			"	14	: † L :	91		: x 8 1	4			31	102			1	
37	"	2						3 5 6 2 3 Y · 4 · · ·	10	1		32	106			5	
3.40	(2-0-8-0)		" (15-4-44-2)	15	9 1	92	7	: x 2† : 6	15	1	† Gd stop Gower. M9 NB - [Cd:3.42	33	107	3	46	5	6

2ND DAY	BOWLERS (BIRD) MAIN STAND END		(SHEPHERD) KIRKSTALL L. END		BATSMEN SCOREBOARD LEFT			SCOREBOARD RIGHT			WEST INDIES 1ST INNINGS NOTES	END-OF-OVER TOTALS					
TIME	BOWLER	O.	BOWLER	O.	SCORING	BALLS	6s/4s	SCORING	BALLS	6s/4s		O.	RUNS	W.	'L' BAT	'R' BAT	EXTRAS
TEA					HAYNES	92	7	LOGIE	15	1	M9 NB-	33	107	3	46	5	6
4.01	PRINGLE	9			: · : 3 ·	97		LB	16		(LB)	34	111		49		7
05			FOSTER	16	. . 1	100		: 1 :	19		HAYNES's 50: 138'	35	113		50	6	
08	"	10			. 1	102		2 . . .	23			36	116		51	8	
12			"	17	. . . 2 . .	108						37	118		53		
16	"	11			1	109		1 4 . 4 1	28	3		38	129		54	18	
20			"	18				. . 4 . . 4	34	5		39	137			26	
24	"	12			W	110	7					39'	137	4	54	26	7
24					ARTHURTON		LHB								0		
26	"	12			: . 4 . .	5					M10	40					
29			"	19				. . 3 6 4 :	40		M11	41					
33	"	13	(19-5-56-2)		. 1 . .	9		2 1	42			42	141		1	29	
37			DILLEY	9	. : :	12		. 4 3	45	6		43	148			36	
42	"	14						. 4 : 4 . W	51	8	DILLEY off (boot repair) – RJ BLAKEY (sub)	44	156	5	1	44	7
46	(14-4-53-2)							HARPER			3 HR					0	
48			"	10	.	13	-		-	-	M11 NB-	44'	156	5	1	0	7
4.49	BLSP		(9.1-2-32-1)								Rain at 4.51		BLSP				
6.02	PLAY ABANDONED												STUMPS				
3RD DAY 11.00	START DELAYED - HEAVY OVERNIGHT RAIN.																
1.00	LUNCH																
2.45			DILLEY	10	LB . : : .	17		LB	1		(LB)(LB) M12	45	158				9
49	FOSTER	20						. : : . 3	7		M13	46					
53			"	11	. : : . 4 1	23	1					47	163		6		
57	"	21			: : . . 1	29						48	164		7		
3.02			"	12	. . 1	32		. . .	10			49	165		8		
06	"	22			2	38						50	167		10		
10			"	13				. : : : : .	16		M14	51					
15	"	23			LB	39		4 . . : .	21	1	(LB)	52	172			4	10
19			"	14	. : . . :	45					M15	53					
23	"	24			1	46		. 1 . . .	26		+ Gd stop (bowler)	54	174		11	5	
27			"	15	. 4 . : : 4	52	3					55	182		19		
31	"	25	(15-5-46-1)		. . . . . .	57		1	27			56	183			6	
35			PRINGLE	15	. . : 2 4	62	4	1	28			57	190		25	7	
39	"	26			. :	64		: . : 1	32		4 HR	58	191			8	
44			"	16				. . : . .	38		M16	59					
47	"	27			. . : 2 :	70					• ? chance long leg (Dilley)	60	193		27		
51			"	17	W	71	4	1	39			60²	194	6	27	9	10*
52					MARSHALL										0		
54			"	17	. . . .	4					+ Diving stop (Gower)	61					
3.56	(28-6-83-2)	28	(17-5-61-3)		1	5	-	4 1 4 . 4	44	4	+ WI in LEAD. M16 • Athey (2nd slip)	62	208	6	1	22	10

3RD DAY	BOWLERS (BIRD) MAIN STAND END		(SHEPHERD) KIRKSTALL L. END		BATSMEN SCOREBOARD LEFT			SCOREBOARD RIGHT			WEST INDIES 1ST INNINGS	END-OF-OVER TOTALS					
TIME	BOWLER	O.	BOWLER	O.	SCORING	BALLS	6s/4s	SCORING	BALLS	6s/4s	NOTES	O.	RUNS	W.	'L' BAT	'R' BAT	EXTRAS
					MARSHALL	5	-	HARPER	44	4	M16 NB.	62	208	6	1	22	10
4.01			PRINGLE	18	2 W	7	-					62^{2}	210	7	3	22	10
02					AMBROSE		LHB								0		
04			"	18	. . 4 .	4	1				• Dr Gower (3rd slip)	63	214		4		
06	FOSTER	29						. 4	50	5	† hit on arm	64	218			26	
09	(29-6-87-2)		"	19	. . 4 W	8	2		50	5		64^{4}	222	8	8	26	10
4.12	TEA		(18.4-5-71-5)		BENJAMIN						M16 NB -			T	E	A	
4.30			PRINGLE	19	2 .	2						65	224		2		
32	FOSTER	30			. . 4 .	6	1	. 1	52		(LB) (LB)	66	231		6	27	12
37			"	20	.	7		. . . . .	57		(LB) M17	67	232				13
41	(30.5-6-97-2)	31	(20-6-73-5)		1	8		4 . . .	61	6	(LB)	67^{5}	238	8	7	31	14
4.44	BLSP												BLSP - RAIN				
5.15	STUMPS										M17 NB -		STUMPS				
4TH DAY 11.00	FOSTER	31						.	62			68					
01	(31-6-97-2)		PRINGLE	21	. . .	11		. . .	65		M18 (LB)	69	239				15
05	DILLEY	16			: : : : 1	16		4	66	7		70	244		8	35	
10			"	22	1 RO	17	1	: : .	70			70^{5}	245	9	9	35	15
13					WALSH										0		
15			"	22	4	1	1					71	249		4		
16	"	17			.	2		. : . . 1	75		5 HR	72	250			36	
21			"	23	: . .	5		. . 1	78		† run refused	73	251			37	
26	"	18			. .	7		2 : : 1	82			74	254			40	
30			"	24				2 : : . 4 1	88	8		75	261			47	
34	"	19						. : . . . 1	94		† Run refused.	76	262			48	
40			"	25	. 1 : :	11		1 1	96		† Run refused. HARPER'S 50: 144'	77	265		5	50	
44	"	20			.	12		2 : . : 1	101		† Run refused	78	268			53	
49	(20-5-59-1)		"	26	. . . :	16		. 1	103		† Run refused	79	269			54	
53	FOSTER	32			. .	18		. . : . 1	107		† Run refused	80	270			55	
57			"	27	. 4 :	21	2	: : 1	110		† Run refused	81	275		9	56	
12.01	(32.2-6-98-3)	33	(27-7-95-5)			21	2	. W	112	8	† Run refused	81^{2}	275	10	9	56	15
12.02	ALL OUT										M18 NB -		ALL OUT				
											488 balls						

4TH DAY	BOWLERS (SHEPHERD) MAIN STAND END		(BIRD) KIRKSTALL L. END		BATSMEN SCOREBOARD LEFT			SCOREBOARD RIGHT			ENGLAND 2ND INNINGS	END-OF-OVER TOTALS					
TIME	BOWLER	O.	BOWLER	O.	SCORING	BALLS	6s/4s	SCORING	BALLS	6s/4s	NOTES SUNNY - STRONG WIND	O.	RUNS	W.	'L' BAT	'R' BAT	EXTRAS
					GOOCH			CURTIS			74 overs left.						
12·13			MARSHALL	1	E2 9 1	2		. . : :	4			1	1		1		
18	AMBROSE	1			. . . : . 7 1	8						2	2		2		
22			"	2	8 3	9		P . . P .	9			3	5		5		
26	"	2			: . . . 2 9	14		T	10			4	6		6		
29			"	3	. 7 x . 5(6) 3 4 4	20	2					5	14		14		
33	"	3			2 3	24		† LB	12		(LB) M1	6	15				1
37			"	4	3 . : . .	28		1 9 . 1	14		CURTIS 24' on 0.	7	16			1	
40	"	4			: 2 x :	31		P 3 8 . . 1	17			8	17			2	
44			"	5				: . . 2 . †	23			9	19			4	
48	"	5			9 1	32		: † . F2B .	28		† Hit on back. (2B)	10	22		15		3
52			"	6	8 6 † 2	38					† Bird - eye problems	11	24		17		
56	(6-2-4-0)	6	(6-0-17-0)			38	2	: G 7 L . . .	34	-	M 2	12	24	-	17	4	3
1·00	LUNCH										10 min RAIN During lunch		LUNCH				
1·50			WALSH	1	(.) 9 9 1 1	42		4 LB . . :	37		delayed resumption. (NB) (LB) NB 1	13	28		19		5
56	AMBROSE	7			4 † . . E1 . 4 x (2)(0)	50					† 1 overthrow (NB) NB 3	14	31		21		6
2·01			"	2	: . 8 1	53		† G 8 . . 1	40		1 HR	15	33		22	5	
04	"	8			L (0) . . 2 E1 . 4 .	60	3				(NB) NB 4	16	38		26		7
10			"	3	4 5(6) 6 6 7 (0) x	66		LB	41		(LB) (NB) NB 5	17	40				9
14	"	9			8E .	67		3 † : † 8 . . 1	46		† [illegible]	18	41			6	
18			"	4				: . 4 6 . 8 . . 2	52			19	43			8	
22	"	10			6 9/9† 1	69		2/1 †.†. 4 4 . . .	56	1		20	48		27	12	
26			"	5	1E 3 7 L 8 4 . . . 1	74	4	P	57		50 p'ship · 83 min.	21	53		32		
31	"	11			2 3	75		YL : 4x 7/8 x W	62	1		22	56	1	35	12	9
34			-					ATHEY								0	
36			"	6	7 1	76		7 L 2 . . .	5			23	59		36	2	
41	"	12			4 †8 : x . 4 . . .	82	5					24	63		40		
45			"	7	: : 7 .	86		: 3	7			25	64			3	
49	"	13			: : † 3	89		P : 7/8 1	10			26	68		43	4	
53	(13-2-29-1)		"	8	7 1 3 : 5(6) 4	94	6	1 3	11		† ENGLAND AHEAD at 2·56.	27	77		49	7	
58	MARSHALL	7			P 3 8 . . 1	97		: 3 † x 2 .	14		† Arthurton misfield 2HR	28	80		50	9	
3·03			"	9	6 4 2 E1 . . . W	101	6				GOOCH'S 50: 117'	28^4	80	2	50	9	9
04					GOWER		LHB								0		
06			"	9	: .	2					M 3	29					
08	"	8			8 † B 2 .	4		: 4 P 7 . . . 1	18		† GOWER 7,000 RUNS in TESTS.	30	84		2	10	10
13			"	10	: . . E1 . 6	10					M4	31					
17	"	9			: 9 W	12		7 1	19			31^3	85	3	2	11	10
19					SMITH										0		
21		9			2 6 6	3					• Dr Logie (sh leg)	32					
3·23	(9-0-24-1)		(11-2-27-2)	11		3	-	7 : E1 W	22	-	M4 NB5 out at 3·25	32^3	85	4	0	11	10

4TH DAY	BOWLERS (SHEPHERD) MAIN STAND END		(BIRD) KIRKSTALL L END		BATSMEN SCOREBOARD LEFT			SCOREBOARD RIGHT			ENGLAND 2ND INNINGS	END-OF-OVER TOTALS					
TIME	BOWLER	O.	BOWLER	O.	SCORING	BALLS	6s/4s	SCORING	BALLS	6s/4s	NOTES	O.	RUNS	W.	'L' BAT	'R' BAT	EXTRAS
					SMITH	3	-	COWDREY	-	-	M4 NB5	32^{3}	85	4	0	0	10
3.27			WALSH	11				6 6 8 · · 1	3			33	86			1	
29	MARSHALL	10			8 1	4		2 4 5 · 1 7 2 · ·	8			34	90		1	4	
34			"	12	8 9 2 1	6		· · 2 ↑ · · · ·	12			35	93		4		
38	(11-0-34-1)	11	(12-2-30-2)		↑ 7/8 · 2 · · 2/3 4 ·	12	1		12	-		36	99	4	10	4	10
3.41	TEA										M4 NB5			T	E	A	
4.00			WALSH	13				↑ ↑ · · · 3	18		M5	37					
05	MARSHALL	12			· 4LB · · · ·	18					(4LB) M6	38	103				14
09			"	14				· · 3 · · ↑	24		M7	39					
13	"	13			· 7 · · 16 1	22		3 5(4) 1	26			40	105		11	5	
18			"	15				4 X 1E P · ·	32		M8 3HR	41					
21	"	14			· · ↑ · L W	26	1					41^{4}	105	5	11	5	14
23					RICHARDS										0		
25	"	14			3 · · ·	2					M9	42					
26			"	16				T 7 3 · · · X W	36	-		42^{4}	105	6	0	5	14
28								LAMB			SMITH as runner					0	
31			"	16				· ·	2		M10	43					
32	"	15			1 3	3		· 2 X 6 3/4 · 4 · · 4	7	2		44	116		3	8	
37			"	17	· 2 7 8 · 2 2 1 L ·	8		6 3	8			45	124		8	11	
42	"	16						· P X · 2 ·	14		M11	46					
46			"	18	· 4 · 6 P4 · ·	14					M12	47					
50	"	17						↑ · · · · ↑6	20		† Round wkt M13	48					
54	(17-4-47-2)		"	19	3 7 · P X L	20					M14	49					
58	AMBROSE	14			· ↑ X W	23	-	Gt · 2 · 3	23		† Hit on wrist. treatment	50	127	7	8	14	14
5.04					PRINGLE										0		
06			"	20				· · 2 7† · ·	29		† Good stop (LOGIE) M15	51					
10	"	15	(20-9-38-3)		3 9 · 1	2		F 3 T 1 · · · ·	33			52	128		1		
15			BENJAMIN	1	3 · · 7 3 5 · ·	8					M16	53					
19	"	16			5(4) · 2 P 2 · · ·	12		2 8↑ · 1	35		4HR	54	131		3	15	
23			"	2	X W	13	-	LB ·	36		(LB)	54^{2}	132	8	3	15	15
24					FOSTER										0		
26			"	2	X 4 · 7 ·	4					M17	55					
29	"	17						· · · · ↑ ↑	42		M18	56					
33			"	3	E1 W	5	-					56^{1}	132	9	0	15	15
33					DILLEY		LHB								0		
36			"	3	7 4 · · 2• 2 7 · ·	5					• Dr gully (Marshall)	57	134		2		
39	"	18						8† P4 3† ↑ 1‡G	48		† Runs refused M19 ‡ AMBROSE warned	58					
43			"	4	· 4 · 4F · ·	11					M20	59					
47	"	19						↑ 2 7 4 ↑ ↑‡ · · 4 · · ·	54	3	AMBROSE named ‡	60	138			19	
51	(19.5-4-40-3)		"	5	Y7 · · † · · ·	17					† Round wicket M21	61					
55			(5-4-2-2)			17	-	3 2† 2† 4† E1 · · · · W	59	3	M21 NB5	61^{5}	138	10	2	19	15
5.58	ALL OUT										376 balls		ALL	OUT			

4TH DAY	BOWLERS (SHEPHERD) MAIN STAND END		BOWLERS (BIRD) KIRKSTALL L. END		BATSMEN SCOREBOARD LEFT			BATSMEN SCOREBOARD RIGHT			WEST INDIES 2ND INNINGS	END-OF-OVER TOTALS					
TIME	BOWLER	O.	BOWLER	O.	SCORING	BALLS	6s/4s	SCORING	BALLS	6s/4s	NOTES	O.	RUNS	W.	'L' BAT	'R' BAT	EXTRAS
					HAYNES			DUJON			Fairbrother sub (LANB)						
6.09	DILLEY	1			·4····	6	1					1	4		4		
14			FOSTER	1	·1	8		1 ··2	4			2	8		5	3	
18	"	2			··22··	14						3	12		9		
22			"	2	:::::	19		1	5			4	13			4	
25	"	3			·:	21		:··3	9			5	16			7	
30			"	3				·42···	15	1		6	22			13	
34	(4-0-16-0)	4	(3-0-11-0)		1	22	1	·4::.	20	2		7	27	-	10	17	-
6.38	STUMPS										M - NB -		S	T	UM	PS	
5TH DAY 11.00			FOSTER	4	··41	26	2	4·	22	3	• Gower (gully) - finger tips.	8	36		15	21	
04	COWDREY	1			:·	28		···2	26		(LB)	9	39			23	1
08			"	5	::·1	32		·4	28	4		10	44		16	27	
11	"	2			····1	37		1	29			11	46		17	28	
14			"	6	·	38		·····	34		(LB) M1	12	47				2
18	"	3						···4··	40	5	+ Round wkt (4 balls) 50 p'ship: 49 min.	13	51			32	
21			"	7	·223	42		:4	42	6		14	62		24	36	
25	(3.3-0-13-0)	4	(7-1-36-0)		1	43	2	:4	44	7		14.3	67	0	25	40	2
11.26	WEST INDIES WON BY 10 WICKETS										M1 NB -						
											87 balls						

Umpire Dicky Bird and the Headingley scene shifters from *Rising Damp*.

ENGLAND 1ST INNINGS v. WEST INDIES (FOURTH TEST) at HEADINGLEY, LEEDS on 21, 22, 23, 25, 26 JULY, 1988.

IN	OUT	MINS	No.	BATSMAN	HOW OUT	BOWLER	RUNS	WKT	TOTAL	6s	4s	BALLS	NOTES ON DISMISSAL TOSS: WEST INDIES
11·51	2·55	37	1	G.A. GOOCH	CT DUJON	MARSHALL	9	1	14	·	2	27	Edged firm-footed defensive push.
11·51	3·52	94	2	T.S. CURTIS	LBW	BENJAMIN	12	2	43	·	1	71	Hit across full length ball.
2·57	5·05	107	3	C.W.J. ATHEY	LBW	AMBROSE	16	4	80	·	1	75	Played back.
3·54	4·10	16	4	D.I. GOWER	CT DUJON	BENJAMIN	13	3	58	·	1	16	Edged ball angled across him. 100TH TEST.
4·31	(11·53)	158	5	A.J. LAMB	RETIRED HURT		64	(4)	183	·	9	91	Tore right calf muscle running quick single.
5·07	12·02	131	6	R.A. SMITH	CT DUJON	AMBROSE	38	5	183	·	5	91	Edged lifting ball outside off stump.
11·55	12·10	15	7	C.S. COWDREY *	LBW	MARSHALL	0	6	183	·	·	12	Late on quicker ball.
12·04	12·22	18	8	C.J. RICHARDS †	BOWLED	AMBROSE	2	8	185	·	·	13	Bowled through gate by fast breakback.
12·12	12·17	5	9	D.R. PRINGLE	CT DUJON	MARSHALL	0	7	185	·	·	3	Gloved lifting ball to 'keeper.
12·19	(12·41)	22	10	N.A. FOSTER	NOT OUT		8			·	1	11	
12·24	12·41	17	11	G.R. DILLEY	CT HOOPER	AMBROSE	8	9	201	·	1	16	Edged drive to second slip.
				EXTRAS	b 1 lb 18	w 6 nb 6	31			-6	214	426 balls (inc 11 no-balls)	

* CAPTAIN † WICKET-KEEPER

TOTAL (69·1 OVERS; 318 MINUTES) 201. ALL OUT at 12·41 pm on 2nd day.

13 OVERS 0 BALLS/HOUR
2·9 RUNS/OVER
47 RUNS/100 BALLS

UMPIRES: H.D. BIRD & D.R. SHEPHERD

BOWLER	O	M	R	W	nb/w
MARSHALL	23	8	55	3	-/2
AMBROSE	25·1	8	58	4	5/4
BENJAMIN	9	2	27	2	-
WALSH	12	4	42	0	6/-
			19		
	69·1	22	201	9	

HRS	OVERS	RUNS
1	14	20
2	13	42
3	14	47
4	13	51
5	11	25

RUNS	MINS	OVERS	LAST 50 (in mins)
50	103	23·1	103
100	170	39·2	67
150	235	52·5	65
200	316	68·5	81

START DELAYED UNTIL 11·51 am. PLAY SUSPENDED - WET RUN-UP
LUNCH: 2-0 2 OVERS - 12 MINUTES (2 LEG-BYES)

TEA: 58-3 [25·3 OVERS 112 MIN] ATHEY 14* (73')

STUMPS (1ST DAY): 137-4 [49 OVERS 218 MIN] LAMB 45* (106') SMITH 23* (70')

WKT	PARTNERSHIP		RUNS	MINS
1st	Gooch	Curtis	14	37
2nd	Curtis	Athey	29	55
3rd	Athey	Gower	15	16
4th	Athey	Lamb	22	34
5th	Lamb	Smith	103*	122
	Cowdrey		0	7
6th	Cowdrey	Richards	0	6
7th	Richards	Pringle	2	5
8th	Richards	Foster	0	3
9th	Foster	Dilley	16	17
10th			201	

WEST INDIES 1ST INNINGS (IN REPLY TO ENGLAND'S 201 ALL OUT)

IN	OUT	MINS	No.	BATSMAN	HOW OUT	BOWLER	RUNS	WKT	TOTAL	6s	4s	BALLS	NOTES ON DISMISSAL
12.52	4.24	154	1	D.L. HAYNES	LBW	PRINGLE	54	4	137	·	7	110	Late on stroke - played outside line.
12.52	1.43	12	2	P.J.L. DUJON †	CT SMITH	DILLEY	13	1	15	·	2	14	Edged drive to cover.
1.45	2.59	74	3	C.L. HOOPER	LBW	FOSTER	19	2	61	·	3	57	Beaten by breakback.
3.01	3.26	25	4	I.V.A. RICHARDS *	CT CURTIS	FOSTER	18	3	97	·	4	20	Pulled hard & low to square-leg (2-handed, diving right).
3.28	4.46	59	5	A.L. LOGIE	CT FOSTER	PRINGLE	44	5	156	·	8	51	Mistimed drive - thick inside edge, head-high, to mid-on.
4.26	3.52	90	6	K.L.T. ARTHURTON	CT RICHARDS	PRINGLE	27	6	194	·	4	71	Edged push at midish ball.
4.48	12.02	164	7	R.A. HARPER	CT GOWER	FOSTER	56	10	275	·	8	112	Skied drive to deep backward point.
3.54	4.02	8	8	M.D. MARSHALL	CT GOOCH	PRINGLE	3	7	210	·	·	7	Edged drive to 2nd slip's right - 2-handed, falling catch.
4.04	4.12	8	9	C.E.L. AMBROSE	LBW	PRINGLE	8	8	222	·	2	8	Beaten by late movement
4.30	11.13	27	10	W.K.M. BENJAMIN	RUN OUT (sub)		9	9	245	·	1	17	Harper attempted run to mid-wicket (N.H. Fairbrother)
11.15	(12.02)	47	11	C.A. WALSH	NOT OUT		9			·	2	21	
				EXTRAS	b - lb 15 w - nb -		15			·6	41 4	488 balls (no n.b)	

* CAPTAIN † WICKET-KEEPER

TOTAL (81.2 OVERS; 342 MINUTES) 275. ALL OUT at 12.02pm on 4th day.

14 OVERS 1 BALLS/HOUR
3.38 RUNS/OVER
56 RUNS/100 BALLS

BOWLER	O	M	R	W
DILLEY	20	5	59	1
FOSTER	32.2	6	98	3
PRINGLE	27	7	95	5
COWDREY	2	0	8	0
			15	1
	81.2	18	275	10

HRS	OVERS	RUNS
1	14	41
2	15	56
3	15	59
4	14	35
5	14	59

RUNS	MINS	OVERS	LAST 50 (in mins)
50	68	16.5	68
100	121	29.4	53
150	174	43.2	53
200	253	61.3	79
250	300	71.5	47

LUNCH:	9-0	2 OVERS, 9 MINS	HAYNES 1*, DUJON 7*
TEA:	107-3	33 OVERS, 131 MIN	HAYNES 46* (131'), LOGIE 5* (14')
STUMPS (2ND DAY):	156-5	44.1 OVERS, 179 MIN	ARTHURTON 1* (23'), HARPER 0* (1')
TEA:	222-8	64.4 OVERS, 266 MIN	HARPER 26* (88')
STUMPS (3RD DAY):	238-8	67.5 OVERS, 280 MIN	HARPER 31* (102'), BENJAMIN 7* (14')

WEST INDIES LEAD BY 74 RUNS

WKT	PARTNERSHIP		RUNS	MINS
1st	Haynes	Dujon	15	12
2nd	Haynes	Hooper	46	74
3rd	Haynes	Richards	36	25
4th	Haynes	Logie	40	37
5th	Logie	Arthurton	19	20
6th	Arthurton	Harper	38	67
7th	Harper	Marshall	16	8
8th	Harper	Ambrose	12	8
9th	Harper	Benjamin	23	27
10th	Harper	Walsh	30	47
			275	

ENGLAND 2ND INNINGS (74 RUNS BEHIND ON FIRST INNINGS)

IN	OUT	MINS	No.	BATSMAN	HOW OUT	BOWLER	RUNS	WKT	TOTAL	6s	4s	BALLS	NOTES ON DISMISSAL
12.13	3.04	121	1	G.A. GOOCH	Ct HOOPER	WALSH	50	2	80	·	6	101	Edged drive to second slip's left.
12.13	2.34	91	2	T.S. CURTIS	BOWLED	AMBROSE	12	1	56	·	1	62	Late on stroke across line – middle and leg stumps hit.
2.36	3.25	49	3	C.W.J. ATHEY	Ct DUJON	WALSH	11	4	85	·	·	22	Edged lifting ball.
3.06	3.19	13	4	D.I. GOWER	Ct DUJON	MARSHALL	2	3	85	·	·	12	7000 RUNS. Edged leg glance – tumbling catch.
3.21	4.23	43	5	R.A. SMITH	LBW	MARSHALL	11	5	105	·	1	26	Beaten by breakback.
3.27	4.28	42	6	C.S. COWDREY*	BOWLED	WALSH	5	6	105	·	·	36	Late on breakback – through 'gate'.
4.25	5.04	39	7	C.J. RICHARDS†	BOWLED	AMBROSE	8	7	127	·	·	23	Breakback.
4.31	5.58	87	8	A.J. LAMB	Ct DUJON	AMBROSE	19	10	138	·	3	59	Top-edged square-cut.
5.06	5.24	18	9	D.R. PRINGLE	BOWLED	BENJAMIN	3	8	132	·	·	13	Off stump – breakback – through 'gate'.
5.26	5.33	7	10	N.A. FOSTER	Ct HOOPER	BENJAMIN	0	9	132	·	·	5	Edged to second slip.
5.36	(5.58)	22	11	G.R. DILLEY	NOT OUT		2			·	·	17	
				EXTRAS	b 3 lb 8 w - nb 4		15			-^{6}	11^{4}	376 balls (inc 5 no-balls)	

* CAPTAIN † WICKET-KEEPER

TOTAL (61.5 OVERS; 276 MINUTES) 138 ALL OUT at 5.58 pm on 4th day.

13 OVERS 2 BALLS/HOUR
2.23 RUNS/OVER
36 RUNS/100 BALLS

BOWLER	O	M	R	W	nb
MARSHALL	17	4	47	2	-
AMBROSE	19.5	4	40	3	3
WALSH	20	9	38	3	2
BENJAMIN	5	4	2	2	-
			11		
	61.5	21	138	10	

HRS	OVERS	RUNS
1	15	33
2	13	47
3	13	25
4	13	26

RUNS	MINS	OVERS	LAST 50 (in mins)
50	83	20.1	83
100	163	37.2	80

LUNCH: 24-0 [12 OVERS, 47 MIN] GOOCH 17*, CURTIS 4*

TEA: 99-4 [36 OVERS, 158 MIN] SMITH 10* (20'), COWDREY 4* (14')

WKT	PARTNERSHIP		RUNS	MINS
1st	Gooch	Curtis	56	91
2nd	Gooch	Athey	24	28
3rd	Athey	Gower	5	13
4th	Athey	Smith	0	4
5th	Smith	Cowdrey	20	37
6th	Cowdrey	Richards	0	3
7th	Richards	Lamb	22	33
8th	Lamb	Pringle	5	18
9th	Lamb	Foster	0	7
10th	Lamb	Dilley	6	22
			138	

WEST INDIES 2ND INNINGS (NEEDING 65 RUNS TO WIN OFF A MINIMUM OF 102 OVERS)

IN	OUT	MINS	No.	BATSMAN	HOW OUT	BOWLER	RUNS	WKT	TOTAL	6s	4s	BALLS	NOTES ON DISMISSAL
6.09	(11.26)	55	1	D.L. HAYNES	NOT OUT		25			·	2	43	
6.09	(11.26)	55	2	P.J.L. DUJON	NOT OUT		40			·	7	44	
			3										
			4										
			5										
			6										
			7										
			8										
			9										
			10										
			11										
				EXTRAS	b - lb 2 w - nb -		2			-^{6}	9^{4}	87 balls (0 no-balls)	

* CAPTAIN † WICKET-KEEPER

TOTAL (14.3 OVERS; 55 MINUTES) 67-0

15 OVERS 5 BALLS/HOUR
4.62 RUNS/OVER
77 RUNS/100 BALLS

BOWLER	O	M	R	W
DILLEY	4	0	16	0
FOSTER	7	1	36	0
COWDREY	3.3	0	13	0
			2	
	14.3	1	67	-

RUNS	MINS	OVERS	LAST 50 (in mins)
50	49	12.4	49

STUMPS (4th DAY): 27-0 [7 OVERS, 29 MIN] HAYNES 10*, DUJON 17*

WEST INDIES WON BY 10 WICKETS at 11.26 am on fifth day

MATCH AWARD: C.E.L. AMBROSE (Adjudicator: E.R. DEXTER)

WKT	PARTNERSHIP		RUNS	MINS
1st	Haynes	Dujon	67*	55

THE OVAL
THE FIFTH TEST

The 'Battersea Bradman' · England's oldest Test ground · Lessons from Leeds · A Jones yorker removes Cowdrey · Enter Captain Gooch · Match report · West Indies complete 'greywash'

Jack Parker was one of Surrey's finest all-round cricketers; a handsome, strongly-built right-hander, he was an aggressive and entertaining stroke-maker, a lively swing bowler and an exceptional slip catcher. Dubbed the 'Battersea Bradman' in tribute to his birthplace and prolific pre-war scoring, he gained selection for the MCC's 1939-40 tour to India only to lose that opportunity and his peak playing years to Hitler's ambitions.

Parker was awarded a benefit in 1951, some nineteen years after making his first-class debut. In those days a benefit consisted mainly of the profits and collections from one county match and the proceeds of a members' donation list. He chose the match against neighbouring Middlesex. I was twelve then, and my father took me by bus and tube from Epsom Downs to watch the second day. Such was the enthusiasm for county cricket in those years that we had to queue for half an hour before I gained my first sight of that enormous expanse of green turf. We watched from the Harleyford Road terracing with the gasometers dominating the background. Rain had allowed only 90 minutes' play on the Saturday and the pitch was still sufficiently lively for Alec Bedser to be an extremely awkward proposition. My first sight of county cricket and all these great players was dominated by an outstanding innings from Denis Compton. He had reached 95 at the tea interval when my father, under stern orders from my mother to be home before six o'clock, ordered our departure. My pleas for us to stay until Compton had reached his hundred were ignored and the return journey was a grim and sulky affair. Next morning I was greeted by a relieved parent brandishing a press report showing that 'Compo' had been dismissed for 97!

The Oval has changed little since Surrey's halcyon title-hogging years although, its recent national fund-raising campaign having borne fruit, it is about to receive a substantial and long-overdue facelift. Through the endeavours of one Charles William Alcock, the ground staged the first Test match in England (1880) and also the first FA Cup Final. Alcock, who had captained England against Scotland in 1875, founded the FA Cup and was a most notable administrator and organizer. In days of primitive communication it must have taken a remarkable talent and considerable stamina to combine the secretarial duties of Surrey County Cricket Club (1872-1907) and the Football Association (1867-96) for such a lengthy period.

Shortly before England and West Indies began their final Test of the series – the 71st to be staged at Kennington Oval – Sir Leonard Hutton returned to celebrate the jubilee of his epic 364. It was a sobering thought that his memorable contribution had proved to be a total well beyond the entire England batting order in their last 39 innings against West Indies since 1980, when they made 370 at The Oval.

Although England had suffered another overwhelming defeat at Headingley, there were signs of improved morale and encouraging performances from Allan Lamb, Graham Gooch, Robin Smith and Derek Pringle. West Indian spirits were visibly drooping after Lamb and Smith had seized control of the match with England's first century partnership since Trent Bridge; then came Lamb's tragic leg injury to herald that extraordinary collapse.

Unless he had discovered a miracle cure for

torn muscles, Lamb would have to be replaced and there were likely to be three other changes. David Gower, Bill Athey and 'Jack' Richards would not have been in my team for Headingley, and all three had predictably disappointed. With Mike Gatting and Graham Gooch unavailable for India, Gower's international career probably had at least one chapter unwritten, but Athey and Richards had surely been found wanting once too often.

As Harry Brind's pitch inevitably provides the best playing surface of any series, The Oval should be the ideal ground on which to blood new batsmen. Two who were currently in superb form were Kim Barnett and Matthew Maynard. Barnett had the advantage of being an obvious successor should Cowdrey fail to raise his game to international level and his leg-spin bowling would be extremely handy in India. Maynard had played many outstanding innings for a struggling county – suitable preparation for a role in this England team.

My recommendations were: Gooch, Curtis, Barnett, Smith, Maynard, Cowdrey, Russell, Pringle, Ellison, Foster, Dilley and Childs.

The selectors substituted 'Jack' Richards for Russell and Small for Ellison in my twelve. They also added Allan Lamb at the player's request in the vain hope that his torn calf muscle would heal in time and thereby qualify for the *Guinness Book of Records*.

Such was the extraordinary and bizarre set of accidents and injuries which befell this chosen band that it bore little resemblance to the final eleven. A swollen knee ruled out Dilley a few hours after the team was surprisingly revealed on Saturday morning, a day ahead of tradition. The very next day Barnett sustained severe bruising to the base of his right thumb while fielding in a Refuge Assurance League match.

Monday brought about the destruction of the captain whilst he was batting at Canterbury in a Britannic Assurance Championship match against Somerset. A fast yorker from Adrian Jones scored a direct hit on his left instep. Although no bones were fractured, the bruising was sufficient to require more than a week's treatment. That single delivery, allied to his hapless performances with the bat at Headingley, almost certainly ended Christopher Cowdrey's

CRICKET ENGLAND v. AUSTRALIA – AT KENNINGTON OVAL

F. Dadd's impressions of the first Test match staged in England. *(Illustrated London News)*

international career. Had he played at The Oval he would have been under less pressure than at Leeds and, on a better batting surface, could well have established his position.

Phillip DeFreitas was recalled for Dilley (another astonishing selection as his county had just dropped him for not trying), Robert Bailey and David Capel of Northamptonshire replaced

England's latest recruits Matthew Maynard and Robert Bailey in action at The Oval.

Neil Foster relishing his role of 'nightwatchman'.

Barnett and Cowdrey, and, after considerable shillyshallying, the selectors invited Graham Gooch to become England's fourth captain of the season.

There had been only three previous instances of a side employing four captains in one series: Australia *v.* England 1884-85; West Indies *v.* England 1929-30; and India *v.* West Indies 1958-59. Gooch, who emulated Ken Higgs (1966), previously the only England player to appear in all five matches of a home series with West Indies, became the fourth Essex player after Johnny Douglas, Frederick Fane and Keith Fletcher to captain England. This was Gooch's 67th Test; only Tom Graveney (74), Bob Willis (70), Geoff Boycott (69) and John Edrich (68) waited longer before leading England. The world record is held by Dilip Vengsarkar who first led India in his 96th Test.

England omitted Small from their makeshift assembly – I did put my gear in the boot in case of any further last-minute withdrawals – and gained first use of a pitch promising pace and even bounce. My scoresheets display the depressing progress of yet another batting shambles, this time in near-perfect conditions. Only brave resistance by Robin Smith who, though battered and bruised by a generous ration of short-pitched deliveries, particularly from the giant Ambrose, evoked memories of Trevor Bailey as he battled heroically for 208 minutes and 57 runs. His main support came from Robert Bailey (no relation) who got well in line and used his height (six foot three inches) to counteract the shorter stuff. Unfortunately, someone forgot to tell Matthew Maynard that he was playing in a five-day match. In an innings lasting only six balls, he managed narrowly to avoid being decapitated by a Marshall bouncer, survive a close run-out appeal, be dropped at short-leg, hit a thumping cover-drive and perish to an attempted slash at a bouncer well outside his off stump.

England's 205 looked an embarrassingly small total on such a good batting surface, but an inspired spell of bowling by the Essex trio of Foster, Pringle and Childs dismissed the mighty Caribbean line-up for a mere 183. It was the first time in thirteen Tests that England had gained a first-innings lead against West Indies and the players looked quite bewildered as they were cheered and applauded from the field by a packed second-day house soon after tea.

Saturday provided another hot and sultry day of the kind better spent relaxing in a swimming pool than working in the grimy confines of the London Borough of Lambeth. Press facilities at The Oval have been of a temporary nature since the old press box was demolished after the 1983 season. Those for this match were situated at the top of a new prefabricated block of hospitality suites at the Vauxhall End. They were extremely cramped and were subjected to fierce sunlight for the first half of each day's play, and my allotted niche also had the top rail of a balcony fence cunningly positioned at eye level. One brief inspection led me to select an alternative site and I reported the third day's play from a deck chair on the balcony below the BBC commentary boxes on top of the pavilion. It was a marvellous open-air vantage point with a perfect view of play exactly down the line of the middle stumps.

As my newspaper contract prevents my assisting commentary teams on Test match Saturdays, my place on the *Test Match Special* bench has been taken on those days for the past two seasons by one of three understudies, selected according to the region – London, Midlands or North – the Test was played in. At first they had to don false beards so that Brian Johnston would not be confused. Although I use a portable computer word processor when covering overseas matches, I return to old-fashioned methods for home Tests. Debbie Brown, deputy headmistress of an Enfield primary school and dubbed 'The Handmaiden' by Don Mosey, has telephoned my copy for many seasons. Her experiences with deaf and cricket-ignorant copy-takers, not to mention inadequate telephone facilities, would make an entertaining read. For several years she had the additional task of deciphering the erratic handwriting of the *Sunday Telegraph*'s cricket correspondent, Tony Lewis. On one occasion, 'Before mercy came to the aid of the toiling Radford' appeared in the paper as 'Before Murphy came . . .' When Bob Taylor's sun-hat fell off revealing his greying locks, the published comment was: 'It was a pregnant moment.' What Tony had actually written was 'poignant'!

That third day's play began in absolutely

Graham Gooch during his heroic captain's crusade.

perfect conditions: a cloudless sky, a capacity crowd and a true pitch. For once it found an England team very much in contention, 86 runs ahead with 7 second innings wickets in hand, including the crucial one of their latest leader.

The tourists were obliged to field without theirs, because Viv Richards, suffering acutely from a recurrence of haemorrhoids, had to undergo surgery before the match ended. He thus finished his tour poised on the threshold of three notable career landmarks, with 98 first-class hundreds and Test aggregates of 99 matches and 99 catches. He had endured by his immense standards only a modest series with the bat, but his stature as a captain and sympathetic father-figure had increased immeasurably.

Gordon Greenidge, his deputy, promoted Winston Benjamin to share the day's opening overs with Marshall, a decision which would have borne immediate fruit if Carl Hooper at second slip had held on to a chance from the Leicestershire all-rounder's very first offering. Hooper reacted late, not the first to discover that The Oval is a less-than-perfect sighting ground.

His spirits boosted by the boundary accruing from that mistake, Neil Foster, who relishes the role of 'nightwatchman', celebrated with a cover-drive of exquisite perfection, a stroke of such power and elegance that it astonished everyone except the perpetrator who, like most bowlers, enjoys great expectations as a batsman. That cover-drive dictated the session's fortunes; it gave Foster the confidence to take on the formidable West Indian pace attack to such an extent that he dominated the strike and the scoring. Gooch was relegated to a watching brief as Foster revelled in his new-found talents. Five times he kept his bemused captain from the strike by demanding a single off the final ball of an over.

Gooch was not the only one to suffer at Foster's expense. When the rampant Marshall, straining to add to his record 35-wicket haul in the series, delivered a spate of bouncers, Foster unflinchingly took him on, hooking a first-bounce boundary. Marshall reacted by stationing a long-leg and deep backward square-leg, only to be no-balled by umpire Bird. When he switched to around the wicket he was imperiously driven to the long-off boundary. Another bouncer, another no-ball, another hook for four. Marshall, now beside himself with frustration, was removed from the attack and poor 'Dicky' Bird was so unnerved by it all that he allowed a five-ball over.

By the time Foster perished to yet another hook, gloving a gentle catch to backward square-leg, he had outscored his captain by 33 to 2. It was good to see him rewarded with a standing ovation for some of the bravest batting of the series.

Gooch had been permitted just 32 balls in 16 overs during his 'nightwatchman' 's eccentric take-over bid and he was unable to recapture his timing. This can happen to any batsman but it is most unusual in the case of a powerful hitter armed with a heavy bat and generous repertoire of strokes. So becalmed was he that his score remained beached on 40 for an extraordinary 69 minutes. Sensibly he just soldiered on, adding only 8 runs in a session which saw the West Indian over-rate drop to a pitiful 12 an hour.

There is no doubt that the ICC policy of decreeing a minimum daily ration of overs merely extends the working day unless it is armed with a penalty clause for non-achievement.

Matthew Maynard again looked frenetically nervous and was given a torrid time by Benjamin and Ambrose. Between several body blows he displayed a sumptuous cover-drive but it was almost a relief when he fell to a tame return catch, an inswinger taking his pad before connecting with the bat's follow through.

Apart from Curtis and Foster, no one survived as long as an hour to partner Gooch in his heroic captain's crusade. John Childs courageously supported him for 10 overs without getting off the mark before Gooch ended his 422-minute vigil with a tired square-drive which carried to deep backward-point. He said afterwards that it must easily have been the longest he had ever batted without scoring a hundred. Had he survived his final partner, he would have become only the second to carry his bat through a completed innings for England in a home Test. That honour remains the exclusive property of Sir Leonard Hutton, who took a public bow during the Saturday tea interval to celebrate the jubilee of his 797-minute innings in the last timeless Test played in England.

Gooch saw little of the tourists' reply when they began their quest for 225 runs. Attempting a slip catch off a no-ball he dislocated the third finger of his left hand and underwent surgery for torn ligaments. Derek Pringle took over the leader's mantle to become England's fifth captain of a bewildering summer. Although he devised some shrewd bowling changes, he was powerless to interrupt a stand of 131 between Greenidge and Haynes, their 12th three-figure opening partnership in Tests. Shortly after tea on the fourth day, West Indies completed their 39th victory in 95 encounters with England.

The most significant outcome of this match was the effect of captaincy at this level on Graham Gooch. It appeared to awaken fresh resolve in him, and he confessed to finding it easier to lead England than it had been to take charge of Essex. We were all forced to revise our views. Looking a season ahead, he appeared to have the right qualities to captain England against Australia.

Although West Indies completed a four-nil 'greywash' with more than a day to spare, England, led by their fourth captain of the summer, had given a more spirited performance and eventually emerged from a frustrating and testing series with some positive gains.

After tentative beginnings at Trent Bridge and a disastrous first day at Lord's, West Indies had gained in confidence and developed into a formidable force to dominate the series

Desmond Haynes (helmet) and Gordon Greenidge during their 12th three-figure partnership in Tests.

in all departments. Gatting's indiscretion had prompted a series of selection blunders which destroyed team morale and confidence. Marshall was then able to expose ruthlessly a sickening lack of technique and resolution in our batting and fully deserved to set a new national record with 35 wickets in the series.

The middle-order batting of Logie and Dujon had proved another major factor and made a stark contrast when compared with that of England. Whilst each of the tourists' last 5 wickets had averaged 33, England's could muster only a paltry 12 apiece. Logie had finally established himself as a Test batsman of genuine class and his fielding was often exceptional. Dujon, a most elegant timer of the ball, had enjoyed an outstanding series on both sides of the stumps. He deservedly gained Fred Trueman's nomination as the Cornhill Player of the Match at The Oval.

Although our quicker bowlers had done all that was asked of them in restricting the formidable West Indies batting to a solitary century in the five matches, our spinners had made virtually no impression.

Without doubt the most irritating feature of the summer's selections had been the futile tactic of employing inferior 'all-rounders' instead of specialists. Capel, Cowdrey, Downton, Richards, and to some extent DeFreitas, were largely the product of one-day cricket; bits-and-pieces players not good enough in any department to hold their own in the highest class. It would have rankled less if such players had actually been in any sort of form.

Surely the most outrageous of many stupid decisions made during the summer was the choice of Paul Downton and 'Jack' Richards because they 'could bat a bit'. This theory had been cruelly exposed by a combined output of 97 runs from nine batting missions. In fairness to the selectors it should be revealed that their presence was largely the choice of the captain of the day, Gatting and Emburey demanding Downton, and Cowdrey insisting upon Richards. The absence of 'Jack' Russell was almost as frustrating to bear as the banishment of Graeme Hick.

England's task was made virtually impossible by the performances of Malcolm Marshall. Although far from peak fitness when the series began, he confirmed his position as the world's most devastating bowler by averaging 7 wickets per Test. During the Fourth Test he became the third West Indian after Sir Garfield Sobers and Lance Gibbs to take 100 wickets against England. It is no surprise to discover that his 290 Test wickets have been taken more cheaply and at a greater frequency than those of any of the nine bowlers ranged above him in the list of leading Test wicket-takers.

As usual, Harry Brind's Oval pitch had provided the truest playing surface of the summer. Had the Gatting affair never occurred and the entire series been staged at Kennington, perhaps the honours would have been more even.

Leading Test Wicket-takers

	Wkts	Tests	Runs/Wkt	Balls	Balls/Wkt	5wI	10wM
I. T. Botham	373	94	27.86	20801	55.7	27	4
R. J. Hadlee	373	74	22.46	19135	51.3	32	8
D. K. Lillee	355	70	23.92	18467	52.0	23	7
Imran Khan	334	73	21.91	17137	51.3	23	6
R. G. D. Willis	325	90	25.20	17357	53.4	16	0
Kapil Dev	319	92	29.63	19225	60.2	19	2
L. R. Gibbs	309	79	29.09	27115	87.7	18	2
F. S. Trueman	307	67	21.57	15178	49.4	17	3
D. L. Underwood	297	86	25.83	21862	73.6	17	6
M. D. Marshall	290	58	20.41	13047	44.9	18	3

1ST DAY	BOWLERS (HD BIRD) PAVILION END		(KEPALMER) VAUXHALL END		BATSMEN SCOREBOARD LEFT			SCOREBOARD RIGHT			ENGLAND 1ST INNINGS	END-OF-OVER TOTALS					
TIME	BOWLER	O.	BOWLER	O.	SCORING	BALLS	6s/4s	SCORING	BALLS	6s/4s	NOTES	O.	RUNS	W.	'L' BAT	'R' BAT	EXTRAS
					CURTIS			GOOCH			cloudy – humid						
11.02			MARSHALL	1				1/2 4 : : :	6	1	† arm GOOCH 1500 v WI	1	4			4	
08	AMBROSE	1			⊙ . . . : : 2	7					(NB) NB1	2	5				1
12			"	2				. : 4 T .	12	2		3	9			8	
16	"	2			P : X :	13					M1	4					
20			"	3	X 3 . EP	18		: ①	14		NB2	5	10			9	
25	"	3						7 4 P : : T	20		M2	6					
28			"	4	3 1	24					sunny. CURTIS 29' on 0.	7	11		1		
32	"	4			1	25		. . . . W	25	2		8	12	1	2	9	1
35								BAILEY								0	
37			"	5	EP : 6 .	31					M3	9					
41	"	5						: : : : P	6		cloudy M4	10					
44			"	6	3 . 4 4 P P 4	37	2					11	20		10		
48	"	6			:	38		L : : : 4/3	11			12	21			1	
52			"	7	. : LB	41		9 1	14		(LB)	13	23			2	2
56	"	7	(7-1-19-0)		X P . P ⊙ :	48					(NB) NB3 1HR	14	24				3
12.01	(7-3-4-1)		WALSH	1	8 :	50		3 X 3 9 1	18			15	25			3	
06	BENJAMIN	1			3 . 1	52		. 3 2 :	22			16	31		11	8	
10			"	2	4 : TE 1	56		P :	24			17	32		12		
14	"	2			. 2 . 3 2 3	62						18	34		14		
18			"	3	3 : P : 4	67		1	25			19	35			9	
22	"	3			. . F6	69		. P X 1	29		† No played on	20	36			10	
26			"	4	. 1	71		P EP 3	33		• sh leg (LOGIE)	21	40		15	13	
31	"	4			L 3 3/2 4 6/7 4 2	77						22	42		17		
35			"	5				⊙ 68 : : :	40		(NB) NB4	23	43				4
40	"	5			: : : 3 6 2	83					M5	24					
44			"	6	4	84	3	4 ⊙ 2 ⊙ . 1	47		(NB)(NB) NB6	25	52		21	16	6
50	"	6	(6-0-17-0)		: :	86		6 : 7 1	51			26	53			17	
54	(6-1-12-0)		HARPER	1				: : 7 :	57		M6	27					
57	HOOPER	1			4 3 P : :	92					M7	28					
59½	(1-1-0-0)		"	2	P .	94	3	. 7 9 8 2 1	61	–	2 HR	29	56	1	21	20	6
1.02	LUNCH		(2-1-3-0)								M7 NB6		LUNCH				
1.42	BENJAMIN	7						6 : 2 1E	67		ARTHURTON sub (RICHARDS) (2 overs) M8	30					
46			MARSHALL	8	. 1	96		4 1 4 L	71		† No played on	31	57		22		
50	"	8			3 LB 2 : P	101		6 1	72		(LB)	32	59			21	7
54			"	9				: . 3 6 1 4	78	1	50 p'ship: 99'	33	63			25	
57	"	9			3/2 6 P/E 7 7/8 1	106			79			34	64		23		
2.02			"	10	3 4 L P 3 3/3 8 1	112	4					35	69		28		
05	"	10			P : 6/5 2	118						36	71		30		
2.09	(10-2-16-0)		(11-1-35-0)	11		118	4	8 2/3 6 2 4 . . .	85	2	M8 NB6	37	77	1	30	31	7

1ST DAY	BOWLERS (BIRD) PAVILION END		(PALMER) VAUXHALL END		BATSMEN SCOREBOARD LEFT			SCOREBOARD RIGHT			ENGLAND 1ST INNINGS	END-OF-OVER TOTALS					
TIME	BOWLER	O.	BOWLER	O.	SCORING	BALLS	6s/4s	SCORING	BALLS	6s/4s	NOTES	O.	RUNS	W.	'L' BAT	'R' BAT	EXTRAS
					CURTIS	118	4	BAILEY	85	2	M8 NB6	37	77	1	30	31	7
2.13	BENJAMIN	11			4 EIY · W	120	4					37²	77	2	30	31	7
14					SMITH										0		
16	"	11			4 3	2	1	: :	87			38	84		7		
19			MARSHALL	12	. : . . .	8					M9	39					
23	"	12						. . : 4 . :	93	3		40	90			35	9
27			"	13	2 . . 1	12		EP 3 :	95			41	93		10		
30	"	13			: 2 . : :	18					Sun	42	95		12		
35			"	14	: 3 1	21		1 3 :	98		† Round wkt to Bailey	43	97		13	36	
39	"	14	(14-2-40-0)		: . . . 4 .	27	2				cloud † diving stop (HAYNES) 3HR	44	101		17		
43	(14-2-33-1)		AMBROSE	8				. : † : . :	104		Sun M10	45					
47	WALSH	7			: ⊙ . . : 3	34					(NB) NB7	46	102				10
52			"	9				2 . : . . .	110		cloud	47	104			38	
56	"	8			: 2/3 . 8 . :	40					M11	48					
3.00			"	10	1	41		. 1 : 1	115		† ball changed	49	107		18	40	
08	"	9						: . ⊙ . .	122		(NB) NB8	50	108				11
13			"	11	: : : 4 : .	47	3				† Hit on back/shoulder	51	112		22		
17	"	10			:	48		. ⊙ . . 1	128		(NB) NB9	52	114			41	12
22	(10-1-21-0)		"	12	: † † : .	53		1	129			53	115			42	
27	HARPER	3						: . 3 . : .	135		Sun M12	54					
29			"	13	: . : . 3 .	59					M13	55					
33	"	4			:	60		: . : . 1	140		† pigeon on pitch. - dismissed by BIRD!	56	116			43	
36	(4-2-4-0)		"	14			3	: . 4/3 × W	145	3		56⁵	116	3	22	43	12
3.39	TEA		(13.5-5-14-2)					MAYNARD			cloud			TEA		0	
4.02			AMBROSE	14				⊙ .	2		† Excellent return (NB) NB10 (HOOPER) 4HR	57	117				13
04	HARPER	5			1 :	63		. : 3	5		• by LOGIE (fh leg)	58	121		23	3	
08			"	15				W	6	–		58¹	121	4	23	3	13
								CAPEL								0	
10			"	15				⊙ . . ⊙ .	7		(NB) (NB) NB12	59	123				15
14	"	6			 3	69					M14	60					
16			"	16	: ⊙	73		: . 1	10		(NB) NB13	61	125			1	16
21	"	7			. :	75		: . 1	14		• Ro chance (BENJAMIN) † overthrow.	62	126			2	
24			"	17				: : ⊙ 4 :	21	1	(NB) NB14	63	131			6	17
29	"	8			: . : . 1	80		:	22		Sun	64	132		24		
31			"	18	: : : : .	86					M15	65					
35	"	9			: 4 1	89	4	: 1 :	25			66	138		29	7	
38			"	19	: . : : 0	95		2	26		NB15	67	141		30	9	
43	"	10			: : 3 4 .	101	5					68	145		34		
45			"	20				: . : 4 :	32	2		69	149			13	
4.49	(11-3-28-0)	11	(20-6-31-3)		4 4 . : :	107	7		32	2	† Walsh torpedoed. M15 NB15	70	157	4	42	13	17

1st DAY TIME	BOWLERS (BIRD) PAVILION END BOWLER	O.	(PALMER) VAUXHALL END BOWLER	O.	BATSMEN SCOREBOARD LEFT SCORING	BALLS	6s/4s	SCOREBOARD RIGHT SCORING	BALLS	6s/4s	ENGLAND 1st INNINGS NOTES	END-OF-OVER TOTALS O.	RUNS	W.	'L' BAT	'R' BAT	EXTRAS
					SMITH	107	7	CAPEL	32	2	M15 NB15	70	157	4	42	13	17
4.53			MARSHALL	15	4 x 2† : :	110		3 x 7 : : 3	35		† Diving stop (Greenidge)	71	160			16	
58	HARPER	12						6† . : : E1 W	40	2	† HARPER 1st warning (PITCH DAMAGE)	71^5	160	5	42	16	17
59								RICHARDS								0	
5.01	"	12						:	1		M16	72					
02			"	16	6 : P . L8 :	116					M17 5HR	73					
06	"	13						. . EP7 : W	4	-		73^3	160	6	42	0	17
07								PRINGLE								0	
09	"	13						: 4 P	3		M18	74					
11			"	17	4 . . 4 6 1	121		6 :	4		Walsh off (Arthurton)	75	161		43		
16	"	14			6 1	122		: 6 4 8 :	9			76	162		44		
19			"	18	† L : 6 1	126		: †x	11			77	163		45		
22	"	15			6 1 :	128		: : 6 1E 1	15			78	165		46	1	
25			"	19				E1 W	16	-		78^1	165	7	46	1	17
								DEFREITAS								0	
27			"	19	: 3/2 3/2 4	131	8	4S . 1	2		SMITH's 50: 172'	79	170		50	1	
31	"	16			6 1	132		: : 6 3 L :	7			80	174		51	4	
34			"	20	LB L † LB	136		3/3E 1 x	9		(LB)(LB)	81	177			5	19
38	"	17			: : 9 2 : : :	142						82	179		53		
40			"	21	9 . .	145		†7• 5 6 1 . 1	12		• Just over LOGIE	83	182		54	7	
45	"	18						: 7/8 . : 4 P	18		M19	84					
47			"	22	: T 4 7 6 : 1 :	150		3/3† 3	19		† running confusion – LOGIE overthrows (2)	85	186		55	10	
51	"	19						: : 7 4 . P 7 4	25	2		86	194			18	
54			" -	23	: † T ⊙⊙ 6 :	158					(NB)(NB) NB17	87	196				21
59	"	20						PG4 W	26	2		87^1	196	8	55	18	21
								FOSTER								0	
6.01	"	20						EB 6 P . P	5		M20 6HR	88					
04			"	24	P† E1 G1 : 2 . W	162	8				† Appeal ct LOGIE.	88^4	198	9	57	0	21
06					CHILDS		LHB								0		
08			"	24	E1 . .	2						89					
10	(21-7-50-3)	21	(24-3-62-2)		: : † :	5	-	7 : 6 4 : 1	8	1	† Harper conceded	90	203	9	0	5	21
6.14	STUMPS										M20 NB17		STUMPS				
2nd DAY 11.01			MARSHALL	25		5	-	4 3/2 . 2 W	11	1	ARTHURTON sub (WALSH)	90^3	205	10	0	7	21
11.02	ALL OUT		(24.3-3-64-3)								M20 NB17		ALL OUT				
											560 balls						

2ND DAY	BOWLERS (BIRD) PAVILION END		(PALMER) VAUXHALL END		BATSMEN SCOREBOARD LEFT			SCOREBOARD RIGHT			WEST INDIES 1ST INNINGS						
											NOTES	END-OF-OVER TOTALS					
TIME	BOWLER	O.	BOWLER	O.	SCORING	BALLS	6s/4s	SCORING	BALLS	6s/4s		O.	RUNS	W.	'L' BAT	'R' BAT	EXTRAS
					HAYNES			GREENIDGE									
11.16			FOSTER	1				·2···1	6			1	3			3	
20	DEFREITAS	1			··:·1	5		1	7			2	5		1	4	
25			″	2	·:1	8		···	10			3	6		2		
29	″	2			······	14					† Hit on shoulder M1	4					
33			″	3	····	18		·1	12			5	7			5	
38	″	3						·:·2·: 2LB	18		(LB) M2	6	9				2
42			″	4	···W	22	–					6[4]	9	1	2	5	2
44					HOOPER										0		
46			″	4	2·	2						7	11		2		
47	″	4						···2·3	24			8	16			10	
52			″	5				W	25	–		8[1]	16	2	2	10	2
53								RICHARDS								0	
55			″	5				::W	3	–		8[4]	16	3	2	0	2
56								LOGIE								0	
59			″	5				·	1		M3	9					
12.00	″	5			2·····	8						10	18		4		
04			″	6	·::	11		4·3	4	1		11	25			7	
09	″	6						···42·	10	2		12	31			13	
14			″	7	::·1	15		·:	12		1HR	13	32		5		
18	″	7			······	21					M4	14					
22	(7-3-15-0)		″	8	6	22	1/–	::2·1	17			15	41		11	16	
26	PRINGLE	1			····	26		·1	19			16	42			17	
31			″	9	W	27	1/–	44241	24	5		17	57	4	11	32	2
34					DUJON										0		
36	″	2			··1	3		1 ·:	27			18	59		1	33	
40			″	10	:··2··	9						19	61		3		
45	″	3	(10-1-41-4)					······	33		M5	20					
49			DEFREITAS	8	·····4	15	1					21	65		7		
52	″	4			··2	18		:·1	36			22	68		9	34	
57	(4-1-6-0)		″	9		18	1	····2·	42	5		23	70	4	9	36	2
1.00	LUNCH		(9-3-21-0)								M5 NB-	LUNCH					
1.41	PRINGLE	5			······	24					M6	24					
45			DEFREITAS	10	·	25		:···1	47			25	71			37	
51	″	6						·:2·:·	53		Boot repairs (Pringle)	26	73			39	
54			″	11	······	31					† Exc stop (Bailey) M7 2HR	27					
58	″	7						···2··	59			28	75			41	
2.02			″	12	23 ·3	35		·1	61			29	84		17	42	
07	″	8			·43	38	2	:::	64			30	91		24		
2.11	(8-2-17-0)		(13-4-33-0)	13	·2····	44	2		64	5	M7 NB-	31	93	4	26	42	2

WEST INDIES 1ST INNINGS

2ND DAY TIME	PAVILION END (BIRD) BOWLER	O.	VAUXHALL END (PALMER) BOWLER	O.	SCOREBOARD LEFT SCORING	BALLS	6s/4s	SCOREBOARD RIGHT SCORING	BALLS	6s/4s	NOTES	O.	RUNS	W.	'L' BAT	'R' BAT	EXTRAS
					DUJON	44	2	LOGIE	64	5	M7 NB-	31	93	4	26	42	2
2·15	PRINGLE	9			4 x : : L 4	49	3	7 1	65			32	98		30	43	
20	(9-2-22-0)		FOSTER	11	: : x 6 3	52		2 1 4 2	68			33	102		33	44	
25	CAPEL	1			: : Y 9/8 1	55		: : P 2 1	71			34	104		34	45	
29			•	12	7/8 1	56		: : L 6S 1 x 2	76			35	106		35	46	
33	•	2			4 4 Y 6 4S/6 3	62					5op'slip: 80'	36	109		38		
37			•	13	4/3 : ↑ 6 4LB3 4 4	68	5				(4LB)	37	121		46		6
41 / 45	DRINKS •	3			: E1 4 2 4 : :	72	6	P 2 : 1	78		• Between 3rd 4 slip. 50: 90'	38	126		50	47	
49			•	14				E1 W	79	5		38¹	126	5	50	47	6
50								HARPER								0	
52			•	14				+ 6 L 4 8 ↑ 2	5		(W) 3HR	39	129			2	7
56	•	4			S/4 4 7 3 : 9 2 2	78						40	133		54		
3.01			•	15				6 4 4 5 4	11		M8	41					
04	•	5			6 6 4 6 4 6 2	84						42	135		56		
09			•	16				2/3 • 4 9 6 : 4 2	17	1		43	141			8	
13	•	6	(16-2-64-5)		: 7/8 4 4 4 2 4	90	7					44	145		60		
19			PRINGLE	10	5 : :	93		• • ⊙ 8 1	21		(NB) NB1	45	147			9	8
23	•	7			x 6	98		7 1	22		FOSTER (sub SMALL) off	46	148			10	
28	(7-0-21-0)		•	11				: : : : . .	28		M9	47					
33	CHILDS	1			: 8 1 8 • 6 2	103		9 1	29			48	152		63	11	
37	(1-0-4-0)		•	12	6 8/7 8 1	107	7	LB 7 1	31	1	(LB)	49	155	5	64	12	9
3.40	TEA		(12-3-26-0)								M9 NB1			T	E	A	
4.02	CHILDS	2						: P P : P :	37		M10	50					
05			PRINGLE	13	: 4 L W	110	7					50³	155	6	64	12	9
07					MARSHALL										0		
09			•	13	2/3 P 4	3					M11	51					
11	•	3			EP P P S W	7		: 1E• 1	39		• No chance.	52	156	7	0	13	9
14					AMBROSE		LHB								0		
16			•	14	x 3 4 4/3 3	4		8E† 1 ↑	41		† N! played on. 4HR	53	160		3	14	
21	•	4			49E S(6) 2• 1	6		P : : P	45		† over wkt to LHB. • Gooch (b. sh leg)	54	163		6		
25			•	15	: 3/2 1 4x x x	11		2 1	46			55	165		7	15	
28	•	5						: P : P P 1 1	52			56	166			16	
31			•	16				1ERO 1	53	1		56¹	167	8	7	17	9
32								BENJAMIN								0	
34			•	16	2E 1	12		x W	1	-		56³	168	9	8	0	9
35								WALSH								0	
37			•	16				x : S(4) 4	3	1		57	172			4	
39	•	6			: 7 : S(6) P 4	18	1					58	176		12		
43	(6-1-13-1)		•	17	4 • 6 4 S(6) ⊙ 4 ①	23	2	9 1 x 4 W	6	1	(NB) NB3	59	183	10	17	5	10
4.47	ALL OUT		(17-4-45-3)								357 balls. M11 NB3			A	LL	OUT	

2ND DAY	BOWLERS (PALMER) PAVILION END		(BIRD) VAUXHALL END		BATSMEN SCOREBOARD LEFT			SCOREBOARD RIGHT			ENGLAND 2ND INNINGS	END-OF-OVER TOTALS					
TIME	BOWLER	O.	BOWLER	O.	SCORING	BALLS	6s/4s	SCORING	BALLS	6s/4s	NOTES	O.	RUNS	W.	'L' BAT	'R' BAT	EXTRAS
					CURTIS			GOOCH			26 OVERS REMAIN						
5.02			MARSHALL	1				7. ↑ 8 2/3 · 2 · · 2 4	6	1	• Fast chance (sh leg)	1	8			8	
07	AMBROSE	1			P ⊙ · P ↑x F/8 F/4↑ 4	7	1				(NB) NB 1	2	13		4		1
12			"	2				8E · · · 5(6) 7 2 · · · 2 3	12			3	20			15	
16	"	2			· ⊙ · 8 1	11		· 3 1/2 · · 3	15		(NB) NB 2	4	25		5	18	2
22			"	3	· 4 · G · 2	17					M1	5					
26	"	3						3/2 3 2 x · · 4 · 4 · ⊙ · ·	22	3	(NB) NB 3	6	34			26	3
31	(3-0-19-0)		"	4	· 2/3 · · 6/5 1	22		·	23			7	35		6		
36	BENJAMIN	1			P 6 L 8 7 · · · · 2 · ·	28						8	37		8		
42			"	5				· · 4 · x · · · · · ·	29		WALSH off (ARTHURTON) M2	9					
46	"	2			· P · 4 7 †8 · · · 4 1	34	2					10	42		13		
50			"	6	· · · · · ·	40					M3	11					
55	"	3			3 P · · ·	43		P · 2 · 1	32		1 HR	12	43			27	
59			"	7	· P	45		4 · 5(4) LB · · 2	36		(LB)	13	46			29	4
6.04	"	4						2LB ↑ 2 · · · · ·	42		(2LB) M4	14	48				6
07			"	8	· L 6 L · · · 2 W	50	2				50 p'ship: 68 min.	14⁵	50	1	15	29	6
11					BAILEY										0		
13			"	8	1	1						15	51		1		
14	"	5			1	2		· · · · 4	47			16	52		2		
20			"	9	· · L 8 1	6		8†4	49		† Good stop (LOGIE)	17	53		3		
25	"	6			· · 1E · · ·	12					M5	18					
29			"	10	L · · LB	16		1 8/7 ·	51		(LB)	19	55			30	7
35	"	7			· Yx · W	18	-					19²	55	2	3	30	7
36					SMITH										0		
38	"	7			x x · L · · · W	4	-				M6	20	55	3	0	30	7
40					FOSTER										0		
42			"	11	·	1		L · P 3/2 9 · · 1	56			21	56			31	
47	"	8	(11-3-24-1)		x 7 · ·	4		6 · · 3/2 ①	60		NB 4	22	57			32	
52			AMBROSE	4				6 2 · 3 6 · 2 · · ·	66			23	59			34	
57	"	9			8 · 1	6		L 4 4 · · ·	70		2 HR	24	60		1		
7.01			"	5	· · YE ↑x · ·	12					M7	25					
05	(10-3-15-2)	10	(5-1-21-0)			12	-	x 3 P 1/2 8 3 · · · 4 · ·	76	4		26	64	3	1	38	7
7.09	STUMPS										M7 NB 4	STUMPS					
3RD DAY 11.02			MARSHALL	12	· ⊙ EP E1 · · 1	18		·	77		RICHARDS off (ARTHURTON) (NB) NB 5	27	66		2		8
09	BENJAMIN	11			E1 · x · 3/4 2 4 · · · 4 1	24	2				• Dr HOOPER (2nd slip)	28	75		11		
13			"	13	· EP · x 2† · · · ·	30					† Exc stop (ARTHURTON) M8	29					
18	"	12			· x ·	33		· · 1	80			30	76			39	
22			"	14	†x ·	34		· · 4 6 LB	85		(LB) M9	31	77				9
27	"	13			1E 3 7 · 3	37		7 1 4 4 · ·	88			32	81		14	40	
11.31	(13-3-29-2)		(15-5-30-1)	15	↑ x x x 4 L 1 ⊙ · ⊙ · ⊙ · 1	45	2	4	89	4	(NB)(NB)(NB) NB 8	33	85	3	15	40	12

3RD DAY	BOWLERS (PALMER) PAVILION END		(BIRD) VAUXHALL END		BATSMEN SCOREBOARD LEFT			SCOREBOARD RIGHT			ENGLAND 2ND INNINGS	END-OF-OVER TOTALS					
TIME	BOWLER	O.	BOWLER	O.	SCORING	BALLS	6s/4s	SCORING	BALLS	6s/4s	NOTES	O.	RUNS	W.	'L' BAT	'R' BAT	EXTRAS
					FOSTER	45	2	GOOCH	89	4	M9 NB 8	33	85	3	15	40	12
11·39	BENJAMIN	14			x x E ! · · 4 1	49	3	! 6	91			34	90		20		
43			MARSHALL	16	6 4 8 † 4 3/7 · 4 ⊙ 4 · ⊙1	56	5				E Toe-end (pull) NB 10 (NB) † Rd wkt (1 ball) (NB)	35	101		29		14
50	·	15	(16-5-41-1)		8 1 3 3 · 1	59		L 4 LB · · ·	94		(LB) 5-ball over (confirmed by PALMER) 3HR	36	104		31		15
55			AMBROSE	6	: x : 2 . x	65					M 10	37					
59	·	16						· · : ⊙ L 8 5 · ·	101		(NB) NB 11 50 (1st Smp) in 87'	38	105				16
12·04			·	7	· x · : : !	71						39	106		32		
08	·	17			· x !	74		6 4 4 · · ·	104			40	107		33		
12			·	8	1E !	76		3 . † x	108			41	108		34		
15 19	DRINKS ·	18			: · P 48 W	80	5					41[4]	108	4	34	40	16
21					MAYNARD										0		
23	·	18			x 1/2 · 1	2						42	109		1		
25			·	9	T 2 2 4 1E 4 E · ⊙ · · 2 · 1	9					(NB) NB 12	43	113		4		17
30	·	19			4 : †† . : †	15					† Hit on arm. M 11	44					
34			·	10	!	16		6 4 x 4 7 · · · · 1	113		69' on 40.	45	114			41	
38	·	20			3†‡ : 7 4 · · 2	20	1	: 9 1	115		‡ Hit on 'box'. † 1000 F-C runs (1988)	46	121		10	42	
43			·	11	: † 4 5 · · · ·	24		: 3/7 1	117			47	122			43	
47	·	21			: EP 6 EPS · · · W	28	1	6/5 · 3	119		4HR	48	125	5	10	46	17
50					CAPEL										0		
53			· ·	12				: 4 x 4 3 3	125		M12	49					
57	(22-4-52-4)	22	(12-3-29-0)		7 6 † : ! 2 · · · · 1	6	–		125	4	M12 NB12	50	128	5	3	46	17
1·00	LUNCH										GOOCH 8 in SESSION	LUNCH					
1·42			AMBROSE	13	. . : 16 x :	12					M13	51					
47	WALSH	1			: . † 6 P	17		7 1	126			52	129			47	
51			·	14				6 † †8 : :	132		M14	53					
54	·	2			: : † † : .	23					M15	54					
58			·	15				. x 4 2 † 4	138		M16	55					
2·02	·	3			. : LB	26		. P .	141		(LB) M17	56	130				18
06			·	16	x 2/3 · 3 3 9 · 4 · 4 · 1	32	2					57	139		12		
10	·	4			L W	33	2					57[1]	139	6	12	47	18
					RICHARDS										0		
12	·	4			† . 8 4 †	5					M 18	58					
15			·	17				†, : x . : :	147		M19	59					
20	·	5			EP 2 · 1	7		5/6/5(4) x 7 4 4 · 1	151	6	GOOCH'S 50: 285'	60	149		1	56	
24			·	18	B ·	8		. 7 . 3 8 · 1	156		(B)	61	151			57	19
28	·	6			P 4 4 : †B · · · · 1	13		·E!	157		• Dr Harper 2nd slip	62	152		2		
32			·	19	x x x x E! :	19					• Dr Harper 2nd slip M20 5HR	63					
37	·	7			:	20		9 · E! 8/7/9 2 : · · 1	162		• Dr Dujon (rt glove)	64	155			60	
41			·	20	! 1	21		4 · 4 x ! · · · · 1	167			65	157		3	61	
2·45	(8-4-15-2)	8	(20-8-41-0)		P P E! · · W	24	–		167	6	Out at 2·47pm M 20 NB 12	65[3]	157	7	3	61	19

3RD DAY	BOWLERS (PALMER) PAVILION END		(BIRD) VAUXHALL END		BATSMEN SCOREBOARD LEFT			SCOREBOARD RIGHT			ENGLAND 2ND INNINGS	END-OF-OVER TOTALS					
TIME	BOWLER	O.	BOWLER	O.	SCORING	BALLS	6s/4s	SCORING	BALLS	6s/4s	NOTES	O.	RUNS	W.	'L' BAT	'R' BAT	EXTRAS
					PRINGLE	-	-	GOOCH	167	6	M20 NB12	65³	157	7	0	61	19
2.49	WALSH	8			x 6 ⋯	3					M21	66					
51			AMBROSE	21				2/3 4	173	7		67	161			65	
56	"	9			1 . P . 1E 4	9	1					68	165		4		
3.00			"	22				. 4 P 3 . .	179		M22	69					
03	"	10			P 2LB . . 4 P	15					(2LB) M23	70	167				21
07			"	23				3 . 4 . 5	185		M24	71					
11	"	11	(23-10-45-0)		. . . 1 1	19		. .	187			72	168		5		
15			MARSHALL	17	⊙⊙ . . 2 . 6	27					(NB)(NB) NB14	73	170				23
22	"	12			.	28		. . x . 7 1	192		AMBROSE off (WILLIAMS)	74	171			66	
26	(12-5-21-2)		"	18	: . . .	32		x 2 . 1	194			75	172			67	
32	HARPER	1						x . P . .	200		M25 6HR	76					
35	(1-1-0-0)		"	19	6 2 . : . 7 1	37	1	.	201	7		77	175	7	8	67	23
3.40	TEA		(19-5-47-1)								M25 NB14			T	E	A	
4.02	HARPER	2			: : : : : x W	43	1				M26	78	175	8	8	67	23
04					DEFREITAS										0		
06			MARSHALL	20	1E : 4 LB	4		3 1 x	203		(LB)	79	177			68	24
11	"	3			4 BP3 . W	6	-					79²	177	9	0	68	24
12					CHILDS		LHB								0		
14	"	3			: : 3 :	4					M27	80					
17			"	21				. x 4 2 9 1	209			81	178			69	
21	"	4			4 . . .	8		7 6 6 1	211	1/7		82	185			76	
25			"	22	2 :	10		. P 4† LB	215		† Run refused (LB) M28	83	186				25
31	"	5			. .	12		. 2 6†6 . . . 1	219		† Run refused	84	187			77	
34			"	23	P . .	14		P : . 1	223			85	188			78	
40	"	6			.	15		8† 2B8† 4 8 1	228		† Runs refused (2B) • St chance	86	191			79	27
45	(6-3-9-2)		"	24	P 4LB . .	17		6† 8† 3† 2 . . . 1	232		† Runs refused (4LB)	87	196			80	31
51	AMBROSE	24						x x P . x 8† . . . . . ⊙ 4	239	1/8	(NB) NB15 7HR	88	201			84	32
55			"	25	8 x 2 x †P . . . . ⊙ . .	24					(NB) NB16 † Round	89	202				33
5.01	" (24.1-10-50-1)	25	(25-6-52-1)			24	-	2/3 W	240	1/8		89¹	202	10	0	84	33
5.01	ALL OUT										M28 NB16 1 5-ball over 550 balls		ALL		OUT		

3RD DAY	BOWLERS (PALMER) PAVILION END		BOWLERS (BIRD) VAUXHALL END		BATSMEN SCOREBOARD LEFT			BATSMEN SCOREBOARD RIGHT			WEST INDIES 2ND INNINGS NOTES	END-OF-OVER TOTALS					
TIME	BOWLER	O.	BOWLER	O.	SCORING	BALLS	6s/4s	SCORING	BALLS	6s/4s	Hot. no cloud.	O.	RUNS	W.	'L' BAT	'R' BAT	EXTRAS
					HAYNES			GREENIDGE			(109th Test partnership) 24 OVERS - 3rd day						
5·16			FOSTER	1				:4 . . :	6	1	NB1	1	4			4	
20	DEFREITAS	1			(1)	1		. . : : :	12		• Dropped 1st slip - Gooch inj left hand	2	5		1		
26			"	2	P : : P : :	7					NR TAYLOR sub. PRINGLE acting capt. M1	3					
31	"	2			1	8		1 . 4 . :	17	2		4	11		2	9	
35			"	3	. . 1	11		. 4 .	20	3		5	16		3	13	
39	"	3			· 1 .	14		2 · 1	23			6	20		4	16	
43	(3-0-11-0)		"	4				4 : . . 4 1	29	5		7	29			25	
48	CHILDS	1						: : : : : 1	35			8	30			26	
51			"	5				: : : : . 4	41	6		9	34			30	
55	"	2	(5-1-22-0)		: : 4 : : :	20					M2	10					
58			DEFREITAS	4				. . . . : (·) .	48		• "ct" at gully. (NB) NB2	11	35				1
6·03	"	3			: : : : : :	26					M3	12					
08			"	5				(·) . . : : 4 :	55	7	(NB) NB3	13	40			34	2
13	"	4			: : : : : .	32					M4 1HR	14					
15			"	6				: : : 4 : :	61	8		15	44			38	
20	"	5	(6-0-21-0)		: : : : : :	38					M5	16					
23			PRINGLE	1	1	39		. : 1 : (·) .	67		(NB) NB4	17	47		5	39	3
28	"	6			: : : : : :	45					M6 •	18					
31			"	2	. 1	47		. 3 2 :	71		50 p'ship: 76'	19	53		6	44	
35	"	7			: : 4 : : :	53	1					20	57		10		
39			"	3	1	54		. . 1 : 4	76	9		21	63		11	49	
42	"	8			1	55		: : ! . 1	81		50 in 89 min	22	65		12	50	
46			"	4				. . : . 2	87			23	67			52	
50	(9-5-11-0)	9	(4-0-17-0)		2 · 1 :	59	1	. 1	89	9		24	71	-	15	53	3
6·54	STUMPS										M6 NB4		STUMPS				
4TH DAY 11·01			DEFREITAS	7				: 2 · 2 : :	95		NR TAYLOR sub (GOOCH)	25	75			57	
06	FOSTER	6			· 1	61		: . : :	99			26	76		16		
10			"	8	4 : : . 1	66	2	:	100			27	81		21		
14	"	7	(8-0-30-0)		· 1 1	69		· 1 :	103			28	84		23	58	
18			CHILDS	10	: 1	71		: 2 : :	107		2HR	29	87		24	60	
22	"	8			· 2 · 1 :	76		LB ·	108		(LB)	30	91		27		4
26			"	11				: : : : : 1	114			31	92			61	
29	"	9						: . : . 4 :	120	10		32	96			65	
33			"	12	: : : : : :	82					M /	33					
36	"	10			1	83		: : : 1 .	125			34	98		28	66	
41			"	13	: 4 · 2 : :	89	3				100 p'ship: 138'	35	104		34		
44	"	11			:	90		: : . : 1	130		2000 • ENG	36	105			67	
49			"	14				: : : : : 1	136			37	106			68	
11·52	(12-1-39-0)	12	(14-6-22-0)			90	3	: : : (·) · 2 ·	143	10	(NB) (LB) NB5 M7	38	110	-	34	70	6

4TH DAY	BOWLERS (PALMER) PAVILION END		BOWLERS (BIRD) VAUXHALL END		BATSMEN SCOREBOARD LEFT			BATSMEN SCOREBOARD RIGHT			WEST INDIES 2ND INNINGS	END-OF-OVER TOTALS					
TIME	BOWLER	O.	BOWLER	O.	SCORING	BALLS	6s/4s	SCORING	BALLS	6s/4s	NOTES	O.	RUNS	W.	'L' BAT	'R' BAT	EXTRAS
					HAYNES	90	3	GREENIDGE	143	10	M7 NB 5	38	110	-	34	70	6
11·57			DEFREITAS	9				2 ⊙ : x . . . 2 3 9E 1	150		(NB) NB 6	39	112			71	7
12·02	CHILDS	15			5 P :	93		6 . 8 1	153			40	113			72	
05			"	10				. . 2 . . 2	159		M8	41					
09	"	16			: 6 4 : 7 1	98		:	160			42	114		35		
12			"	11	2 ⓵	99		4 : 2 x 4 :	166		NB 7	43	115		36		
18	"	17			: . : P : :	105					over wkt. M9 3HR	44					
20			"	12				. : 3 P 8 3 2 .	172			45	117			74	
24	"	18			5 : : : : P	111		.			M10	46					
28			"	13	6s 1	112		3 : 4 4 1	177			47	119		37	75	
32	"	19			: P . : 8 .	118					M11	48					
35			"	14	. . † . 4	122		⊙ . 8 1	180		(NB) † Round wkt NB 8	49	121			76	8
40	"	20	(14-1-39-0)					: : : P : P	186		M12	50					
43			PRINGLE	5	2 G L . : T	128					M13	51					
47	"	21						Fx . . . 9 8 1	192			52	122			77	
50			"	6				. x : 7 : .	198		M14	53					
54	"	22			5(4 3/2E 4 3	130	4	5 P : :	202			54	129		44		
58	(22-10-32-0)		"	7	: 2B 8/7 . L :	136	4		202	10	(2B) M15 NB 8	55	131	-	44	77	10
1·01	LUNCH		(7-3-17-0)									LUNCH					
1·42	CHILDS	23						G3/2 W	203	10		55¹	131	1	44	77	10
43								HOOPER			McKENDRICK sub (FOSTER)					0	
45	"	23						4/5 P . 2 4† 4 3	5	1	† Diving save (KENDRICK)	56	138			7	
48			PRINGLE	8				. : ! : 7 7/6	11		M 16	57					
52	"	24			P P P P† P P	142					† Appeal ct slip. M17	58					
55			"	9	: : :	145		5P : 2/1 1	14			59	139			8	
59	"	25						P 7 2 G 9E† P	20		† nr played on. 4HR • nr silly point (BAILEY)	60					
2·02			"	10	P ! 1	147		L L . P	24		M18	61	140		45		
06	"	26			P P 3 P P :	153					M19	62					
09			"	11	P . :	156		7 2 . 1	27		KENDRICK sub (FOSTER) (2 overs)	63	141			9	
12	"	27			:	157		P 5 . P 4 1	32			64	142			10	
15			"	12	x 5	159		P . P 8 1	36			65	143			11	
19	"	28						2 5(6) 5/4 6/5 4/5P 4 6	42	1/2		66	153			21	
22			"	13	1E 7 : 2S 1	163		1 L 2 .	44			67	156		46	23	
26	"	29	(13-4-24-0)		P P : P 2 4 :	169	5				50 : 264'	68	160		50		
29			FOSTER	13				x 7 8E : x .	50		M 20	69					
33	"	30			. : : . E1. L 2	175					Round wkt • Left of slip (MAYNARD)	70	162		52		
37			"	14				. L ! . EX W	55	1/2		70⁵	162	2	52	23	10
39								LOGIE								0	
41			"	14				5	1		M21	71					
2·42	(31-14-56-1)	31	(14-3-39-1)		P P : : : P	181	5		1	-	M22 NB 8	72	162	2	52	0	10

4TH DAY	BOWLERS (PALMER) PAVILION END		(BIRD) VAUXHALL END		BATSMEN SCOREBOARD LEFT			SCOREBOARD RIGHT			NOTES	WEST INDIES 2ND INNINGS END-OF-OVER TOTALS					
TIME	BOWLER	O.	BOWLER	O.	SCORING	BALLS	6s/4s	SCORING	BALLS	6s/4s		O.	RUNS	W.	'L' BAT	'R' BAT	EXTRAS
					HAYNES	181	5	LOGIE	1	-	M22 NB8	72	162	2	52	0	10
2.45			FOSTER	15	7S 4 / 1 :	183		1E 4 L 8EP / 1 · · 1	5			73	165		53	2	
49 51	DRINKS CHILDS	32			: : :	186		8 x 3 / 4 · 1	8	1	over wkt	74	170			7	
55			"	16				↑ · x x7S / · · · · · 1	14			75	171			8	
58	"	33						8 · · P · E1 / · · · · · ·	20		M23 5HR	76					
3.02			"	17	G 6 9 x3S / · 2 1 · 1	191		2/3 / 1	21			77	176		57	9	
06	"	34			: : : : : P	197					M24	78					
09			"	18				EP YP 2 5(6) 5 3 / · · 4 · · ·	27	2		79	180			13	
13	"	35	(18-3-52-1)		P P : : † 3 / · · · · · 1	203					† over wkt	80	181		58		
17			CAPEL	1	4 6 YL 4/5 / 3 · · · 4	208	6	4 / 1	28			81	189		65	14	
22	"	36			x : P : P / · · · · · ·	213		8 / 1	29			82	190			15	
25			"	2	1 ½ / 2 1	215		E1 : 4 1 / · · 4 1	33	3		83	198		68	20	
29	"	37			8 / 1	216		: x 8 1 : / · · · 2 ·	38			84	201		69	22	
33			"	3	2 1 6 3 / · 3 · · ·	221		3 / 1	39			85	205		72	23	
37	(38-16-71-1)	38	(3-0-20-0)		† · P P / · · · ·	225	6	6 8 / 4 1	41	4	† Round	86	210	2	72	28	10
3.40	TEA										M24 NB8			T	E	A	
4.02			DEFREITAS	15				2/3 4 3/2 7 3/2 / · · · · · ·	47		M25	87					
06	CHILDS	39			3E P P P 9 / · · · · · 2	231					over wkt 50 p'ship: 65'	88	212		74		
09			"	16	3 / · ·	233		4 x : 2 / · · · 1	51			89	213			29	
13	"	40			4S / 1	234		6 · P 3 8 / · · · 4 1	56	5	† Good stop (SMITH)	90	219		75	34	
16	(40-16-79-1)		" (17-2-46-0)	17	: 2 6 / · 1 1	237	6	LB 6 6 / · · 4	59	6	(LB)	91	226	2	77	38	11
4.20	WEST INDIES WON BY 8 WICKETS										M25 NB8						
											554 balls						

ENGLAND 1ST INNINGS v. WEST INDIES (FIFTH TEST) at KENNINGTON OVAL, LONDON on 4, 5, 6, 8, ~~9~~ AUGUST, 1988.

IN	OUT	MINS	No.	BATSMAN	HOW OUT	BOWLER	RUNS	WKT	TOTAL	6s	4s	BALLS	NOTES ON DISMISSAL TOSS: ENGLAND
11.02	11.35	33	1	G.A. GOOCH *	CT LOGIE	AMBROSE	9	1	12	·	2	25	Fended bouncer to short square-leg (lobbed catch).
11.02	2.14	153	2	T.S. CURTIS	CT DUJON	BENJAMIN	30	2	77	·	4	120	Edged yorker. HS in Tests. Late on stroke - inswinger.
11.37	3.39	202	3	R.J. BAILEY	CT DUJON	AMBROSE	43	3	116	·	3	145	Edged cover-drive at widish ball which lifted.
2.16	6.06	208	4	R.A. SMITH	CT HARPER	MARSHALL	57	9	198	·	8	162	Failed to avoid lifting ball which touched glove. (2ND SLIP) HS in Tests
4.02	4.08	6	5	M.P. MAYNARD	CT DUJON	AMBROSE	3	4	121	·	·	6	Top-edged cut at bouncer - much-juggled catch.
4.10	4.59	49	6	D.J. CAPEL	CT MARSHALL	HARPER	16	5	160	·	2	40	Edged to slip - quicker 'arm' ball.
5.01	5.07	6	7	C.J. RICHARDS†	CT LOGIE	HARPER	0	6	160	·	·	4	Edged via pad to short square-leg.
5.09	5.25	16	8	D.R. PRINGLE	CT DUJON	MARSHALL	1	7	165	·	·	16	Edged firm-footed swish at widish ball.
5.27	5.59	32	9	P.A.J. DEFREITAS	CT HAYNES	HARPER	18	8	196	·	2	26	Pad/glove catch to silly mid-off.
6.01	11.02	14	10	N.A. FOSTER	CT SUB (ARTHURTON)	MARSHALL	7	10	205	·	1	11	Skied drive to square-cover. MARSHALL'S 34TH WICKET - WI RECORD
6.08	(11.02)	7	11	J.H. CHILDS	NOT OUT		0			·	·	5	
				EXTRAS	b - lb 6	w - nb 15	21			-6	22 4	560 balls (including 17 no-balls)	

* CAPTAIN † WICKET-KEEPER

TOTAL (90.3 OVERS; 370 MINUTES) 205 ALL OUT at 11.02 am on second day.

14 OVERS 4 BALLS/HOUR
2.26 RUNS/OVER
36 RUNS/100 BALLS

UMPIRES: H.D. BIRD AND K.E. PALMER

BOWLER	O	M	R	W	nb
MARSHALL	24.3	3	64	3	3
AMBROSE	20	6	31	3	8
WALSH	10	1	21	0	6
BENJAMIN	14	2	33	1	-
HARPER	21	7	50	3	-
HOOPER	1	1	0	0	-
			6		
	90.3	20	205	10	

HRS	OVERS	RUNS
1	14	24
2	15	32
3	15	45
4	13	16
5	16	43
6	15	36

RUNS	MINS	OVERS	LAST 50 (in mins)
50	107	25	107
100	179	43.5	72
150	284	69.1	105
200	365	89.1	81

LUNCH: 56-1 [29 OVERS, 120 MIN] CURTIS 21* (120') BAILEY 20* (85')

TEA: 116-3 [56.5 OVERS, 237 MIN] SMITH 22* (83')

STUMPS: 203-9 [90 OVERS, 369 MIN] FOSTER 5* (13') CHILDS 0* (6')

WKT	PARTNERSHIP		RUNS	MINS
1st	Gooch	Curtis	12	33
2nd	Curtis	Bailey	65	118
3rd	Bailey	Smith	39	83
4th	Smith	Maynard	5	6
5th	Smith	Capel	39	49
6th	Smith	Richards	0	6
7th	Smith	Pringle	5	16
8th	Smith	DeFreitas	31	32
9th	Smith	Foster	2	5
10th	Foster	Childs	7	7
			205	

WEST INDIES 1ST INNINGS [IN REPLY TO ENGLAND'S 205 ALL OUT]

IN	OUT	MINS	No.	BATSMAN	HOW OUT	BOWLER	RUNS	WKT	TOTAL	6s	4s	BALLS	NOTES ON DISMISSAL
11·16	11·53	37	1	C.G.GREENIDGE	CT DEFREITAS	FOSTER	10	2	16	·	·	26	Mistimed pull – simple catch to wide mid-on.
11·16	11·44	28	2	D.L.HAYNES	CT RICHARDS	FOSTER	2	1	9	·	·	22	Edged push at widish ball that lifted and left him.
11·46	12·34	48	3	C.L.HOOPER	CT GOOCH	FOSTER	11	4	57	1	·	27	Edged push at lifting outswinger to 1st slip.
11·55	11·56	1	4	I.V.A.RICHARDS*	CT CURTIS	FOSTER	0	3	16	·	·	3	Edged breakback via thigh pad to short square-leg.
11·59	2·50	130	5	A.L.LOGIE	CT GOOCH	FOSTER	47	5	126	·	5	79	Edged push to 1st slip – followed lifting ball.
12·36	4·07	148	6	P.J.L.DUJON †	LBW	PRINGLE	64	6	155	·	7	110	Beaten by breakback – played round front leg.
2·52	4·32	78	7	R.A.HARPER	RUN OUT [FOSTER/CAPEL PRINGLE]		17	8	167	·	1	53	Ambrose failed to respond to call for 2nd run to third man.
4·09	4·14	5	8	M.D.MARSHALL	CT AND BOWLED	CHILDS	0	7	156	·	·	7	Mistimed on-drive at leg-break – leading edge.
4·16	(4·47)	31	9	C.E.L.AMBROSE	NOT OUT		17			·	2	23	
4·34	4·35	1	10	W.K.M.BENJAMIN	BOWLED	PRINGLE	0	9	168	·	·	1	First ball – off stump. Missed straight ball – yorked.
4·37	4·47	10	11	C.A.WALSH	CT DEFREITAS	PRINGLE	5	10	183	·	1	6	Skied drive to deep mid-off – excellent leaping catch.
				EXTRAS	b - lb 7	w 1 nb 2	10			1[6]	16[4]	357 balls (Including 3 no-balls)	

* CAPTAIN † WICKET-KEEPER

TOTAL (59 OVERS; 268 MINUTES) 183 ALL OUT at 4.47 p.m. on second day.

13 OVERS 1 BALLS/HOUR
3.10 RUNS/OVER
51 RUNS/100 BALLS

BOWLER	O	M	R	W	nb/w
FOSTER	16	2	64	5	-/1
DEFREITAS	13	4	33	0	-
PRINGLE	17	4	45	3	3/-
CAPEL	7	0	21	0	-
CHILDS	6	1	13	1	-
			7	1	
	59	11	183	10	

HRS	OVERS	RUNS
1	13	32
2	14	41
3	12	56
4	14	31

RUNS	MINS	OVERS	LAST 50 (in mins)
50	76	16·2	76
100	146	32·4	70
150	218	47·3	72

LUNCH: 70-4 [23 OVERS 104 MIN] LOGIE 36* (61') DUJON 9* (24')

TEA: 155-5 [49 OVERS 223 MIN] DUJON 64* (143') HARPER 12* (48')

ENGLAND'S FIRST FIRST-INNINGS LEAD OF THE SERIES (22 RUNS)

(FIRST v. WEST INDIES SINCE LORD'S, 1984)

WKT	PARTNERSHIP		RUNS	MINS
1st	Greenidge	Haynes	9	28
2nd	Greenidge	Hooper	7	7
3rd	Hooper	Richards	0	1
4th	Hooper	Logie	41	35
5th	Logie	Dujon	69	92
6th	Dujon	Harper	29	53
7th	Harper	Marshall	1	5
8th	Harper	Ambrose	11	16
9th	Ambrose	Benjamin	1	1
10th	Ambrose	Walsh	15	10
			183	

ENGLAND 2ND INNINGS (22 RUNS AHEAD ON FIRST INNINGS)

IN	OUT	MINS	No.	BATSMAN	HOW OUT	BOWLER	RUNS	WKT	TOTAL	6s	4s	BALLS	NOTES ON DISMISSAL
5.02	5.01	422	1	G.A. GOOCH *	CT GREENIDGE	AMBROSE	84	10	202	1	8	240	Last out – cut to deep backward point. 69 MIN ON 40. 50 in 285'
5.02	6.11	69	2	T.S. CURTIS	LBW	MARSHALL	15	1	50	·	2	50	Late on vast breakback. On back foot – played across line.
6.13	6.36	23	3	R.J. BAILEY	BOWLED	BENJAMIN	3	2	55	·	·	18	Inswinger (via pads) through 'gate'.
6.38	6.40	2	4	R.A. SMITH	LBW	BENJAMIN	0	3	55	·	·	4	Padded up to inswinger.
6.42	12.21	106	5	N.A. FOSTER	CT LOGIE	BENJAMIN	34	4	108	·	5	80	'Nightwatchman' Gloved hook at bouncer to backward sq. leg.
12.23	12.50	27	6	M.P. MAYNARD	CT AND BOWLED	BENJAMIN	10	5	125	·	1	28	Inswinger hit pad before bat – caught at second attempt.
12.53	2.10	35	7	D.J. CAPEL	LBW	WALSH	12	6	139	·	2	33	Beaten by low-bounce – played back – inswinger – 'plumb'.
2.12	2.47	35	8	C.J. RICHARDS†	CT DUJON	WALSH	3	7	157	·	·	24	Outside edge – driving
2.49	4.04	53	9	D.R. PRINGLE	BOWLED	HARPER	8	8	175	·	1	43	Bamboozled by off-break – played back – through 'gate'.
4.06	4.12	6	10	P.A.J. DEFREITAS	CT HAYNES	HARPER	0	9	177	·	·	6	Egged sweep via pad to diving silly-point.
4.14	(5.01)	47	11	J.H. CHILDS	NOT OUT		0			·	·	24	
				EXTRAS	b 3 lb 15	w – nb 15	33			1 6	19 4	550 balls (inc 16 no-balls + 1 five-ball over)	

*CAPTAIN †WICKET-KEEPER

TOTAL (89.1 OVERS; 422 MINUTES) 202. ALL OUT at 5.01 pm on third day.

12 OVERS 4 BALLS/HOUR
2.26 RUNS/OVER
RUNS/100 BALLS

BOWLER	O	M	R	W	nb
MARSHALL	25	6	52	1	9
AMBROSE	24.1	10	50	1	5
BENJAMIN	22	4	52	4	2
WALSH	12	5	21	2	·
HARPER	6	3	9	2	·
			18		
	89.1	28	202	10	

HRS	OVERS	RUNS
1	12	43
2	12	17
3	12	44
4	12	21
5	15	27
6	13	20
7	12	29

RUNS	MINS	OVERS	LAST 50 (in mins)
50	68	14.4	68
100	173	34.4	105
150	289	60.5	116
200	416	88	127

STUMPS (2ND DAY): 64-3 [26 OVERS 127 MIN] GOOCH 38* (127') FOSTER 1* (27') LEAD: 86

LUNCH: 128-5 [50 OVERS 245 MIN] GOOCH 46* (245') CAPEL 3* (7')

TEA: 175-7 [77 OVERS 363 MIN] GOOCH 67* (363') PRINGLE 8* (51')

WKT	PARTNERSHIP		RUNS	MINS
1st	Gooch	Curtis	50	69
2nd	Gooch	Bailey	5	23
3rd	Gooch	Smith	0	2
4th	Gooch	Foster	53	106
5th	Gooch	Maynard	17	27
6th	Gooch	Capel	14	35
7th	Gooch	Richards	18	35
8th	Gooch	Pringle	18	53
9th	Gooch	DeFreitas	2	6
10th	Gooch	Childs	25	47
			202	

WEST INDIES 2ND INNINGS

REQUIRING 225 TO WIN

IN	OUT	MINS	No.	BATSMAN	HOW OUT	BOWLER	RUNS	WKT	TOTAL	6s	4s	BALLS	NOTES ON DISMISSAL
5.16	1.43	219	1	C.G GREENIDGE	CT RICHARDS	CHILDS	77	1	131	·	10	203	Leaping leg-break took glove & ballooned towards point.
5.16	(4.20)	354	2	D.L. HAYNES	NOT OUT		77			·	6	237	
1.45	2.39	54	3	C.L. HOOPER	BOWLED	FOSTER	23	2	162	1	2	55	Played on – attempted steer at short ball.
2.41	(4.20)	77	4	A.L. LOGIE	NOT OUT		38			·	6	59	
			5										
			6										
			7										
			8										
			9										
			10										
			11										
				EXTRAS	b 2 lb 3	w - nb 6	11			1	24	554 balls (inc 8 no-balls)	
				TOTAL	(91 OVERS; 354 MINUTES)		226-2						

* CAPTAIN † WICKET-KEEPER

15 OVERS 2 BALLS/HOUR
2.48 RUNS/OVER
40 RUNS/100 BALLS

BOWLER	O	M	R	W	nb
FOSTER	18	3	52	1	1
DEFREITAS	17	2	46	0	6
CHILDS	40	16	79	1	-
PRINGLE	13	4	24	0	1
CAPEL	3	0	20	0	-
			5		
	91	25	226	2	

2ND NEW BALL NOT TAKEN.

HRS	OVERS	RUNS
1	14	40
2	15	47
3	15	28
4	16	24
5	16	32

RUNS	MINS	OVERS	LAST 50 (in mins)
50	76	18.2	76
100	138	34.2	62
150	257	65.5	119
200	328	83.5	71

STUMPS 3RD DAY: 71-0 (154 to win) [24 OVERS, 98 MIN] GREENIDGE 53*, HAYNES 15*

LUNCH: 131-0 (94 to win) [55 OVERS, 218 MIN] GREENIDGE 77*, HAYNES 44*

TEA: 210-2 [86 OVERS, 336 MIN] HAYNES 72* (326'), LOGIE 28* (59')

WEST INDIES WON BY 8 WICKETS at 4.20 pm on fourth day

MATCH AWARD: P. J. L. DUJON (Adjudicator: F.S. TRUEMAN)

MEN OF SERIES: G.A. GOOCH and M.D. MARSHALL

WKT	PARTNERSHIP		RUNS	MINS
1st	Greenidge	Haynes	131	219
2nd	Haynes	Hooper	31	54
3rd	Haynes	Logie	64*	77
			226	

LORD'S
THE SRI LANKA TEST

Enter the Sri Lankans · Starved of Test cricket · Gooch keeps everyone guessing · Russell at last · Match report · Elusive victory

England's selectors scarcely had time to lick their wounds or draw breath after the West Indies series before they were compelled to choose a team to contest a one-off Test against Sri Lanka. There was no question of being able to use this fixture as a trial for the winter tour of India. Memories of a similar match in 1984 were still painfully fresh; on that occasion the fledgling Sri Lankan batsmen had ambushed England with an object lesson in technique and strokeplay, achieving an emphatic first-innings lead of 121 runs in a drawn game.

The latest Sri Lankans arrived equally determined to do everything within their power to extend England's unprecedented sequence of eighteen matches since their last victory. Their attainment of full membership of the ICC in 1981, with its accompanying Test match status, had been remarkable for a nation with such meagre playing resources. Their elevation had owed much to their performances in the limited-overs game, particularly in the World Cup tournaments of 1975 and 1979. Within five years of their inaugural Test against England in February 1982, Sri Lanka had won Test matches against India and Pakistan. Both those victories had been gained in the capital city of Colombo. I doubt if any world capital dominates the commerce of a country to the extent that Colombo does that of Sri Lanka. This domination has dictated the format of the country's cricket; the capital houses all the major clubs and produces virtually all of its Test cricketers.

Seven years after the country gained Test status, political infighting continued to prevent the organization of a much-needed and long overdue provincial first-class tournament. Sri Lanka's domestic cricket continued to be limited to Saturday club matches and based entirely in Colombo. Civil war against the Tamils had taken a heavy toll of their international programme, depriving them of three home series. They had played only two Tests in the eighteen months prior to touring England and were in desperate need of regular international cricket.

During a warm-up match against Indian Gymkhana at Osterley, their captain, Ranjan Madugalle, emphasized the importance of their visit:

> This tour is vital and we aim to play to the best of our ability and make maximum use of this opportunity. This may be our last overseas tour for some considerable time. We desperately need practice against top opposition; we have just completed a special six-week tournament of three-day matches in Colombo and have seven county matches before the Test. It is every player's dream, the world over, to play for their country at Lord's. If we cannot win, we are going to make it as difficult as possible for England to get the victory they want so badly.

Madugalle was making his fifth tour of England and most of their sixteen-man party were familiar with English conditions. Such an abbreviated tour allowed little time for acclimatization and it had been essential to select players who had this experience. The team included six survivors from that epic 1984 Lord's Test side, including five batsmen (century-makers Mendis and Silva, vice-captain Ranatunga, Madugalle and De Silva) and seamer Ravi Ratnayeke. Missing was stylish opening batsman Sidath Wettimuny, who had scored a memorable 190 in that match but had subsequently retired. Brendon Kuruppu, his replacement, seemed more than adequate, having celebrated his Test debut with Sri Lanka's first double century. The line-up would have been even stronger if star batsman Asanka Gurusinha had recovered from recent knee surgery.

The tourists' bowling was very much an unknown quantity in English conditions. There was little variety in the seam attack; Ratnayeke, Labrooy, Ramanayake and Samarasekera were all right-handers whose top speed was little more than a lively medium. This gentle attack was augmented by Ranatunga's little seamers and the leg-breaks of either Rajadurai or left-armer Anurasiri.

The full party, with batting and bowling categories, was:

	Bat	Bowl
Saliya Ahangama	L	RMF
Don Anurasiri	R	SLA
Aravinda De Silva	R	OB
Brendon Kuruppu	R	WK
Graeme Labrooy	R	RMF
Ranjan Madugalle	R	OB
Ranjith Madurasinghe	L	OB
Roshan Mahanama	R	–
Duleep Mendis	R	–
Brian Rajadurai	R	LB
Champaka Ramanayake	R	RMF
Arjuna Ranatunga	L	RM
Ravi Ratnayeke	L	RMF
Athula Samarasekera	R	RMF
Amal Silva	L	WK
Hashan Tillekeratne	L	OB

Key: L – left-handed; R – right-handed; LB – leg-breaks; OB – off-breaks; RM – right-arm medium; RMF – right-arm medium-fast; SLA – slow left-arm leg-breaks; WK – wicket-keeper.

The selectors decided that the Sri Lanka Test would be treated quite independently from the winter tour and that there would be no embargo on players who had declared themselves unavailable for India. Having failed to find a combination capable of winning any of England's last eighteen matches, the selectors were understandably keen to grab a victory to end England's humiliating record sequence.

At this time only Mike Gatting and 'Jack' Richards had declared themselves unavailable for the winter tour, and Gatting had already ruled himself out of consideration for the Sri Lankan match. The key question concerned the England captaincy. Ideally whoever led the side at Lord's would also captain the touring team. After his successful introduction at The Oval, Graham Gooch was seen by some of the selectors as the best man for the winter job and for the all-important 1989 Ashes campaign. Until he had sampled the England captaincy in the Fifth Test, there was never the slightest hope of the Essex opener even considering another tour. Gooch much preferred the company of his wife, Brenda, and three infant daughters – Hannah, and the twins Megan and Sally. After enjoying the 1987 World Cup, he had bitterly regretted his decision to remain in Pakistan for the subsequent misery of a Test series. He had made no secret of the fact that he very definitely intended that to be his last England tour. At that time he can never have entertained any glimmer of ambition to captain England. Gatting had survived the hideous row with an umpire and seemed reasonably secure in the role. If he did fall, then John Emburey was the obvious successor. After that the mantle would probably go to one of the younger county skippers. Moreover Gooch had just resigned the Essex captaincy after only one season because the cares of the job had wrecked his batting form.

Everything changed at The Oval when Gooch discovered that, in many ways, captaining a Test team was a far less demanding task than looking after a county day in and day out. Moreover, he found himself enjoying the challenge and thriving upon the responsibility to such an extent that he batted for over seven hours to achieve an heroic and fatherly 84. That experience prompted him to reconsider winter touring – but only if he were in charge.

Rumours abounded when the selectors' promised appointment of the captain for Lord's was delayed, but neither Gooch nor the selectors would make any statement. Sir Garfield Sobers was highly amused by the machinations and mystery when I met him in the sponsor's box at Lord's during the Cockspur Cup Final on the Friday when the Test team was due to be chosen. 'Gooch knows he has the Board where he wants them. They have got themselves in an awful mess. He is your only world-class player and he can name his own terms,' said Sobers.

Later we discovered that the delay had been caused by Gooch's contractual responsibilities with Western Province. It was believed that he had an agreement to play another season for them, but that this would be deferred until the 1989-90 season when England were due to tour the Caribbean. It transpired that he was negotiating for his release from a contract he had signed in respect of the coming winter.

Gooch's unexpected aptitude for the job and change of touring heart also presented the selectors with a slightly embarrassing situation. What were they to do about Chris Cowdrey? Despite his poor batting performances at Headingley, he had been appointed for two matches, and would have captained at The Oval but for his foot injury. Rightly or wrongly, the selectors took the view that, although Cowdrey had been appointed for two Tests, they had been specifically the last two against West Indies; it was his bad luck that injury had prevented him from completing the contract. Certainly there was no obligation to persevere with him in the light of Gooch's change of mind, and it seemed inevitable that he would emulate Ken Cranston, whose only Test as captain was also against West Indies. It was yet another messy situation, and I felt much sympathy for Christopher Cowdrey. Undoubtedly he would have done a good job in India but, on his current form as both batsman and bowler, he did not merit a place in a Test team.

Before I was required to suggest a team for the Sri Lanka Test, Graham Gooch had been appointed captain and the team announced: Gooch, Curtis, Robinson, Lamb, Barnett, Smith, Pringle, Emburey, Newport, Foster and Lawrence.

It was such a logical selection that it smacked of the combined thinking of Graham Gooch and Micky Stewart rather than being the product of a bungling five-man committee. This was indeed the first team that Gooch had helped to select; the one he inherited for the Fifth West Indies Test had been chosen by Cowdrey before his injury. The captain must inevitably have the final say when there is divided opinion over a particular player. This is not unreasonable, considering that any misgivings about the side must affect his performance as a leader.

Peter May insisted that this latest combination was just a one-off special designed to defeat Sri Lanka. This suggested that actually picking a side to win a Test represented new enlightened thinking, and that perhaps the summer's five previous permutations were just to provide the West Indies with a bit of practice before their tour of Australia.

The team's composition revealed a dramatic change of selection policy and confirmed my suppositions. The committee had obviously decided that Cowdrey did not merit a place as a player and had also abandoned the futile tactic of employing inferior 'all-rounders' in preference to top-class specialists. They had almost certainly persuaded Gooch to go to India even if it was to be on his own terms – as captain.

I was delighted that 'Jack' Russell was about to win his first England cap; it was at least a year overdue. At the beginning of the season I had decided to use an action photograph of him on the cover of the 1989 *Playfair Cricket Annual*. A consensus of expert opinion anticipated that Russell would become the best wicket-keeper in international cricket and remain an automatic choice for the next decade. A chirpy, quick-witted character, he relaxes by sketching.

It was also gratifying to see 'Syd' Lawrence and Phil Newport given an opportunity at Test level. No bowlers have worked harder at their technique or fitness and their efforts had been amply rewarded with the impressive combined tally of 145 wickets at the time of their selection. Lawrence conveys the supreme enthusiasm of a Tony Lock; after charging in for 25 overs on a hot day, he will still chase hits to the boundary and throw his vast frame around in the field. His favourite forms of relaxation are boxing and break-dancing. Newport credited Ian Botham for the motivation which led to his ousting Richard Ellison as the best of our medium-fast bowlers who can swing the ball late both ways.

Lawrence (Gloucester) and Russell (Stroud) were the first Gloucestershire-born players from that county to represent England since 1966, when David Allen made the last of his 39 Test appearances (in my first Test as scorer for the BBC). Not since 1961-62 had an England team included two Gloucestershire players; in that season, Allen and David Smith appeared together in all five Tests of the series in India.

The one surprise selection was Tim Robinson. Unless England planned to play a sixth specialist batsman against the weakest bowling attack in international cricket, the Nottinghamshire captain could only gain a place at the expense of Tim Curtis, who had battled long and bravely against the West Indian pace battery. Robinson had not been selected for that series, presumably because of his abject showing against fast bowling on the 1985-86 tour of the Caribbean.

Emburey had earned his recall with two recent six-wicket analyses at Lord's. Dilley was unavailable because of his damaged knee.

England preferred Robinson to the unlucky Curtis, won the toss, invited Sri Lanka to bat, and reduced them unceremoniously to 63 for 6 and 130 for 9 before their number eleven astounded everyone, including himself, by contributing 42 to a Sri Lankan record last-wicket stand of 64.

The day was cheerless, the crowd negligible and silent, and the atmosphere gave no hint that we were witnessing a Test match. For once, identifying the England side gave commentators as much trouble as sorting out the opposition. There were seven changes from the last England team, four new caps and a first appearance of the season for Robinson bringing the total number of players employed in six Tests to an astonishing 28, nine of whom made their debut in Test cricket. Add Fairbrother, French, Hemmings and Radford from the antipodean tour and you have a grand total of 32 players – almost three complete teams – who played Test cricket for England in the space of seven months.

The match produced no fewer than seven debutants with Samarasekera and Madurasinghe making their first appearance for the tourists and umpire John Holder standing in his first Test. Holder's promotion was especially historic; he was the first black umpire to officiate in a Test match in England. A former Hampshire fast bowler now domiciled in Rochdale, he had impressed at county level and done extremely well to graduate during only his sixth season on the first-class list.

Lawrence began his international career with the fastest new-ball spell achieved by an England bowler all year. It was probably a major reason for the Sri Lankans' capitulation. He should have had the first wicket when Russell dropped a difficult low chance diving to his left. He said afterwards that in a county match he would have taken it one-handed but, as it was a Test, he thought he should use two. As a result of this afterthought he was a fractionally late on it. He made amends eight balls later when Silva edged a drive at a late outswinger from Foster.

Athula Samarasekera's first innings gave the commentators problems of pronunciation and identification – he was very similar in appearance to Kuruppu, and both wore blue helmets. I passed a note to Brian Johnston pointing out that Samarasekera had a long-sleeved sweater, a white helmet peak and smiled more than his sleeveless-sweatered partner. 'Johnners' seemed pleased, and solved the other problem by dubbing him 'Big Sam'. Brian, incidentally, who made his television debut in 1946, was broadcasting his 250th Test match. It was the 150th Test that I had scored; I doubt if I shall catch him up.

Sri Lanka lunched mournfully at 69 for 6, the wickets shared between Foster and Newport, both of whom had bowled a perfect line and length, moving the ball late in the overcast conditions. Duleep Mendis revived brief memories of his two captain's innings (111 and 94) in the 1984 fixture, before Ravi Ratnayeke and Graeme Labrooy produced the most entertaining cricket of the day.

Russell, having disappointed himself and his many supporters by dropping two difficult chances on the opening day, dominated the second (Sir Donald Bradman's 80th birthday), by amassing the highest score of his first-class career. A nimble-footed left-hander, he is no mug with the bat and came into the match with his average for the season standing at 31.65. With Gooch, he registered England's first three-figure partnership in three Tests against Sri Lanka. He was about to become only the third 'nightwatchman' to score a century in a Test when he sliced a gentle skier to cover during the second over of the second new ball. His 94 was the sixth-highest innings by a 'nightwatchman'

'Jack' Russell celebrates his long-overdue selection by amassing the sixth-highest score by a Test match 'night-watchman'.

in Test cricket:

105	A. L. Mann		
	Australia *v*. India	Perth	1977–78
101	Nasim-ul-Ghani		
	Pakistan *v*. England	Lord's	1962
101*	S.M.H. Kirmani		
	India *v*. Australia	Bombay	1979–80
98	H. Larwood		
	England *v*. Australia	Sydney	1932–33
95	E. E. Hemmings		
	England *v*. Australia	Sydney	1982–83
94	R. C. Russell		
	England *v*. Sri Lanka	Lord's	1988

The last England wicket-keeper to make a hundred on his Test debut was Paul Gibb at Johannesburg in 1938-39. 'Billy' Griffith, also a 'keeper, had done so at Port-of-Spain in 1947-48, but he was playing as a batsman while Godfrey Evans kept wicket.

With Kim Barnett also celebrating his first cap with a half-century, England ended the second day with a lead of 84 and 7 wickets in hand. On paper it was a highly satisfactory position and one which we had seldom even dreamt of during the West Indies series. In reality it was a hollow performance against such mediocre opposition. The Sri Lankans were desperately short of international competition. To be brutal, their cricket seldom seemed worthy of even first-class status on the first two days at Lord's, and it was painfully obvious that the playing standard of both sides had regressed since they last met.

Doubtless the tourists realized this, and they certainly fought back with a vengeance on the Saturday, removing England's last 7 wickets for 151 runs before substantially reducing their first innings deficit of 235 with a flamboyant assault which saw 16 boundaries in just 25 overs. When bad light ended play 16 overs prematurely, Sri Lanka were 143 runs behind with eight second-innings wickets intact.

Barnett and Lamb began the day with a series of crisp strokes and swift singles, the latter stolen with an ease which belied the fact that this was their first partnership together at any level. Ratnayeke and Ramanayake ran in with all the enthusiasm of bowlers sentenced to a lengthy day of slaughter on a slow pitch offering minimal help. Just as we were contemplating an England total of 500 by tea, Labrooy ended Barnett's impressive baptism with his very first ball, an away-seamer taking the edge and just carrying to a lone slip. Derbyshire's fidgety captain had cut, pulled and driven with authority on a pitch that allowed him ample scope to play off his front foot.

Lamb, as perky as ever, tested his repaired calf muscle with some sharp running in a spirited innings which brought him a 61-ball fifty. The only England batsman to score a hundred against Sri Lanka, he looked certain to repeat the feat when Labrooy floated a slower ball through a gap between bat and pad.

Labrooy, with an approach modelled on that of Richard Hadlee, acquired his best figures in Test cricket when he lured Pringle to destruction. When Robin Smith provided Ranatunga with his first wicket of the tour it was left to the fast bowlers to extend England's lead towards their captain's ambitions.

Sri Lanka stormed into action after tea, Kuruppu and Silva taking five boundaries off Newport's first two overs. When they fell, 'Big Sam' launched a spectacular assault on some short-pitched stuff from Foster, hooking a six and two fours in the space of four balls. He went on to complete a well deserved fifty on the Monday and, with Ranatunga, who became the first Sri Lankan to score 1,500 runs, and Mendis sharing a century partnership, England were kept in the field until nearly six o'clock. There was just time for Gooch to score the single he required to complete 2,000 first-class runs in a season for the third time.

With Essex involved in a vital round of four-day Britannic Assurance Championship matches starting on the Tuesday, Gooch, Foster, Pringle and Childs were all anxious for the game to be finished in four days. Even though it was obvious that he would not be available until lunchtime, Essex named Gooch in their team against Surrey across the Thames at The Oval, while Middlesex named Emburey for their game against Sussex at more distant Hove. Both eventually enjoyed the unusual distinction of appearing in two first-class matches on the same day, although only Gooch took the field in both. The last man to achieve this was E. M. Grace during the 1865 Canterbury Festival.

Accurate seam bowling and a slow pitch compelled England to struggle for their remaining 89 runs, and the last pre-lunch over began with 8 still required and Gooch, car keys in hand, glowering from the dressing room. After three balls the scores were level but Robinson was unable to score from 'Big Sam's' last three balls. With dark clouds approaching, the Sri Lankans gleefully trotted off for lunch. It would have been worth eavesdropping on the England dressing room as Gooch and Emburey gave vent to their feelings.

Four balls after the interval it was all over. A bewildering season of misadventure and selectorial chaos thus ended with England's elusive first victory anywhere since Melbourne 1986-87. Their last win in England had taken place three years earlier, against Australia at The Oval; five years had elapsed since their last victory at Lord's, against New Zealand.

All of those donning the crown and three lions for the first time in this unequal contest had made their mark and ensured selection for the winter tour. Lawrence always gave maximum effort, bowling flat out on a sluggish pitch; with a little more luck he could have doubled his tally of wickets. Barnett batted with assurance and fielded bravely at 'Boot Hill'. Russell, after missing two difficult chances

Kim Barnett (England captain of the near-future?) cut, drove and pulled with authority on a pitch which allowed ample scope for his front-foot technique.

on the first day, confirmed his reputation as the best wicket-keeper in the country ('in the world', according to 'Dickie' Bird), and made a career best 94. Newport took seven wickets in the match, batted usefully and won England's Cornhill Match Award.

Sri Lanka fought hard after a disastrous first morning, but looked a shadow of the side that had dominated a similar fixture four years earlier. They were again a most popular touring side, well-led by the friendly and erudite Madugalle. They hope to be given a three-match series on their next visit in 1992. Before then they must institute a three-day inter-provincial tournament which encourages cricketers throughout the country and not just in Colombo.

Philip Newport – a fine all-round performance and worthy winner of the Cornhill match award in his first Test.

1ST DAY	BOWLERS (DJ CONSTANT) PAVILION END		(JW HOLDER) NURSERY END		BATSMEN SCOREBOARD LEFT			SCOREBOARD RIGHT			NOTES	SRI LANKA 1ST INNINGS END-OF-OVER TOTALS					
TIME	BOWLER	O.	BOWLER	O.	SCORING	BALLS	6s/4s	SCORING	BALLS	6s/4s		O.	RUNS	W.	'L' BAT	'R' BAT	EXTRAS
					KURUPPU			SILVA		LHB							
11.01			FOSTER	1	P : LB	3		. : .	3		(LB) M1	1	1				1
05	LAWRENCE	1			: . . . . . G	9					M2	2					
09			"	2	1 2 P : . .	12		P : 8 : . 1	6			3	2			1	
13	"	2						↑ x x · 2E	12		M3	4					
17			"	3	. . 4 7 8/7 : 2 2 :	18						5	6		4		
21	"	3						↑ . . 1E	18		• Dropped Russell M4	6					
26			"	4	. 9E 1	20		: . T E1 W	22	–		7	7	1	5	1	1
29								SAMARASEKERA								0	
31	"	4			9 · 5/6 4 · 1	23	1	: : :	3			8	12		10		
36			"	5	4 3/4.7S . 2 1	26		3 L :	6			9	15		13		
40	"	5			4 4 RT3 2 4 1	29	2	P 2 :	9			10	22		20		
44			"	6	. P . : . L .	35					M5	11					
47	"	6	(6-2-9-1)					. ↑ · 3/2 6 3	15		M6	12					
52			NEWPORT	1	2 8/7 2 1 9 · 4 · · 4 1	41	4					13	31		29		
56	"	7			. 5(6)LB : 4 ·	44	5	: . .	18		(LB) 1HR	14	36		33		2
12.00	(7-4-16-0)		"	2	: 6 2/3 5 X 1E 2 2 · · 4	50	6					15	44		41		
05	FOSTER	7						1E W	19	–		15[1]	44	2	41	0	2
								DE SILVA								0	
08	"	7						: . : : .	5		M7	16					
11			"	3	. 4 . : RP3 2 .	56						17	46		43		
15	"	8			1/3 3	57		: . 8 T LB 2 · ·	10		(LB)	18	52		46	2	3
19			"	4	1E W	58	6					18[1]	52	3	46	2	3
20					MADUGALLE										0		
22			"	4	P	5					M8	19					
25	"	9						. : . : : 9 1	16			20	53			3	
29			"	5				: E1 W	18	–		20[2]	53	4	0	3	3
30								RANATUNGA		LHB						0	
32			"	5				2 : 1 : . 4	4	1		21	57			4	
36	"	10			: P LB	8		. : P	7		(LB) M9	22	58				4
39			"	6	: 4 : 7/8 3	12		L 4 :	9			23	61		3		
44	"	11			· L W	14	–					23[2]	61	5	3	4	4
44					MENDIS										0		
46	"	11			7S 1 : .	3		8 1	10			24	63		1	5	
50			"	1				· L W	12	1		24[2]	63	6	1	5	4
51								RATNAYEKE								0	
53			"	7				. : E1 2 (4)	5	1	NB1	25	67			4	
56	" (12-4-19-3)	12	(7-1-30-3)		Y : Y. RE X . . . . 2 ·	9	–		5	1		26	69	6	3	4	4
1.00	LUNCH										M9 NB1		LUNCH				

1ST DAY	BOWLERS (CONSTANT) PAVILION END		(HOLDER) NURSERY END		BATSMEN SCOREBOARD LEFT			SCOREBOARD RIGHT			SRI LANKA 1ST INNINGS	END-OF-OVER TOTALS					
TIME	BOWLER	O.	BOWLER	O.	SCORING	BALLS	6s/4s	SCORING	BALLS	6s/4s	NOTES	O.	RUNS	W.	'L' BAT	'R' BAT	EXTRAS
	LUNCH				MENDIS	9	-	RATNAYEKE	5	1	M9 NB1 2HR	26	69	6	3	4	4
1.40			NEWPORT	8				: : 4 4 : :	11	3		27	77			12	
44	FOSTER	13			: 2 : : : 4	15	1					28	81		7		
48			"	9				: 4 · 4 2	17	5		29	91			22	
52	"	14			4 : 2 : : :	21	2					30	97		13		
56			"	10	: : 1	24		4 : (1) : :	21		• Dropped Russell. NB2 – diving right.	31	99		14	23	
2.00	"	15			1 1	26		: : : :	25		† Just short of 3rd man (B)	32	102		16		5
05			"	11	: : : (·) : :	33					(NB) NB3	33	103				6
09	"	16						: : : : : :	31		M10	34					
13			"	12	1 · 4	36	3	4 : 1	34	6	50 p'ship: 43 min	35	113		21	28	
17	"	17						: : · 4 · 1	40	7	† 2 overthrows (stumps)	36	118			33	
21	(17-5-36-3)		"	13	· : : :	40		· :	42		(LB) M11	37	119				7
25	LAWRENCE	8						: · · · : 1	48			38	120			34	
29			"	14	: :	42		: · : 1	52			39	121			35	
34	"	9			W	43	3	: 1	54			39[3]	122	7	21	36	7
36					MADURASINGHE		LHB								0		
38	"	9			: 1	2		:	55		3HR	40	123		1		
40			"	15	· 2 : : · :	8						41	125		3		
44	"	10	(15-2-64-3)		: : 1	11	-	1 ·	57			41[5]	127	8	4	37	7
47					RAMANAYAKE										0		
49	"	10			·	1						42					
51			PRINGLE	1	: ·	3		· : : 1	61			43	128			38	
54	"	11			: : : :	7		: 1	63			44	129			39	
59			"	2	W	8	-	· : 1	66			44[4]	130	9	0	40	7
3.01					LABROOY										0		
03			"	2	· :	2						45					
04	"	12			: 1	4		1 · : :	70			46	132		1	41	
08			"	3	· : 4 · 2 2	10	1	(1)	71		NB4	47	142		9	42	8
13	"	13			: : : : 4	15	2	1	72			48	147		13	43	
18			"	4	: : · 2	19		· 1	74			49	150		15	44	
21	"	14	(4-0-14-1)		· 1	21		1 4 · :	78	8		50	156		16	49	
26			NEWPORT	16	: : : : : :	27					M12	51					
30	"	15			: : 1	30		1 : :	81		RATNAYEKE'S 50: 118'	52	158		17	50	
34	(15-4-37-1)		"	17	: : : : : :	36					M13 4HR	53					
39	FOSTER	18						· 2 : : 4 ·	87	9		54	164			56	
43			"	18	: 1 :	39		: : 1	90			55	166		18	57	
47	"	19			: : : 1	43		· 1	92			56	168		19	58	
52			"	19	· : : 4 1	49	3					57	173		24		
56	"	20	(19-4-71-3)		4 : : 1	53	4	: :	94		† stoppage for repairs.	58	178		29		
4.02	(20-5-49-3)		EMBUREY	1	: : : : : :	59	4		94	9	M14 NB4	59	178	9	29	58	8

1ST DAY	BOWLERS (CONSTANT) PAVILION END		(HOLDER) NURSERY END		BATSMEN SCOREBOARD LEFT			SCOREBOARD RIGHT			SRI LANKA 1ST INNINGS	END-OF-OVER TOTALS					
TIME	BOWLER	O.	BOWLER	O.	SCORING	BALLS	6s/4s	SCORING	BALLS	6s/4s	NOTES	O.	RUNS	W.	'L' BAT	'R' BAT	EXTRAS
					LABROOY	59	4	RATNAYEKE	94	9	M14 NB4	59	178	9	29	58	8
4.05	FOSTER	21			3 · 4 Y1 · · · 1	63		L 7 · 1	96			60	180		30	59	
09	(21-5-51-3)		EMBUREY	2	: P P 3 P : · · · 4 · ·	69	5		96	9		61	184	9	34	59	8
4.11	TEA		(2-1-4-0)								M14 NB4			T	E	A	
4.30	PRINGLE	5						P : x 4 4 4 · · · · · ·	102		M15	62					
33			NEWPORT	20	3 · LB · 4 · ·	73	6	5(4) · :	104		(LB)	63	189		38		9
37	·	6			3 1	74		4 x · · · · · · · ·	109		(NB) NB5	64	190		39		
41			·	21	x 4 x 9 · · · 1	78		5(4) 2 P · (·) ·	112		SRI LANKA'S HIGHEST 10th WKT STAND (prev 60)	65	192		40		10
45	(6.5-1-17-2)	7	(21-4-77-3)		x 6 7 2/3 L · · 2 · W	83	6		112	9		65⁵	194	10	42	59	10
4.48	ALL OUT										M15 NB5		ALL		OUT		
											400 balls						

1ST DAY	BOWLERS (CONSTANT) PAVILION END		(HOLDER) NURSERY END		BATSMEN SCOREBOARD LEFT			SCOREBOARD RIGHT			ENGLAND 1ST INNINGS NOTES	END-OF-OVER TOTALS					
TIME	BOWLER	O.	BOWLER	O.	SCORING	BALLS	6s/4s	SCORING	BALLS	6s/4s		O.	RUNS	W.	'L' BAT	'R' BAT	EXTRAS
					GOOCH			ROBINSON									
4.59			RATNAYEKE	1	· · · 1 ·	5		1	1			1	2		1	1	
5.03	LABROOY	1						· : : : : :	7		M1	2					
07			"	2	· 1	7		: : 2 ·	11			3	5		2	3	
10	"	2			: : : · · 4	13	1				† Appeal ct wk (leg-side)	4	9		6		
14			"	3	: : · · :	18		1	12			5	10			4	
18	"	3			: :	20		: : · 1	16			6	11			5	
22			"	4	1	21		4 : 1 : :	21	1		7	17		7	10	
25	"	4	(4-0-12-0)		1	22		: : · 2 ·	26		† 1 overthrow	8	20		8	12	
30			RAMANAYAKE	1	: : : : : :	28					M2	9					
34	"	5			: 3	30		1 : · :	30			10	24		11	13	
38			"	2	1	31		: : : : :	35			11	25		12		
41	"	6			: : : : · ·	37					M3	12					
45			"	3	· ·	39		: · : 1	39			13	26			14	
49	"	7			1	40		1 : · 2 ·	44			14	30		13	17	
53	(7-2-16-0)		"	4	· 4 : · ⊙ ·	47	2				(NB) NB1 1HR	15	35		17		1
58	RATNAYEKE	5			· : 1	50		1 : :	47			16	37		18	18	
6.02			"	5	: : ⊙ 1	54		: · :	50		(NB) NB2	17	39		19		2
07	"	6	(5-1-9-0)		· : · : : :	60					M4	18					
11			MADURASINGHE	1				· : : : : 1	56			19	40			19	
13	"	7						: W	58	1		19²	40	1	19	19	2
14								RUSSELL		LHB						0	
16	"	7			1	61		: 1 ·	3			20	42		20	1	
19			"	2	4 : : : : :	67	3					21	46		24		
21	" (8-1-17-1)	8	(2-0-5-0)			67	3	: : · · : 1	9	-		22	47	1	24	2	2
6.25	STUMPS										M4 NB2		STUMPS				
2ND DAY 11.00			MADURASINGHE	3				: : : : : :	15		† Round wkt M5	23					
03	LABROOY	8	(3-1-5-0)		1	68		· : · · 1	20			24	49		25	3	
07			RATNAYEKE	9				4 · · · ·	26	1		25	53			7	
11	"	9			LB	69		· : : : ·	31		(LB) M6	26	54				3
15			"	10	: · : 1	73		: :	33			27	55		26		
19	"	10			· : · ⊙ · ⊙ 1	80		:	34		(NB) (NB) NB4	28	58		27		5
24			"	11	: ⊙ : · · ·	87					(NB) NB5	29	59				6
29	"	11			: : · :	91		: · ③	37		NB6 2HR	30	62			10	
34			"	12				· : · : · 4	43	2	• Dr wk (Silva)	31	66			14	
38	"	12			1	92		· · : · 2	48			32	69		28	16	
42	(12-3-27-0)		"	13	: : ⊙ · 1	97		: 3	50		(NB) NB7	33	74		29	19	7
49	RAMANAYAKE	6			:	98		· : 4 · 1	55	3		34	79			24	
53			"	14				: : : : · :	61		M7	35					
11.57	" (7-1-16-0)	7	(14-2-32-1)		· : : : · 2	104	3		61	3	M7 NB7	36	81	1	31	24	7

2ND DAY	BOWLERS (CONSTANT) PAVILION END		(HOLDER) NURSERY END		BATSMEN SCOREBOARD LEFT			SCOREBOARD RIGHT			NOTES	ENGLAND 1ST INNINGS END-OF-OVER TOTALS					
TIME	BOWLER	O.	BOWLER	O.	SCORING	BALLS	6s/4s	SCORING	BALLS	6s/4s		O.	RUNS	W.	'L' BAT	'R' BAT	EXTRAS
					GOOCH	104	3	RUSSELL	61	3	M7· NB7	36	81	1	31	24	7
12.01			RATNAYEKE	15	6 4 4 3 : · · · 4 :	109	4	9 1	62			37	86		35	25	
05	RAMANAYAKE	8	(15-2-37-1)		8/7 4 x 2 · : : :	114		8/9 1	63			38	89		37	26	
10			SAMARASEKERA	1				4 : : : 4 3 4	69	4	Partnership 50: 83'	39	93			30	
14	"	9			· · L 6 1	117		: 4 3	72			40	94		38		
18			"	2	· 9 1	119		8 3 4 3 2 · · ·	76			41	97		39	32	
22	"	10			8 3E 6 9 · 2 · 2 1	124		2 1	77			42	103		44	33	
26			"	3				4 4 7 · P :	83		M8	43					
29	"	11			· 6 E1 4 5 6 · 4 · ·	130	5				•Dropped c-b. 3HR	44	107		48		
34			"	4	: 4 :	133		7 · 1E 2 · 1	86			45	110			36	
39	"	12						3 3 3 3 · 6	92		M9	46					
42	(12-2-30-0)		"	5	4 2 · 4 · 4	139					M10	47					
46	LA BROOY	13	(5-2-10-0)		4 4 · 4 ⊙ · · ·	143		P 4 8E · · 1	95		(NB) NB 8	48	112			37	8
51			MADURASINGHE	4				: : : : 4 :	101		M11	49					
54	"	14			6 1	144		· PE 4 ⊙ · · P	107		(NB) NB 9	50	114		49		9
58	(14-3-31-0)		"	5	3 4 : · 1	148	6	: :	109	4	GOOCH'S 50: 205'	51	119	1	54	37	9
1.01	LUNCH		(5-2-10-0)								M11 NB9		LUNCH				
1.41	LABROOY	15			· : L 5(4) 3	152		· 4 ·	111			52	122		57		
45			MADURASINGHE	6	3/4 4 : 6 : 4 1	157	7	:	112			53	127		62		
48	"	16			: 2 1	159		3 3 3 3 4 · · 1	116	5		54	133		63	42	
52			"	7				4 : : : : 4	122		M12	55					
55	"	17			3 2 : 2 : · ⊙ ·	166					(NB) NB 10	56	138		67		10
59			"	8	: ·	168		7 2 : : 3 3	126		100 p'ship: 149'	57	143			47	
2.02	"	18						: : 4 9/8 · ⊙ : Y ·	133	6	(NB) NB 11 RUSSELL'S 50: 153'	58	148			51	11
07	(18-3-50-0)		"	9	3/4 : : : 4 1	173		:	134			59	149		68		
11	RATNAYEKE	16			3 · 7 6 2 3	179					M13 4HR	60					
15			"	10	6 1	180		6/7 4 : : 2 6 4 1	139	8		61	159		69	60	
19	"	17			4 4 : 2 6 4 1	185	8	4 1	140			62	165		74	61	
23			"	11	: 4 :	188		: 3 6 1	143			63	166			62	
26	"	18			:	189		: 3 6 1 3 2 1	148			64	169			65	
30			"	12	: x : 4/5 1	193		3 1 ·	150			65	171		75	66	
33	"	19			L W	194	8					65'	171	2	75	66	11
					BARNETT										0		
35	"	19			1 3	1		· 4 2 4	154			66	174		3		
39			"	13	x : : P P :	7					M14	67					
42	"	20			: : 2/3 1	10		6 3 4 1 :	157	9		68	180		4	71	
46			"	14	: : : : 8 2 P ·	16						69	182		6		
50	"	21	(14-4-36-0)		: : : 8 1	20		6 1 ·	159			70	184		7	72	
55			LABROOY	19	: 2 4 : 4 7 :	26	1					71	188		11		
2.59	(22-3-59-2)	22	(19-3-54-0)		7 1	27	1	x 4 2 7 1 2 :	164	9	M14 NB 11	72	190	2	12	73	11

2ND DAY	BOWLERS (CONSTANT) PAVILION END		(HOLDER) NURSERY END		BATSMEN SCOREBOARD LEFT			SCOREBOARD RIGHT			ENGLAND 1ST INNINGS	END-OF-OVER TOTALS					
TIME	BOWLER	O.	BOWLER	O.	SCORING	BALLS	6s/4s	SCORING	BALLS	6s/4s	NOTES	O.	RUNS	W.	'L' BAT	'R' BAT	EXTRAS
					BARNETT	27	1	RUSSELL	164	9	M14 NB11	72	190	2	12	73	11
3.03			LABROOY	20	134 6 5 ::·2:	33						73	192		14		
07	RATNAYEKE	23			P ·	34		3 3 ·:·:1	169			74	193			74	
11	(23-3-60-2)		"	21				2:434:	175		M15 5HR	75					
16	RAMANAYAKE	13			:7::⊙ 42 ·1	41					(NB) NB12 LEAD	76	195		15		12
21			"	22	46 41	43	2	4674 ·6·4	179	10		77	204		20	78	
26	"	14	(22-4-65-0)		3S 1 :2 2	47		4 ½ 41	181	11		78	212		23	83	
30			MADURASINGHE	15	P ::::	51		4 9 ·3	183			79	215			86	
34	"	15						4·2245	189		M16	80					
38	(15-3-40-0)		"	16	:::7 6/7 2:	57	2		189	11		81	217	2	25	86	12
3.41	TEA		(16-4-41-0)								M16 NB12			T	E	A	
4.00	RAMANAYAKE	16			L::EB7 4 1	62		4 1	190			82	219		26	87	
05			SAMARASEKERA	6	L::45P	68					M17	83					
08	"	17			46 ·::	71		::2 1	193		umpires discussed light.	84	220			88	
13	(17-3-43-0)		"	7	6 2	72		3 7E 2 2 3 ···21	198		50 p'ship: 80'	85	225		28	91	
17	RATNAYEKE	24	(7-3-15-0)		33 8 4½ ::2·1	77		†5(4) 1	199		† NEW BALL	86	229		31	92	
23			LABROOY	23	L:7 6 (1)	81		3 x 3 2⊙W	202	11	(NB)(NB) NB14	86⁵	233	3	32	94	13
27								LAMB								0	
29			"	23				† ·	1		† Beamer 6HR	87					
31	"	25			6 8 ··(4)1	85	3	7 4·⊙⊙·	6	1	(NB)(NB) NB17	88	244		37	4	15
37			"	24	7/6 334·6/7 2·44·1	91	5					89	255		48		
41	"	26			P 44 ··1	95		L:	8			90	256		49		
45			RAMANAYAKE	18	xP:6 6 ··1·	100		4 1	9		BARNETT'S 50: 114'	91	258		50	5	
50	"	27			·	101		8/7 6 ·1 6···1	14	1/1		92	265			12	
54			"	19				EB3 6 2 L3 ·····1	20			93	266			13	
58	"	28						x·xP4 2† ·····2	26		† 1 overthrow	94	268			15	
5.02			"	20	6E 1 4·	103		L:43 ···1	30			95	270		51	16	
07	"	29			5 2 2 ·21	106		6 1 3 :1	33			96	275		54	18	
11	(29-3-90-2)		"	21	L9P ·1·	109	5	:3 5S 1 ①	37	1/1	NB18	97	278	3	55	20	15
5.16	BLSP		(21-3-51-0)								M17		B	L	SP		
6.06	PLAY ABANDONED												STUMPS				
3RD DAY 11.02	RATNAYEKE	30			::·4S 1	113		3 6 1 3	39		50 p'ship: 51'	98	283		56	24	
06			RAMANAYAKE	22	Y x 3 3 :·4:	117	6	4 3S +·1	41		(W)	99	289		60	25	16
11	"	31			6S L26 1···	121		6 4S 1 1	43			100	292		61	27	
15			"	23	x3 ·:	123		7 :66 2··1	47		7HR	101	295			30	
19	"	32			6 2/3 ·4	125	7	P4 7½ ·4·1	51	1/2		102	304		65	35	
24	(32-3-107-2)		"	24	1 1	126		64 LB 68 ·(4)4·42	57	1/5	(LB) NB19	103	320		66	49	17
29	LABROOY	25	(24-3-75-0)		E1 W	127	7					103'	320	4	66	49	17
30					SMITH										0		
11.32	(25-4-84-2)	25			4 ··:4:	5	1		57	1/5	M17 NB19	104	324	4	4	49	17

3RD DAY	BOWLERS (CONSTANT) PAVILION END		(HOLDER) NURSERY END		BATSMEN SCOREBOARD LEFT			SCOREBOARD RIGHT			ENGLAND 1ST INNINGS	END-OF-OVER TOTALS					
TIME	BOWLER	O.	BOWLER	O.	SCORING	BALLS	6s/4s	SCORING	BALLS	6s/4s	NOTES TILLEKERATNE sub for RANAWAKE (hand)	O.	RUNS	W.	'L' BAT	'R' BAT	EXTRAS
					SMITH	5	1	LAMB	57	1/5	M17 NB 19	104	324	4	4	49	17
11.36			SAMARASEKERA	8	4 8 · 1	7		· : 2 8 1	61	1/5	LAMB's 50: 83'	105	326		5	50	
41	LABROOY	26			6 8 · 2 : : 3 8 1	13						106	329		8		
45			"	9	7 · 1 35 1	17		2/3 7/8 4 1	63	1/6	(NB) NB 21	107	336		10	55	
49	"	27			: x 4 3/2 · 3 ⊙ ⊙ ·	25					• Dr Madurasinghe (cover - to left) · (NB)	108	338				19
54			"	10	: 7 P : 3 2	30		2 1	64			109	342		13	56	
58	"	28			: 2 7 : · ·	36					M18	110					
12.02			"	11	: 9 1	38		x 4 · 1 · 3 1	68			111	345		14	58	
06	"	29			6 : 2	41		8 P 4 2 · 1	71			112	348			61	
11				12	: : 8 3 7 1	45		+ 1/2 1 2 1	73		(W) 8HR	113	355		18	63	20
15	"	30			7 3	46		x x · W	75	1/6		113³	358	5	21	63	20
17								PRINGLE								0	
19	"	30						6 : ·	3			114					
22			"	13	· 8 1	48		8/7 7 6 2 · ·	7			115	361		22	2	
25	"	31			15 : 4F 2/3 : 4 2	54						116	363		24		
29			"	14	· · 3 1	57		· : 4 1	10			117	365		25	3	
34	"	32			: : 1 · 5 1	62		S(4)F	11			118	367		26	4	
38	(32-5-99-3)		"	15	P :	64		3 : : 6 1	15			119	368			5	
42	RANATUNGA	1						4 : : : : L	21		M19	120					
46			"	16	· 8/7 3 · 4 4 : 1	69	2	5 :	22			121	373		31		
49	"	2			6X W	70	2					121¹	373	6	31	5	20
					EMBUREY										0		
51	"	2			· 3 : · ·	5					M20	122					
54			"	17				5(6) 6 4 6 4 · · · ·	28	1		123	377			9	
57	(3-3-0-1)	3	(17-3-53-0)		3 : : : : :	11	–		28	1	M21	124	377	6	0	9	20
1.00	LUNCH										M21 NB21		LUNCH				
1.40			SAMARASEKERA	18	: 1 : : :	16		4 1	29		Ranawake back.	125	378			10	
44	LABROOY	33						· : : x · 3	35		M22	126					
48			"	19	: 3 W	18	–					126²	378	7	0	10	20
49					NEWPORT										0		
51			"	19	· 4 : ·	4					M23	127					
53	"	34						6f 7 E1 ⊙ 4 W	38	2	(NB) NB 22	127²	383	8	0	14	21
54								FOSTER								0	
56	"	34			4 4 ·	6	1	1 : 1	2		9HR	128	388		4	1	
59			"	20				: : · 6 3 5 1	8		M24	129					
2.03	"	35			3 3 : 2/1 1 :	11		1/2 1	9			130	390		5	2	
07			"	21	· 4 3 4	14	2	: : 2 8 ② 1	13		NB 23	131	397		9	5	
11	"	36						3/2 · · 4 3	19		M25	132					
15			"	22	: 4 1 4 3	17		· 35 1 2 1	22			133	402		13	6	
2.19	(37-7-112-4)	37	(22-5-66-1)		· 3 · 3 1	21	2	2 :	24	–	M25 NB 23	134	403	8	14	6	21

3RD DAY	BOWLERS (CONSTANT) PAVILION END		(HOLDER) NURSERY END		BATSMEN SCOREBOARD LEFT			SCOREBOARD RIGHT			ENGLAND 1ST INNINGS NOTES	END-OF-OVER TOTALS					
TIME	BOWLER	O.	BOWLER	O.	SCORING	BALLS	6s/4s	SCORING	BALLS	6s/4s		O.	RUNS	W.	'L' BAT	'R' BAT	EXTRAS
					NEWPORT	21	2	FOSTER	24	-	M 25 NB 23	134	403	8	14	6	21
2.23			RANATUNGA	4	3 · 1	23		· · : ·	28			135	404		15		
26	LABROOY	38			3 : : 1	26		2 3 : 2 ·	31			136	407		16	8	
31	(38-7-115-4)		"	5	4 3 9 : · 3	29		7 4 · : :	34			137	410		19		
34	RAMANAYAKE	25			1E 4F 1 1	31		6 4 7 : 1 · ·	38			138	413		21	9	
39			"	6	3 4 4 1 · ·	34		4 5 6S · • 1	41		• NT c ✓b.	139	415		22	10	
42	"	26	(6-3-6-1)		2/3 3 · 8W 4 · W	38	3	4 4 1 · · (1)	44		NB 24	140	420	9	26	11	21
47					LAWRENCE						crossed.				0		
49			LABROOY	39	3 x · 3 x 2 2 · · · · 1	6						141	423		3		
53	"	27			6 8 LB 1	8		7 4 1 : · :	48		(LB) 10 HR	142	426		4	12	22
58			"	40	6 B 4 · · ·	11		4 3 : · 1	51		(B)	143	428			13	23
3.02	" (27.2-3-86-2)	28	(40-7-119-4)		6 W	12	-	3 1	52	-		143[2]	429	10	4	14	23
3.03	ALL OUT										M 25 NB 24		ALL		OUT		
											884 balls						

David 'Syd' Lawrence begins his Test career with a spell of awesome ferocity.

3RD DAY	BOWLERS (HOLDER) PAVILION END		(CONSTANT) NURSERY END		BATSMEN SCOREBOARD LEFT			SCOREBOARD RIGHT			SRI LANKA 2ND INNINGS	END-OF-OVER TOTALS					
TIME	BOWLER	O.	BOWLER	O.	SCORING	BALLS	6s/4s	SCORING	BALLS	6s/4s	NOTES	O.	RUNS	W.	'L' BAT	'R' BAT	EXTRAS
					KURUPPU			SILVA									
3.15	FOSTER	1			8 5(4) ·43	3	1	···	3			1	7		7		
19			LAWRENCE	1	7 4LB 5/4 2··4·	9	2				(4LB)	2	17		13		4
24	"	2						·9 2 2· ·4···	9	1		3	21			4	
28			"	2	⊙·····P	16					(NB) NB 1	4	22				5
33	"	3						·P 2 1· ······	15		M1	5					
36	(3-1-11-0)		"	3	2 P 2 x 76 ······	22					M2 NB1	6	22	-	13	4	5
3.40	TEA		(3-1-7-0)											T	E	A	
4.00	FOSTER	4						x x P x x ······	21		M3	7					
04			NEWPORT	1	6 4 3 1 4·4··4	28	5					8	34		25		
09	"	5						1 P · ↑ · ······	27		M4	9					
12			"	2	LB ·	29		P 1 2 ··44·	32	3	(LB)	10	43			12	6
16	"	6			:↑7 :W	31	5					10[2]	43	1	25	12	6
17					SAMARASEKERA										0		
20	"	6			8· ·····	4					M5	11					
22			"	3				P· ······	38		M6	12					
26	"	7			6 : ↑ 3 ···1	8		2 ·4	40	4		13	48		1	16	
29			"	4	P5 6 ··.3	12		E1/9 W	41	4		13[5]	51	2	4	16	6
32								DE SILVA								0	
35			"	4				·	1		1HR	14					
36	"	8			··8 ···1	16		2 9E ·2	3			15	54		5	2	
40			"	5	··· 5(4) 6· ···4··	22	1					16	58		9		
44	"	9						··L 8·↑x ······	9		M7	17					
48			"	6	3· 6·· ······	28					M8	18					
52	"	10			9 1 :	30		·7 :8 ·1 :1	13			19	61		10	4	
56			"	7	9 1	31		··:·7 ····1	18			20	63		11	5	
59	"	11	(7-2-29-1)		x↑8 5↑8↑9 ··4·64	37	1/3					21	77		25		
5.03			PRINGLE	1	6 5 6 ···1	41		5 1 :	20			22					
07	"	12			P↑ ↑ P·· ······	47					† Hit on box. M9	23					
13			"	2	1 L 4··	50	1/4	··9 ··1	23			24					
16	(12.5-6-44-1)	13	(2-0-7-0)			50	1/4	4 7 6† ··44·	28	2	† all run	24[5]	92	2	30	15	6
5.20	BLSP										M9		B	L	S	P	
6.15	PLAY ABANDONED												STUMPS				
4TH DAY 11.00	FOSTER	13						2 :	29			25					
01	(13-6-44-1)		NEWPORT	8	L 1E · 8EP ···1 :	55		6 3	30			26	96		31	18	
06	LAWRENCE	4						L W	31	2		26[1]	96	3	31	18	6
								MADUGALLE								0	
08	"	4						3 8 ::42·	5	1		27	102			6	
12			"	9	x x · ······	61					M10 2HR	28					
11.16	(5-1-14-1)	5	(9-3-33-1)			61	1/4	··3 1 ↑ ···⊙·	12	1	• Low to 3rd slip (LAMB) (NB) M10 NB2	29	103	3	31	6	7

4TH DAY	BOWLERS (HOLDER) PAVILION END		(CONSTANT) NURSERY END		BATSMEN SCOREBOARD LEFT			SCOREBOARD RIGHT			SRI LANKA 2ND INNINGS NOTES	END-OF-OVER TOTALS					
TIME	BOWLER	O.	BOWLER	O.	SCORING	BALLS	6s/4s	SCORING	BALLS	6s/4s		O.	RUNS	W.	'L' BAT	'R' BAT	EXTRAS
					SAMARASEKERA	61	1/4	MADUGALLE	12	1	M 10 NB 2	29	103	3	31	6	7
11.21			NEWPORT	10	4	67					M 11	30					
24	LAWRENCE	6						. . . x . .	18		M 12	31					
29			"	11	. 6 P . . .	73					M 13	32					
33	"	7	(11-5-33-1)		P 7 6 1 . . ⊙ 3	77		6 ③ . 8 1	22		(NB) NB 4	33	111		34	10	8
39			FOSTER	14				. P 2 4 . . 3	28	2	PRINGLE off – 4 overs sub: A. van Lindt (MCC)	34	115			14	
43	"	8			9 4 . 4 3	80	1/5	. . .	31			35	122		41		
47			"	15	L . . 6 3	84		2/3 . 4	33	3		36	129		44	18	
52	"	9			† 6s 1	86		. . 6 .	37			37	130		45		
57			"	16	1 † 3s 4 . 1	89	1/6	P 3 . .	40		SAMARASEKERA's 50: 118'	38	135		50		
12.01	"	10	(16-6-60-1)		. . . 2 4 x 2 ⊙	96					(NB) NB 5	39	138		52		9
06	(10-2-33-1)		EMBUREY	1				4 . . 2 . 4	46		M 14	40					
09	FOSTER	17			7 x . 6 . 1	100		. .	48			41	139		53		
13			"	2	P . P 4 . 2/3 4	106	1/7				3 HR	42	143		57		
16	"	18						5(6) x 2 W	50	3		42²	145	4	57	20	9
17								RANATUNGA		LHB						0	
19	"	18						. . †4‡ 2	4		† box ‡ 1 overthrow	43	147			2	
23			"	3	x 6 6 L W	110	1/7					43⁴	147	5	57	2	9
24					MENDIS										0		
26			"	3	. .	2					M 15	44					
27	"	19						3 . . x 4	10		M 16	45					
31			"	4	7 8 . 1	4		P . . .	14			46	148		1		
34	"	20			† . 4 P . x	10					M 17	47					
38			"	5				. . . . P	20		M 18	48					
40	"	21			3 . 4† 1 . . 1	14		3 3	22		† Appeal ct wk (leg side)	49	149		2		
44			"	6	. . 9 ! . . 2	20						50	151		4		
47	"	22	(6-3-7-1)		1 7 4 2	22	1	. . 6 1	26			51	158		10	3	
51			NEWPORT	12	. . . P	26		P LB	28		(LB) M 19	52	159				10
55	"	23			† x † . x	31		6 1	29			53	160			4	
59	(23-8-74-2)		"	13	3 . . P	36	1	9 1	30	-		54	161	5	10	5	10
1.02	LUNCH		(13-6-34-1)								M 19 NB 5		LUNCH				
1.41	LAWRENCE	11			. . 4	39		3 2 . 8 ③	34		NB 6	55	164			8	
47			EMBUREY	7				. . . . P .	40		M 20	56					
49	"	12			4 . 3 5(6) 4 . ⊙ 2 3	44		4 . .	42		(NB) NB 7 4 HR	57	170		15		11
54			"	8	. 6 4	50	2					58	174		19		
57	"	13						. 3 4 x 4 7	48		M 21	59					
2.01			"	9	. . 5(6) ① .	54		† . L 9 . 1	51		† Round wkt NB 8	60	176		20	9	
04	"	14						x 7 2 3† 4 . .	57	1	† over cover (Barnett)	61	180			13	
08			"	10	. 7 . 1 . .	58		P 1 . 1	59			62	182		21	14	
2.11	(15-3-55-1)	15	(10-4-15-1)		9 3 4 4 . .	61	3	2 2 8 ④ . 1	63	2	NB 9 M 21	63	191	5	25	19	11

4TH DAY TIME	BOWLERS (HOLDER) PAVILION END BOWLER	O.	(CONSTANT) NURSERY END BOWLER	O.	BATSMEN SCOREBOARD LEFT SCORING	BALLS	6s/4s	SCOREBOARD RIGHT SCORING	BALLS	6s/4s	SRI LANKA 2ND INNINGS NOTES very dark cloud	END-OF-OVER TOTALS O.	RUNS	W.	'L' BAT	'R' BAT	EXTRAS
					MENDIS	61	3	RANATUNGA	63	2	NB 9 M21	63	191	5	25	19	11
2.17			EMBUREY	11	: :	63		: 4 . LB	67		(LB) M22	64	192				12
20	LAWRENCE	16						: 3 8 : 2 : 20 : :	74		(NB) NB 10	65	195			21	13
25	(16-3-58-1)		"	12	8 1	64		: : 9 2 : 2 3	79		50 p'ship: 82'	66	201		26	26	
29	NEWPORT	14			7/8 2 . 5(6) 4 : :	68	4	9S 1 8 2	81			67	209		31	29	
34			"	13	7 6 6 6 7/8 7 4 4 : :	74	6					68	217		39		
37	"	15	(13-5-29-1)					x 6/7 2† x . 4 . 4	87	4	† over gully.	69	225			37	
41			PRINGLE	3	3 : 1 P 6 4 : 2 : 1	80						70	228		42		
45	"	16			7 : 3 1E†8 : 4 1	85	7	.	88		† over 2nd slip	71	233		47		
49			"	4	8 1 4 2 . 4	88	8	: : 9† 3	91		† Deficit removed. MENDIS 50: 109' 5HR	72	241		52	40	
54	"	17			.	89		. . 3/2 5† 4E 4 . 1	96	5	† Hit stumps (bowler's)	73	246			45	
58			"	5				3 x 4E : :	102		M23	74					
3.01	"	18			: 6 4 . 1	93		: .	104		100 p'ship: 119'	75	247		53		
05	(18-6-61-1)		"	6	6 9 8L . 2W	98	8	LB .	105		(LB)	76	251	6	56	45	14
08					RATNAYEKE		LHB				sunny				0		
11	EMBUREY	14						: P : 6 2 :	111		M24	77					
13			"	7	x : : : : 4	6					M25	78					
16	"	15			: :	8		: P 9 3S 4 1	115	6		79	256			50	
20			"	8				: : . . : 1	121			80	257			51	
23	"	16						: : : : : :	127		M26	81					
26			"	9	. x . 2 1	12		: 7	129			82	258		1		
29	"	17			: : : 2 : :	18					M27	83					
31			"	10				5(6) x . 5† 6 8 4 . . . 1	135	7	† Hit bowler's stumps.	84	263			56	
35	"	18						: : : 2 :	141		M28	85					
38	(18-9-34-1)		"	11	2 1 P :	21	-	: . 1/2 1	144	7		86	265	6	2	57	14
3.41	TEA		(11-2-30-1)								M28 NB 10			T	E	A	
4.00	FOSTER	24						†. 8 P . 3/4 2 . 1	150		† NEW BALL	87	268			60	
05			LAWRENCE	17				x . 6 . 6 7	156		M29	88					
09	"	25			: : . 4 . :	27	1				6HR	89	272		6		
14			"	18	. 1 (1)(0)	29		. 7 . . 4 (1) 4 . 4	163	8	(NB) NB 13	90	279		7	65	15
20	"	26			: x 4 . 3	35					M30	91					
24			"	19				2E† 7 . 5†8 7 3 4	169	9	† Just short of gully (LAMB). ‡ Hit stumps.	92	283			69	
29	"	27	(19-4-69-1)		4 3 5 1/2 4 1	40		2 1	170			93	285		8	70	
38			NEWPORT	19	1P . 3 L . 2 .	45		†7S 1	171		† Ball changed.	94	288		10	71	
43	"	28			4/5 2† 4 . . 1	49	2	1E 1 P	173		• Narrow hit cut to gully's right (BARNETT)	95	294		15	72	
47			"	20	4 T 7/8 4 : 2 2 .	55						96	298		19		
51	"	29			†7S 1	56		3 9 4 1 . : .	178	10	50 p'ship: 81'	97	304		20	77	
55			"	21	P 4 3 : 7 1	60		P 9 . 1	180			98	309		24	78	
59	"	30			. . . † . :	66					† Round wkt. M31	99					
5.04	(30-10-95-2)		(22-6-74-2)	22		66	2	x W	181	10	M31 NB 13	99'	309	7	24	78	15

4TH DAY	BOWLERS (HOLDER) PAVILION END		(CONSTANT) NURSERY END		BATSMEN SCOREBOARD LEFT			SCOREBOARD RIGHT			SRI LANKA 2ND INNINGS NOTES	END-OF-OVER TOTALS					
TIME	BOWLER	O.	BOWLER	O.	SCORING	BALLS	6s/4s	SCORING	BALLS	6s/4s	NOTES	O.	RUNS	W.	'L' BAT	'R' BAT	EXTRAS
					RATNAYEKE	66	2	MADURASINGHE	-	LHB	M31 NB13	99[1]	309	7	24	0	15
5.07			NEWPORT	22				4 4 : : ½ 1	5			100	310			1	
10	FOSTER	31			† 2 :	68		x 3 : 1	9		† Round wkt 7HR	101	311			2	
14			〃	23				x x : W	11	-		101[2]	311	8	24	2	15
15								LAMBRODY								0	
17			〃	23	: 6 ½E 4	71	3	6	1			102	316		28	1	
20	〃	32			:	72		T : P x 8 1	6			103	317			2	
25			〃	24	: T 4 P P 4	77	4	S(4) 1	7			104	322		32	3	
29	〃	33			†G : : :	81		· 1	9		† Round wkt	105	323			4	
34	(33-10-98-2)		〃	25				6 : 3 x x4	15		M32	106					
38	LAWRENCE	20			: : 3E E1 W	85	4					106[4]	323	9	32	4	15
40					RAMANAYAKE										0		
42	〃	20			Y x	2					M33	107					
44			〃	26	x x 3 4 x	7		7S 1	16			108	324			5	
48	〃	21						: : 3 (·) : 1E 4	23	1	(NB) NB14	109	329			9	16
53	(21-5-74-2)		〃	27	8/7 E1 · 2 W	10	-		23	1		109[3]	331	10	2	9	16
5.55	ALL OUT		(26.3-7-87-4)								M33 NB14		ALL OUT				
											671 balls						

4TH DAY	BOWLERS (HOLDER) PAVILION END		(CONSTANT) NURSERY END		BATSMEN SCOREBOARD LEFT			SCOREBOARD RIGHT			ENGLAND 2ND INNINGS	END-OF-OVER TOTALS					
TIME	BOWLER	O.	BOWLER	O.	SCORING	BALLS	6s/4s	SCORING	BALLS	6s/4s	NOTES	O.	RUNS	W.	'L' BAT	'R' BAT	EXTRAS
					GOOCH			ROBINSON			Tillekeratne sub for Ramanayake						
6.04	LABROOY	1			6 6 8 . . . . . ⊙	7					(NB) NB 1	1	1				1
08			RATNAYEKE	1				7 . . 4 1 . . . 4 .	6	1		2	5			4	
12	" (2-0-4-0)	2	(1-0-4-0)		6 1	8	-	4 . . . 5 P 7 ⊙⊙ 1	13	1	(NB)(NB) NB 3	3	8	-	1	4	3
6.17	STUMPS										M - NB3	STUMPS					
5TH DAY 11.00			RATNAYEKE	2	4 1	9		. . 6P . 4	18			4	9		2		
05	LABROOY	3			. P 8BP 1	12		. P L ⊙	22		(NB) NB 4	5	11		3		4
09			"	3	. . . . 4 4	18					M 1	6					
13	"	4						6P L . 2LB 9 4 . . . . 2 .	28		(2LB)	7	15			6	6
17			"	4	6 . . 6 1	22		. .	30			8	16		4		
21	"	5			8 1E 4 . 6 . 2 . . .	28						9	18		6		
24			"	5	L 2LB 6 . 4 . .	33		7 1	31		(2LB)	10	21			7	8
28	"	6						. . . 3 . 4 .	37		(W)	11	22				9
32			"	6	5(4) 4 7 5LB	37	1	6 . 1	39		(LB)	12	28		10	8	10
37	"	7						8 4 7 6 8 X . 2 . 2 . . .	45			13	32			12	
41			"	7	. . 2 4 2LB 3 4	43	2				(2LB) 1HR	14	38		14		12
45	"	8	(7-1-16-0)		7 1	44		. 3S P 8 1 . 2 .	50			15	42		15	15	
49			SAMARASEKERA	1	. . 2 1	47		5 . 4 . 4	53		(W)	16	44		16		13
53	"	9			. 4 7 6 (4) 1	51	3	. 4 3 .	56		NB 5	17	49		21		
57	(9-0-24-0)		"	2	3 1	52		8 4 2 . . .	61		50 p'ship: 70'	18	52		22	17	
12.01	RANATUNGA	1			3 1	53		. X . . .	66			19	53		23		
04			"	3	3 1 7 4	55	4	. 4 3S 1	70			20	59		28	18	
08	"	2						 4	76		M2	21					
11			"	4	. 5 6 1 6 7 . . . 2 .	61						22	61		30		
14	"	3						3 L 7 7 4 . . . . 1 .	82		M3	23					
16			"	5	5(4) 6 3 . . 1	64		. 4 .	85		† Diving stop (MADUGALLE)	24	62		31		
20	"	4			4 . 4 3 1 1 4	69	5	3S 1	86			25	68		36	19	
22			"	6	E1 W	70	5	6 3S . 4 1	88	2		25^3	73	1	36	24	13
24					BARNETT										0		
26			"	6	L E1 W	2	-					25^5	73	2	0	24	13
27					LAMB										0		
28			"	6	:	1						26					
29	"	5						. . 2/3 . 3 .	94		M4	27					
32			"	7	4 3 3 8 4 . . . . 2 .	7						28	75		2		
36	"	6			4 . 3S 1	10		4 3 . 1 .	97			29	77		3	25	
39			"	8	3 X 5(6) 3 . . 4 1	14	1	P . .	99			30	82		8		
43	"	7			7 W	15	1					30^1	82	3	8	25	13
					SMITH										0		
45	"	7			2/2	5					M5 2HR	31					
48			"	9	LB	6	-	. 1 1E 3S 3 . 4 1	104	3	(LB)	32	88	3		30	14
52	"	8			. . L . 8 1	12						33	89		1		
56	(8-4-10-1)		"	10	6 3	13	-	6 5(6) 7 2 6 . 4 . . .	109	4		34	96	3	4	34	14
1.00	LUNCH		(10-0-38-2)								M5 NB5	LUNCH					
1.40	RANATUNGA	9			. . . 3 4	17	1		109	4	M5 NB5	34^4	100	3	8	34	14
1.41	(8-4-4-14-1) ENGLAND WON BY 7 WICKETS										213 balls						

SRI LANKA 1ST INNINGS v. ENGLAND (ONLY TEST) at LORD'S, LONDON on 25, 26, 27, 29, 30 AUGUST, 1988.

IN	OUT	MINS	No.	BATSMAN	HOW OUT	BOWLER	RUNS	WKT	TOTAL	6s	4s	BALLS	NOTES ON DISMISSAL (TOSS: ENGLAND)
11.01	12.20	79	1	D.S.B.P. KURUPPU	CT GOOCH	NEWPORT	46	3	52	.	6	58	Edged back-foot push to 2nd slip
11.01	11.29	28	2	S.A.R. SILVA †	CT RUSSELL	FOSTER	1	1	7	.	.	22	Edged off-drive.
11.31	12.05	34	3	M.A.R. SAMARASEKERA	CT RUSSELL	FOSTER	0	2	44	.	.	19	Edged off-drive at widish ball.
12.08	12.30	22	4	P.A. DE SILVA	CT GOOCH	NEWPORT	3	4	53	.	.	18	Edged outswinger to 2nd slip.
12.22	12.44	22	5	R.S. MADUGALLE*	LBW	FOSTER	3	5	61	.	.	14	Hit across line – 'plumb'.
12.32	12.51	19	6	A. RANATUNGA	LBW	NEWPORT	5	6	63	.	1	12	Pushed across line – beaten by swing.
12.46	2.36	70	7	L.R.D. MENDIS	CT SMITH	LAWRENCE	21	7	122	.	3	43	Skied edged drive to third man – held low.
12.53	(4.48)	176	8	J.R. RATNAYEKE	NOT OUT		59			.	9	112	3rd fifty in Tests.
2.38	2.47	9	9	A.W.R. MADURASINGHE	RUN OUT (LAWRENCE)		4	8	127	.	.	11	Run out by bowler following through – direct throw.
2.49	3.01	12	10	C.P.H. RAMANAYAKE	LBW	PRINGLE	0	9	130	.	.	8	Late on breakback.
3.03	4.48	86	11	G.F. LABROOY	LBW	PRINGLE	42	10	194	.	6	83	Slower ball – missed hit towards mid-wicket. HS in TESTS
				EXTRAS	b 1 lb 7	w - nb 2	10			.6	25	400 balls (including 5 no-balls).	

* CAPTAIN † WICKET-KEEPER

TOTAL (65.5 OVERS; 288 MINUTES) 194 ALL OUT at 4.48 pm on first day.

13 OVERS 4 BALLS/HOUR
2.94 RUNS/OVER
48 RUNS/100 BALLS

UMPIRES: D.J. CONSTANT and J.W. HOLDER

BOWLER	O	M	R	W	nb
FOSTER	21	5	51	3	.
LAWRENCE	15	4	37	1	.
NEWPORT	21	4	77	3	4
PRINGLE	6.5	1	17	2	1
EMBUREY	2	1	4	0	.
			8	1	
	65.5	15	194	10	

HRS	OVERS	RUNS
1	14	36
2	12	33
3	14	54
4	13	35

RUNS	MINS	OVERS	LAST 50 (in mins)
50	78	18	78
100	140	31.1	62
150	219	49	79

	Score	Overs / Minutes	Not out
LUNCH:	69-6	26 OVERS, 119 MINUTES	MENDIS 3* (14'), RATNAYEKE 4* (7')
TEA:	184-9	61 OVERS, 270 MIN	RATNAYEKE 59* (158'), LABROOY 34* (63')

‡ RECORD SRI LANKAN 10TH-WICKET PARTNERSHIP IN ALL TESTS (previously 60 v N.Z.)

WKT	PARTNERSHIP		RUNS	MINS
1st	Kuruppu	Silva	7	28
2nd	Kuruppu	Samarasekera	37	34
3rd	Kuruppu	De Silva	8	12
4th	De Silva	Madugalle	1	8
5th	Madugalle	Ranatunga	8	12
6th	Ranatunga	Mendis	2	5
7th	Mendis	Ratnayeke	59	63
8th	Ratnayeke	Madurasinghe	5	9
9th	Ratnayeke	Ramanayake	3	12
10th	Ratnayeke	Labrooy	64‡	86
			194	

ENGLAND 1ST INNINGS (IN REPLY TO SRI LANKA'S 194 ALL OUT)

IN	OUT	MINS	No.	BATSMAN	HOW OUT	BOWLER	RUNS	WKT	TOTAL	6s	4s	BALLS	NOTES ON DISMISSAL
4.59	2.33	259	1	G.A. GOOCH *	LBW	RATNAYEKE	75	2	171	·	8	194	Played across line – 1 run short of 2,000 for season (f-c).
4.59	6.14	75	2	R.T. ROBINSON	CT SAMARASEKERA	RATNAYEKE	19	1	40	·	1	58	Swatted bouncer to mid-wicket – took eyes off ball.
6.16	4.27	277	3	R.C. RUSSELL †	CT SAMARASEKERA	LABROOY	94	3	233	·	11	202	'NIGHTWATCHMAN'. HS in F.C CRICKET. Sliced drive to cover. Gentle skier.
2.35	11.30	170	4	K.J. BARNETT	CT RANATUNGA	LABROOY	66	4	320	·	7	127	Edged off-drive to 1st slip – away-seamer moved up slope.
4.29	12.17	122	5	A.J. LAMB	BOWLED	LABROOY	63	5	358	1	6	75	Beaten by slower ball floated 'through gate'.
11.32	12.49	78	6	R.A. SMITH	BOWLED	RANATUNGA	31	6	373	·	2	70	Played on – edged square-drive at ball 18" wide of wicket.
12.19	1.54	55	7	D.R. PRINGLE	CT SILVA	LABROOY	14	8	383	·	2	38	Edged away-seamer.
12.51	1.49	18	8	J.E. EMBUREY	CT DE SILVA	SAMARASEKERA	0	7	378	·	·	18	Drilled short, midish ball to cover.
1.51	2.47	56	9	P.J. NEWPORT	CT DE SILVA	RAMANAYAKE	26	9	420	·	3	38	Hooked short ball to long-leg.
1.56	(3.03)	67	10	N.A. FOSTER	NOT OUT		14			·	·	52	
2.49	3.03	14	11	D.V. LAWRENCE	CT MENDIS	RAMANAYAKE	4	10	429	·	·	12	Drove to mid-on.
				EXTRAS	b 1 lb 3	w 2 nb 17	23			1	40	884 balls (including 24 no-balls).	
				TOTAL	(143.2 OVERS; 604 MINUTES)		429						All out at 3.03 pm on third day.

* CAPTAIN † WICKET-KEEPER

14 OVERS 1 BALLS/HOUR
2.99 RUNS/OVER
48 RUNS/100 BALLS

BOWLER	O	M	R	W	nb/w
RATNAYEKE	32	3	107	2	5/-
LABROOY	40	7	119	4	12/-
RAMANAYAKE	27.2	3	86	2	6/1
MADURASINGHE	16	4	41	0	-
SAMARASEKERA	22	5	56	1	1/1
RANATUNGA	6	3	6	1	-
			4		
	143.2	25	429	10	

2ND NEW BALL taken at 4.17 pm on 2nd day – ENGLAND 225-2 after 85 overs.

HRS	OVERS	RUNS
1	15	35
2	15	27
3	14	45
4	16	42
5	15	44
6	12	40
7	14	62
8	12	60
9	15	33
10	14	38

RUNS	MINS	OVERS	LAST 50 (in mins)
50	94	24.2	94
100	170	4.4	76
150	241	60.1	71
200	308	76.2	67
250	366	88.3	58
300	422	101.4	56
350	473	112.1	51
400	559	132.5	86

STUMPS (1ST DAY):	47-1	22 OVERS 86 MIN	GOOCH 24* (86') RUSSELL 2* (9')
LUNCH:	119-1	51 OVERS 207 MIN	GOOCH 54* (207') RUSSELL 37* (130')
TEA:	217-2	81 OVERS 327 MIN	RUSSELL 86* (250') BARNETT 25* (66')
STUMPS (2ND DAY):	278-3 (84 AHEAD)	97 OVERS 403 MIN	BARNETT 55* (142') LAMB 20* (47')
LUNCH:	377-6	124 OVERS 521 MIN	PRINGLE 9* (41') EMBUREY 0* (9')

235 LEAD

WKT	PARTNERSHIP		RUNS	MINS
1st	Gooch	Robinson	40	75
2nd	Gooch	Russell	131	182
3rd	Russell	Barnett	62	93
4th	Barnett	Lamb	87	75
5th	Lamb	Smith	38	45
6th	Smith	Pringle	15	30
7th	Pringle	Emburey	5	18
8th	Pringle	Newport	5	3
9th	Newport	Foster	37	51
10th	Foster	Lawrence	9	14
			429	

SRI LANKA 2ND INNINGS (235 RUNS BEHIND ON FIRST INNINGS)

IN	OUT	MINS	No.	BATSMAN	HOW OUT	BOWLER	RUNS	WKT	TOTAL	6s	4s	BALLS	NOTES ON DISMISSAL
3.15	4.17	42	1	D.S.B.P. KURUPPU	CT BARNETT	FOSTER	25	1	43	·	5	31	Fended lifting ball to short square-leg.
3.15	4.32	57	2	S.A.R. SILVA †	CT RUSSELL	NEWPORT	16	2	51	·	4	41	Edged off-drive low to 'keeper's left.
4.20	12.24	144	3	M.A.R. SAMARASEKERA	LBW	EMBUREY	57	5	147	1	7	110	Missed sweep at 'arm' ball.
4.35	11.06	51	4	P.A. DE SILVA	LBW	LAWRENCE	18	3	96	·	2	31	Played across Lawrence's first ball of fourth day.
11.08	12.17	69	5	R.S. MADUGALLE*	BOWLED	FOSTER	20	4	145	·	3	50	Played back to ball which clipped off stump.
12.19	5.04	227	6	A. RANATUNGA	BOWLED	NEWPORT	78	7	309	·	10	181	1st SRI LANKAN to score 1,500 in Tests. Played on.
12.26	3.08	124	7	L.R.D. MENDIS	LBW	PRINGLE	56	6	251	·	8	98	Missed pull.
3.11	5.40	130	8	J.R. RATNAYEKE	CT LAMB	LAWRENCE	32	9	323	·	4	85	Edged lifting ball to third slip.
5.07	5.15	8	9	A.W.R. MADURASINGHE	BOWLED	NEWPORT	2	8	311	·	·	11	Late on inswinger - bowled through 'gate'.
5.17	(5.55)	38	10	G.F. LABROOY	NOT OUT		9			·	1	23	
5.42	5.55	13	11	C.P.H. RAMANAYAKE	CT GOOCH	NEWPORT	2	10	331	·	·	10	Edged lifting away seamer to 2nd slip.
				EXTRAS	b - lb 8	w - nb 8	16			1[6]	44[4]	671 balls (including 14 no-balls)	

* CAPTAIN † WICKET-KEEPER

TOTAL (109.3 OVERS; 462 MINUTES) 331. ALL OUT at 5.55pm on fourth day.

14 OVERS 1 BALLS/HOUR
3.02 RUNS/OVER
49 RUNS/100 BALLS

BOWLER	O	M	R	W	nb
FOSTER	33	10	98	2	-
LAWRENCE	21	5	74	2	13
NEWPORT	26.3	7	87	4	·
PRINGLE	11	2	30	1	·
EMBUREY	18	9	34	1	1
			8		
	109.3	33	331	10	

2ND NEW BALL taken at 4.00pm on 4th day - SRI LANKA 265-6 after 86 overs.

HRS	OVERS	RUNS
1	14	51
2	14	51
3	14	41
4	15	27
5	15	71
6	17	31
7	12	39

RUNS	MINS	OVERS	LAST 50 (in mins)
50	56	13.4	56
100	115	26.4	59
150	210	49.3	95
200	275	66	65
250	314	75.5	39
300	398	96.1	84

TEA: 22-0	6 OVERS 25 MINUTES	KURUPPU 13* SILVA 4*
STUMPS (3RD DAY): 92-2	24.5 OVERS 105 MIN	SAMARASEKERA 30*(60') DE SILVA 15*(45')
LUNCH: 161-5 (74 BEHIND)	54 OVERS 227 MIN	RANATUNGA 5*(43') MENDIS 10*(36')
TEA: 265-6	86 OVERS 347 MIN	RANATUNGA 57*(163') RATNAYEKE 2*(30')

WKT	PARTNERSHIP		RUNS	MINS
1st	Kuruppu	Silva	43	42
2nd	Silva	Samarasekera	8	12
3rd	Samarasekera	De Silva	45	51
4th	Samarasekera	Madugalle	49	69
5th	Samarasekera	Ranatunga	2	5
6th	Ranatunga	Mendis	104	124
7th	Ranatunga	Ratnayeke	58	94
8th	Ratnayeke	Madurasinghe	2	8
9th	Ratnayeke	Labrooy	12	23
10th	Labrooy	Ramanayake	8	13
			331	

ENGLAND 2ND INNINGS — REQUIRING 97 RUNS TO WIN OFF 98 OVERS (MINIMUM).

IN	OUT	MINS	No.	BATSMAN	HOW OUT	BOWLER	RUNS	WKT	TOTAL	6s	4s	BALLS	NOTES ON DISMISSAL
6.04	12.24	97	1	G.A. GOOCH *	Ct SILVA	SAMARASEKERA	36	1	73	·	5	70	Edged drive at widish ball.
6.04	(1.41)	134	2	R.T. ROBINSON	NOT OUT		34			·	4	109	
12.26	12.27	1	3	K.J. BARNETT	Ct SILVA	SAMARASEKERA	0	2	73	·	·	2	Edged push at outswinger.
12.28	12.43	15	4	A.J. LAMB	Ct DE SILVA	RANATUNGA	8	3	82	·	1	15	Clipped short ball to mid-wicket.
12.45	(1.41)	16	5	R.A. SMITH	NOT OUT		8			·	1	17	Made winning hit off fourth post-lunch ball.
			6										
			7										
			8										
			9										
			10										
			11										
				EXTRAS	b - lb 8	w 2 nb 4	14			·6	11 4s	213 balls (including 5 no-balls)	

* CAPTAIN † WICKET-KEEPER

TOTAL (34.4 OVERS; 134 MINUTES) 100-3

15 OVERS 3 BALLS/HOUR
2.88 RUNS/OVER
46 RUNS/100 BALLS

BOWLER	O	M	R	W	nb/w
LABROOY	9	0	24	0	5/1
RATNAYEKE	7	1	16	0	-
SAMARASEKERA	10	0	38	2	·
RANATUNGA	8.4	4	14	1	·
	34.4	5	8 100	3	

HRS	OVERS	RUNS
1	14	38
2	17	44

RUNS	MINS	OVERS	LAST 50 (in mins)
50	70	17.1	70
100	134	34.4	64

STUMPS: 8-0 (NEEDING 89 TO WIN) [3 OVERS, 13 MINUTES] GOOCH 1*, ROBINSON 4*

LUNCH: 96-3 (SCORES LEVEL) [34 OVERS, 133 MINUTES] ROBINSON 34* (133'), SMITH 4* (15')

ENGLAND WON BY 7 WICKETS OFF FOURTH POST-LUNCH BALL

ENDING SEQUENCE OF 18 TESTS WITHOUT A WIN (SINCE DECEMBER 1986).

FIRST HOME WIN SINCE 1985. FIRST LORD'S WIN SINCE 1983.

MEN OF THE MATCH: P.J. NEWPORT & J.R. RATNAYEKE

WKT	PARTNERSHIP		RUNS	MINS
1st	Gooch	Robinson	73	97
2nd	Robinson	Barnett	0	1
3rd	Robinson	Lamb	9	15
4th	Robinson	Smith	18*	16
			100	

EPILOGUE

Chronicle of a tour aborted · Summary of 1988 · Bottom of the World League · Grass roots · Surfeit of international cricket · Pitches

Graham Gooch was duly appointed captain for the eleven-week, five-Test tour of India. On Tuesday 6 September, exactly one week after leading England to victory against Sri Lanka, he joined Peter May's final selection committee in the TCCB conference room at Lord's to select his team. The following sixteen names were announced the next day: G. A. Gooch (captain), J. E. Emburey (vice-captain), R. J. Bailey, K. J. Barnett, J. H. Childs, G. R. Dilley, N. A. Foster, D. I. Gower, E. E. Hemmings, A. J. Lamb, D. V. Lawrence, P. J. Newport, S. J. Rhodes, R. T. Robinson, R. C. Russell and R. A. Smith.

Two days later, on the morning of Friday 9 September, an official in the Indian Foreign Ministry in New Delhi announced:

> We must make it abundantly clear that we would not permit entry into India for the purpose of the tour any player having, or likely to have, sporting contacts with South Africa.

The Board of Control for Cricket in India subsequently confirmed that visas would not be issued to the eight England tourists whose names appeared on the United Nations 'black list'. They were: Gooch, Emburey, Bailey, Barnett, Dilley, Lamb, Newport and Robinson.

After many deadlines, cables and attempts at negotiating a solution, the TCCB formally cancelled the tour on Friday 7 October. Their chief executive, Alan Smith, made the following statement:

> The TCCB is disappointed that members of its team, selected entirely in accordance with unanimously agreed International Cricket Conference rules, should find themselves ineligible for visas to enter India. This is particularly regrettable noting the impending special meeting of the ICC in January.

All sixteen members of the selected party had signed contracts expressly prohibiting them from playing anywhere without the Board's permission between 18 September and 15 April. In return they were to be paid an undisclosed proportion of their basic tour fee of £12,000.

The TCCB announced that it would 'seek other opponents for this winter, though it is accepted that with the congested programme already arranged this may not be easy'.

England's cricketers were left to await the special ICC meeting at Lord's on 23 January which would debate the thorny problem of their continued contact with South Africa.

Less than a year had passed since Gooch and Co. were being welcomed to India with open arms to take part in the highly lucrative Reliance World Cup. Whilst he was in Jaipur, Gooch purchased some diamonds for his wife from a jeweller, and asked where they came from. 'South Africa' was the answer. Marvellous thing, expediency.

Thus ended one of the most catastrophic years in the history of English cricket. Starting in the wake of a thoroughly abrasive and unpleasant tour of Pakistan, it ended with England's team virtually ostracized by the four non-white cricket powers and the future of integrated Test cricket in jeopardy.

The results of England's ten Tests of 1988 could be summed up as a drawn birthday bun-fight in Sydney, a stalemate series of unremitting tedium in New Zealand, a customary thrashing by West Indies, and finally the slim consolation of a hollow victory against a weak Sri Lankan team that had been starved of first-class, let alone Test cricket.

Graham Gooch, England's current captain. The Oval was saved but not the tour of India.

That victory brought to an end England's all-time record sequence of non-success but, as the accompanying table shows, even the West Indies have endured worse runs. Let us hope that England never threaten to eclipse the ultimate record set by New Zealand, who waited 26 years for their first win (against West Indies in Auckland).

Most Consecutive Matches Without Victory

44	New Zealand	Christchurch 1929-30 to Wellington 1955-56
31	India	Bangalore 1981-82 to Faisalabad 1984-85
28	South Africa	Leeds 1935 to Port Elizabeth 1949-50
24	India	Lord's 1932 to Kanpur 1951-52
23	New Zealand	Auckland 1962-63 to Dunedin 1967-68
22	Pakistan	Lahore 1958-59 to Christchurch 1964-65
20	West Indies	Wellington 1968-69 to Port-of-Spain 1972-73
18	New Zealand	Dacca 1969-70 to Wellington 1973-74
18	England	Sydney 1986-87 to The Oval 1988
16	South Africa	Melbourne 1910-11 to Cape Town 1921-22
16	Pakistan	Lord's 1967 to Wellington 1972-73

More relevant as a guide to England's standing in a league table of Test playing countries is an analysis of results during the past three years, from 4 September 1985 to 3 September 1988:

Test Match Results Since 1985

	Tests	Won	Lost	Tied	Drawn	% won	% lost
West Indies	23	13	4	–	6	56.5	17.3
Pakistan	25	8	3	–	14	32.0	12.0
New Zealand	19	5	3	–	11	26.3	15.7
India	24	5	3	1	15	20.8	12.5
Australia	22	4	5	1	12	18.1	22.7
Sri Lanka	15	2	7	–	6	13.3	46.6
England	34	3	15	–	16	8.8	44.1

Pro rata, England have the worst immediate record of any country; even Sri Lanka have managed a higher percentage of wins. In terms of series results during this period, England have won only one (Australia 1986-87), lost six and drawn one.

Many of England's problems could be laid at the feet of Peter May and his selection committee comprising Philip Sharpe, Micky Stewart and Fred Titmus. Their vacillation knew no bounds, with 32 players, including 10 new caps, being employed during 10 Tests. They were frequently divided in their views on discipline and choice of key personnel. Their ham-fisted handling of delicate situations and lack of communication with players is now legendary. With the creation of the office of a permanent team manager employed by the TCCB, the amateur post of chairman of selectors should have been abolished. If the committee structure is to be retained, it should include at least one and preferably two current senior county cricketers.

In the selectors' defence, one could argue that English cricket at all levels is at an extremely low ebb. County cricket is mortgaged by sponsors who have produced an excess of limited-overs matches. This pop-art version of a balanced, subtle game has destroyed technique and stifled individuality. Even the traditional domestic competition, the county championship, has degenerated into a hotchpotch of three- and four-day matches with some counties playing each other once and others twice. Club cricket is obsessed with league positions; mostly it is conducted under limited overs rules which promote negative bowling and discourage the building of an innings. Cricket in state schools is verging on non-existent, and it is declining in the fee-paying establishments too.

There is far too much international cricket. Winter schedules like that inflicted upon England in 1987-88 can only kill the spirit of players and produce tedium for spectators and correspondents. The ICC should apportion a reduced annual quota of Test and limited-overs internationals equally around the circuit of full member countries. England's compulsory rest during the 1988-89 winter must, through the law of scarcity, encourage greater interest in the forthcoming Ashes series.

The key to any game of cricket is the pitch, and many of the surfaces I saw on the county circuit in 1988 were a disgrace. I was delighted to learn that the TCCB plans to take positive action by deducting points from those counties who deliberately under-prepare playing surfaces. It is blatant cheating which can destroy the confidence of batsmen and produce a horde of automatic seamers who become cannon-fodder when they have to bowl on decent pitches. it does not require years of training to acquire the art of pitch preparation. One of the best batting surfaces of the season was produced for Glamorgan's three-day match against Worcestershire at Abergavenny. I asked the groundsman about his method. He had to find 90 pitches from his square each season; first he chose the best three to expend extra effort on, and, once he had selected the strip for the county match, he gave it 60 hours of rolling. He told me he had been groundsman at Abergavenny for four years and I asked where he had been before that. 'I was a long-distance lorry driver,' he revealed.

That match was won, like many others in the most successful season in the history of Worcestershire County Cricket Club, by a thunderous hundred from Graeme Ashley Hick. When other countries have a compulsory qualification period of four years, it seems ludicrous that the TCCB insists upon seven for a player of such genius who has no birth qualification for any full member of the ICC. How different England's fortunes might have been in 1988 had Hick and a fit and eager Botham been available.

REGISTER OF ENGLAND TEST CRICKETERS 1988

Details of the 16 England representatives who toured Australia and New Zealand are given on pages 17-20. Statistics for the remaining 16 players who appeared against West Indies and Sri Lanka are to the end of the 1988 English season. ★ denotes not out.

BAILEY, Robert John. Born Biddulph, Staffordshire 28 October 1963. 6ft 3in tall. Educated at Biddulph High School. Right-handed batsman who can bowl medium-paced seamers or off-breaks. Northamptonshire debut 1982; capped 1985. Represented Staffordshire 1980. Cricket Writers' Club Young Cricketer of 1984. One Test appearance against West Indies at The Oval in August 1988 (highest score 43). 1,000 runs in a season five times; most – 1,915 in 1986. Highest first-class score 224★ Northants *v*. Glamorgan (Swansea) 1986, best bowling 3-27 Northants *v*. Glamorgan (Wellingborough) 1988.

BARNETT, Kim John. Born Stoke-on-Trent, Staffordshire 17 July 1960. 6ft 1in tall. Educated at Leek High School. Right-handed opening batsman and leg-break bowler. Derbyshire debut 1979; cap 1982; captain since 1983. Represented Staffordshire 1976 and Boland from 1982-83 to 1987-88. One of *Wisden*'s Five Cricketers of 1988. One Test appearance against Sri Lanka at Lord's in August 1988 (highest score 66). Tours: New Zealand 1979-80 (D. H. Robins' XI); Sri Lanka 1985-86 (England B). 1,000 runs in a season six times; most – 1,734 in 1984. Highest first-class score 239★ Derbyshire *v*. Leics (Leicester) 1988; best bowling 6-115 Derbyshire *v*. Yorks (Bradford) 1985.

CHILDS, John Henry. Born Plymouth, Devon 15 August 1951. 6ft tall. Educated at Audley Park Secondary Modern School, Torquay. Orthodox left-arm slow bowler and left-handed tail-end batsman. Essex debut 1985; cap 1986. One of *Wisden*'s Five Cricketers of 1986. Represented Devon 1973-74 and Gloucestershire 1975-84 (cap 1977). 2 Test appearances against West Indies, making his debut at Old Trafford in June 1988; highest Test score 2★; best bowling 1-13. Highest first-class score 34★ Glos *v*. Notts (Cheltenham) 1982; best bowling 9-56 Glos *v*. Somerset (Bristol) 1981.

COWDREY, Christopher Stuart. Born Farnborough, Kent 20 October 1957. 6ft 1in tall. Educated at Tonbridge School. Right-handed all-rounder: middle-order batsman and medium-paced bowler. Brother of G. R. Cowdrey (Kent), son of M. C. Cowdrey (Kent and England 1950-76) and grandson of E. A. Cowdrey (Europeans). Kent debut 1977; cap 1979; captain since 1985. 6 Tests (1 as captain) making his debut against India at Bombay in November 1984. Highest Test score 38 *v*. India (Delhi) 1984-85; best bowling 2-65 *v*. India (Madras) 1984-85. Tours: New Zealand 1979-80 (D. H. Robins XI); India/Sri Lanka 1984-85; Sri Lanka 1977-78 (D. H. Robins' XI). 1,000 runs in a season three times; most – 1,364 in 1983. Highest first-class score 159 Kent *v*. Surrey (Canterbury) 1985. best bowling 5-46 Kent *v*. Hampshire (Canterbury) 1988.

CURTIS Timothy Stephen. born Chislehurst, Kent 15 January 1960. 5ft 11in tall. Educated at Worcester Royal Grammar School; Durham University; Magdalene College, Cambridge University. Right-handed opening batsman and very occasional leg-break bowler. Worcestershire debut 1979; cap 1984. Represented Cambridge University 1983 (blue). Two Test appearances against West Indies, making his debut at Headingley in July 1988; (highest score 30 at The Oval). 1,000 runs in a first-class season five times; most – 1,601 in 1987. Highest first-class score 153 Worcs *v*. Somerset (Worcester) 1986; best bowling 2-58 Cambridge U. *v*. Notts (Cambridge) 1983.

DOWNTON, Paul Rupert. Born Farnborough, Kent 4 April 1957. 5ft 10in tall. Educated at Sevenoaks School; Exeter University. Wicket-keeper, right-handed middle-order batsman and occasional off-break bowler. Son of G. C. Downton (Kent 1948). Played for Kent 1977-79 (cap 1979). Middlesex debut 1980; cap 1981. 30 Test appearances, making his debut against West Indies at Port-of-Spain in February 1981; highest Test score 74 *v*. India (Delhi) 1984-85. Tours: West Indies 1980-81, 1985-86; New Zealand 1977-78; India/Sri Lanka 1984-85; Pakistan 1977-78; Zimbabwe 1980-81 (Middlesex). 1,000 runs in a first-class season once: 1,120 in 1987. Highest first-class score 126★ Middlesex *v*. Oxford U. (Oxford) 1986.

GOOCH, Graham Alan. Born Leytonstone, Essex 23 July 1953. 6ft tall. Educated at Norlington Junior High School. World-class right-handed opening batsman, medium-paced outswing bowler. Essex debut 1973; cap 1975; benefit 1985; captain 1986-87. One of *Wisden*'s Five Cricketers of 1979. Represented Western province 1982-83 and 1983-84. 68 Test appearances (2 as captain), making his debut against Australia at Edgbaston in July 1975; highest Test score 196 *v*. Australia (The Oval) 1985; best bowling 2-12 *v*. India (Delhi) 1981-82. Tours: Australia 1978-79, 1979-80; South Africa 1981-82 (SA Breweries XI); West Indies 1980-81, 1985-86; India 1979-80, 1981-82; Sri Lanka 1981-82. 1,000 runs in a first-class season 12 times in UK and once overseas; most – 2,559 in 1984. Highest first-class score 275 Essex *v*. Kent (Chelmsford) 1988; best bowling 7-14 Essex *v*. Worcs (Ilford) 1982.

GOWER, David Ivon. Born Tunbridge Wells, Kent 1 April 1957. 6ft tall. Educated at Kings School, Canterbury; London University. World-class left-handed early-order batsman and eccentric off-break bowler. Leicestershire debut 1975; cap 1977; captain 1984-86 and 1988; benefit 1987. One of *Wisden*'s Five Cricketers of 1978. Cricket Writers' Club Young Cricketer of 1978. 100 Test appearances (26 as captain), making debut against Pakistan at Edgbaston in 1978 and scoring four off his first ball; highest test score 215 *v*. Australia (Edgbaston) 1985; best bowling 1-1. Tours (C = Captain): Australia 1978-79, 1979-80, 1982-83, 1986-87; West Indies 1980-81, 1985-86C; New Zealand 1983-84; India 1979-80, 1981-82, 1984-85C; Pakistan 1983-84; Sri Lanka 1977-78 (D. H. Robins' XI), 1981-82, 1984-85C. 1,000 runs in a first-class season eight times; most – 1,530 in 1982. Highest first-class score 215 (above); best bowling 3-47 Leics *v*. Essex (Leicester) 1977.

LAMB, Allan Joseph. Born Langebaanweg, Cape Province, South Africa 20 June 1954. 5ft 8in tall. Educated in South Africa at Wynberg High School; Abbotts College. Right-handed middle-order batsman and very occasional right-arm medium-pace bowler. Northamptonshire debut/cap 1978; benefit 1988. One of *Wisden*'s Five Cricketers of 1980. Represented Western Province 1972-73 to 1981-82, and Orange Free State 1987-88. 56 Test appearances, making his debut against India at Lord's in June 1982; highest Test score 137★ *v*. New Zealand (Trent Bridge) 1983; best bowling 1-6. Tours: Australia 1982-83, 1986-87; West Indies 1985-86; New Zealand 1983-84; India/Sri Lanka 1984-85; Pakistan 1983-84. 1,000 runs in a first-class season eight times; most – 2,049 in 1981. Highest first-class score 294 Orange Free State *v*. Eastern province (Bloemfontein) 1987-88; best bowling 1-1.

LAWRENCE, David Valentine ('Syd'). Born Gloucester 28 January 1964. 6ft 2in tall. Educated at Linden School. Right-handed fast bowler and tail-end batsman. Gloucestershire debut 1981; cap 1985. Cricket Writers' Club Young Cricketer of 1985. One Test appearance against Sri Lanka at Lord's in August 1988 (highest score 4; best bowling 2-74). Tours: Sri Lanka 1985-86 (England B); 1986-87 (Glos). Highest first-class score 65★ Glos *v*. Glamorgan (Swansea) 1987; best bowling 7-47 Glos *v*. Surrey (Cheltenham) 1988.

MAYNARD, Matthew Peter. Born Oldham, Lancashire 21 March 1966. 5ft 10½ in tall. Educated at Ysgol David Hughes, Anglesey. right-handed early-order batsman and medium-pace bowler. Glamorgan debut 1985, scoring 102 out of 117 in 87 minutes *v*. Yorkshire (Swansea), completing hundred with three sixes off successive balls (first Glamorgan hundred on f-c debut since 1921). Cap 1987. 1 Test appearance against West Indies at The Oval in August 1988 (highest score 10). 1,000 runs in a first-class season three times: most – 1,626 in 1987. Highest first-class score 160 Glamorgan *v*. Somerset (Weston) 1987; best bowling 3-21 Glamorgan *v*. Oxford U. (Oxford) 1987.

NEWPORT, Philip John. Born High Wycombe, Buckinghamshire 11 October 1962. 6ft 3in tall. Educated at High Wycombe Royal Grammar School; Portsmouth Polytechnic. Right-arm fast-medium swing bowler and late-order right-handed batsman. Worcestershire debut 1982; cap 1986. Represented Buckinghamshire 1981-82. One Test appearance against Sri Lanka at Lord's in August 1988 winning match award (highest score 26; best bowling 4-87). Highest first-class score 86 Boland *v*. Transvaal B (Stellenbosch) 1987-88; best bowling 8-52 Worcs *v*. Middlesex (Lord's) 1988.

PRINGLE, Derek Raymond. Born Nairobi, Kenya 18 September 1958. 6ft 4½ in tall. Educated at Felsted School; Fitzwilliam College, Cambridge University. Right-handed all-rounder: medium-fast seam bowler and middle-order batsman. Son of D. J. Pringle (East Africa). Essex debut 1978; cap 1982. Represented Cambridge University 1979-82; blue 1979-80-81; captain 1982. 19 Test appearances, making debut against India (Lord's) 1982; highest Test score 63 *v*. India (Lord's) 1986; best bowling 5-95 *v*. West Indies (Headingley) 1988. Tours: Australia 1982-83; Sri Lanka 1985-86 (England B). Highest first-class score 128 Essex *v*. Kent (Chelmsford) 1988; best bowling 7-32 Essex *v*. Middx (Chelmsford) 1983.

RUSSELL, Robert Charles ('Jack'). Born Stroud, Gloucestershire 15 August 1963. 5ft 8½ in tall. Educated at Archway Comprehensive School. World class wicket-keeper and handy left-handed middle-order batsman. Gloucestershire debut 1981; cap 1985. One Test appearance against Sri Lanka at Lord's in August 1988 (highest score 94). Tours: Pakistan 1987-88; Sri Lanka 1986-87 (Glos). Highest first-class score 94 (above).

SMALL, Gladstone Cleophas. Born St George, Barbados 18 October 1961. 5ft 11in tall. Educated at Moseley School; Hall Green Technical College. Right-handed fast-medium bowler and late-order batsman. Debut 1979-80 for D. H. Robins' XI in New Zealand. Warwickshire debut 1980; cap 1982. Represented South Australia 1985-86. Five Test appearances, making his debut against New Zealand at Trent Bridge in August 1986; highest Test score 21★ and best bowling 5-48 *v*. Australia (Melbourne) 1986-87. Tours: Australia 1986-87; New Zealand 1979-80 (D. H. Robins' XI); Pakistan 1981-82 (International XI). Highest first-class score 70 Warwicks *v*. Lancashire (Old Trafford) 1988; best bowling 7-15 Warwicks *v*. Notts (Edgbaston) 1988.

SMITH, Robin Arnold. Born Durban, South Africa 13 September 1963. 5ft 11in tall. Educated at Northlands High School, Durban. Right-handed early-order batsman and occasional leg-break bowler. Brother of C. L. Smith (Hampshire, Natal and England) and grandson of Dr V. L. Shearer (Natal). Represented Natal 1980-81 to 1984-85. Hampshire debut 1982; cap 1985. Three Test appearances, making his debut against West Indies at Headingley in July 1988 (highest score 57). 1,000 runs in a first-class season three times; most – 1,533 in 1985. Highest first-class score 209★ Hampshire *v*. Essex (Southend) 1987; best bowling 2-11 Hampshire *v*. Surrey (Southampton) 1985.

RELEVANT STATISTICS

SERIES AVERAGES
NEW ZEALAND *V.* ENGLAND 1987–88

NEW ZEALAND – BATTING AND FIELDING

	M	I	NO	HS	Runs	Avge	100	50	Ct/St
M. J. Greatbatch	2	3	1	107*	186	93.00	1	1	–
K. R. Rutherford	2	3	1	107*	138	69.00	1	–	–
I. D. S. Smith	3	4	2	33*	92	46.00	–	–	10
J. G. Wright	3	5	0	103	221	44.20	1	–	1
M. D. Crowe	3	5	0	143	216	43.20	1	–	2
J. G. Bracewell	3	5	1	54	152	38.00	–	1	2
T. J. Franklin	3	5	0	62	125	25.00	–	1	1
D. K. Morrison	3	2	1	14*	14	14.00	–	–	2
M. C. Snedden	2	3	0	20	34	11.33	–	–	–
J. J. Crowe	2	4	0	28	40	10.00	–	–	2
E. J. Chatfield	3	2	1	10	10	10.00	–	–	–

Played in one Test: S. L. Boock did not bat; R. J. Hadlee 37; A. H. Jones 8, 54* (4 ct), R. H. Vance 47.

ENGLAND – BATTING AND FIELDING

	M	I	NO	HS	Runs	Avge	100	50	Ct/St
M. D. Moxon	3	4	1	99	208	69.33	–	2	4
B. C. Broad	3	4	0	114	204	51.00	1	1	–
J. E. Emburey	3	3	0	45	106	35.33	–	–	–
M. W. Gatting	3	4	1	42	106	35.33	–	–	–
R. T. Robinson	3	4	0	70	126	31.50	–	2	–
P. W. Jarvis	2	3	1	14	34	17.00	–	–	–
G. R. Dilley	3	3	2	8*	17	17.00	–	–	–
P. A. J. De Freitas	2	2	0	16	20	10.00	–	–	1
B. N. French	3	3	0	13	23	7.66	–	–	11
D. J. Capel	3	3	0	11	16	5.33	–	–	3
N. H. Fairbrother	2	1	0	1	1	1.00	–	–	2

Played in one Test: C. W. J. Athey 22,19 (1 ct); E. E. Hemmi did not bat; N. V. Radford 8.

NEW ZEALAND – BOWLING

	Overs	Mdns	Runs	Wkts	Avge	Best	5wI	10wM
E. J. Chatfield	126.1	51	198	13	15.23	4–36	–	–
D. K. Morrison	80.2	14	269	8	33.62	5–69	1	–
M. C. Snedden	90	31	202	6	33.66	4–45	–	–
J. G. Bracewell	68	18	148	3	49.33	3–88	–	–

Also bowled: S. L. Boock 26-9-53-1; R. J. Hadlee 18-3-50-0; K. R. Rutherford 6-1-9-0.

ENGLAND – BOWLING

	Overs	Mdns	Runs	Wkts	Avge	Best	5wI	10wM
G. R. Dilley	104.5	33	210	15	14.00	6–38	2	–
M. W. Gatting	23	5	61	2	30.50	1–21	–	–
P. W. Jarvis	98	31	201	6	33.50	2–43	–	–
P. A. J. DeFreitas	91.1	33	175	4	43.75	2–39	–	–
D. J. Capel	109.2	22	274	5	54.80	2–57	–	–
J. E. Emburey	133.5	48	236	3	78.66	1–28	–	–

Also bowled: N. H. Fairbrother 2-0-9-0; E. E. Hemmings 45-107-0; M. D. Moxon 2-0-3-0; N. V. Radford 50-8-132-1.

ENGLAND *V.* WEST INDIES 1988

NGLAND – BATTING AND FIELDING

	M	I	NO	HS	Runs	Avge	100	50	Ct/St
A. Gooch	5	10	0	146	459	45.90	1	3	6
J. Lamb	4	8	2	113	254	42.33	1	1	–
I. Gower	4	8	1	88*	211	30.14	–	1	2
A. Smith	2	4	0	57	106	26.50	–	1	1
R. Downton	3	5	1	27	84	21.00	–	–	9/-
W. Jarvis	2	3	1	29*	42	21.00	–	–	–
C. Broad	2	4	0	54	71	17.75	–	1	–
S. Curtis	2	4	0	30	69	17.25	–	–	2
A. Foster	2	4	1	34	49	16.33	–	–	1
D. Moxon	2	4	0	26	55	13.75	–	–	1
R. Dilley	4	7	1	28	58	9.66	–	–	1
W. Gatting	2	4	0	29	38	9.50	–	–	1
E. Emburey	3	5	0	30	46	9.20	–	–	3
R. Pringle	4	7	0	39	52	7.42	–	–	–
J. Capel	2	4	0	16	29	7.25	–	–	1
A. J. DeFreitas	3	5	0	18	36	7.20	–	–	2
J. Richards	2	4	0	8	13	3.25	–	–	3/-
H. Childs	2	4	4	2*	2	–	–	–	1

yed in one Test: C. W. J. Athey 16, 11; R. J. Bailey 43, 3; S. Cowdrey 0, 5; M. P. Maynard 3, 10; G. C. Small 5*, 7.

WEST INDIES – BATTING AND FIELDING

	M	I	NO	HS	Runs	Avge	100	50	Ct/St
A. L. Logie	5	7	2	95*	364	72.80	–	2	6
P. J. L. Dujon	5	7	1	67	305	50.83	–	4	20/–
R. A. Harper	3	3	0	74	147	49.00	–	2	5
C. G. Greenidge	4	6	0	103	282	47.00	1	1	4
D. L. Haynes	4	7	2	77*	235	47.00	–	3	3
I. V. A. Richards	5	6	0	80	223	37.16	–	2	3
M. D. Marshall	5	6	1	72	135	27.00	–	1	1
C. L. Hooper	5	7	0	84	166	23.71	–	1	3
C. E. L. Ambrose	5	6	2	43	75	18.75	–	–	–
R. B. Richardson	3	4	0	26	71	17.75	–	–	4
C. A. Walsh	5	5	3	9*	26	13.00	–	–	–
W. K. M. Benjamin	3	2	0	9	9	4.50	–	–	1
B. P. Patterson	2	2	0	2	2	1.00	–	–	–

Played in one Test: K. L. T. Arthurton 27.

NGLAND – BOWLING

	Overs	Mdns	Runs	Wkts	Avge	Best	5wI	10wM
R. Dilley	136.1	26	403	15	26.86	5-55	1	–
A. Foster	73.2	12	250	9	27.77	5-64	1	–
R. Pringle	119	33	326	11	29.63	5-95	1	–
C. Small	37.5	6	140	4	35.00	4-64	–	–
W. Jarvis	57.1	6	217	6	36.16	4-107	–	–
H. Childs	86	29	183	3	61.00	1-13	–	–
E. Emburey	62	14	228	3	76.00	2-95	–	–
A. J. DeFreitas	92	16	253	3	84.33	2-93	–	–

o bowled: D. J. Capel 22-2-79-1; C. S. Cowdrey 5.3-0-21-0.

WEST INDIES – BOWLING

	Overs	Mdns	Runs	Wkts	Avge	Best	5wI	10wM
W. K. M. Benjamin	67	17	151	12	12.58	4-52	–	–
R. A. Harper	29	11	63	5	12.60	3-50	–	–
M. D. Marshall	203.1	49	443	35	12.65	7-22	3	1
C. E. L. Ambrose	203.1	56	445	22	20.22	4-53	–	–
C. A. Walsh	157.2	40	412	12	34.33	4-46	–	–
B. P. Patterson	74.5	13	270	4	67.50	2-100	–	–

Also bowled: C. L. Hooper 24-3-57-0; I. V. A. Richards 10-1-28-0.

ENGLAND TEST CAREER RECORDS

BATTING AND FIELDING

Records and ages of the 32 England Test representatives of 1988 on the last day of the Sri Lanka Test.

	County	Age	M	I	NO	HS	Runs	Avge	100	50	Ct/St
C. W. J. Athey	Glos	30	23	41	1	123	919	22.97	1	4	13
R. J. Bailey	N'hants	24	1	2	0	43	46	23.00	–	–	–
K. J. Barnett	Derbys	28	1	2	0	66	66	33.00	–	1	1
B. C. Broad	Notts	30	23	40	2	162	1579	41.55	6	6	8
D. J. Capel	N'hants	25	10	16	0	98	272	17.00	–	2	4
J. H. Childs	Essex	37	2	4	4	2*	2	–	–	–	1
C. S. Cowdrey	Kent	30	6	8	1	38	101	14.42	–	–	5
T. S. Curtis	Worcs	28	2	4	0	30	69	17.25	–	–	2
P. A. J. DeFreitas	Leics	22	12	17	1	40	182	11.37	–	–	4
G. R. Dilley	Worcs	29	39	55	18	56	479	12.94	–	2	10
P. R. Downton	Middx	31	30	48	8	74	785	19.62	–	4	70/5
J. E. Emburey	Middx	36	57	84	17	75	1409	21.02	–	7	33
N. H. Fairbrother	Lancs	24	4	4	0	3	5	1.25	–	–	3
N. A. Foster	Essex	26	25	37	5	39	342	10.68	–	–	6
B. N. French	Notts	29	16	21	4	59	308	18.11	–	1	38/1
M. W. Gatting	Middx	31	67	115	14	207	3848	38.09	9	18	51
G. A. Gooch	Essex	35	68	123	4	196	4541	38.15	8	27	69
D. I. Gower	Leics	31	100	172	13	215	7000	44.02	14	35	68
E. E. Hemmings	Notts	39	8	12	3	95	207	23.00	–	1	4
P. W. Jarvis	Yorks	23	4	6	2	29*	76	19.00	–	–	–
A. J. Lamb	N'hants	34	56	98	9	137*	2969	33.35	8	12	53
D. V. Lawrence	Glos	24	1	1	0	4	4	4.00	–	–	–
M. P. Maynard	Glam	22	1	2	0	10	13	6.50	–	–	–
M. D. Moxon	Yorks	28	9	15	1	99	437	31.21	–	3	10
P. J. Newport	Worcs	25	1	1	0	26	26	26.00	–	–	–
D. R. Pringle	Essex	29	19	33	3	63	479	15.96	–	1	7
N. V. Radford	Worcs	31	3	4	1	12*	21	7.00	–	–	–
C. J. Richards	Surrey	30	8	13	0	133	285	21.92	1	–	20/1
R. T. Robinson	Notts	29	28	47	5	175	1589	37.83	4	6	7
R. C. Russell	Glos	25	1	1	0	94	94	94.00	–	1	3
G. C. Small	Warwks	26	5	7	3	21*	61	15.25	–	–	1
R. A. Smith	Hants	24	3	6	1	57	145	29.00	–	1	2

* denotes not out

BOWLING

	Balls	Runs	Wkts	Avge	Best	5wI	10wM
B. C. Broad	6	4	0	–	–	–	–
D. J. Capel	1112	527	10	52.70	2-13	–	–
J. H. Childs	516	183	3	61.00	1-13	–	–
C. S. Cowdrey	399	309	4	77.25	2-65	–	–
P. A. J. DeFreitas	2338	1080	23	46.95	5-86	1	–
G. R. Dilley	7682	3789	133	28.48	6-38	6	–
J. E. Emburey	13315	4763	130	36.63	7-78	6	–
N. H. Fairbrother	12	9	0	–	–	–	–
N. A. Foster	5079	2376	76	31.26	8-107	5	1
M. W. Gatting	752	317	4	79.25	1-14	–	–
G. A. Gooch	1431	550	13	42.30	2-12	–	–

	Balls	Runs	Wkts	Avge	Best	5wI1
D. I. Gower	36	20	1	20.00	1-1	–
E. E. Hemmings	2332	876	16	54.75	3-53	–
P. W. Jarvis	931	418	12	34.83	4-107	–
A. J. Lamb	30	23	1	23.00	1-6	–
D. V. Lawrence	216	111	3	37.00	2-74	–
M. D. Moxon	48	30	0	–	–	–
P. J. Newport	285	164	7	23.42	4-87	–
D. R. Pringle	3232	1501	43	34.90	5-95	2
N. V. Radford	678	351	4	87.75	2-131	–
R. T. Robinson	6	0	0	–	–	–
G. C. Small	1083	454	20	22.70	5-48	2